Otherwise Than the Binary

SUNY series in Ancient Greek Philosophy

Anthony Preus, editor

Otherwise Than the Binary

New Feminist Readings in Ancient Philosophy and Culture

Edited by
Jessica Elbert Decker, Danielle A. Layne,
and Monica Vilhauer

Published by State University of New York Press, Albany

Printed in the United States of America

For information, contact State University of New York Press, Albany, NY
www.sunypress.edu

Library of Congress Cataloging-in-Publication Data

Names: Decker, Jessica Elbert, editor. | Layne, Danielle A., editor. | Vilhauer, Monica, editor.
Title: Otherwise than the binary : new feminist readings in ancient philosophy and culture / [editors] Jessica Elbert Decker, Danielle A. Layne, Monica Vilhauer.
Description: Albany : State University of New York, [2022] | Series: SUNY series in ancient Greek philosophy | Includes bibliographical references and index.
Identifiers: LCCN 2022003295 (print) | LCCN 2022003296 (ebook) | ISBN 9781438488790 (hardcover : alk. paper) | ISBN 9781438488813 (ebook)
Subjects: LCSH: Philosophy, Ancient | Greece—Civilization—To 146 B.C. | Gender nonconformity. | Feminist criticism.
Classification: LCC B111 .O84 2022 (print) | LCC B111 (ebook) | DDC 180—dc23/eng/20220218
LC record available at https://lccn.loc.gov/2022003295
LC ebook record available at https://lccn.loc.gov/2022003296

10 9 8 7 6 5 4 3 2 1

Contents

Part Two: Platonic Transformations

Part Three: Late Antique Destabilizations

Introduction

Jessica Elbert Decker and Danielle A. Layne

A now common critique of the Western philosophical tradition is that it harbors an inherent sexism wherein "universal reason" is far from neutral but is, rather, positively masculine, setting itself against the feminine domain of irrationality, madness, magic, and mystery. Theorists like Genevieve Lloyd or feminists like Luce Irigaray have argued that Greek modes of thought, particularly Pythagorean, Platonic, and Aristotelian, insofar as they appear to privilege identity over difference, *logos* over *pathos*, the intelligible over the bodily, form over matter, and so on, all harbor a gendered hierarchy that reinforces sexist and racist oppression not only in antiquity but also in the present age. As our title suggests, this volume hopes, to think otherwise than this binary and to examine whether the Greek worldview neatly falls within this exclusionary form of thinking. Overall, we will ask if there are ways of thinking antiquity differently, namely, as possibly expounding and even celebrating philosophies of difference, and we will see if we may discover rare moments when authors of antiquity valorize and uphold the necessity of all that has been coded as feminine, foreign, and/or irrational. This volume does not aim to address every figure or period of antiquity; rather, it proceeds thematically through selected texts that invite interpretation that is otherwise than the binary. As contemporary thinkers are turning toward new ways of reading antiquity, we hope that these selected studies will inspire other readings of ancient texts through this critical lens. When examining the philosophers and notable figures of antiquity alongside their overt patriarchal and masculinist agendas, we will attempt to rethink our current methodologies while also questioning how we receive and read these texts.

Is it possible to interrogate particular authors, texts, and social practices of antiquity for ideas, theories, and/or images that are complementary to feminist and intersectional concerns? While not a work of apologetics that dismisses or neglects exclusionary practices and beliefs of classical authors so as to safeguard the value of the "perennial tradition," the following does hope to respond to the question in the affirmative, analyzing the works of problematic thinkers and texts anew, seeing if we can engage their philosophy and practices in ways that might expose their own deep-seated tensions and contradictions. In other words, insofar as feminists wish to argue that patriarchal logic is inherently problematic, we will expose how there are moments, strains of thinking, in which masculinist authors fail to be fully consistent in their misogyny—fail, despite their agendas, to support their own attempts to delegitimize the feminine/Other—showing how the systems and ideas of antiquity may contain internal struggles and possible whispers of revolution that dismantle and subvert patriarchal thinking.

Of course, this anthology of essays in which we reinterpret select authors from antiquity through a feminist perspective would not be possible without the important works of the scholars before us. One of the most influential works to turn a feminist critical lens on Ancient Greek culture and thought is Nicole Loraux's groundbreaking *Children of Athena: Athenian Ideas about Citizenship and the Division between the Sexes* (1984). In this text, Loraux examines the Athenian idea of autochthony (nativeness) in the Ancient Greek imagination and analyzes the figure of Pandora as the "first woman" created by Hephaestus at Zeus's command. Loraux approaches these myths as fantasies, arguing that myth—often disregarded in much of the classical tradition of scholarship that preceded her—plays a significant political role in the context of the *polis*.[1] Loraux is working in a genre of scholarship influenced by the ideas of Lévi-Strauss, and often refers to the texts of Jean-Pierre Vernant and Marcel Detienne, thinkers working in the tradition of structuralist anthropology that attempted to understand Ancient Greek mythical narratives within their cultural, civic, and religious contexts. *Children of Athena* is a rich and complex work, and cannot be exhaustively summarized here, so we will focus on crucial aspects of Loraux's treatment of autochthony and the myth of Pandora as emblematic analyses that demonstrate her method and critical feminist orientation toward the texts, especially as she reads them in ways that would support our "otherwise than the binary" reorientation toward classical antiquity.

Loraux argues that the Athenian tradition of autochthony "dispossesses the women of Athens of their reproductive function. This dispossession, of course, belongs to the realm of the imaginary, and it looks like the expression of a dream or a denial of reality rather than a definite program or an Athenian theory of reproduction."[2] Athenians adopted this origin myth, where they are born directly from the soil, out of the earth, and they do not originate in the womb of a woman. This denial of the female reproductive body is further evident in the myth of Erichthonios, who is born from the earth after Hephaestus' failed attempt to rape Athena; Hephaestus' seed falls to the earth and from her Erichthonios is born. It is significant that Athena remains a virgin goddess, echoing the erasure of the sexually autonomous female reproductive body that the myth of autochthony properly accomplishes. Loraux reads these Ancient Greek myths and their effects in the civic life of the Athenian people, while remarking on the myth of Erichthonios as an expression of male desire.

> The doctrine of autochthony is something like the satisfaction of a desire, rather than a misunderstanding of the laws of reproduction. The desire of a society of men to deny the reality of reproduction is vested in the story of Erichthonios, since masculine experience dictates that what really counts takes place among men.[3]

Athenian autochthony has, of course, been discussed in traditional scholarship, but as Loraux points out, only insofar as it is historically significant. Loraux emphasizes the meaning of this doctrine with regard to sexual difference and the social and cultural markers of gender as they appear in the everyday lives of ancient Athenian people.[4]

One of the most enduring legacies of Loraux's work is her innovative reading of the myth of Pandora. Just as the myth of autochthony inevitably implicates Athena (as a kind of "virgin mother" of Erichthonios), the story of Pandora also crucially involves Athena, who presides over the creation of the alleged first woman.[5] Pandora is the mother of all women, indeed, mother of the "race of women," but she, herself, is not born but created by father Zeus and the craftsman Hephaestus. In other words, she is not human in two respects. First, insofar as she is not man but woman, she is separated from *anthropoi*, marked by an ominous otherness; and, further, she is created rather than born. Loraux asks how this separation of women from *anthropoi*, from human beings, is even possible, and compares it to the political structure of the Athenian *polis* where women are excluded.

> The reference to Hesiod allows us to raise a perennial question in the Greek ideology of citizenship: that is, the exclusion of women, the paradoxical "half" of the Greek *polis*, an exclusion that is necessary and impossible at the same time. The consistency of this discourse about women deserves to be emphasized.[6]

The creation of Pandora essentially gives Zeus credit for all human birth, since the race of women is descended from this alleged first woman. Pandora is not born; she is built by the craftsman god Hephaestus, the forger of weapons—and Pandora herself is just such an arsenal, a Trojan horse, a deceptive trap (*dolon*). In both the *Theogony* and *Works and Days*, this "beautiful evil" or *kalon kakon*, is explicitly a deception and a trap.[7] Female sexuality and beauty are constructed as dangerous illusions wherein the female body itself is threatening—and this is Loraux's brilliant insight—because Pandora cannot even be said to have a "real" body. Again, like the Trojan horse, she is hollow, empty, simply a deceptive outside. She is all surface with a shining and appealing facade but concealing *nothing*.

In describing her finery and accoutrements, Athena gives Pandora a shimmering veil; Hephaestus gives her a glittery diadem; but where is Pandora herself?

> It is a trap of finery, a trap of an exterior that is too beautiful. Is woman, then, a trap of simple appearances? I suspect that such a reading of the text might lead us to miss an important question: indeed, what makes the woman into a wholly exterior being in the first place? Certainly the notion of disguise is an essential part of the veil, and likewise a part of the word *kalyptre* (the word for veil, from the verb "to conceal"). Yet . . . the creature in the *Theogony* is no hidden

> form beneath a deceitful disguise. Her veil does not conceal anything other than a woman: not a god, a demon, or a man. It hides nothing, because the woman has no interior to conceal. In short, in the *Theogony*, the first woman *is* her adornments—she has no body.[8]

So, in short, what is woman? For Loraux, she is multiple things, and none of them easy to pin down. Is she a mother or is she a virgin? Indeed, she *looks* like a virgin: "*parthenos aidoie ikelon*," "the likeness of a chaste virgin,"[9] and it is through this emphasis on *likeness* that she is revealed to be a resemblance, an illusion, a specter of the real. In other words, she exists not as original, despite being the first, but as eternal image, an *ikelon*; "she is a copy that does not have an original."[10] Moreover, insofar as Pandora is not a human being but a specter of deceit, an empty cosmetic womb, one may ask how she can give birth or be the mother of anything, let alone the future generations of men? In other words, Loraux's work highlights how the question of sexual difference and the origin of women clearly leave us with an ambiguous persona wherein the feminine is both a problematic snare while still being an instrumental part of human reproduction and society.

This theme has been taken up by Froma Zeitlin (1996) and more recently by Elissa Marder, who argues "Pandora's function is to suppress, rather than express, the link between women and reproduction."[11] Marder emphasizes Loraux's suggestion that Pandora's function as a mother is not natural, and argues that she is an artifice, a replicant, a product of *techne*.[12] With regard to Pandora's famously dangerous box, or jar (*pithos*), Marder cites Loraux and Zeitlin for their recognition of the decidedly unnatural character of Pandora and rejects the assumption that the jar/box is merely linked with birth, death and fertility (as suggested by Vernant).[13] Marder suggests that Pandora's *pithos* is not a representation of her but a *mechanical reproduction* of the womb.

> A fabricated replica of Pandora's fabricated duplicitously empty body. As a prosthetic, externalized replication of Pandora's womb (within which lurks the figure of "Anxiety," here bearing the name Elpis), the jar opens up the disturbing possibility that the maternal function is not a natural operation and that it cannot be so easily contained.[14]

Indeed, this image of unruly but instrumental container/receptacle (as in Plato's *Timaeus* or Aristotle's *Generation of Animals*) often appears whenever female sexuality and reproduction is at issue in antiquity. Here one need only refer to the work of Page Dubois, whose *Sowing the Body: Psychoanalysis and Ancient Representations of Women* (1988) helped uncover how the female body was consistently compared to fertile soil, the wandering womb of the monstrous mother earth. Meanwhile masculinity and its *techne* became the desired plow, the steady hand that would heroically domesticate the feminine, reduce her to a container/receptacle—the land or the earth laid bare, waiting the inscription that would allow her finally to bear legitimate fruit.

The question of sexual difference in ancient Greek philosophy is also a major theme in the work of Luce Irigaray, whose influence on the study of sexual difference in the Western philosophical canon has been prodigious. Irigaray argues that sexual difference underlies the massive dualistic structures of Western metaphysics, epistemology, and ethics—all the way back to ancient Greek thinkers like Plato and Aristotle. In *Speculum of the Other Woman*, Irigaray suggests, "Any theory of the subject has always been appropriated by the 'masculine.'"[15] The so-called universal subject, or transcendental ego, is imagined to be both no one and anyone, while in reality it is an image of the dominant masculine subject, masquerading itself as the universal. What we know as rationality is a guise, a specific determination dreamed up and codified so as to set the masculine up as that which can "legitimately" excise, exclude, regulate, and order all that is categorized as other, the feminine, the slave, the body, the emotional, and so forth.

Adopting Lacanian terminology (in order to subvert it), Irigaray points out that the category of woman is coded and perceived as "lack." "Subjectivity is denied to women," writes Irigaray: Women are nothing but a mirror in which the masculine subject can narcissistically regard his own reflection from a perverse upside-down angle. The woman is lacking the organ of agency (because only male penetration counts as agency), of speech (in Lacan's system, where the phallus is the master signifier), and she is a monster, as Aristotle has it, or a mutilated creature, according to Freud.[16] In approaching this binary coding of the masculine with the transcendent soul and the feminine with immanent body, Irigaray argues that sexual difference is the key element of this organization—and sexual reproduction is deeply implicated. Just as Loraux discovers the myth of autochthony as a masculine fantasy, Irigaray describes the masculine subject in similar terms.

> The "subject" plays at multiplying himself, even deforming himself, in this process. He is father, mother, and child(ren). And the relationships between them. He is masculine and feminine and the relationships between them. What mockery of generation, parody of copulation and genealogy, drawing its *strength* from the same model, from the model of the same: the subject.[17]

The mythological imagination of the ancient Greek world repeatedly demonstrates this masculine tendency to appropriate female generativity, giving birth to all that reinforces its superiority. Consider again the myth of autochthony and the birth of Erichthonios, Zeus's ingestion of his first wife Metis and the resultant "birth" of Athena, and Zeus's creation of Pandora as the "first woman." Here, we see the intents of crafting narratives that reinforce the allegedly motherless status of goddesses such as Athena and Aphrodite, the domestic taming of Gaia, the slaughter (or, perhaps, "castration") of Medusa and other monsters by male gods and heroes, and so forth.[18] Suffice to say that these narratives tend to privilege the heroic masculine subject, and often present female figures as treacherous, chaotic, and monstrous.[19] The rare "good woman" is praised, while the "bad woman" is often portrayed as a kind of cautionary tale, conditioning women to accept masculine proscription of their behavior. For example, Penelope and Alcestis are cast as the faithful wives, while figures like Medea, Helen, and Clytemnestra are models of the "bad woman"—and their failure is directly caused by their refusal to fulfill their roles as wives and mothers.[20] As Cristiana Franco's *Shameless: The Canine and the Feminine in Ancient Greece* demonstrates, women in antiquity are thought to lack *aidos*, self-restraint, and require male masters—much like dogs.[21]

So, it seems then that female sexuality, in the ancient Greek imagination, is excessive and chaotic and in need of dominance. Nevertheless, the symbolic constellation of female/matter/body/earth/nature signifies to many contemporary feminist authors not masculine power or positivity but, rather, masculine fear and anxiety, his need for an "other" to make him mean something. Overturning the trope of "penis envy" some scholars of antiquity, following Irigaray and Loraux, observe in masculinity a kind of psychotic insecurity, suggesting in such diagnosis that the binary, and all its exclusionary practices, was born of *birth envy* and the fear of impotence and powerlessness.[22] In this reception of feminist scholarship on antiquity, the binary between the subject and the other, the masculine and the feminine, is now being read anew, exposing not mere sexism in the system but, rather, more paradoxically, the frightened boy. As feminist author Hélène Cixous invited readers to reimagine the relationship between Medusa and Perseus in her illustrious *The Laugh of Medusa* (1976), we ask: "Is it possible that masculinity trembles while she smiles? Is it possible that women/the other have been the site of power all along?" Medusa knows what she is—a site of authentic generative power, and Perseus only appropriates it for himself because he sees in her reflection his own lack. In decapitating the monster, castrating and appropriating her power, he only *seems* to complete the job because, much like the hydra, woman and all she bears within herself will constantly regrow, fighting against the true terror of masculinity and its power born of impotence and fear.

Assuredly, much recent scholarship has begun this task of attempting to reread the classical binary, either subverting from within or showing how the reception of antiquity has unfortunately covered over or neglected to analyze both the ambiguity of the binary in the Greek imagination or the explicit transgression of it in particular authors and cultural practices. In this we would like to emphasize the work of E. Bianchi who in her book, *The Feminine Symptom: Aleatory Matter in the Aristotelian Cosmos* (2014), stresses the crucial importance of Aristotle's *Generation of Animals* for understanding his overall system, and finds that there is a "glitch"—a symptomatic constellation—created within Aristotle's system by the aleatory motion of (feminine-coded) matter; in other words, an unpredictable agency that is not subject to male mastery, that doesn't follow the fabricated masculinist order. This reading offers feminist thinkers an exciting revolutionary model: *aleatory feminism*, which Bianchi compares to the spiraling tendency that Goethe found in his work on plants and their growth patterns.

> A manifestation of the aleatory feminine may be found also in Goethe's botanical writings of the early nineteenth century, in which he writes of the "spiral tendency" of plants as contrasted with their tendency for vertical growth. The

> spiral system which causes plant growth to turn in on itself governs development, nourishment, and reproduction, but it is prone to excess and as such is also the source of "the extremely diverse misgrowths that appear as deviations from the law of definite forms." The spiral tendency is thus also symptomatic in the sense I have developed here, in that it both "fosters completion" but also occurs erratically, prematurely, and destructively.[23]

The spiral system that "governs development, nourishment, and reproduction" is a system that can rightly be dubbed *kata phusin*, according to nature, and it is a system of generation *and* destruction on which the masculine is dependent.[24] Alongside Bianchi's aleatory feminism, there is also the work of Jill Gordon who, instead of rehearsing the standard arguments regarding the Demiurgic Father or the masculinist insistence on reason, demonstrates the necessity of eros for Plato's system, showing how eros is not merely an expedient in the *Symposium*, but the thickest cable drawing humans back toward their divine source.[25] In the insistence on the erotic aspect of Plato's entire system, Gordon breaks down the myth of a transcendent separation between what has often been coded in feminine and masculine terms, that is, the sensible and the intelligible, the particular and the universal. Rather, the bridge of longing that drives human activity and transcendence takes center stage in Plato's metaphysics. In this same vein, Coleen P. Zoller's *Plato and the Body: Reconsidering Socratic Asceticism*, has attempted to analyze the so-called disparagement of the body, what she calls an austere dualism, in works like the *Phaedo*, *Gorgias*, and the *Republic*. While recognizing the political and feminist implications of her thesis, Zoller calls for utilizing Plato less as an obstacle to feminism and more as a resource.

> Misreading Plato as a philosopher who ignores or demeans the physical results in failing to see Plato as a resource for those working on a wide variety of women's issues. Let's consider several dimensions. Women have borne the brunt of the austere dualist interpretation's influence in part because the austere dualist account of ascetism became pervasive throughout Western culture as the epitome of purity and goodness. The prevalence of this interpretation in effect established a standard sexual morality. . . . Maybe we would not live in

> a culture of rape, violence, and female disempowerment if austere dualism had not appeared to condone the degradation of anything associated with the physical. Now that we can push aside that misguided view, scholars and others working on contemporary problems surrounding sexual morality would benefit from utilizing Plato as a resource.[26]

Similar to Zoller's worry that the austere dualist approach to authors like Plato reinforce contemporary oppression, Donna Zuckerberg's *Not All Dead White Men*[27] turns to the rise of Stoic philosophy in the hands of white nationalists and sexist groups like the "Manosphere" or the "Red Pill" community.[28] Indeed, Stoic philosophy cannot pretend that it is not susceptible to such appropriation when many authors from within the tradition explicitly decry all things feminine, particularly the emotions and the body, while also, in turn, consigning women's natural duty to the role of being domestic shadows of men.[29] Yet, despite this, Zuckerberg leans on the research of scholars like Scott Aikin and Emily McGill-Rutherford,[30] as well as Lisa Hill[31] to emphasize that Stoicism cannot be so easily relegated to the trash bin. Rather, one can legitimately read the Stoics in a way that is more consistent with feminist theory. Aikin and McGill-Rutherford maintain the following:

> [W]e have argued that despite the fact that the individual Stoics themselves failed the liberal requirement, Stoicism as a philosophical program is not inherently anti-liberal (and thereby anti-feminist) . . . The liberal Stoicism we've proposed respects autonomy, but it recognizes the fact that the world is not ideal, and so there must be the familiar Stoic virtues of endurance. And these virtues of endurance needn't be inherently socially conservative or misogynist.[32]

As Zuckerberg emphasizes, this way of reading Stoic philosophy additionally brings Stoicism into greater consistency with itself and, as a consequence, she reassesses the interpretation of Stoicism as inherently antifeminist insofar as overly narrow readings lend themselves to the dangerous appropriation of classical authors for harmful ends in our own contemporary social spheres and cultural conversations. But what happens when we begin to reimagine the power differentials in particular classical authors so as to make such narrow appropriations, like those of the "Red Pill" community, into obvious failings to creatively and impactfully resuscitate a philosophical worldview. Is it possible we can reread such traditions in a way that can change the course of oppression today rather than reinforcing it?

The reimagining of the power differentials and the invitation to read classical authors of antiquity as open-ended, ambiguous, and not necessarily regulative of sex discrimination, ultimately suggests that we can engage the texts of antiquity with cautionary awareness of how these texts have been used and, perhaps, abused by patriarchal and imperial logic. Is it now possible to think and imagine systems in which the subject does not need to be in a hostile or combative relationship with its "other"—systems that do not relegate the other to the category of mere reflection, lack, or the monstrous, bestial thing that either needs to be destroyed or tamed? Overall, we can see in this new strain of contemporary readings of antiquity that scholars are beginning to emphasize less the reality of the binary in its neat separation, reinforcing the obvious fact of sexism and exclusion, and instead are moving more to theorize the contingency and liminality of borders as well as question the methods for reading the texts/authors as participating in or reinforcing patriarchal political orders—themes that resonate throughout this volume.

The task, then, in the present volume is to further this work of reading antiquity and its relation to gender as otherwise than the binary that reinforces patriarchal and sexist practices—practices that demarcate a divide between terms like form and matter, the intelligible and sensible, and the logical and the mythical. Rather, following the path set out by scholars like Loraux, Zeitlin, Bianchi, Gordon, and Zoller, we will look to see the tensions in antiquity that invite readers to see the complexity embedded in select Greek thinkers and texts regarding that which was coded feminine. Again, this project is not an apologetics. Rather, the goal is to discover ways out of the binary, new *methodologies* that allows us to explore ways in which the marginalized may discover tools in which they can move from the domain of the excluded and demonized. In this way we can shift the perspective to the world of value and empowerment, a move both possible to uncover in antiquity as well as in our own present age. To do this, we have organized the essays into four historical sections.

The mythical and religious conceptions of binary thinking explored in the first section of this volume emphasize the liminality of borders between mortals and the divine and attempt to read these mythical and religious symbols and practices within their cultural context, rather than frame them within modern metaphysical models that obscure the ambiguity inherent in these archaic binary distinctions.[33] The second section of this volume takes up the logic of opposition as it appears in Presocratic thinking and highlights the manner in which Presocratic thinkers were engaged in nuanced understandings of opposites as permeable and in motion, rather than logically distinct and separate from one another. In particular, the essays in this section approach Presocratic conceptions of "mixture"—especially visible in the texts of Empedocles and Anaxagoras—and emphasize the subtle and precise manner in which opposites are understood in relation rather than as "essence." This distinction is significant because Aristotelian thinking of "prime matter" and "substance" tends to obscure the complexity of these early physical accounts of the *kosmos*. The philosophical conception of "mixture" is taken up in the third section in the context of Plato's texts, particularly with regard to cosmology and the relation between the soul and the body. The final section of the volume focuses on this question of binaries and mixture in the context of gender and sexual difference in later antiquity, emphasizing both the value of the feminine and eroticism in late Platonic texts, both pagan and Christian.

In part 1, "Myth, Divination, and the Pre-Platonic," each essay deals with a perennial figure or theme related to Greek prose, religion, and culture. Andrew Gregory's essay "Was Homer's Circe a Witch?" problematizes the characterization of the infamous Homeric figure, showing how only in modernity is Circe characterized as a witch while in antiquity she retained the status of a divine figure. Sasha Biro's "The Oracle as Intermediary" engages in the age-old debate about mythological speech and its association with irrationality and the feminine, arguing that in opposition to scholars who wish to exclude myth and divination from philosophical *logos*, the Greeks intimately accepted and valorized the speech of the Sibyl as a place to think through the reality of ambiguity, paradox, and difference. Jessica Elbert Decker's "The Roots of Life and Death in the Homeric Hymns and Presocratic Philosophy," wherein she investigates how sexual difference plays out in early cosmological narratives argues that, while these narratives operate within binary structure, they can also show a sensitivity to the liminality of borders and the permeability of apparent oppositions. Holly Moore's "The Intelligibility of Difference: Anaxagoras' and Lugones' Ontologies of Separation" brings together the theories of Anaxagoras and feminist Latina philosopher María

Lugones, showing how both are resistant to philosophies that presuppose the values of purity and homogeneity and seek to rehabilitate a notion of relationality versus masculine sovereignty.

In part 2, "Platonic Transformations," we have three essays that analyze key Platonic dialogues via diverse feminist perspectives, for example, the *Phaedo*, the *Symposium*, the *Timaeus*, and the *Republic*. In Hilary Yancey and Anne-Marie Schultz's "As Much Mixture as Will Suffice: Socrates' Embodied Intermediacy in Plato's *Phaedo* and *Symposium*," readers are invited to rethink Socratic asceticism via the erotic and embodied components of philosophical life. Along these lines, Monica Vilhauer's "Overturning Soul-Body Dualism in Plato's *Timaeus*" attempts to show the value of the receptacle and nurse of becoming, underscoring the importance of this feminine paradigm in the life of the individual animal. Mary Townsend's "The Argument of Socrates' Action in *Republic* V" revisits a timeless feminist concern and argues that Socrates' response to the "woman question" in his ideal city is much richer and more aporetic than is generally imagined. Overall, by focusing on the dramatic action, Townsend reevaluates the status of Socrates' claims about women's relative weakness.

Finally, part 3, "Late Antique Destabilizations," spans over 400 years of thinking and addresses the work of the Neoplatonists and early Christianizing Greek philosophers. Danielle A. Layne's "Divine Mothers: Plotinus' Erotic Productive Causes" explicitly calls out Plotinus' sexist views regarding matter as the impotent mother of the *kosmos*. Nevertheless, the main thrust of the essay focuses on two other feminine principles in his system, mythologically framed as Aphrodite and Penia (Poverty from Plato's *Symposium*). Layne argues that these principles ultimately trouble a univocal understanding of the Neoplatonist's degradation of the feminine. Next, Jana Schultz's essay, "Beyond Maleness and Femaleness? The Case of the Virgin Goddesses in Proclus' Metaphysics," examines the subversive role that feminine deities and metaphysical principles—for example, otherness, difference, and life—have in Proclus' theological metaphysics. William Koch's "Hekate and the Liminality of Souls" focuses on the depiction of the goddess Hekate, arguing that throughout antiquity but, most especially in its reception in late antique texts like the *Chaldean Oracles*, she occupies a liminal place in the pantheon of the Greeks, retaining the importance of the magical and the mysterious—a place of movement that ultimately constitutes the human soul. Finally, Ilaria L. E. Ramelli's essay, "Christian Platonists in Support of Gender

Equality: Bardaisan, Clement, Origen, Gregory of Nyssa, and Eriugena" focuses on these thinkers so as to surprisingly confirm that these Christian Platonists insisted on the genderless nature of divinity, which, in its transcendence (theorized within a solid Platonic framework) lies beyond any gender distinction.

Overall, all these essays complement one another and will guide readers into seeing that binary/gendered thinking in antiquity was much more complex than scholars have previously argued, allowing for the opportunity to engage a variety of texts in ways that might be subversive for our own contemporary discussion of sex, gender, and sexuality. For our contemporary world, looking back at these texts is crucial. It allows us to recognize ourselves in reflections and pastiche, in echoes from earlier mothers and sisters, and to see that while there is sameness, there is always difference. The binary divisions that have modeled and molded our culture for so long are in transition; their borders becoming more transparently permeable and open to becoming otherwise.

Notes

1. Nicole Loraux, *Children of Athena: Athenian Ideas about Citizenship and the Division Between the Sexes* (Princeton: Princeton University Press, 1993), see especially 5–8 and 37–71 on autochthony as a "civic myth."

2. Loraux, *Children of Athena*, 9.

3. Loraux, 17.

4. Loraux, 4–10, 37–71.

5. Loraux discusses Athena's role in Pandora's creation at 10–11, 18–21, and 114–17; see also 123–43 for her analysis of Athena's birth.

6. Loraux, 75.

7. See Hesiod, *Theogony* 585, where Pandora is called a *dolon*, or trap; she is also described as *amechanon* at 589, a word used by Sappho to describe "unmanageable" *eros* (Fragment 130), as well as used by Parmenides to express the helpless, paralyzed state of mortal beings (in the "third way" section of the poem, DK 6.5–9). The description of Pandora as *dolon aipun amechanon* appears in both tales, in *Theogony* 589 and *Works and Days* 83. Beauty as a trap has a long history, and is associated with Aphrodite, Helen of Troy, and Pandora. See Loraux, 80n45. See also Elbert Decker's discussion of *thauma edesthai* in this volume.

8. Loraux, 81.

9. Loraux, 81–83; in Hesiod, *Theogony* 572.

10. Loraux, 82. For this body as a copy with no original, see also the work of Judith Butler, *Gender Trouble* (New York: Routledge, 2006) and *Bodies That Matter* (New York: Routledge, 1993).

11. See Elissa Marder, *The Mother in the Age of Mechanical Reproduction* (New York: Fordham University Press, 2012), 15, where she cites Froma Zeitlin for this argument.

12. Marder, *The Mother*, 9.

13. Marder, 13–16 for discussion of the *pithos* and its possible interpretations.

14. Marder, 16.

15. Luce Irigaray, *Speculum of the Other Woman* (New York: Cornell University Press, 1995), 133.

16. Aristotle refers to female offspring as monsters in *Generation of Animals*, see Emanuela Bianchi, *The Feminine Symptom: Aleatory Matter in the Aristotelian Cosmos* (New York: Fordham University Press, 2014). Consider also Freud wherein all libido is masculine, while women are associated instead with masochism and the death instinct.

17. Irigaray, *Speculum*, 136. Italics in original. See Paul Miller, *Diotima at the Barricades: French Feminist Read Plato* (Oxford: Oxford University Press, 2016) for an in-depth account of Irigaray's engagement with Platonism, specifically her interpretation of the Allegory of the Cave.

18. For the various appropriations of birth, particularly the ingestion of Metis, birth of Athena, doctrine of autochthony, and creation of Pandora, see Jessica Elbert Decker, "Manufacturing the Mother: Technical Appropriations of Birth in Ancient Greek Thought," in *Bearing the Weight of the World*, ed. Alys Einion and Jen Rinaldi (Bradford: Demeter Press, 2018).

19. For female figures as monstrous in the *Odyssey*, see Beth Cohen, *The Distaff Side: Representing the Female in Homer's Odyssey* (Oxford: Oxford University Press, 1995).

20. For female figures in tragedy, see Helene P. Foley, *Female Acts in Greek Tragedy* (Princeton: Princeton University Press, 1991), and Ruby Blondell, *Women on the Edge. Four Plays by Euripides* (New York: Routledge, 1999).

21. Cristiana Franco, *Shameless: The Canine and the Feminine in Ancient Greece* (Oakland: University of California Press, 2014).

22. See Jessica Elbert Decker (as Jessica Elbert Mayock) "The Medusa Complex: Matricide and the Fantasy of Castration," *PhiloSOPHIA* Vol. 3.2 (New York: SUNY Press, 2013) for analysis of Freud's castration theory as male fantasy.

23. Bianchi, *The Feminine Symptom* 233.

24. In DK 1, Heraclitus says he will speak *kata phusin*, according to nature.

25. Jill Gordon, *Plato's Erotic World: From Cosmic Origins to Human Death* (Cambridge: Cambridge University Press, 2012).

26. Coleen Zoller, *Plato and the Body: Reconsidering Socratic Ascetism* (New York: SUNY Press, 2018), 10.

27. Donna Zuckerberg, *Not All Dead White Men: Classics and Misogyny in the Digital Age* (Cambridge: Harvard University Press, 2018).

28. Zuckerberg, *Not All Dead*, 1–2 defines these groups succinctly stating: "These online communities go by many names—the Alt-Right, the manosphere, Men Going Their Own Way, pickup artists—and exist under the larger umbrella of what is known as the Red Pill, a group of men connected by common resentments against women, immigrants, people of color, and the liberal elite. The name adopted from the film *The Matrix*, encapsulates the idea that society is unfair to men—heterosexual white men in particular—and is designed to favor women."

29. Some peak examples of Stoic sexism or disparagement of women include Musonius *Lectures* 12.4, Epictetus *Discourses* 3.24.53, 3.7.20 and *Enchiridion* 40, Cicero *Tusculan Disputations* 3.17.36 and *De Officis* I, 55, and Seneca *Ad Helviam* 14 2.

30. Scott Aikin and Emily McGill-Rutherford, "Stoicism Feminism and Autonomy," in *Symposium* 1 (1):9–22, 2014. For other discussions of Stoicism and gender/sex issues see C. E. Manning, "Seneca and the Stoics on the Equality of the Sexes." Mnemosyne 26: 170–77, 1973; Martha Nussbaum, "The Incomplete Feminism of Musonius Rufus," in *The Sleep of Reason*, ed. M. C. Nussbaum and J. S. Hivola, 283–325 (University of Chicago Press, 2002); Sarah Pomeroy, *Goddesses, Whores, Wives and Slaves* (New York: Schocken Books, 1975).

31. Lisa Hill, "The First Wave of Feminism: Were the Stoics Feminists?" *History of Political Thought* 22: 13–40, 2001.

32. Aikin and Emily McGill-Rutherford, "Stoicism Feminism and Autonomy," 26.

33. To some extant this section follows the goals of Vanda Zajko and Miriam Leonard's *Laughing with Medusa: Classical Myth and Feminist Thought* (Oxford: Oxford University Press, 2006), an excellent collection of essays devoted to feminist readings of myth—covering everything from psychoanalytic interpretations and reinterpretations of the Olympians to new readings of *Antigone* as well as interesting attempts to integrate cyberfeminism into a reading of Homer's *Iliad*.

Bibliography

Aikin, Scott, and Emily McGill-Rutherford. "Stoicism Feminism and Autonomy," *Symposium* 1, no. 1 (2014): 9–22.

Bianchi, Emanuela. *The Feminine Symptom: Aleatory Matter in the Aristotelian Cosmos*. New York: Fordham University Press, 2014.

Blondell, Ruby, Mary-Kay Gamel, Nancy Sorkin Rabinowitz, and Bella Vivante (eds.). *Women on the Edge: Four Plays by Euripides*. New York: Routledge, 1999.

Butler, Judith. *Gender Trouble*. New York: Routledge, 2006.

———. *Bodies That Matter*. New York: Routledge, 1993.

Cohen, Beth. *The Distaff Side: Representing the Female in Homer's* Odyssey. Oxford, UK: Oxford University Press, 1995.

Dubois, Page. *Sowing the Body*. Chicago, IL: University of Chicago Press, 1988.

Elbert Decker, Jessica. "Manufacturing the Mother: Technical Appropriations of Birth in Ancient Greek Thought." In *Bearing the Weight of the World*, edited by Alys Einion and Jen Rinaldi. Bradford, ON: Demeter Press, 2018.

———. [as Jessica Elbert Mayock]. "The Medusa Complex: Matricide and the Fantasy of Castration," *PhiloSOPHIA*, Vol. 3.2, Albany: State University of New York Press, 2013.

Foley, Helene P. *Female Acts in Greek Tragedy*. Princeton: Princeton University Press, 1991.

Franco, Cristiana. *Shameless: The Canine and the Feminine in Ancient Greece*. Oakland: University of California Press, 2014.

Gordon, Jill (2012). *Plato's Erotic World: From Cosmic Origins to Human Death*. Cambridge, UK: Cambridge University Press, 2012.

Hill, Lisa. "The First Wave of Feminism: Were the Stoics Feminists?" *History of Political Thought* 22 (2001): 13–40.

Irigaray, Luce. *Speculum of the Other Woman*. Ithaca, NY: Cornell University Press, 1995.

———. *This Sex Which Is Not One*. Translated by Catherine Porter with Carolyn Burke. Ithaca, NY: Cornell University Press, 1985.

Loraux, Nicole. *Children of Athena: Athenian Ideas about Citizenship and the Division between the Sexes*. Princeton, NJ: Princeton University Press, 1993.

———. *Tragic Ways of Killing a Woman*. Cambridge, MA: Harvard University Press, 1993.

Manning, C. E. "Seneca and the Stoics on the Equality of the Sexes." *Mnemosyne* 26 (1973): 170–77.

Marder, Elissa. *The Mother in the Age of Mechanical Reproduction*. New York: Fordham University Press, 2012.

Miller, Paul. *Diotima at the Barricades: French Feminist Read Plato*. Oxford, UK: Oxford University Press, 2016.

Most, Glenn W., ed. *Hesiod: Theogony, Works and Days, Testimonia*. Cambridge, MA: Harvard University Press, 2006.

Nussbaum, Martha, "The Incomplete Feminism of Musonius Rufus." In *The Sleep of Reason*, edited by M. C. Nussbaum and J. S. Hivola, 283–325. Chicago, IL: University of Chicago Press, 2002.

Pomeroy, Sarah. *Goddesses, Whores, Wives and Slaves*. New York: Schocken Books, 1975.

Rawlinson, Mary, Sabrina Hom, and Serene Khader, eds. *Thinking with Irigaray*. New York: State University of New York Press, 2011.

Tuana, Nancy, ed. *Feminist Interpretations of Plato*. College Station: Pennsylvania State University Press, 1994.

Zajko, Vanda, and Miriam Leonard, eds. *Laughing with Medusa: Classical Myth and Feminist Thought*. Oxford, UK: Oxford University Press, 2006.

Zeitlin, Froma. *Playing the Other: Gender and Society in Classical Greek Literature*. Chicago, IL: University of Chicago Press, 1996.

Zeitlin, Froma, David Halperin, and John Winkler, eds. *Before Sexuality: The Construction of Erotic Experience in the Greek World*. Princeton, NJ: Princeton University Press, 1990.

Zuckerberg, Donna. *Not All Dead White Men: Classics and Misogyny in the Digital Age*. Cambridge, MA: Harvard University Press, 2018.

Part One

Myth, Divination, and the Pre-Platonic

Chapter One

Was Homer's Circe a Witch?

Andrew Gregory

It is widely accepted by many scholars, commentaries, and translations that Homer's character Circe was a witch, indeed the first in the Western literary tradition.[1] This paper will argue that neither Homer nor his characters considered Circe to be a witch, and nor should we. The modern Western conception of a witch has involved and still does involve substantial gender issues, which it is inappropriate to impose on Homer.[2] I will be interested in two gender related binaries in this paper. First, there is the question of why male gods in Homer have been treated simply as gods while some Homeric goddesses have been accused of witchcraft. Second, I will be interested in how the "good women, bad women" bifurcation has allowed an unjustified differentiation of female Homeric deities into goddesses and witches.[3] This paper's contribution lies in opening up these gender issues, in posing a key and hitherto unaddressed question about the abilities of Homeric deities, in questioning what supposedly differentiates Circe from other Homeric deities, and in a close and objective reading of the text, from which there is surprisingly much to be gained. There is a need to deal with the issues in some length and detail, as the Circe passages have been much discussed, the Circe-as-witch paradigm is deeply ingrained, and there appears to be, but in fact there is not, much interlocking evidence that Circe was a witch.[4] There is also a need to get back to the Greek, as a great deal of importance has been obscured in the standard English translations, virtually all of which treat Circe as a witch.

Important for this paper will be two questions of symmetry. If Circe acts in the same manner with similar intentions as the other Homeric deities, what is it then that differentiates her as a witch? Second, if words used to describe Circe have a clear meaning elsewhere in Homer, is there any justification for giving them a more sinister meaning when applied to her? Ultimately, this paper will pose a dilemma. If we do consider Circe to have been a witch, then there are many more witches, and many more warlocks in Homer, perhaps a whole pantheon of them. Conversely, if these Homeric deities were not witches and warlocks, then Circe was not a witch either. I argue we should reject the first lemma as anachronistic, misleading, and unjustified by the text.

Also, at stake are some broader issues concerning how we read Homer, how we read the portrayal of women in ancient literature, and how we read ancient texts where, to the modern Western eye, there appears to be some magical element. This paper also has some philological import, in that some words in Homer (exclusive to Homer or originating with Homer) have been ascribed a meaning on the assumption that Circe was a witch. Remove that assumption and we need to rethink the meanings of those words.

Circe the Goddess and Magic

It is an important fact that Circe was a Homeric goddess. She is always referred to as a goddess, both by the narrative and by the characters. Odysseus' men, when they first meet Circe, wonder if she is a woman or a goddess (X, 227, 255),[5] without considering the option of witch.[6] Circe is immortal, *athanatê* (XII, 302). Circe's genealogy is that of a goddess, daughter of Helios the sun god (X, 138) and Perse who is the daughter of Okeanos (X, 139). At XII, 155 she is a *dia theaôn*, divine goddess. Her handiwork is that of a goddess, *hoia theaôn* (X, 222). It is also significant that Circe's house is a "sacred dwelling," *hiera dômata* (X, 426, 444), and is within a "sacred grove" *hieras bêssas* (X, 275).[7] Circe has four handmaidens (X, 348), who are children of the springs and groves and of the sacred rivers (*hierôn potamôn*). This is all appropriate for a goddess but not a witch.[8] One might argue here that *hieros* can also mean "enchanted" or "haunted," but in Homer's use elsewhere it exclusively means "sacred." So at *Iliad* I, 99 (passim) the *hekatombê* and other sacrifices are sacred. The gods collectively and individually are described as *hieros* (passim). More specific to the cases here, at *Iliad* VI, 89 Athene has a sacred dwelling. At *Iliad* II, 506 there is sacred Onchestus, the bright grove of Poseidon, and at *Odyssey* VI, 322 a grove sacred to Athene. At *Iliad* XI, 276 there is the sacred stream of Alpheius. Only if we already assume Circe to be a witch are there grounds to translate *hieros* in a sinister manner unattested elsewhere in Homer.

Circe then is not a woman who works magic. Is she a goddess who works magic? The key questions are as follows:

1. When Zeus gathers clouds, or generates a thunderbolt, are those magical acts, or is Zeus simply doing what a Homeric god is capable of doing?
2. Are any of Circe's actions magical, or is Circe simply doing what a Homeric goddess is capable of doing?

The intuitive, and in my view correct answer to 1 is that Zeus is simply doing what a Homeric god is capable of doing. One can ask this question of other Homeric deities with similar results. If we answer "Zeus magical, Circe magical" (with all the Homeric deities being magical), then I would ask why Zeus is not a warlock and why we single out Circe as a witch.[9] If Zeus is capable, what of Circe? Is there something different in the nature of Circe's actions? I will argue that there is not. Indeed many similar or identical actions are performed by other Homeric gods and goddesses, particularly by Athene and Hermes. Is there something different about the morality of Circe's actions? This may be contentious given Circe's modern reputation, but I argue that Circe's actions are not egregious in the context of the *Odyssey*. An important point made by Dickie is that there is no indication from Homer that Circe's actions are in any way impious or sacrilegious, and I would add there is no sense that Circe is or should be punished for her actions.[10]

The issue of abilities is highly important. At no time does Circe call on or invoke other powers outside herself. That is important relative to some general definitions of magic: "Magic may be said to be the exercise of preternatural control over nature by human beings, with the assistance of forces more powerful than they."[11]

Circe is neither human nor does she call on any assistance from any external force or power at any stage. I do not propose to defend this as an absolute definition of magic. Rather, my point is that against a plausible definition of magic it is questionable whether Circe does anything magical. One commentator has remarked that

> The Odyssey is unusually cognizant of the charm and subtle power, the potential helpfulness and dangerousness of woman; and Circe embodies in concentrated form the complex ambiguity of the Odyssean female. If not yet la belle dame sans merci, she is still never quite free of the awesome, non-human, or even subhuman, distance of a demonic power.[12]

Circe may be awesome and nonhuman but she is not subhuman and she does not have, nor is she in league with, any demonic power. That is so either in the Christian sense of demon, as there is no devil or anything similar in Homer, or the Greek sense of daemon, as a lesser deity (not necessarily evil) that still has abilities beyond those of humans. Indeed, in the *Odyssey* some characters (but not Circe) refer to daemons while the narrator does not, and they do not seem to be part of the ontology.[13] Our modern intuition, influenced by Christian thinking, may be that in order to do something beyond what we take to be natural, a human must access some other power.[14] It would be thoroughly anachronistic though to impose that idea on pre-Christian pagan mythology.[15]

Homer and Magic?

Distinctions such as normal and magical, or natural and supernatural,[16] are not to be found in Homer.[17] This is not a criticism of Homer, more a recognition that Homer was a very early Greek thinker, prior to the early Greek natural philosophers. In the mythology of many early cultures, what we would consider to be normal and magical were mixed together without any distinction between them. It is significant that the standard Greek terms of *magos* and its cognates (magician, wizard) or *goês* and its cognates (sorcerer, wizard, juggler, cheat) are not to be found anywhere in Homer. Homer has no other term for witch or for magic. Compare here the range of terms for something that does interest Homer, which is fate or one's lot in life. We have *moira*, *aisa*, and *kêra* (fate, fate, and death/doom), and we also have a range of *kata moiran* and *ou kata moiran* (passim, according to fate, not according to fate), *para moiran* (XIV/509, against fate), *huper moiran, ou huper moiran* (I/34, 35, V/46, *Iliad* XX/30, 336, XXI/517, beyond or not beyond fate), and *ammoira* (XX, 76 Zeus knows what is and what is not the fate of mortals). Similarly, we find *kat' aisan* at *Iliad* X/445 and XVII/716, and we find *kat' aisan . . . oud' huper aisan* at *Iliad* III/59 and VI/333. Nowhere do we find *kata phusin*, "according to nature," a phrase that is very common among the Presocratic natural philosophers.

This is not to deny that there are things that we might consider to be magical in the world of Homer's poems. It does, though, question whether Homer would consider them to be magical and whether he treated them differently compared to other phenomena. The world of Homer's poems is not chaotic. Clearly there are important regularities, for example, of the heavens and seasons. However, there are not exceptionless laws of nature either. The gods can and do intervene in the world on their own caprice, manipulating the weather to help or hinder Odysseus (passim). Athene can hold back the dawn, breaching the regularities of time and the heavens (XXIII, 242). It is perhaps significant that Homer's only use of the term *phusis*, nature (X, 303), in the *Odyssey* is in relation to something we might consider to be magical. Homer never uses *kosmos* and its cognates in its sense of cosmos, a well-ordered universe.[18] Without a strong conception of or vocabulary for what is normal or natural (and that is hardly Homer's main concern in his poems), it is difficult to develop a strong conception of or vocabulary for what is beyond or contrary to the normal or natural (again, not a major concern for Homer). I agree with scholars who reject the idea of any global, ahistorical definition of magic.[19] Rather, I take the view that magic is best understood through local contrasts of what is and is not considered to be magic. I do not see Homer contrasting what he takes to be magical or supernatural with what he takes to be normal or natural. Arguably, it is the early Greek natural philosophers who generate both the conception of and vocabulary for an invariant natural world, in which ideas of *phusis* and *cosmos* loom large.[20] So, for example, we have a report that

> Concerning thunder, lightning, thunderbolts, hurricanes and typhoons: Anaximander states that all these come about because of wind. Whenever it is enclosed in a thick cloud and then forcibly breaks out, due to its fineness and lightness, then the bursting makes the noise, and the rent against the blackness of the cloud is the lightning flash.[21]

So in contrast to meteorological phenomena being explained in terms of the caprice of the gods, typical in Homer and Hesiod, all of these phenomena are explained naturally.[22] Once this is in place, along with the *phusis/cosmos* vocabulary, then it is possible to develop an intellectual conception of the magical.[23] A corollary of this is that it is incorrect to speak of a unitary ancient, or even ancient Greek conception of magic or witchcraft. By the fourth century BCE, there may have been reasonable (though still developing) conceptions of both, but the time span from Homer is roughly equivalent to our own from the witch hunt of the fifteenth and sixteenth centuries CE, ample time for significant changes of attitude.

A simple example of how we can apply this analysis to Homer begins when Odysseus and his crew are preparing to leave Aiaia. Circe gets to the ship first (easily she passed us by, X, 574). This has led to speculation that in common with witches: Circe could make herself invisible, fly, or make a soul journey.[24] Typically a witch was supposed to apply some unguent or potion to make themselves invisible or fly,[25] and Circe knew many *pharmaka* (X, 276), the suggestion runs.[26] There is no mention of any such journey or potion though. What the text simply tells us is that "Against the will of a god who could see them with eyes as they go to and fro?" (X, 574). So, Circe as a Homeric goddess has the ability to make herself invisible to humans at will, without calling on any external power or using any potion, as do all Homeric deities. No magic, no witchcraft, just a Homeric goddess doing what any Homeric deity can do. If Circe is a witch on these grounds, then every goddess in Homer is a witch and every god a warlock.[27]

The *Rhabdoi*

Circe is possibly most famous for turning some of Odysseus' crew into pigs. Commonly, she is supposed to do this with a *rhabdos*, often translated as, "magic wand" or "witch's wand," first administering a *pharmakon* to make Odysseus' crew pliable.[28] The alternative is that she turns them into pigs with the *pharmakon* and then drives them into the pens with the *rhabdos*, here being given the alternative translation of "herding stick." The latter view is correct, not least because when Circe turns the pigs back into men again, she first drives them with her *rhabdos* (X,

388ff.) and then administers another *pharmakon* to each to turn them back into men again.[29]

No spell is involved here. After the attempt to transform Odysseus, Circe says "go now to the sty, and lie with your comrades" ("*ercheo nun supheonde, met' allôn lexo hetairôn*" [X, 320]). I take that as a herding instruction, Odysseus having just been hit with a herding stick, rather than as a verbal spell. I would expect a spell to be phrased differently.[30] There is no mention of Circe saying any spell when she works a successful transformation or when Hermes warns Odysseus of what she will do.[31] X, 326–28 has Circe saying,

> I am amazed that you have drunk this *pharmakon* and not been beguiled. No other man at all has resisted this *pharmakon*, once he has drunk it past the barrier of his teeth.

The critical point here is that Circe is amazed that the *pharmakon* has not worked, not that the blow of the *rhabdos* or any supposed spell has failed.

Circe is not the only deity in the *Odyssey* to have a *rhabdos*, though Circe's is very long, *perimêkei*, and more appropriate for a herding stick. Hermes has a beautiful *rhabdos* made of gold (*chrusos rhabdos* V, 47; XXIV, 2; *chrusorrapis* V, 87; X 277, 331). He lulls people to sleep with it and wakens them when he wishes (V, 47–48; XXIV, 3; *Iliad* XXIV, 343),[32] and he rouses and leads the ghosts of the suitors (XXIV, 5). Athene has a *rhabdos* (XIII, 429; XVI; 172, and XVI, 456), again a golden one. At XIII, 429 she withers Odysseus' flesh, destroys his hair, gives him the skin of an old man, and dims his eyes. At XVI, 172 she increases his stature and youth. At XVI, 455 she makes Odysseus into an old man again.[33] It is interesting to compare how these *rhabdoi* are used. We are not told that Hermes touches anyone or anything with his *rhabdos*. At XIII, 429 and at XVI, 172 Athene touches, *epemassat'*, Odysseus with her *rhabdos*, while at XVI, 456 Athene strikes him, *peplêguia*. Odyssey X varies between *elaunein*, to drive, and *plêssein*, to strike, for Circe's *rhabdos*. So at X, 238 we have *peplêguia* (transforming the crew to pigs), at X, 293 *elasê* (warning from Hermes of what Circe will try), at X, 319 *peplêguia* (attempt to transform Odysseus), and at X, 390 *elasen* (transforming the crew back). So generally, Athene touches with her *rhabdos* while Circe drives. It would be clearer if Athene only touched with hers and Circe only drove with hers, though there is a reasonable contrast even though Homer uses *plêssein*, to strike, for both.[34]

The *Pharmaka*

Circe administers *pharmaka* to Odysseus' men and is described at X, 276 as *Circês . . . polupharmakou*. The Loeb here gives "Circe, expert in poisons," which is too pejorative as Circe has healing as well as harmful *pharmaka*. The usual terms for harmful *pharmaka*, *kakos*, and *lugros*, are absent here but are often used elsewhere. As Stratton has pointed out, *pharmakos* itself is neutral as a term and needs to be qualified by good or bad.[35] Butler gives "the enchantress Circe," the Penguin "sorceress." All *Circês . . . polupharmakou* says is "Circe of many *pharmaka*," which I take to mean that Circe knows many *pharmaka*, or possesses many *pharmaka*, or quite possibly both.[36]

Helen (IV, 219ff.) casts a *pharmakon* into the wine that will cause humans to forget all ills. Helen knows of more *pharmaka*, as she has *pharmaka mêtioenta*, *esthla*, drugs that are useful and good (IV, 227–28). She knows of these from the Egyptian woman Polydamna. Egypt produces the most *pharmaka* (IV, 228ff.), from the "grain giving earth," "*zeidôrus aroura*" (IV, 229), which strongly suggests these are natural.[37] Many of these are good when mixed, many of these harmful (*polla men esthla memigmena polla de lugra*). Here each is a doctor (or perhaps healer, *iêtros*) having knowledge above humans. Not a sorcerer or witch, but a doctor/healer. At *Iliad* XVI, 28 there are *iatroi polupharmakoi*, doctors/healers knowing many *pharmaka*. There is a good deal of simple medical use of *pharmaka* for wounds in the *Iliad*.[38]

After Homer, one Greek term for witch is *pharmakis*, clearly derived from *pharmakon*.[39] Ogden has argued that it would be "disingenuous to attempt to dissociate *poly-pharmakos* and *pharmakis* in meaning,"[40] so Circe is not fully characterized as a goddess but is at least in part characterized as a witch. On the grounds that there are *iatroi polupharmakoi* in Homer, I disagree. Both Circe and these healers know many *pharmaka*, and those *pharmaka* are natural (see below). In Homer, *polupharmakos* does not pick out witches, merely those with good knowledge of *pharmaka*.

Agamede is an interesting and important parallel to Circe. By the fourth century BCE she was considered by some sources to be a witch.[41] Yet all we are told about Agamede by Homer is that she "knew so very many *pharmaka* which were nourished by the broad surface of the earth" (*Iliad* XI, 741). I do not see that Homer or his characters treat her as a witch on these grounds and nor should we. She is merely an herbalist who is later portrayed as a witch, in an era when conceptions of witchcraft and magic had developed considerably after Homer.[42] Neither Homer[43] nor Hesiod[44] have a bad word to say about Hekate, but she too is soon seen as a witch in some sources. So too by the fourth century BCE, Circe was considered to be a witch in some sources. There are more grounds to consider with Circe, but we should not consider her to be a witch because she knew of, possessed or employed *pharmaka*.[45] We should beware this effect, though, and the "witch hunting mentality" that attempts to impose a stereotypical or anachronistic account of what it is to be a witch on otherwise innocent actions.[46]

Hermes has knowledge of *pharmaka*, too. He intercepts Odysseus as he is going to attempt to rescue his men who have been turned into pigs. He warns Odysseus that he is likely to fail and gives him a *pharmakon esthlon*, a good *pharmakon*, to counteract the *pharmaka* of Circe. The Loeb here translates *pharmakon esthlon* as "potent herb," the Oxford "herb of magic virtue." Hermes pulls the *pharmakon* from the ground (X, 302ff) and shows its nature, *phusin*, to Odysseus. It is hard (*chalepon*, X, 305, or perhaps dangerous) for men to dig, but "the gods can do all things." It is significant here that Odysseus does not need to do anything magical with this herb. He merely has to be shown its nature.[47] So too while only a god can dig it easily/safely, both gods and humans can use it. I have left *pharmaka* untranslated so far to bring out the fact that Circe has *pharmaka*, Hermes has a *pharmakon*, and Helen and many others have *pharmaka*. English translations of the *Odyssey* tend to obscure this by rendering Circe's *pharmaka* as "drugs" or "poisons" and everyone else's *pharmaka* as "herbs," with no justification.[48] If Hermes' *pharmakon* that counteracts the *pharmaka* of Circe is a naturally occurring plant that has a *phusis*, then Circe's *pharmaka* may well be something similar.[49]

I agree with Naddaf that the use of *phusis* at X, 303 (*moi phusin autou edeixe*) is interesting, as Homer might have used *eidos*, *morphê*, or *phuê* instead. So perhaps *phusis* intends something more than external appearance, and perhaps *edeixe* indicates more than show, perhaps demonstrate or instruct.[50] However, I disagree with Naddaf on Circe being a witch, having a magic wand, and using a spell, so do not see that Odysseus needs to know everything about the Moly in order to combat her, and all we are in fact told is that Moly is what this is called by the gods and that it has a black root and a white flower.[51] It is interesting that the discussion of the extent of the knowledge here has centered on the men, and no one has been concerned with what knowledge Circe might have, even though her *pharmaka* are on a par with the Moly and Circe is described as *polupharmakou*. This is significant, as we might make similar points about the knowledge that Agamede, Helen, and Poludamna, along with the Greek and Egyptian healers, might possess. In my view all of these characters have a knowledge of the *phusis* of *pharmaka*, which goes beyond the external appearance that would be indicated by *eidos*, *morphê*, or *phuê*, but is probably not as extensive as the later Presocratic sense of *phusis* as origin, development, and current constitution.

Are *pharmaka* natural in Homer, in the sense that they are not made by gods or humans? There is strong evidence to suggest that *pharmaka* are either naturally occurring plants or that they are simple preparations thereof. This is clear in the case of Hermes' *pharmakon* but should also be evident in the case of Agamede, where *pharmaka* are "nourished by the broad surface of the earth" (*Iliad* XI, 741), and Helen, where Egypt produces the most *pharmaka*. One might argue, though, that Circe's *pharmaka* are different in that they are *kaka* (X, 213) and *lugra* (X, 236). However, *pharmaka* that are *kakos* or *lugros* are also naturally occurring. The snake of *Iliad* XX, 94 is described as *bebrôkôs kaka pharmak'*, "having eaten *kaka pharmaka*," presumably plants. The *pharmaka esthla* and *pharmaka lugra* produced by Egypt may well be naturally occurring, or at most be produced by a simple mixing of naturally occurring ingredients, or a mixing with water or wine. Does Circe do something strange with the ingredients she has? She makes a *kukeô* (X, 290, 317), a simple mix of barley, cheese, and wine.[52] The verb used is *teuchô*, a standard verb of making in Homer for manufacturing, handiwork, or cooking. According to Hermes, she will simply throw, *baleei*, the *pharmaka* into the *kukeôn*. This is the same verb as when Helen puts *pharmaka* in the wine (IV, 221). Circe simply gives, *edôken*, the *pharmaka* that transformed the wild animals (X, 213), at X, 235 she mixes up, *anemisge*, *pharmaka* with food, and at X, 317 she simply throws, *hêke*, the *pharmakon* into Odysseus' drink. When Circe turns some of Odysseus' crew back into men, she smears, *prosaleiphen*, each of them with a *pharmakon* (X, 392). It does not appear that Circe enchants her *pharmaka* any more than Hermes or Helen do. Homer's poems may credit plants with more powers than we would, but these are natural powers in the sense that they are inherent to the plants and are not induced by any magical action of gods or humans.

Here we might consider the following question. If we can analyze a supposedly magical act into nonmagical components, does that entail that the act is not magical? My own intuition on this is yes. All, or some part of an act must be irreducibly magical for the whole act to be considered magical. No collection of natural actions can produce something beyond or contrary to nature. There is an alternative though, which takes a holistic view or a syndrome view of magic, insisting it is the nature of the whole act which is critical, not the nature of the parts. Here one would need to be very careful in specifying what precisely is considered to be magical about the whole and on what grounds. It is significant here that when Circe fails to transform Odysseus, she does not wonder that the supposed whole process failed, or even that each of the individual elements of *pharmaka*/*rhabdos*/spell failed, but only that the *pharmakon*, a simple preparation of a naturally occurring herb, failed.

There are some issues in relation to the Moly given by Hermes to Odysseus.[53] It is not clear what Odysseus is supposed to do with the Moly (possess it, eat it, put it in Circe's *kukeôn*, or something else) in order to guard against Circe's *pharmaka*.[54] Nor is it entirely clear why, if Odysseus has the Moly, he makes Circe swear an oath to do him no further harm. If Odysseus is meant to eat it raw, or perhaps consume some simple preparation of it, and if it is proof against one administration of Circe's *pharmaka*, that would make reasonable sense of the narrative.[55]

A second issue here is why Homer gives us so little information on the Moly. One view is that Homer is attempting to suppress magical elements in the *Odyssey*.[56] However, this imposes a modern Western view of what is and is not magical and a rationalization agenda, which are not necessarily shared by Homer. I would also be suspicious of any attempt to bring Homer into a *muthos* to *logos* account, which sees a gradual and linear rationalization and suppression of magic beginning with Homer, passing through Hesiod, and culminating in the Milesian natural philosophers. My alternative is simple and deflationary, but ties into my solution to the first Moly issue. Homer is not particularly interested in events we would consider to be magical. The *pharmaka* of Hermes and Circe are naturally occurring. Odysseus simply consumes the Moly. There is nothing here for Homer to make a great fuss about, especially as this is marginal to the drama of the interaction between Circe and Odysseus. Homer may, to a modern eye, tell us disappointingly little when Hermes gives us the *phusis* of the Moly, but the interest is modern and not Homer's.[57] Homer is more interested in what Odysseus must do to show bravery and leadership. It is also significant here that Hermes tells Odysseus "all of the cunning plans of Circe" ("*panta de toi ereô olophôia dênea Kirkês*," X, 287), but all that amounts to is saying that Circe will mix and *kukeôn* and throw *pharmaka* in it (X, 290). Perhaps that's disappointing for something magical, but it's understandable for natural *pharmaka*. A further parallel here is the bag of winds given by Aeolus, which Odysseus' crew foolishly opens only to be buffeted at random. As with the Moly, Homer gives us very little on the nature or use of the bag of winds.[58]

The verb that Homer uses when Circe administers her *pharmaka* is *thelgein*.[59] In later Greek certainly this comes to mean "enchant" or "bewitch," but it could also have a sense of beguile, as with humans being beguiled by the gods or being beguiled by words. It is very significant that when Circe transforms some of Odysseus' crew back into men again, we do not get *thelgein*. This is just as much an act of supposed witchcraft as the initial transformation is (especially as the men are taller and more handsome than before), so if *thelgein* indicates bewitchment it should be there. However, if *thelgein* indicates beguilement, it should not be there with the countertransformation, as there is no need for any subterfuge. Circe is not the only person to beguile in the *Odyssey*. This is what the God Hermes does with his *rhabdos* (*thelgei* V, 47; XXIV, 3; *Iliad* XXIV, 343), beguiling humans to sleep. The Sirens also beguile when they sing (*thelgousin*, XII, 40, 44). Elsewhere there is beguilement by words/lies (I, 57; III, 264; XIV, 387; XVII, 514; XVII, 521; *Iliad* XXI, 276), the gods can beguile (XVI, 195; 298; *Iliad* XII, 255), Zeus and Athene beguile the suitors (XVI, 298), hearts can be beguiled (XVIII, 212, 282; *Iliad* XV, 322, 594), and there can be beguilement by craft (*Iliad* XXI, 604).[60] There are no grounds to translate *thelgein* as "bewitched" or something similar in *Odyssey* X. It does not fit Homer's use of *thelgein* in that chapter, nor does it match Homer's usage elsewhere.[61]

Apollonius of Rhodes' *Argonautica* provides some interesting parallels on *pharmaka*. They are "generated/grown from the ground and full flowing waters," *êpeiros te phuei kai nêchuton hudôr*,[62] so again ought to be seen as natural and the preferred translation ought to be herbs rather than drugs. A consequence of this is that there is then no case that Circe, Hekate, or Medea are witches in the *Argonautica*. Circe is treated quite positively, as someone who can cleanse suppliants of murder.[63] At *Argonautica* IV, 666–67, there is a construction with *pharmaka* and *thelgein*, but this should be translated as "beguiled with herbs," rather than the Loeb's "bewitched with drugs." Hekate is a goddess with a sacred temple,[64] who is prayed to in the *Argonautika*.[65] At *Argonautika* III, 479, she guides a girl "to treat with herbs," *pharmassein*, not the Loeb's "concocts drugs." Medea is not mentioned by Homer and is a once-mentioned goddess in Hesiod.[66] Medea does instruct Jason in the use of herbs in the *Argonautika*, but that is unproblematic as these are natural, Jason speaks of *menoeikea pharmaka*, "suitable herbs," and there is no distinction with her instruction to Jason on how to use a rock to defeat the earth-born soldiers.[67] At *Argonautica* IV, 1677, Medea is *polupharmakou*, which should be rendered as "having/knowing many herbs," rather than the Loeb's "sorceress." The *Argonautica* is dated to the third century BCE, so it is interesting that while some of these characters are treated as witches from around the fourth century BCE on, there is not unanimity here. One might argue that Apollonius is deliberately echoing Homer in generating an epic poem, to which I would reply that he does so correctly in not treating these characters as witches and, echoing or not, he can do so in the context of the third century BCE.

Circe's Beasts

Circe's house has attendant tame wolves and lions. There is a question as to whether the wolves and lions are wild animals that Circe has tamed, or whether they are humans that she has transformed. The former is correct, as the wolves and lions are treated differently from the pigs (free not penned), they behave differently (fawn, beg, tail-wag), and are described differently (no residual human attributes, mental or physical). The fact that the wolves and lions tail-wag, beg, and fawn to strangers may indicate they are well treated by their keeper. The comparison drawn is to good masters who give treats to their dogs (X, 216). These may simply be Circe's exotic pets. The best formulation here is that of de Jong, bringing out an interesting contrast. These animals are changed in mind but not in shape (they've become tame), while the crew is changed in shape but not in mind.[68] The wolves and lions do not fit the pattern of witches' familiars. These would usually be small animals, would have magical powers, would be used for channeling demonic powers, and would often be fed by the witch by a special witches' treat.

It is significant that Artemis is "queen of the wild beasts," *potnia therôn* at Homer, *Iliad* XXI 470ff. Circe is also *potnia*, "revered" or "queenly"

(X, 394, 549). This is a term of high praise for women/goddesses in Homer. Aphrodite clearly has power over all animals, birds, land animals, sea animals (*Homeric Hymn to Aphrodite* I, 3–5). Fierce gray wolves, lions, bears, and leopards fawn on her (*Homeric Hymn to Aphrodite* I, 69–72). Circe's wolves and lions also fawn; in each case the verb is *sainein*. The same verb is used for dogs in relation to human masters (X, 217) and dogs in relation to Telemachus (XVI, 6), so there is nothing mysterious about this fawning.

The alternative view relies on the testimony of Eurylochus, who is concerned that if they return to the house of Circe, she will "make us all into pigs or wolves or lions" (X, 431–32). Eurylochus' fear for the future, though, does not mean that in the past Circe has worked a human to wolf or lion transformation. How reliable is Eurylochus' testimony? He is clearly afraid, as he was earlier (X, 266ff.). Does he exaggerate the peril to convince others not to go? That is certainly possible. He does get it wrong that Circe will transform them in order to have them guard her house. If the wolves and lions are guards, they are very poor ones, as they neither attack the crewmen, oppose them going further, or alert Circe to the presence of strangers (the crew have to call to Circe, X, 228–29).[69] Also significant are the reactions to Eurylochus' testimony. Odysseus considers whether or not to cut his head off while the rest of the crew go (X, 438ff.). Evidently they do not put great store by Eurylochus' testimony. It may be significant that Homer uses *katathelgein* for these animals and *thelgein* for humans into pigs, perhaps indicating different changes.[70] Eurylochus uses *poiêsetai* (X, 433), she will make, for a change into pigs, wolves, or lions in his speech, but I take that to be symptomatic of his incomprehension, exaggeration, and panic.

Ogden has suggested that the only reason people kept pigs in the ancient world was to eat them.[71] It can hardly be for want of food that Circe works this transformation though, as after she transforms the pigs back she still feeds Odysseus and all his crew for a year. Ogden has suggested that all the animals on Circe's island are transformations from humans, such that Odysseus and his crew are tricked into an act of cannibalism in eating the stag that Odysseus hunts.[72] However, there is nothing in the text to suggest that this animal is any different from any other hunting success that Odysseus has in the *Odyssey*. The stag is free to roam, rather than tied to the house like the wolves and lions, and it does not approach Odysseus and fawn on him (it is coming down from pasture in the wood to drink, X, 158–59). Also significant is that the stag is god sent (X, 157) and the meal is an *erikudea daita* (X, 182), a splendid meal.[73] We can compare other splendid meals at III, 66; XIII, 26; and *Iliad* XXIV, 802, and contrast the *aterpea daita* (X, 124), the loathsome meal that the cannibalistic Laestrogonians make of Odysseus' men, spearing them like fish and carrying them home to eat. Where there is cannibalism, it is made clear that such a thing happens and that it is abhorrent (X, 123–24). I would expect to see either some sense of condemnation or at the very least some tragic drama to be wrought out of these supposed acts. There is no sense of impiety or sacrilege here.[74]

Circe: Deeds and Descriptions

There are several deeds of Circe (real or imagined) that are supposed to be characteristic of a witch, such as weather working. Circe certainly has some control of the weather, at least in the proximity of Aiaia. Each time Odysseus leaves, Circe gives him a northerly wind to help him on his way. Calypso, like Circe gives Odysseus a favorable wind when he departs (V, 167, 268). Witches were supposed to use the weather to create *maleficia*, to sink ships or to destroy crops. Circe, though, uses her control of the weather in a manner that is beneficial to Odysseus. It hardly needs pointing out that other Homeric deities can control the weather (Zeus, Poseidon), and often do so in a manner that is not beneficial to Odysseus![75] Athene, when offended (V, 108) generates *anemon te kakon kai kumata makra*, an evil wind and huge waves, though she is also able to give a favorable wind (II, 420; XV, 292). Athene is also able to generate mist to hide Odysseus (VII, 140; XIII, 90).

It is held by some commentators that witches can cause men to fall from heights, so Circe has been implicated in the death of Elpenor, one of Odysseus' crewmen.[76] Odysseus tells us that Elpenor (X, 552ff.), who is not mentally the best equipped, lay down on the roof of Circe's house when he was very drunk to get some cool air. The movements of his comrades roused him and, forgetting he came up by ladder, he fell off the roof and broke his neck. Elpenor (XI, 60ff.) confirms this account of his death. He blames the evil will of some god and a vast amount of wine, but does not blame Circe, even though he is now in Hades. Ogden has quite reasonably questioned why Circe did not bury Elpenor,[77] but it is not her job to do so. Is it proper for a goddess to bury a mortal? Odysseus believes it is for himself and his crew to perform the burial rites (XI, 50ff.). So does Elpenor, who asks Odysseus to bury his corpse so that Odysseus does not incur the wrath of some god (XI, 71ff.). There is no sense here that Circe failed to do something she should have done.[78]

Is Elpenor critical to a successful consultation with the dead for Odysseus? It adds some dramatic tension to the tale if Elpenor is first, so we have to wait for Teiresias. It is a nice piece of tragedy/irony (Odysseus says "coming on foot you have outstripped me in my black ship" [XI, 58]) and it may help to illustrate who can say what and why when necromancy is performed. I do not see, though, that Elpenor is in any way necessary for Odysseus to get the information he needs from Teiresias. So, I cannot subscribe to Ogden's view that Circe deliberately contrived Elpenor's death and left him unburied in order that Odysseus could have a successful consultation.[79]

Circe certainly has foresight (X, 472ff.; XII, 37ff.). However, this seems to be a straightforward ability she has as a Homeric goddess. When Odysseus is about to tell his crewmen what Circe has prophesied to him, he describes her as a *dia theaôn*, divine goddess (XII, 155). She does not call on any power, object, or person, nor cast any spell, in order to have this foresight. She uses this foresight solely to advise Odysseus how to accomplish his aims. Hermes tells Odysseus of what Circe will do (X, 281ff.), and Circe says that Hermes prophesied to her that she would meet with Odysseus (X, 331ff.). Athene prophesies the death of the suitors (I, 252). So, too, there is Teiresias, the blind seer of XI, 90ff.

Circe is said to be spinning a web at X, 221ff. Even if we take this as a metaphor for planning, many other people, both humans and deities have plans in the *Odyssey*.[80] Circe's web is *ambroton*, divine/immortal; it is the handiwork of a goddess and it is an accomplished and beautiful piece of work. Other goddesses and women are often found spinning or doing allied activities, such as Calypso (V, 62), Odysseus' wife Penelope (II, 90; XIX, 150), and the Phaeacian women (VII, 110). In relation to fate, your fate can be spun at birth by the personified Fates, Moira, Aisa, or Klothes, or gods can spin your fate.[81]

There are several descriptions of Circe that have been taken to be negative descriptions, or to imply that she is some form of witch, when there are alternative, more plausible interpretations. At X, 289, Hermes warns Odysseus of the *olophôia denea* of Circe. The Loeb translation of the *Odyssey* gives this as "deadly wiles," but this is harsh as Circe has not killed anyone, does not plan to kill anyone, and indeed does not kill anyone.[82] Her use of a *kukeôn* may be deceptive but is not deadly. The Penguin version translates *olophôia denea* as "black magic," the Oxford as "witches' arts," while Butler translates it as "wicked witchcraft." The description *olophôios* is used four times in the *Odyssey*, once of Circe, twice of the shape changer in *Odyssey* IV (410, 460), and once at XVII, 248. With the shape changer, *olophôios* is much better rendered as "cunning" or "deceptive" than deadly.[83] He is able to change shape when he is ambushed by Odysseus, but he does not kill him or attempt to do so. Also, significant here is that the shape changer at IV, 455, is said to have a "*doliês technês*," a "crafty" or "deceitful" skill. At X, 339, Circe is *dolophroneousa*, crafty minded. Compare this with *Iliad* XIX, 97, 112 where Hera is said to have craft or cunning. It is also worth noting that at IX, 30, Circe is referred to as the guileful woman, *doloessa*, of Aiaia. At XIX, 137, Penelope's robe is *dolos*.[84] At X, 258, Eurylochus does not enter Circe's house as he suspects some *dolon*, some cunning or deceit. Circe may well have cunning, guileful or deceptive plans, but she does not have deadly plans, nor does she employ black magic or wicked witchcraft.

Circe is described three times as "beautiful haired Circe," "*deinê theos audêessa*," first at X, 136. The Loeb translation renders this as "dread goddess of human speech." However, *deinê* can mean fearful, or strong, or skillful. I would suggest "awesome" or Butler's "formidable" as the best translations here, giving the sense that Circe is a Homeric goddess with powers beyond those of humans. One consideration that may help here is how we understand *oloophronos* at X, 137, when Circe is first described in *Odyssey* X. I would translate "beautiful haired Circe, awesome goddess of human speech, sister to sagacious [*oloophronos*] Aetes."[85] I would also accept *crafty* or *cunning* here, but not *baneful* with its negative connotations. Calypso at I, 52 and Ariadne at XI, 322 are also described as *oloophronos*. Circe is by no means alone in being described as *deinê*, as almost a whole pantheon of gods are described in this manner.[86] That the *deinê theos audêessa* description is used twice directly after Circe has been extremely generous to Odysseus and his crew (XI, 7–8 and XII, 149–150) speaks against the idea that *deinê* is a negative description here.

One might argue that in the main, Circe uses *pharmaka* for her ends and does not exert the powers of a goddess. That I think is mainly due to Circe's role in the plot of the *Odyssey* rather than any lack of powers. Circe does exert her goddess powers in her weather working, journeying without being seen by humans, influence over animals, knowing Odysseus has returned to Aiaia, and knowing the content of Odysseus' meeting with the ghosts. Circe was not an Olympian deity and that may mean that she had fewer powers or could not exert those powers as forcefully as some other deities. However, she shared the same sorts of powers as the Olympians and the powers were clearly of the same nature. As we have seen, Circe had similar descriptions to the other goddesses, whether they were Olympians or not.

Circe's Morality

So far, I have argued that there is nothing in the nature of Circe's actions that warrant us calling her a witch. What, though, of the morality of her actions? I do not intend any absolute defense of Circe. Rather, the key question is whether, in the context of Homer's poems, Circe does anything egregious enough to warrant different treatment from other Homeric deities. My first point here may seem obvious, but it nevertheless needs to be stated in this context. As stated in Xenophanes Fragment 11,

> Homer and Hesiod have ascribed to the gods all those things which are shameful and reproachful among men: theft, adultery and deceiving each other.

Homeric deities are not omnibenevolent. Throughout I have used "Homeric goddess" and cognate terms, as it is important to keep in mind the difference between Homeric deities and deities of the Abrahamic religions and even those of Xenophanes, Plato, and Aristotle. It is not enough simply to point out that Circe does some bad things, when virtually all of the Homeric deities do things as bad or worse. Unlike Athene, Circe neither kills nor plots to kill, and unlike at the beginning of the *Iliad*, she does not send a deadly pestilence on the Greek army (*Iliad* I, 10). In this context it is interesting to consider Athene, whose actions are usually given a very positive gloss. Athene does a great number of things that, from the modern point of view, would be considered magical and the actions of a witch. She has a *rhabdos*, and at VI, 229; VIII, 20;and XXIII, 156, she makes Odysseus taller, sturdier, and improves his hair. At XIII, 429, she withers Odysseus' flesh, destroys his hair, gives him the skin of an old man, and dims his eyes. At XVI, 172, she increases his stature and youth. At XVIII, 70, she increases the size of his limbs, and at XXIV, 520 gives him great strength. She is also able to transform herself (XIII, 221). She is capable of weather working (winds, waves, mists, II, 420; V, 108ff. VII; 140 XIII, 190; and XV, 292). She is able to beguile (*thelgein*) humans (XVI, 298). She has foresight (I, 252). She is capable of bestowing grace (II, 12; VII, 18, passim), sleep (I, 364; V, 491; XVI, 451; XIX 604; XXI, 358), and knowledge (II, 116) in humans. She can generate and control a phantom (IV, 795ff.). She is capable of holding back the dawn (XXIII, 242). As with all Homeric deities, she is invisible to humans if she wills it (X, 574). On issues of morality, she generates bad winds and huge waves to kill mortals who have offended her (V, 108ff.), she plots the death of the suitors with Odysseus (XIX, 1ff.), she binds Amphinomous so that he can be killed (XVIII, 155), and she approves of the acquisition and use of the "man slaying" *pharmakon* (I, 252ff.). Judged by the standards of modern morality, I would say that Athene acts worse than Circe. In an ancient context moral comparison here is more difficult, but what is clear is that Circe does nothing egregious in this context that would warrant her being classified as a witch when others are not.

So why are Circe, and to a lesser extent Calypso thought of as witches, but not Athene?[87] One reason may be that they are the females who hinder Odysseus' quest using what we perceive to be magic.[88] That, though, would be to define the merits of the female characters' actions in terms of their relationship with the male lead, and it hardly needs pointing out that that is a distinctly patriarchal approach. On a more feminist reading that treats Homer's females as independent characters in their own right, a radically different picture emerges.[89] If in addition to the split between female characters who help and those who hinder Odysseus, the good women/bad women dichotomy is applied, we then see the emergence of Circe the witch. Everything Circe does is given a negative interpretation and she is castigated as a witch, while everything Athene does is given a positive interpretation and so Athene has an unsullied reputation. Again, if we treat Circe (and Athene) more objectively, we can generate a radically different view. So too we must be cautious not to overplay any comparison between Penelope and Circe.[90]

Against the good women/bad women dichotomy, it is worth listing Circe's acts of generosity to Odysseus and his men as these are often ignored or underestimated. When Circe transforms the crew back again, she makes them younger, more handsome, and larger (X, 396). She pities the crew (X, 399). Circe bathes, anoints, clothes, and feeds Odysseus (X,

348ff.). Circe bathes, anoints, and clothes the crew (X, 449ff.). She also feeds them and gives them wine for a year (X, 466ff.). Circe does not obstruct Odysseus when he wants to leave Aiaia, but in fact gives him considerable aid.[91] Circe provisions the ship and gives them a favorable wind. Circe gives considerable good advice, and the means to carry it out, by giving Odysseus the ram and black ewe he will need in order to summon the ghosts.

When Odysseus and his men return to Aiaia from Hades in *Odyssey* XII, they busy themselves with the funeral rights for Elpenor and do not seem to be expecting to see Circe. However, Circe is aware of them and comes quickly with her handmaidens. Circe is again generous to Odysseus and his crew, and this generosity is both unsolicited and free from any compulsion. Circe and her handmaidens bring meat, bread, and wine. Circe gives Odysseus a great deal of good advice on what he needs to do next. When Odysseus' ship leaves, she gives them a good wind again. There is a view, expressed by Austin and others, that "Circe's generosity appears only under compulsion."[92] I disagree entirely. All of Circe's generosity in *Odyssey* XII is unsolicited and she is under no compulsion there at all. In *Odyssey* X, Circe swears to do no further harm to Odysseus, but her generosity there goes far beyond what that oath would compel, nor is there any threat or compulsion from Odysseus or his crew. We must be extremely cautious of the good women/bad women dichotomy and how that can be used to give a negative interpretation for everything concerning Circe. If it exists in Homer, it must be properly represented, not further imposed or amplified. It certainly should not be employed to generate a goddess/witch distinction between Circe and her fellow goddesses that is simply not there in Homer.

Drug Morality

Let us take it that Circe possesses *pharmaka*, which are *kakos* and *lugros*. Are there worse *pharmaka* in the Odyssey? At I, 261, we have the *pharmakon androphonon*, the man-slaying *pharmakon*, *androphonos*, being used by Homer for some of the exploits of Hector and Achilles (see, e.g., *Iliad* XVIII 317; XXIV 724). At II, 329, we have the *thumophthora pharmaka*, the life-taking *pharmaka*, or perhaps more literally soul-destroying *pharmaka*. Are these used, or are these intended to be used for nefarious purposes? At I, 252ff., Odysseus wants the man-slaying *pharmakon* to put on his arrows. Ilus will not give it to him, but Zeus does, with the apparent approval of Athene who is relaying the story. At II, 325ff., it is said that Telemachus plans murder, that he will bring men or he will go to the land of Ephyre to bring back the *thumophthora pharmaka* to put in the wine. Compared to this, Circe's acts of transforming men into pigs and back again seem relatively small misdemeanors.

Some of Circe's *pharmaka* are without doubt described as bad. But who describes them as bad and for what reason? We can answer the first part definitively. It is Odysseus and his allies (Hermes and the crew) who describe them as bad, not Circe, nor the narrator of the *Odyssey*.[93] Do they do so because these *pharmaka* are intrinsically bad or because they will hinder Odysseus in his quest? That is a more open question. Are withering the flesh, making someone old, and making their eyesight deteriorate intrinsically bad? This is what Athene does to Odysseus at XIII, 429, albeit with Odysseus' consent and to aid him in his quest. If Circe's men-to-pigs *pharmakon* was used to Odysseus' benefit would it still be described as bad? I do not wish to defend the idea that there are no bad *pharmaka* in Homer. Circe's wild beast *pharmaka* are described as bad when they have little bearing on Odysseus' quest; the snake of *Iliad* XXII, 94 eats *kaka pharmaka*; and some Egyptian *pharmaka* are *lugra*, though further debate is possible in all these cases. I merely want to point out that the *Odyssey* is relayed in large part through the speech of its characters, and we should be cautious of how those characters, with their own interests and agendas, evaluate entities and actions. In context, there is nothing egregious about Circe's knowledge, possession, or use of *pharmaka*.

Necromancy

At the beginning of XI, 23ff., Odysseus performs a ritual to summon ghosts, in particular the ghost of Teiresias, as he is advised to do by Circe (X, 504ff.). Circe does not perform an act of necromancy. Hermes does, leading the ghosts of the suitors (XXIV, 1ff.), as does Persephone (XI, 226ff.), sending ghosts to Odysseus and his mother and scattering ghosts (XI, 385ff.).[94] Is Circe present in some way when the necromancy takes place? Ogden has argued this on the basis that Circe knows what Teiresias has said without Odysseus telling her at the beginning of *Odyssey* XII.[95] One might add that at XII, 17 Circe is in some unknown way aware of

Odysseus' return to Aiaia. It is possible that Circe was present for the necromancy, though it is also possible that Circe has either foresight or some telepathic power.

What I would question here is whether necromancy had the same connotations for the Greeks of Homer's time, or for Homer himself, as it does for the modern Christian-influenced West. It may be a momentous act (showing bravery and leadership) for a mortal to summon ghosts (it seems much less momentous for Hermes or Persephone), but I do not have the sense in Homer that this is an intrinsically evil act. Neither Hermes nor Odysseus are treated as warlocks, and Persephone is not treated as a witch, either by Homer or later commentators, as she is aiding Odysseus. As is well documented, the Greeks had a very different relation to the dead than in modern Western thinking. Leviticus 20:27 is very clear on the status of necromancy,

> A man or a woman who is a medium or a necromancer shall surely be put to death. They shall be stoned with stones; their blood shall be upon them.[96]

There is also the important tale of the Witch of Endor, in Samuel 28:8–14, where Saul disguises himself and gets a female medium to summon the ghost of Samuel, contrary to the law, whose punishment is death. However, in ancient Greece, Empedocles Fr. 111, says that

> All the *pharmaka* which exist as a defence against evils and old age
> You will learn, as for you alone will I accomplish all these things
> You will stop the might of tireless winds which over the earth
> Sweep and destroy fields with their gusts
> Then again, if you wish, you will bring on the requiting winds
> You will make, from a black rainstorm seasonal drought
> for men, and out of a summer drought you will generate
> Tree nourishing streams that dwell in the aether
> and you will bring back from Hades the strength of a man who has died.

There is a debate here about how literally this passage should be taken,[97] but my point here is that Empedocles could commit such a statement to writing and escape any moral or legal censure for having done so. Necromancy was neither a major moral issue in Homer, nor for the early Greeks more generally. It is bold and heroic that Odysseus undertakes what is dangerous and frightening but necessary to get him home. There is, though, no sense of impiety or sacrilege.[98] There is also no sense that anyone, divine or human, is or ought to be punished by the gods for their role in any necromancy in Homer.

Sexual Morality

Circe initiates a sexual relationship with Odysseus. It is Circe who suggests they go to bed after she has tried to transform Odysseus and he has attacked her. That a goddess initiates a relationship is, I take it, nothing exceptional in Homer, nor that a goddess has a relationship with a mortal, Aphrodite's seduction of Anchises being a good example here. At V, 116, Calypso begins a complaint that the gods are envious of goddesses who have relationships with mortals and gives a list of those who have done so. There are some issues here though. Odysseus refuses to go to bed with Circe unless she swears a great oath that she will not plan some other harm for him, as he is advised to by Hermes (X, 301 and 344). The worry is that when Odysseus is naked/without weapons, Circe may render him unworthy and unmanned. As expressed by Hermes, "*s'apogumnôthenta kakon kai anênora thêê*," and as expressed by Odysseus, "*gumnôthorenta kakon kai anênora*." It is not clear here whether *apogumnôthenta/gumnôthorenta* means that Odysseus will be naked or just stripped of his weapons. He has just threatened Circe with his sword, so the latter is probably the best interpretation, and Hermes' *apogumnôthenta* too leans in that direction. Nor is it clear precisely what *kakon kai anênora thëës* means. One view is that Odysseus thinks it worthy and manly to rescue his crew. He believes that if he is unguarded with Circe, she may prevent that and so Odysseus will be made unworthy and unmanly. Certainly, he thinks she has some crafty or deceptive purpose (*dolophroneousa*, X, 339) in asking him to bed. Later, when he is offered food before his crew has been released, Odysseus says, "For what man, who is right minded," "*tis gar ken anêr, hos enaisimos eiê*," could eat before his comrades are freed?

Ogden has argued that Circe is not fully characterized as a goddess, as she has to swear an oath by the blessed gods, and gods do not swear oaths by the gods.[99] Who or what else, though, would a Homeric deity swear by? Calypso gives us the answer to this. She is asked by Odysseus to swear an oath exactly as he asks Circe. *Odyssey* X, 343–344 is an exact repeat of V, 178–179. Calypso swears by earth, broad heaven, and the River Styx, and this is according to her the greatest oath for the blessed gods, *makaressi theoisi*. This does not compromise her status as a goddess. We see similar oaths from Homeric deities at *Iliad* XIV, 271ff. and XV, 36ff. With that in mind, I would read X, 299 as "Command her to swear a great oath of the blessed gods" ("*Kelesthai min makarôn megan orkon omossai*"). Calypso is referred to as a goddess just before she swears this oath, as is Circe by both Hermes and by Odysseus in a similar context. There is a further nuance here in that while Hermes includes a reference to the blessed ones in his advice to Odysseus, this is not what Odysseus actually asks Circe to swear, nor, implicitly, what she does swear. Odysseus says, "*Thea, megan orkon omossai*," "Goddess, swear a great oath" (X, 343), without any reference to the blessed gods, and it is this that Circe immediately swears to.

Circe has been accused of using erotic magic and that is of course something that fits with the Western conception of a witch.[100] However, there is nothing explicit in the text about the use of erotic magic, and there is no need to suppose the use of erotic magic. Why does Odysseus have sex with Circe? Hermes advises him to in order to save his men, Circe is beautiful, she invites him to have sex with her, and she has a nice bed. Do we need more than that to explain Odysseus' actions? He has already had an affair with Calypso, so this will not be the first time he is unfaithful to Penelope. Alternatively, one might ask, what need does Circe have of erotic magic, when she is naturally attractive?[101] It is also important to be clear on the sequence of events. Circe attempts to transform Odysseus, he makes as if to attack her, she invites him to bed, Odysseus refuses and requires an oath. If the Moly is still active, why does Odysseus require an oath? If it is not, how is it that Odysseus can refuse to have sex with Circe when she has supposedly deployed some erotic magic? When Circe's attempt at transforming Odysseus fails, she is amazed (X, 325ff.) and says so openly. Yet Circe is not amazed when Odysseus initially refuses her and her supposed erotic magic has failed. Where there is some supplement to natural attractiveness, Homer makes that explicit, as at *Iliad* XIV, 197ff. But there is no mention of any such means here. Hermes has made clear that Odysseus has to sleep with Circe before their rescue. Odysseus is in an important sense a willing party in this.[102] Although it is not explicit in the text, it is highly likely that Circe and Odysseus have an affair while he is on Aiaia. Circe cannot deploy any erotic magic after she has made her oath, yet there is still a natural sexual attraction there without any erotic magic.

More radical views of *kakon kai anênora thêês* are possible. So *anênora* may mean that Odysseus is unmanned in the sense of losing his virility, becoming impotent, or even losing his penis.[103] If the latter sounds a little far-fetched, here are some passages from Kramer and Sprenger's *Malleus Maleficarum* (Hammer of the Evildoers), first published in 1487, effectively the seminal manual of witch hunting, and highly influential in thinking about witches for many years. Witch trials were rare in the Christian West until the late fifteenth century, until Innocent X's Papal Bull *Summis desiderantes affectibus* of 1484, and the subsequent publication of the *Malleus*. These are all section headings:

> Whether witches may work some illusion so that the male member appears to be entirely removed from the body.[104]
>
> How, as it were, they deprive man of his virile member.[105]
>
> Remedies prescribed for those who by the prestidigitatory arts have lost their virile members or have seemingly been transformed into beasts.[106]

If one has that conception of what witches do, then Circe is a prime candidate and one might want to read *anênora* in this manner. So too Circe's advances fit the Kramer and Sprenger pattern. In their view, "All witchcraft comes from carnal lust, which is in women insatiable. See Proverbs XXX; There are three things that are never satisfied; yea a fourth thing which says not 'it is enough': that is the mouth of the womb. Wherefore for the sake of fulfilling their lusts they consort even with devils."[107] Their view of women is that "Since they are feebler both in mind and body, it is not surprising that they should come more under the spell of witchcraft."[108] I would agree that "The Malleus probably contributed more than any other text to the perception that witchcraft was primarily a female crime."[109]

As many commentators have noticed, there is a strong tendency in Kramer and Sprenger toward a binary account of women. Either they are impossibly good, as with the Virgin Mary, or they have a tendency to be very bad, as with Eve, who is held to be the woman who let evil into the world. Brauner comments that "Kramer and Sprenger develop a powerful gender-specific theory of witchcraft based on a hierarchical and dualistic view of the world. Everything exists in pairs of opposites: God and Satan, Mary and Eve, and men (or virgins) and women."[110] At the root of the Western construction of the idea of a witch then are two binaries, between men and women, and between good women and bad women. These may not be as blatantly or misogynistically expressed now as they were in Kramer and Sprenger, but they remain implicit in many conceptions of witchcraft. It is only by differentiating Circe as a female and as a bad female that the accusation of witchcraft can generate any traction. This section also highlights the relative nature of the construction of witchcraft. It is clear that in some periods of history a woman's sexuality could be held against her in a way in which hopefully it would not be today. One could say something similar of intelligence, the cunning woman being open to accusations of witchcraft in the past, in the way that an intelligent woman today (hopefully) would not. In terms of reading ancient texts, we must be open to the possibility that female characters could be powerful, attractive, sexually active, and able to pursue their own agenda and interests in an intelligent manner without magic and without being witches.

Our Conception of a Witch?

It should now be clear that neither Homer nor any of Homer's characters treat Circe as a witch. One might argue though that Circe's character and actions fit the pattern of what we in the modern West understand to be a witch. Whether that is justified and whether that is an enlightening thing to say may depend on the following considerations.

The conception of a witch is not something ahistorical and given.[111] It is something that has been constructed and there are many variations on that construction. The modern Western idea of a witch has been generated within a patriarchy and there are many gender assumptions implicit in that construction. Those gender assumptions are necessary for the construction of Circe as a witch. She has to be differentiated from male gods and then other goddesses where there is no such differentiation in Homer, and she has to be treated as a bad woman. It is our construction that Homer's Circe fits our pattern of a witch, one that says more about the nature of the Western conception of a witch than it does about Circe or Homer.

It is important to recognize that however we construe the idea of a witch within broad modern Western parameters, on an objective analysis and a close reading of the text, Circe fits those conceptions much less well than is generally supposed. Circe is a goddess, not a woman working magic. There is no magic wand, there are no enchanted drugs, there are no spells, there is no soul flight, there is no causing people to fall from heights, there is no erotic magic, her beasts are not familiars, there is no cannibalism. She is not *La Belle Dame Sans Merci*. She is generous and helpful to Odysseus. Critically for any conception of a witch based on Christianity, Circe calls on no power outside of herself. Her actions and morality are not egregious either by ancient or modern standards. Phrases and terms supposedly attributing witchcraft to Circe in fact do not do so. There is not so very much left that does fit a supposed pattern. That Circe calls on no other power is critical. Are the categories of goddess and witch mutually exclusive? Here I agree with Ogden that they are not.[112] It is possible to imagine a world where a goddess can, and does, call on evil powers that are not her own. However, that is not the world of Homer's poems. No goddess calls on such a power and there is no such power to call on. So, Circe is neither goddess/witch nor goddess and witch. Even if we broaden the conception of witchcraft here to include any further power, so allowing "white" witches as well, still we see none of this in Homer.[113] If the notion of magical action is intrinsic to witchcraft, then even when Circe does engage in an activity that superficially matches a later pattern of witchcraft, such as weather working, in fact there is a deeper and critical mismatch.[114] So too there is a moral mismatch, as, for example, witches' weather working produces *maleficia*, evil deeds, whereas Circe's weather work produces something good for Odysseus.

If Circe is held to fit some supposed modern pattern of witchcraft, then it must be recognized that many other Homeric deities fit this pattern as well, perhaps a whole pantheon of them. To single out Circe is unjustified and unjustifiable. One objection to this "proliferation" argument might be that being a witch requires not one, but several criteria to be met, or there is a holism/syndrome applicable to witchcraft.[115] Circe meets these criteria, but others implicated by one criterion applicable to Circe do not. I would reply in three ways. My analysis of Circe's descriptions and supposed deeds suggests that Circe meets fewer of these criteria than is generally supposed. Second, throughout I have taken Athene (able to transform herself and Odysseus, malicious weather working, beguilement, foresight, able to bestow sleep, can generate and control phantoms, involved with *pharmaka*, can hold back dawn, invisible at will, has *rhabdos*, etc.) and Hermes (flying, rousing and leading the dead, foresight, lulling to sleep, involved with *pharmaka*, invisible at will, has *rhabdos*, etc.) as interesting comparisons with Circe, as they clearly do meet multiple criteria for being a witch or warlock if Circe is supposed to be a witch. Other Homeric deities would join them on further analysis. Finally, I see no sense in Homer of what, collectively, is required to be a witch. Any such "syndrome" criterion would have to be a later imposition, and I would ask who defines such a syndrome, how it is defined, and why it is defined like that when there are many alternatives.

Does Homer's Circe fit some ancient folklore paradigm of what it is to be a witch? In Homer's time, I very much doubt that there was anything as concrete as a paradigm here.[116] We may group together some folktales and literature on the basis of an affinity to modern conceptions of witchcraft, but whether the authors would have recognized such a grouping, or subscribed to a paradigm, let alone articulated what that paradigm might be, would be further issues. As with the idea of a witch syndrome, who defines the paradigm they are supposed to fit, and how and why they do so, are key questions.[117] As a perfectly plausible alternative to a rigid ancient witch paradigm, I propose instead a loose tradition or rough commonality of females with strange powers prior to Homer. Second, I would argue that key parts of this discussion of Circe are generic, in the sense that they can be applied to other situations where characters in ancient literature have later been interpreted as witches but were not witches in the original context. Third, the fit between Circe and any supposed witch paradigm/tradition is not particularly strong, much less than is generally supposed. Fourth, even if there were an ancient witch paradigm, that need not bind Homer. Homer was quite capable of originality, transformation, and generating his own coherent worldview where goddesses have powers but are not witches.

One merit I claim for the view I have argued for is that it credits Homer with a coherent picture of his character Circe. She is not some confused mix of woman, witch, and goddess, but is simply a Homeric goddess. On this issue, the text we have is clear, however, the Homeric tradition may have developed before it. My view also allows us a reasonably univocal reading of many terms in Homer. Terms such as *hieros* and *deinos* do not mean one thing when applied to some deities and something far more sinister and unattested elsewhere in Homer when applied to Circe.

Conclusion

Circe was a Homeric goddess, with the powers of a Homeric goddess. She was not a woman who worked magic, nor was she a goddess who worked magic. She was part of the Homeric pantheon, and there is nothing in Homer that differentiates her in terms of the nature of her actions or her morality from other Homeric deities. The idea that she is a witch is a later construction, requiring a binary differentiation of gods from goddesses and goddesses from witches not to be found in Homer. Homer did not treat Circe as a witch and that is not accidental. The world of Homer's poems gave intrinsic powers to goddesses who need not, did not, and indeed could not call on other powers. Modern Western notions of magic and witchcraft simply do not map well onto Homer's pagan epic poetry. In broader terms, we can apply the analysis of this paper to Calypso, Agamede, Helen, and other Homeric females, as well as Hekate and Medea in the *Argonautika*. If Homer's Circe is not a witch, neither are these characters. It is important that we consider Homer's Circe as a character in her own right and not judge her actions by her relation to the male hero. So, too, we ought to consider what Circe and other female characters might know, rather than look at knowledge entirely in terms of the male characters. Beyond this, there is also an important application of this sort of analysis to the folk tradition of other cultures. There may be rather fewer witches there than is generally supposed. There is also the issue of how females are portrayed in Homer. It would of course be naive to suggest that there are no patriarchal or sexist assumptions in Homer or other ancient authors. We should be careful, though, not to import those associated with the witch tradition in our culture, especially the good women/bad women bifurcation. We need to reconsider how we evaluate Circe, who has suffered from this, and Athene, who has benefited from it. An awareness of this effect is critically important for our understanding of the portrayal of women and goddesses in ancient literature.

Notes

1. I would like to thank Prof. Daniel Ogden, Dr. Jessica Elbert Decker, Dr. Danielle A. Layne, Dr. Helen Perdicoyianni-Paleologou, Dr. Sarah Feldman, Jonathon Griffiths, Chiara D'Agostini, two anonymous referees and audiences at University of Bristol, the London Ancient Science Conference, University College London, University of South Florida and *The Otherwise Than the Binary* online conference for their comments on this piece.

Daniel Ogden, *Magic, Witchcraft and Ghosts in the Greek and Roman Worlds: A Sourcebook* (Oxford: Oxford University Press, 2002), and *Night's Black Agents* (Hambledon: Continuum, 2008) has put forth the best academic case for Circe being a witch. See, e.g., commentaries by Alfred Heubeck and Arie Hoekstra, *A Commentary on Homer's Odyssey* (Oxford: Oxford University Press, 1989); Irene De Jong, *Narratological Commentary on the Odyssey* (Cambridge: Cambridge University Press, 2001), translations by Samuel Butler; *Odyssey* (London: Cape 1922), widely available online; A. T. Murray, *Homer Odyssey* (New York: Heinneman, 1919); Emile Rieu, *Homer: Odyssey* (London: Penguin 2003); Walter Shewring, *Homer: Odyssey* (Oxford: Oxford University Press 2008). Histories of witchcraft/magic also treat Circe as a witch. See for example, Venetia Newall, *Encyclopedia of Witchcraft and Magic* (London: Hamlyn, 1974), Rosemary Guiley, *The Encyclopedia of Witches and Witchcraft* (New York: Checkmark, 1989), Bengt Ankarloo and Stuart Clark *Witchcraft and Magic in Europe: Ancient Greece and Rome* (London: Athlone, 1999).

2. There may of course be ancient gender issues in Homer, but we should not assume these are identical to our own or impose later issues on Homer.

3. I mean nothing contentious or heavily theoretical here, just a recognition that such a bifurcation can be found.

4. See Ogden, *Night's Black Agents*, 7–26. Ogden argues that Circe knows drugs, controls weather, extends and renews life, makes incantations, manages summoning and control of ghosts and divination, changes forms, makes disappear, has the power of erotic attraction, and that these characterize her as a witch.

5. References to the *Odyssey* are given by chapter and line number.

6. Cf. Ogden, *Night's Black Agents*, 26. "Goddess or woman" in my view presents a simple exclusive choice, not some worry that Circe may be something in-between.

7. The sacred nature of these places is obscured in many English translations.

8. Especially as they only do good things for Odysseus and his crew (X, 351ff.).

9. Gods capable, goddesses magical would be an extraordinarily sexist view, generated by our own ideas of magic/witchcraft and religion with no basis in Homer.

10. Matthew Dickie, *Magic and Magicians in the Greco-Roman World* (London: Taylor and Francis, 2001), 23.

11. Valerie Flint, *The Rise of Magic in Early Medieval Europe* (Princeton: Princeton University Press, 1991).

12. Charles Segal, "Circean Tempations," *Transactions of the American Philological Association*, 99 (1968): 419.

13. Eric Dodds, *The Greeks and the Irrational* (Berkeley: University of California Press, 1951), 11. The *Iliad* treats deities and daemons quite closely, so Athene goes back to Olympus among the other daemons, *Iliad* I, 222.

14. Augustine, *De Civitate Dei* is seminal here. See, for example, X, 9 and XXI, 6, cf. Aquinas, *Summa Theologicae*, II, II, 96, and Heinrich Kramer and James Sprenger, *Malleus Maleficarum* (1487, Dover ed., 1971, trans, Montagu Summers, passim).

15. In the anthropological literature, there is a distinction between witches, humans who depend on external powers for magic, and sorcerers, humans who have magical powers themselves—a more common view outside the West. Neither is applicable to Circe the Homeric goddess.

16. See Andrew Gregory, *The Presocratics and the Supernatural* (London: Bloomsbury, 2013) on such distinctions in an ancient context.

17. I am not the only scholar to question whether there is magic in Homer, but this reason for doing so is new. Cf. Fritz Graf, *Magic in the Ancient World* (Cambridge: Harvard University Press, 1997), 30ff.; Dickie, *Magic and Magicians in the Greco-Roman World* 18ff.; Kimberley Stratton, *Naming the Witch: Magic, Ideology, and Stereotype in the Ancient World* (New York: Columbia University Press, 2008), 43.

18. Usually he uses such terms for military organization or similar order, or for seemliness.

19. See Ogden, *Night's Black Agents*, 5ff. Dickie, *Magic and Magicians in the Greco-Roman World*, chs. 1 and 2, Derek Collins, *Magic in the Ancient Greek World* (Oxford: Blackwell, 2008), ch. 1.

20. See Andrew Gregory, *Ancient Greek Cosmogony* (London: Bloomsbury, 2007). *The Presocratics and the Supernatural*, Anaximander: A *Re-Assessment* (London: Bloomsbury, 2016).

21. DKA23, Pseudo-Plutarch III, 3, 1.

22. See Gregory, *The Presocratics and the Supernatural*, Anaximander: A *Re-Assessment* on this being a specific contrast to Hesiod *Theogony*.

23. This is not to suggest a binary between myth and reason (see Sasha Biro, ch. 2 in this volume), or between poets and philosophers (see Jessica Elbert Decker, ch. 4 in this volume), as there are important commonalities of topics, arguments, epistemologies, and modes of expression, as well as a rich set of allusions from later to earlier thinkers (see Gregory, *The Presocratics and the*

Supernatural). There is, though, important new thinking about *phusis*—what its contraries might be, and how it might be investigated. Arguably the language and concepts of *phusis/kata phusin/para phusin* for the world about us are rooted in Homer's language of *moira/kata moiran/para moiran* (so too *aisa*) for the social order of gods and humans. Some attributes of the gods (immortal, etc.) became attributes of the *archai* of the early thinkers about nature, and the social order generated by the gods was transformed into the natural order of the cosmos. See Andrew Gregory, *Early Greek Philosophies of Nature* (London: Bloomsbury, 2021).

24. Ogden, *Night's Black Agents*, 18.

25. See Kramer and Sprenger, *Malleus Maleficarum*, 107.

26. *Pharmaka*—drugs? herbs? See below on translation.

27. The god Hermes can fly (V, 47 and *Iliad* XXIV, 343), but that is something that particular Homeric god is capable of.

28. So Butler, *Odyssey*, "she turned them into pigs with a stroke of her wand."

29. Cf. Ogden, *Night's Black Agents*, 15, Heubeck and Hoekstra, *A Commentary on Homer's Odyssey*, 57, 61. See also W. B. Stanford, "That Circe's *Rhabdos* Was Not a Magic Wand," *Hermathena* 66 (1945): 69–71.

30. In later Greek I would expect *katadesmeuô*, I bind, as a verb here, typically used in Greek spells and curses (see Collins, *Magic in the Ancient Greek World*, 64ff.). Homer uses *desmeuô*, but only in the ordinary sense of bond and does not use *katadesmeuô*.

31. After the successful transformation, the men/pigs may be more compliant and move off when struck with the herding stick, without instructions.

32. Athene also has the ability to give sleep, I, 364; V, 491; XVI, 451; XIX, 604; XXI, 358.

33. Other uses of *rhabdos* in Homer: XII, 251, a fishing rod which is *perimêkei*; *Iliad* XII, 297 is unclear but the *rhabdoisi* are probably small rods (rivets?) holding hide to a shield.

34. Many English translations obscure these differences.

35. Stratton, *Naming the Witch: Magic, Ideology, and Stereotype in the Ancient World*, 26.

36. Note that Odysseus is often described by *polu-* words, most typically *polumêchanê, polutropos, polumêtis* (of many devices, much traveled/turned, of many counsels). So, too, there is Poludamna (literally subdues many, who gives Helen *pharmaka*).

37. The alternative translation of "life giving earth" would lead to the same conclusion.

38. The standard phrase is "sprinkle soothing *pharmaka*" on the wound, with variations, *Iliad* IV, 218; XI 514; XV 394.

39. First use, Aristophanes, *Clouds*, 749, 423 BCE; see Ogden, *Night's Black Agents* 26. Note that *pharmakis* has the feminine *-is* ending, cf. my later note on the *Malleus Maleficarum*.

40. Ogden, *Night's Black Agents*, 26–27.

41. Dickie, *Magic and Magicians in the Greco-Roman World*. 23, Ogden *Night's Black Agents*, 21ff.

42. Ogden, *Night's Black Agents*, 100 considers Helen to be a witch as well.

43. Homeric Hymn to Demeter, 25, 52, 59, 60, 438, 440.

44. Hesiod, *Theogony*, 410ff.

45. With the introduction and development of ideas of magic and witchcraft post-Homer, we cannot take the view of some later Greeks that Circe was a witch as evidence that Homer thought she was.

46. In the European witch hunt of the fifteenth and sixteenth centuries, witches were questioned (tortured) until they confessed to a stereotypical account of witchcraft.

47. Gerard Naddaf, *The Greek Concept of Nature* (New York: State University of New York, 2005), 13–14.

48. Compare, for example, the Loeb's "Circe, expert in poisons," with its rendering of *Iliad* XVI, 28, where the *iatroi polupharmakoi* are "healers skilled in many herbs."

49. Cf. Ogden, *Night's Black Agents*, 20.

50. Naddaf, *The Greek Concept of Nature*, 13–14.

51. In my view it is the *polumêchanê*, *polutropos*, *polumêtis* hero Odysseus, with the aid of the god Hermes, confronting a minor, *polupharmakou* goddess, not man against witch.

52. Cf. Homer, *Iliad* XI 624, 641.

53. See Denys Page, *Folktakes in Homer's Odyssey*. Cambridge: Harvard University Press, 1973), 55, 57.

54. Cf. the bag of winds.

55. Cf. Ogden, *Night's Black Agents*, 20.

56. See Page, *Folktakes in Homer's Odyssey*, 69.

57. See Page, *Folktakes in Homer's Odyssey*, 55, 69.

58. Homer also gives us little on the nature or use of the *rhabdoi*.

59. X, 214; X, 291; X, 318; X, 326.

60. *Iliad* XIII, 435 is the only debatable passage, where *thelxas hosse phaeina* might mean "cast a spell on his gleaming eye" (Murray, Loeb) but could equally be "beguiled his gleaming eyes."

61. Is this special pleading in relation to Circe and *thelgein*? The view that Circe is a witch has been so dominant that this might appear so, but actually I believe the reverse is the case. As *thelgein* means to beguile elsewhere in Homer, there needs to be good reason (not just the supposition that Circe is a witch) why it does not mean to beguile with Circe. I see no such reason.

62. Apollonius of Rhodes, *Argonautica*, III, 530.

63. Apollonius of Rhodes, *Argonautica*, IV, 559, 587ff., 691ff.

64. Apollonius of Rhodes, *Argonautica*, III, 251; IV, 842, 915.

65. Apollonius of Rhodes, *Argonautica*, III, 915, 985, 1035; IV, 247.

66. Hesiod, *Theogony*, 961.

67. Apollonius of Rhodes, *Argonautica*, III, 1246 on herbs, 1364 on rock.

68. Irene De Jong, *Narratological Commentary on the Odyssey* (Cambridge: Cambridge University Press, 2001), 258.

69. Eurylochus also exaggerates Odysseus' supposed recklessness in dealing with the Cyclops—see De Jong, *Narratological Commentary on the Odyssey*, 265.

70. I take *katethelxen* to have a sense of "beguiled down," colloquially to "have got one over on." This is the only use of *katathelgô* in Homer. Cf. Heubeck and Hoekstra, *A Commentary on Homer's Odyssey*.

71. Ogden, *Night's Black Agents*, 16–17. I agree with Ruth Scodel, "Odysseus and the Stag," *Classical Quarterly* 44 (1994): 530–34, that the stag episode is integral to the plot and so does not demand elaborate interpretation.

72. Ogden, *Night's Black Agents*, 17–18.

73. Note that *erikudês* is often used for gifts of the gods, which in a way this stag is.

74. Dickie, *Magic and Magicians in the Greco-Roman World*, 23.

75. So, for example, in XII, 313ff., Zeus raises winds against Odysseus.

76. See, for example, Ogden, *Magic, Witchcraft and Ghosts in the Greek and Roman Worlds: A Sourcebook* and *Night's Black Agents*.

77. Ogden, *Magic, Witchcraft and Ghosts in the Greek and Roman Worlds: A Sourcebook*, 140, *Night's Black Agents*, 19.

78. Following Dickie, *Magic and Magicians in the Greco-Roman World*, 23, there is no sense of impiety or sacrilege.

79. Ogden *Magic, Witchcraft and Ghosts in the Greek and Roman Worlds: A Sourcebook*, 140, *Night's Black Agents*, 20.

80. Cf. Penelope weaving by day and unpicking by night.

81. *Iliad* XX/127; XXIV 209; *Odyssey* VII/195, for the Fates, Gods; *Iliad* XXIV/525; *Odyssey* I/17; III/208; XI/139; XX/195; VIII/579, Zeus, *Odyssey*; IV/208, a daemon; XVI/64.

82. Cf. the Sirens, Athene, assorted gods.

83. See Hesychius' Lexicon, which supports this view and is excellent evidence for how the Greeks understood this term. My thanks to Chiara D'Agostini for this point.

84. My thanks to Sarah Feldman for this point.

85. Butler gives "magician Aeetes," the Oxford has Circe with "strange powers" and Aeetes as a magician.

86. In the *Iliad* at IV, 514, we have Apollo; at V, 839, Diomedes; at VI, 380, 385, Athene; at XVII, 211, Ares. In the *Odyssey* at III, 145 and VII, 41, Athene; at VII, 246, Calypso.

87. Ogden *Magic, Witchcraft and Ghosts in the Greek and Roman Worlds: A Sourcebook* has Circe, Calypso, Helen, and the Sirens as witches, but does not mention Athene or Persephone in this context.

88. Note here that Homeric gods who hinder Odysseus are not thought of as warlocks, but are simply gods.

89. See Danielle A. Layne and Jessica Elbert Decker, Introduction, in this volume on "good" and "bad" women and how they are constructed.

90. We also need to be conscious of whose expectations and evaluations of female behavior is being used in such a comparison (Homer's? or modern ones?) if modern, feminist, or prefeminist (?) Circe will clearly fare better with feminist ideas than, say, Victorian ideals of womanhood.

91. Cf. Calypso.

92. Norman Austin, *Archery at the Dark of the Moon* (Berkeley: University of California Press, 1975), 153.

93. At X, 317, when Circe gives Odysseus the *pharmakon*, she has "an evil purpose in her heart," but note that it is Odysseus who says this.

94. Does necromancy involve magic? Later in antiquity, yes; in the Christian tradition, yes; but not for Homer.

95. Ogden, *Magic, Witchcraft and Ghosts in the Greek and Roman Worlds: A Sourcebook*, 140, *Night's Dark Agents*, 19.

96. Cf. Deuteronomy 18:10.

97. See Gregory, *The Presocratics and the Supernatural.*

98. Cf. Dickie, *Magic and Magicians in the Greco-Roman World*, 23.

99. Ogden, *Night's Black Agents*, 26.

100. See Ogden, *Magic, Witchcraft and Ghosts in the Greek and Roman Worlds: A*

Sourcebook, 139.

101. Circe is certainly not an ugly old woman living on her own as with the common witch stereotype.

102. See Andrew Dyck, "The Witches Bed but Not Her Breakfast," *Rheinisches Museum fur Philologie* 124 (1981): 196–98.

103. There is an issue of translation here as well. If we follow the Loeb, Oxford, or the Penguin translations, then "deprive/rob me of my courage and manhood" will sit better with ideas of loss of virility/penis, and so on. I don't think that is a good translation of *tithêmi* in this context, though, so I follow Butler's "render thee a weakling and unmanned."

104. Kramer and Sprenger, *Malleus Maleficarum*, 58ff.

105. Kramer and Sprenger, *Malleus Maleficarum*, 118ff.

106. Kramer and Sprenger, *Malleus Maleficarum*, 173ff.

107. Kramer and Sprenger, *Malleus Maleficarum*, 47.

108. Kramer and Sprenger, *Malleus Maleficarum*, 44.

109. Judith Burnett and Ruth Karras, *The Oxford Handbook of Women and Gender in Medieval Europe* (Oxford: Oxford University Press, 2013), 31. Even the title may be taken as an indication of attitude. *Malleus Maleficarum*, hammer of the (female) evildoers, not *maleficorum*.

110. Sigrid Brauner, *Fearless Wives and Frightened Shrews: The Construction of the Witch in Early Modern Germany* (Amherst: University of Massachusetts Press, 2001), 33.

111. Unless one seriously wants to defend the idea that there are/have been real witches and that witches form some sort of natural kind which is ahistorical. But even then our knowledge of that natural kind is clearly historical and changing.

112. Ogden, *Night's Black Agents*, 25.

113. I avoid attempting to "reclaim" Circe as a white witch or positive role model feminist magic user.

114. In my view the idea of magical action is intrinsic to witchcraft. Weather working on its own cannot simply be witchcraft, as science can "weather work" by, for example, seeding clouds to create rain.

115. See my earlier discussion of whether there is a holism or syndrome about magical acts.

116. One problem with the Kuhnian "paradigm" language, especially in an ancient context, is that it can imply a greater coherence of and compliance to some supposed set of ideas than actually existed. So, too, it can imply a greater stability over time than actually occurred. Kuhn himself was much more cautious (though not always entirely consistent!) in applying the idea of paradigms to antiquity than many who have subsequently used his work. See Andrew Gregory "Kuhn and Taxonomies of History," *Philosophy Study* 3 (2013), 412–30.

117. One weakness in Kuhn's account of paradigms is that he treats the content of paradigms as relatively self-evident and there is no decision-making procedure if there is disagreement about the content of a paradigm. This is problematic for the ancient world where there can be quite radical disagreement about the content of a supposed paradigm. See Gregory "Kuhn and Taxonomies of History."

Bibliography

Ankarloo, Bengt, and Stuart Clark. *Witchcraft and Magic in Europe: Ancient Greece and Rome*. London: Athlone, 1999.

Brauner, Sigrid. *Fearless Wives and Frightened Shrews: The Construction of the Witch in Early Modern Germany*. Amherst: University of Massachusetts Press, 2001.

Butler, Samuel. *Odyssey*. London: Cape, 1922.

Clay, Jennifer. "Demas and Aude: The Nature of Divine Transformation in Homer." *Hermes* 102 (1974): 129–36.

Cohen, Beth. *The Distaff Side: Representing the Female in Homer's Odyssey*. Oxford, UK: Oxford University Press, 1995.

Collins, Derek. *Magic in the Ancient Greek World*. Oxford, UK: Blackwell, 2011.

De Jong, Irene. *Narratological Commentary on the Odyssey*. Cambridge, UK: Cambridge University Press, 2001.

Dickie, Matthew. *Magic and Magicians in the Greco-Roman World*. London: Routledge, 2001.

Dyck, Andrew. "The Witches Bed but Not Her Breakfast." *Rheinisches Museum fur Philologie* 124 (1981), 196–98.

Flint, Valerie. *The Rise of Magic in Early Medieval Europe*. Oxford, UK: Oxford University Press, 1991.

Graf, Fritz. *Magic in the Ancient World*. Cambridge, MA: Harvard University Press, 1997.

Gregory, Andrew. *Ancient Greek Cosmogony*. London: Bloomsbury, 2007.

———. *The Presocratics and the Supernatural*. London: Bloomsbury, 2013.

———. "Kuhn and Taxonomies of History." *Philosophy Study* 3 (2013): 412–30.

———. *Anaximander: A Re-Assessment*. London: Bloomsbury, 2016.

———. *Early Greek Philosophies of Nature*. London: Bloomsbury 2021.

Guiley, Rosemary. *Witches and Witchcraft*. New York: Checkmark, 1989.

Hesychii Alexandrini Lexicon (Heyschius of Alexandria), edited by M. Schmidt. Jena, Germany: Maukii, 1863; Andesite Press reprint, 2020.

Heubeck, Alfred, and Arie Hoekstra. *A Commentary on Homer's Odyssey*. Oxford, UK: Oxford University Press, 1989.

Karras, Ruth, and Judith Bennett. *The Oxford Handbook of Women and Gender in Medieval Europe*. Oxford, UK: Oxford University Press, 2016.

Kramer, Heinrich, and James Sprenger. *Malleus Maleficarum*. Translated by Montagu Summers. New York: Dover (1487) 1971.

Murray, A. T. *Homer Odyssey*. 2 vols. Loeb Edition. New York: Heinemann, 1919.

Naddaf, Gerard. *The Greek Concept of Nature*. Albany: State University of New York, 2005.

Newall, Valerie. *Witchcraft and Magic*. London: Hamlyn, 1974.

Ogden, Daniel. *Greek and Roman Necromancy*. Princeton, NJ: Princeton University Press, 2001.

———. *Magic, Witchcraft and Ghosts in the Greek and Roman Worlds: A Sourcebook*. Oxford, UK: Oxford University Press, 2002.

———. *Night's Black Agents*. Hambledon, UK: Continuum, 2008.

Page, Denys, *Folktakes in Homer's Odyssey*. Cambridge, MA: Harvard University Press, 1973.

Rieu, Emile. *Homer: Odyssey*. London: Penguin, 2003.

Scodel, Ruth. "Odysseus and the Stag." *Classical Quarterly* 44 (1994): 530–34.

Segal, Charles. "Circean Tempations." *Transactions of the American Philological Association*, 99 (1968): 419–42.

Shewring, Walter. *Homer: Odyssey*. Oxford, UK: Oxford University Press, 2008.

Stanford, W. B. "That Circe's *Rhabdos* Was not a Magic Wand." *Hermathena* 66 (1945): 69–71.

Stratton, Kimberley. *Naming the Witch: Magic, Ideology, and Stereotype in the Ancient World.* New York: Columbia University Press, 2006.

Thompson, Stith. *Motif-Index of Folk Literature*. Bloomington: Indiana University Press, 1955.

Yarnall, Judith. *The Transformations of Circe*. Urbana: University of Illinois Press, 1994.

Chapter Two

The Oracle as Intermediary

Sasha Biro

I Sibylla, Phoibos' wise woman,
Am hidden under a stone monument:
I was a speaking virgin but voiceless
In this manacle by the strength of fate.
I lie close to the Nymphs and to Hermes:
I have not lost my sovereignty.

—Sibylline epitaph[1]

To think antiquity differently is an invitation to revisit and recast traditional narratives. This includes the possibility to think outside of long-standing oppositions, such as the *muthos-logos* divide, a framework to which the Western philosophic tradition is indebted. Rational argumentation's identification as the discourse of truth traces back to antiquity, in which reason provides one legitimate form of thinking, while demythologizing and denigrating other modes of thought that aren't purely rational or scientific. The following analysis explores the possibility of thinking otherwise, taking up the question of what it might mean to think beyond the bounds of one reason and to include rather than exclude a thinking that is mythic—which is to say, thinking through a logic that is capable of expressing ambiguity and paradox, and that operates on the threshold of an experience both rational and ethical. This will mean thinking myth otherwise, as outside of the binary that opposes myth to reason.

The language of myth contains imaginative elements: it is magical, suggestible, ambiguous, capable of contradiction, lending to excess and transformation. Its transformative power takes place in language, and is often necessarily violent. Not simply explanation or story, myth offers a logic other than the logic of rational veracity. Myth enacts such difference by disturbing the distribution of sense, inviting a struggle with ambiguity and uncertainty. If the work of myth[2] in fact elides this definition as the hither side of reason, as a placeholder for nonsense and the irrational, it is possible to study myth—its violence, disruption, displacement—as having an inescapable role in the creation and foundation of reality. In myth, as in literature, one encounters imaginative elements: the fabulous, the irrational, the vibrant. Perhaps literature shares a sameness with myth that is not identical, even as each is bound together. Jean-Luc Nancy will tell us that myth is fiction that founds; a founding that is fiction. And Roberto Calasso suggests the possibility that truth is metaphor, which would make it an accomplice of knowledge rather than enemy, where metaphor, like fiction, binds the world.[3] For instance, that myths leave their traces within the texts of philosophy and literature, pointing us in the direction of disruption. The mythic presents us with the possibility of thinking subversively, thinking, that is, among other things, deviant. The work of myth could then be thought, as Calasso suggests, not only as a form of literature, but also as a deformation of literature. Likewise, in the essay "*Khōra*," Derrida speaks of "a detour . . . signal[ing] toward a genre beyond genre . . . beyond categories, and above all beyond categorical oppositions."[4] Derrida goes on to indicate that "each narrative content—fabulous, fictive, legendary, or mythic . . . becomes in its turn the content of a different tale. Each tale is thus the *receptacle* of another. There is nothing but receptacles of narrative receptacles, or narrative receptacles of receptacles."[5] Each of these interpretations points to a necessary reevaluation of the relationship between myth and literature as themselves separate and distinct ontological forms.

This reevaluation is most clearly demonstrated by turning to the divination of the sibylline oracles, notably the representations of the Delphic Pythia and the Cumaean Sibyl, who are of mythic status.[6] The intermediary state of mind of the oracle, her relation to ambiguity and truth, indicates a subversive power as direct conduit to the divine. A closer look at the suggestive language used to depict the figure of the oracle in the works of Aeschylus, Ovid, and Virgil, including the gestures of the sibylline body, reveals the manifestation of a voice closer to madness and unreason than exactitude. The following analysis limits its scope to these three authors, as each in their own way expropriates the female speech act in their representations of the Pythia and the Cumaean Sibyl, particularly in the suggestive language used by each when depicting these prophetesses. Identifying in these classical representations a connection between ambiguity and authority in female prophetic speech opens up a space to examine how certain gender constructions in antiquity helped to shape a contemporary conception of the oracle (as, for instance, inspired or mad). While acknowledging the many historical and cultural differences among these texts, such canonical representations make visible the relationship between knowledge production and the authority of language/location of voice. Honoring the prophetess as a figure of alterity, one who divines a source of knowledge that is intimate, sensual, and liminal (rather than abstract, universal, or artificial), is to celebrate a way of knowing that transcends binary divisions, transforming our reception of the transmission of knowledge, and the relation between the mortal and divine. The following analysis of the reception of the oracle, in her varying titles of Pythia, Sibyl, and Prophetess, will trace the denigration of this formidable figure, whose divinely authoritative knowledge was subsumed by the masculine economy of the *logos*. An alternate reading, one that recovers, celebrates, and transforms our understanding of the relation between the mortal and the divine, situates the figure of the oracle as central to a thinking through of difference.

The Reason of Myth

Jean-Paul Vernant's discussion of "The Reason of Myth," found in *Myth and Society in Ancient Greece*, provides an in-depth analysis of the cultural role and function of myth in antiquity. Vernant interrogates myth's "reason" as a work valid in and of itself, not merely as a precursor to rational discourse. *Muthos* and *logos* were not always separate and contrasting terms, but our contemporary conception of myth derives from their opposition.[7] Vernant frames his discussion on the contrast between *muthos* and *logos* around speech and writing and the transition from an oral to a written culture, emphasizing how this influenced the arrangement of discourse and, moreover, how the traditional narratives acquired a new function and meaning in the transition.[8] The crux of his analysis centers on a shift in expression (signaling a cosmological shift that becomes certain over time), whereby a form of reasoning that appeals to the reader's "critical intelligence" is employed. Vernant calls this "demonstrative rationality," an abstract form of thinking that differs from the mimetic processes involved in spoken narrative, and it is in part because of this differentiation in form and meaning that the *logos* separates and is eventually wholly distinguished from *muthos* as two differing types of thought.[9] Vernant suggests that speech and writing operate according to differing logics, wherein "the organization of written discourse goes hand-in-hand with a more rigorous analysis and a stricter ordering of conceptual material."[10] In other words, the *logos* acts on the mind at a different level from the spoken word (*muthos*) when assuming the written form—a differing level due to differing mental operations and logical processes.[11]

Another way of describing this shift in expression is through a discussion of philosophical as opposed to mythical language. Philosophical language employs abstract concepts, ontological terminology, a strict ordering of terms and greater rigor in reasoning, and is in short an explanatory discourse in contrast to the narrative discourse of myth.[12] It is the demonstrative logic of noncontradiction, best known through Aristotle and mathematics, where "It is no longer a matter of overcoming one's opponent by spell-binding or fascinating him with one's own superior power over the spoken word."[13] Philosophical language, whose "purpose is to establish the truth following a scrupulous inquiry and to express it in a manner that should, by rights at least, appeal to the reader's critical intelligence alone,"[14] is the language of argument, sophistry, Socrates. In contrast, mythic language does not reason in this way because it does not pose the same questions nor formulate in the same terms the problems that it does tackle.[15] It is a different mode of thinking entirely, one that, through the setting up of an opposition between *muthos* and *logos*, is exiled from the realm of philosophical discourse.

> It is fair to say that throughout Greek tradition—whenever, that is, it does not simply ignore myth—the attitude is the same and myth is seen in one of two ways: Either it expresses in a different, allegorical, or symbolic form the same truth as

> the *logos* expresses directly or, alternatively, it conveys what is not the truth—that which, by its nature, lies outside the domain of truth and which consequently eludes knowledge and has nothing to do with speech articulated according to the rules of demonstration.[16]

At stake is the question of contrasting logics, whereby one mode of thought takes hold, is exemplified, and idealized, whereby "every other form of existence has to struggle laboriously upwards alongside it, as tolerated but not intended."[17] As the logic of the philosophers became that preferential mode of reasoning, what became of the reason of myth? Early in his account Vernant references the infamous scene in the *Republic* where Plato's Socrates distinguishes between the marvelous (which does not provide knowledge) and truthful discourse (which does), the former being suited to poets and storytellers whose stories "may well beguile . . . childish minds . . . by the spectacle of feuding, fighting, reconciliation, marriage, and procreation provided by mythical tales; but have nothing to offer to anyone who seeks to understand, in the strict sense of the word, because understanding refers to a form of intelligibility that *muthos* does not encompass and that only explanatory discourse possesses."[18] According to Vernant, it is this Socratic inheritance and its "stamp of rationalism" that pervades the understanding of myth in contemporary times, where myth is now exiled, its meaning emptied of all richness, and its truth value eyed with a suspiciousness that borders on disregard.

> In the tradition of thought that has come down to us from the Greeks, marked as this is with the stamp of rationalism, myth, despite its place, its impact, and its importance, finds its own specific aspects and functions effaced when it is not purely and simply rejected in the name of *logos*. In one way or another myth, as such, is always exorcised . . . [However] if myth is saying not "something else" but that very thing that it is quite impossible to say in any other way a new problem arises and the entire scope of the study of mythology is transformed: What then is myth saying and what is the connection between the message it bears and the manner in which it expresses it?[19]

Socrates' infamous words, "that there is an old quarrel between philosophy and poetry (607c)," recapitulates this scene, and his claim that "imitation is a kind of play and not serious (602b)" may be read as one example of that tendency toward a rationalism that excludes the magic and suggestibility that mythmaking provides.[20] Traditionally the quarrel between philosophy and poetry is read as the triumph and authority of reason. It is an ancient quarrel that repeats itself indefinitely for all time. The exclusion, or loss, of poetry, which signals a shift in significance and meaning on myriad levels, is the exiling of the gods. To exile the poets is to exile the gods. But this choice—of exclusion—yet invites the question of what is the relation of humanity to its gods and myths and how this relation changes in time. For the myths, though banished, return, even in *The Republic*. Their survival and return become another story, interrupting the first, interrupting the quarrel of old, and its traditional representation. As Derrida holds, "Each tale is thus the receptacle of another."[21]

The representation is as follows: The image of myth that persists today in science and philosophy reflects the contrast between the language of myth and philosophical language, the latter being what Nietzsche will define as Socratic rationalism.[22] Plato's Socrates clears the ground for philosophy by exiling poetry and myth, so that myth stands opposed to reality and rationality; it is but a fiction and an untruth.[23] Again, this shift in significance lies a long way from the original connections between *muthos* and *logos*, connections that have weakened so that the two terms now stand in opposition to one another. Vernant succinctly states the root of the problem.

> There is now such a gap between *muthos* and *logos* that communication between the two breaks down; dialogue becomes impossible since the break is complete. Even when they appear to have the same object, to be directed toward the same end, the two types of discourse remain mutually impenetrable. From now on to choose one of the two types of language is in effect to dismiss the other.[24]

The movement away from an understanding of myth as a valid mode of thinking has continued historically under what may be described as the history of rationalism—witnessed as the Enlightenment, the Age of

Reason, and of technology. A peculiar dialectic is at play, whereby myth is either "dismissed" (as untruth) or upheld as a fable. On the one hand, myth is dismissed in favor of a reasoning that explains and deduces, proposition by proposition, as though this "explanatory discourse" were the only way in which to reason. Seen in this sense, myth can only convey untruth because its mode of exposition isn't through the formulations and demonstrations of philosophical discourse; it is dismissed in the name of philosophy. On the other hand, philosophical discourse continuously returns to and relies on mythic images in order to explicate philosophical concepts, so that even as myth is rejected as untruth, it is simultaneously appropriated (by philosophy) and transposed in order to say something else in the name of reason. Consequentially, "Myth was thus purged of its absurdities, implausibilities, and immorality, all of which scandalized reason. But this was achieved only at the cost of jettisoning myth's own fundamental character, refusing to take it literally and making it say something quite different from what it actually told."[25] This is the work of demythologization. But if we take myth seriously, what myth fundamentally shows us is how philosophy needs myth in order to reason philosophically.

As Socrates says to Glaucon in Book X of *The Republic*, "We are, at all events, aware that such poetry mustn't be taken seriously as a serious thing laying hold of truth, but that the man who hears it must be careful, fearing for the regime in himself" (608b), at once effectively dismissing poetry and raising both a cultural and political issue, where alongside the question of what modes of thinking are best suited to portray true knowledge are the questions of who will rule society, educate the young, and determine what is good. The invitation to believe in the transition from "myth to reason" can be viewed in the light of this dismissal of poetry as that which is not serious, that is, as that which does not provide truth in the manner that explanatory discourse does. However, the implications are grave when considering poetry and myth seriously, as serious and truth bearing.

To choose philosophy over poetry, reason over myth, truth over fiction, is to think within a binary opposition, whereby "identity and difference divide each other endlessly."[26] One is asked to choose, to weigh in on the opposition: Either I choose philosophy or myth, reason or madness, the sacred or the mundane. The choice is indicative of the ancient quarrel that demands we choose "where we cannot, must not, choose."[27] It is a quarrel, as Stephen David Ross suggests in *The Gift of Beauty*, "repeatedly carried out on reason's terms . . . under reason's constraints . . . and repeatedly, the quarrel is undermined by poetry's gifts."[28] It is a quarrel that belongs to reason, or as Ross elaborates, to *technē*, as the production of objects that work toward some end, or are shaped by some goal, and have a use value.[29] Demarcations such as hot and cold may be understood in this respect, whereas terms such as the good, justice, or truth are in fact more multifaceted, and unable to be expressed in terms of profit and use. Such is the case also with poetry and myth. Whereas *technē* introduces categories and distinctions, the matter of poetry and myth suggests something otherwise than a binary opposition.[30] Poetry doesn't lend itself to bearing on this quarrel, setting itself in opposition to reason: The quarrel belongs to reason alone, even as it defines what philosophy and poetry are. "Poetry knows nothing of the diaphora, does not bother with such distinctions."[31] It cannot be measured in terms of profit and use and it fails to give the reader reason, but then reason cannot grant more than the impossibility of reaching the divine and making it ready to hand. In contrast, poetry, *poiēsis*, can be understood as that which includes, to excess.[32] The ambiguous speech of the oracle offers an illustration of such excess, as her replies express a multiplicity of meaning, where truth is multivalent rather than direct and univocal.

The quarrel of old may then be understood otherwise as belonging solely to reason, where choice equates to some exclusion (in this case myth is excluded in favor of reason). But the work of poetry and myth, of *poiēsis*, interrupts and disturbs every technical reduction, "circulating against the authority of any categorical opposition."[33] Myth may not provide useful knowledge in the strict sense, because it is otherwise to the domain of use value, but it bears the mark of the gods, as well as suggesting the impossibility of a measurement between limit and unlimited, finite and infinite, sacred and mundane.[34] Socrates raises the quarrel between philosophy and poetry in his exploration of the precise and the technical. But music, poetry, metaphor, and art are otherwise and incomparable with this precision. "Passing away from measure to the divine, with a care for what may be included where we cannot live except by exclusion" brings into question the oppositional structure of the quarrel itself.[35] Opposition and quarrel belong to reason, to *technē*. Poetry and myth can be thought of outside this oppositional structure, as otherwise to it. "This otherwise haunts every opposition, interrupting its authority. It does not inhabit another opposition."[36] As Derrida points out in his exegesis on *khōra* as that which gives place to such opposition (while yet exceeding opposition), "the concepts of this rhetoric [metaphor, image, simile] appear to be constructed on the basis of 'Platonic' oppositions (intelligible/sensible, being as *eidos*/image, [truth/imitation, serious/nonserious] etc.), oppositions from which *khōra* precisely escapes. The apparent multiplicity of metaphors (or also of mythemes in general) signifies in these places not only that the proper meaning can only become intelligible via these detours, but that the opposition between the proper and the figurative, without losing all value, encounters here a limit."[37]

For instance, Plato offers a means of thinking otherwise about the *muthos-logos* binary and contributes to the discourse of interruption of Western philosophy's *logos*, by writing mythically.[38] That the myth of Er closes *The Republic*, indicates the centrality of the importance of myth as a mode of informing philosophy. The mythic is neither abandoned nor truly exiled. All along it traces through the text, despite textual claims to have banished it. When Plato enters the mythic register, numerous concepts such as the soul, the beautiful, the sun, the good, and the beyond being appear. Each is indefinable without some appeal to the imagination, and each in its own manner describes things beyond ordinary human experience. Plato's writing is itself ambiguous, blurring the very binary (proper/figurative, truth/imitation) it seeks to describe. Reading Plato, one encounters what Vernant describes as the reason of myth, that *muthos* and *logos* weren't always separate and contrasting terms, and that a "logic other than the logic of the *logos*" is operative.[39] To this point, while Vernant describes the sociohistorical conditions that shape the development of the *muthos-logos* binary, Derrida reminds the reader that all binary oppositions are in need of deconstruction, that the poles of any binary are situational, that placing "our trust in the alternative *logos/mythos*" does not allow for a thinking through of "that which, while going outside of the regularity of the *logos*, its law, its natural or legitimate genealogy, nevertheless does not belong, *stricto sensu*, to *mythos*."[40] Derrida identifies the *khōra* as that which "would trouble the very order of polarity, of polarity in general . . . because in carrying beyond the polarity of sense (metaphorical or proper), it would no longer belong to the horizon of sense, nor to that of meaning as the meaning of being."[41] Similarly, in the speech act, the oracle exceeds the *muthos-logos* binary and destabilizes the distribution of sense.

It is, therefore, possible to understand the quarrel between philosophy and poetry otherwise; not as a choice between two polarities. It is for philosophy to choose, the choice of reason, of *technē*. "Do we imagine that the truth of the gods is a truth to be told in *technē*, a truth to be told, to be possessed?"[42] The defense that Socrates expects of poetry, in order that it may return from exile, cannot be given in *technē*'s terms: As poetry is not simply pleasant but dangerous, mad, erotic; nor is poetry useful, for it stands closer to immortality and inspiration than to profit and advantage. *Poiēsis*, poetry, the domain of myth and its mimetic function, speaks of what must remain unknown to *technē*, because *technē* rules through division, conflict, opposition. *Poiēsis* interrupts, displaces *technē* and its oppositional structures, instead bringing "the good unknown to *technē*," a relation to the good, the beautiful, to madness, sensuality, and the sacred.[43] Poetry and myth displace through interrupting the drive for making of truth a useful and practical experience. They disclose something other, beyond the technical, expressing truth as multiplicity.[44]

The Oracle at Delphi

Plato, in the *Phaedrus*, identifies madness (of which there are four types) as a great blessing, provided that it is divinely inspired (244a). Inspiration has its source in the divine, a wellspring beyond human measurement. Prophetic madness in particular involves a transgression of rationality, as the prophetic trances of the oracle involve a possession that is simultaneously a divestment, as "the prophetess of Delphi and the priestesses at Dodona are out of their minds when they perform that fine work of theirs for all of Greece, either for an individual person or for a whole city, but they accomplish little or nothing when they are in control of themselves" (244b). Plato appears to celebrate the divine source of inspiration as a source of knowledge beyond the calculable and the technical.[45] He also offers a glimpse into a vestigial representation of the prophetess as a frenzied, mad woman, whose gift of prophecy is accomplished precisely because she is "out of control." And yet, a variety of sources portray the oracle as "weighed and spoken with measure."[46] As Fontenrose points out, there is "no reliable evidence in ancient literature or art for a frenzied and raving Pythia . . . the Pythia no more takes leave of her senses or enters into violent emotional outbursts than, as a rule, do poets or lovers in the inspiration or emotion that they experience."[47] Her mantic gift is attributed to the god Apollo *and* positions the oracle as an authoritative source of knowledge, with a voice that is simultaneously female and divine.[48]

The *Phaedrus* is also one of several Socratic dialogues in which Socrates ponders the Delphic maxim, "Know thyself."[49] Having been asked to opine on the truth value of the mythic legend of Boreas and Orithuria, Socrates responds that while it would not be out of place for him to reject the myth, he has "no time for such things; and the reason, my friend, is this. I am still unable, as the Delphic inscription orders, to know myself; and it really seems to me ridiculous to look into other things before I have understood that" (230a). Plato here, as elsewhere,[50] appropriates the Delphic maxim as an invitation to self-knowledge, and in doing so decidedly refuses a rationalization of the mythic.[51]

The inscription of this maxim is found in the temple of Apollo at Delphi.[52] Here, the Delphic Oracle, or Pythia, a priestess of the earth, uttered this aphorism that Plato later appropriated in his philosophical quest for truth, being, and universals. The maxim appears in Plato's writing, abstract and disassociated from its original source. Socrates recognizes the inscription itself as a command, but does not allude to its speaker, who was, for more than 2,000 years an important religious authority in classical Greece.[53] Her oracles were words sent from the god; she held right of access to a knowledge that was divine, as the Pythia herself was in direct contact with the divinity. It would not be expected of Plato to name the Pythia, as these ancient priestesses remained nameless, though there were many who held the title and performed the functions of the Pythia. These virginal women dedicated themselves to a life of piety, concerned with reliving "daily the great human dramas of Earth: motherhood, virginity and purity, health and defilement, sacrifice and service, water and forgetfulness, funeral rites and death, earth and fertility, protest and injustice, suffering and sacrilege, and the defense of children."[54] The Pythia is consecrated in the service of the god Apollo; she births prophecy, and her connection to the god is often figured as a sexual union: "the conception of the *unio mystica* as sexual intercourse between a god and a human being. . . . The priestess who was blessed by the favor of the god was also able to tell his will."[55]

Extensively, image-making shapes our understanding of mythic figures. "Historians have always written the story of mankind's past via records, buildings, chronologies, genealogies, wars, monuments, sculpture, art objects, customs, religions, and biographies."[56] The image of the oracle that survives today typifies a manic woman who sits on a tripod above a chasm whose vapors induce her into a state of wild, incoherent utterances.[57] Whereas little is known about the Pythias themselves—to serve the god they left behind all that was worldly, including their own namesake—the liminal figure of the Pythia is archetypal, and surviving accounts shed light on her function in the cultural imaginary of antiquity. Divested of individuating characteristics, the Pythia underwent a series of purifying rituals in preparation.

> [S]he bathed, probably in Castalia, and perhaps drank from a sacred spring; she established contact with the god through his sacred tree, the laurel, either by holding a laurel branch, as her predecessor Themis does in a fifth-century vase painting, or by fumigating herself with burnt laurel leaves, as Plutarch says she did, or perhaps sometimes by chewing the leaves, as Lucian asserts; and finally she seated herself on the tripod, thus creating a further contact with the god by occupying his ritual seat.[58]

The Pythia occupied a liminal space in antiquity, not fully belonging to this world, not fully of the beyond, yet bridging both. This is further emphasized by the role she assumes, as "Apolline mediumship . . . aims at knowledge, of the future or of the hidden present."[59] The Pythia's power as a producer of meaning is attributed to her possession by the god. Here, madness signals the manifestation of the deity; it is a form through which the god appears, a creative, life begetting force.[60] The Pythia's vision is yet bound up with the body—she engenders form through a speech act that is fecund, enigmatic, and suggestible. The form that possession takes, as direct and immediate sensual experience, informs an understanding of what E. R. Dodds describes as the nonrational aspects of human experience.[61] The Pythia gave voice to a knowledge that was earthly and divine, a knowledge that was traditionally refused to women. Access to the Pythia implied access to (divine) knowledge. Whereas males of the town of Delphi had privileged access to the Pythia herself, women were refused this access, unable to enter the temple and worship.[62] The Pythia elucidates an interdicted knowledge:[63] The mark of the god authorizes her as a producer of meaning in a space traditionally refused to women.

The Pythia offers access to regions unknown and unexplored, and does so in a voice that is ambiguous, thus stretching the limits of language and opening a space for a production of knowledge that proliferates in meanings. Her inspiration by the god is physical: a shifting state that is unsustainable, but joins what is above with what is below through the female voice, which is also a divine voice.[64] The oracles defied traditional attempts at sense-making, as they were oral transmissions cryptically spoken, full of promises but without providing direct and obvious answers, offering impossible descriptions. Through linguistic indeterminacy (via metaphor, fragmentation, lack of order, word choice which was often multivalent and ambiguous) the Pythian oracles deferred a straightforward economy of meaning, thus opening the language of the Pythia to multiple interpretations, and engaging in a production of meaning that was nonlinear and determined. The Pythia's ambiguous style "sanctioned the attempt to move beyond the known world by advising clients to seek seemingly impossible objects, landscapes, animals . . . to search . . . for a new understanding of the world embodied in the ambiguous command."[65] According to Maurizio, "Since ambiguous oracles suggested that all knowledge was unstable and in need of interpretation . . . they freed their [male] clients from tradition, from oral stories celebrating heroes' virtues . . . and modeled ways of reinterpreting both the known and the unknown."[66] Vernant's framework contextualizes the significance of the language of the Pythia. If we do not read her oracles as merely allegorical, nor try to rationalize them in order to make sense,[67] and, with the ancients, refuse to see them as falsehoods or untruths, it is clear that the Pythia, a woman at the center of the world, is a producer of ambiguous knowledge, and that ambiguity was respected in the ancient world.

Expropriation

Through the Pythia, Apollo indicated his meaning, commanding a reputation for truth-telling. Men went to the Oracle "to receive advice and sanctions, believing in the sanctity of the place and in Apollo's special authority when he spoke there through the Pythia."[68] "As Phoebus guides my lips, so I pronounce his truth," states the Pythian Priestess of Aeschylus' *Eumenides*. Possession itself, the mark of the god, authenticates the Pythian speech act, whereas the interpretation of the oracle on the part of the male seeker is an act of appropriation that orders and defines on a human and thus measurable scale. Ambiguity is revered so long as it is sanctioned by the god, but without Phoebus' validation, knowledge production is interrupted: its truth value rendered meaningless, as in the case of Cassandra; the constraints of mortality affecting its production altogether, as in the case of the Cumaean Sibyl. While the historical, social, political, and sometimes mythic circumstances that situate the experiences of the priestess Cassandra, the Cumaean Sibyl, and the Delphic Pythia differ, similar motifs concerning language and knowledge production surround these oracles.[69]

Aeschylus provides an account of the prophetess, Cassandra, which illustrates this paradigm. Apollo has offered the gift of prophecy to Cassandra, a Trojan princess, in exchange for her love. She agrees, only to then refuse his embrace. Her punishment is to be robbed of the power to convince others. She foretells the sack of Troy and the murder of Agamemnon, but her words lack authority, those around her see her as mad, taunting and objectifying her.[70] Cassandra may not be authorized by the god, but her speech reveals a liberating component as well. Cassandra's prophecies in the *Agamemnon* involve a voice that is direct, spontaneous, and passionate, contrasting her prophetic speech with the measured and weighed speech of the Pythia.[71] Ambiguity is lacking from her prophetic utterances, which unfold from visions of both past and future events: "Listen. Now my prophecy shall no more peep from under shy veils like a new-made bride, but blow a bounding gale towards the sunrise . . . Without more mystery I will instruct you."[72] While the content of her speech appears nonsensical to those who interpret (the Chorus), it nonetheless displaces the traditional, sanctioned model of prophecy as knowledge production, as she speaks her mind publicly on an array of matters: filicide, conspiracy, mariticide, affairs of war, her fear of imminent death. In doing so, Cassandra's prophecy offers a critique of the dominant discourse of power, even as the speaker herself is subordinated and objectified. The expropriation of Cassandra's voice is also a dispossession of the speech act as power and prophecy and as the production of meaning, for her words are rendered meaningless. However, the figure of Cassandra presents a model for challenging the traditional conception of women's roles in antiquity, as she occupies an ambiguous position between the public and the private sphere and represents a reality that is concurrently past and present.[73]

A similar paradigm ensnares the Sibyl of Cumae. Ovid recounts her story in Book XIV of his *Metamorphoses*, where the "long-lived" Sibyl serves Aeneas as a maternal guide in his descent to the underworld, where he will find the spirit of his deceased father, Anchises, who will teach Aeneas "the laws which govern Avernus and also the dangers facing his people in wars to come."[74] Whereas Anchises teaches Aeneas the law, the Cumaean Sibyl tells him a story, in part admonishment (out of gratitude, Aeneas calls her a goddess, which she is quick to disavow), in part a declaration of defiant sovereignty. The story that the Sibyl recounts takes place within a liminal space—that of the underworld—during the uphill journey back to earth. She tells Aeneas that Apollo had fallen in love with her, with the hope that she would accept his love and offer him her maidenhood (itself a form of dispossession) in exchange for anything she wanted. "I showed him a pile of dust that I gathered and foolishly asked for my birthdays to equal the number of sand-grains."[75] The Sibyl's virginity is commodified by the god, and while she asks to live forever, she fails to ask for eternal youth. Phoebus Apollo grants her immortality and offers eternal youth, "if I let him enjoy my body"—a "gift" the Sibyl in turn refused. Seven hundred years have passed, and as the Sibyl foresees,

> The time will arrive when the length of days shall shrink my body from all it has been to a tiny frame, and my age-worn limbs be reduced to the weight of a feather. Then no one will ever believe that I once was adored and desired by a god. Yes, even Phoebus may fail to recall me, or else he'll deny that he loved me. So changed, so invisible! Yet, the fates will leave me my voice, and by my voice I shall be known.[76]

The Sibyl here recounts a story of the past that also speaks of a futurity where her body, as the vessel of her sovereign voice, will not withstand the depredations of time. The Sibyl's perception, as a vision of what is destined to be, is intimately bound up with her body. While retaining her authority throughout the ages, the Cumaean Sibyl figures as an inversion of the prophetess Cassandra, yet she too is marginalized by the god. Her production of knowledge is constrained by the dislocation of her voice from her body. Language, or voice, as a source of meaning is here shown to be intricately tied to the body. The Sibyl's voice is the embodiment of a knowledge that is immortal, and thus fecund. This would explain the proliferation of sexual and child-birthing imagery surrounding the mantic ritual.[77] So, too, at Delphi, where "the divinatory ritual was figured as an impregnation of the Pythias by Apollo." Even the contested vapors at Delphi are in some sense validated when thought of in terms of possession, as the vapors "which enter the Pythias on their tripod from below . . . are an attempt to realize and explain this constellation of ideas about Apollo and the Pythia's interaction—the action of outside winds upon the human *splancha*—that was implicit and that explained human and divine interaction as impregnation. The delivery of oracles from the Pythia's mouth is simply a displacement upward."[78] The prophetess engenders form, as "the potency of oracles as divine speech could call the world into being,"[79] as well as unite the mortal with the divine.

Virgil's account of the Sibyl in *Aeneid* Book VI speaks to the violence endemic to inspiration, and offers an authoritative account of the expropriation of the speech act, as the Sibyl speaks for others but never for herself. Traditionally, the Sibyl utters the words of the god in the form of oracles, or cryptic language. Heroes, like Aeneas, who need guidance for future actions, seek out the oracle. She takes on the maternal role of guidance and revelation, while repeatedly reminding Aeneas of his divine heritage, confirming and reaffirming his identity. Aeneas is directed to the Cumaean Sibyl by the seer Helenus, son of Priam. Aeneas asks of Helenus, "tell me what dangers am I first to avoid?" and is led by the hand into Apollo's temple, where Helenus reveals "a few things out of many" to Aeneas.[80] Restrictions are placed on Helenus by the Fates and by Juno, but he is able to tell Aeneas the signs that will reveal to Aeneas the future site of Lavinium. Helenus' function is to provide directions, though he also warns Aeneas of the dangers he will face and the routes he should avoid. His final direction is that Aeneas should consult the Sibyl once he reaches Italy, so that he may obtain favorable passage.

The descriptive language through which Helenus portrays the Sibyl (Book III) is clothed in highly suggestive sexual imagery, illustrating a phenomenon that continues into Book VI, whereby the Cumaean Sibyl is relegated to a position of alterity. She is defined as "an ecstatic," "a seeress" who, from her cave "communicates destiny."[81] Cumae is depicted as a marshy region, with adjectives such as haunted, deep, soughing, conveying the double sense of mystery and sexuality, doubly sexual since the Sibyl resides in a cave, an antre "deep in a soughing wood."[82] Helenus elaborates on the Sibyl's literary activity: She writes the runes, but lets them alone, impassive to the ordering of the leaves. When their logic is disturbed by the elements, she lets them flow where they will to resettle in an indeterminate position, perhaps implying a lack of fixation in terms of the future that will be. For this reason, Aeneas implores the Sibyl to speak her prophecies aloud: He is looking for solid, logical facts that proceed in a sequential order that he can follow. Here, the spoken word is given primacy over the written word, which is deemed indeterminate because it is subjected to the forces of nature, including that it is written by a woman's hand.

After receiving Helenus' directions, Aeneas' father, Anchises, appears to him in a dream. Again, Aeneas is told that the Sibyl will serve as a guide for his journey through the underworld. Aeneas' description of the Sibyl's shrine is defined in terms of darkness and depth: a "vasty cave," a "deeply recessed crypt," "huge," with "a hundred wide approaches" and "a hundred mouths from which there issue a hundred voices, the Sibyl's answers." Virgil's cave, and its Sibyl within, serve as a metaphor that functions to transport the initiate (Aeneas) toward the illumination of knowledge. The Sibyl's power is the power of prophecy, the utterance of truth. The price of prophecy is possession by the god: The Sibyl herself serves as a vessel, an intermediary who communicates sacred meaning between the god and mortals. Paradoxically, her own experience is not verbally represented; it is as vacuous as the cave she dwells in. However, through Virgil's portrayal of the Sibyl's body, we see that *it* speaks, manifesting itself in gestures that are sensual and earthly: "Her features, her color were all at once different, her hair flew wildly about; her breast was heaving, her fey heart swelled in ecstasy; larger than life she seemed, more than mortal her utterance: the god was close and breathing his inspiration through her."[83] Submission to the god is described metaphorically, as the sibyl is compared to the taming of a wild horse, "Not yet submissive to Phoebus . . . the Sibyl prodigiously struggled, still trying to shake from her brain the powerful God who rode her, but all the more he exhausted her foaming mouth and mastered her wild heart, breaking her in with a firm hand."[84] Sexual imagery colors the moment of submission, as once she is overcome, the "hundred immense doors of the place fly open of their own accord, letting out the Sibyl's inspired responses."[85]

The Sibyl's power is double-sided. She divines truth, yet her visionary power involves the loss of self in the prophetic moment. Her ability to prophecy is tied to the sexual act as the possession of the god, accessible through the exchange of the Sibyl herself, whose identity and experience is subsumed by the force of the god. Her prophetic utterances are ambiguous: fragmentary, metaphorical, suggestive in that they delineate an unknown—the future that can only be understood by way of the past. Her language, though linguistically indeterminate, is not nonsensical, but the hero Aeneas responds condescendingly: "Maiden, there's nothing new or unexpected to me in such trials you prophecy. All of them I have forecast, worked out in my mind already."[86] Yet Aeneas needs the Sibyl to show him the way through the Underworld, to his father. Maternally, the Sibyl acts as guide to Aeneas in his katabasis, protecting him along the way, charting the unknown for him. She leads him to his father, who speaks to Aeneas in a recognizable language that he understands, a language of exactitude that holds a use value: He tells a *history* and *names* what will be, in contrast to the Sibyl's poetic diction, steeped in metaphor and riddle. It is Anchises who *shows* Aeneas his destiny. Aeneas seeks the father tongue; he operates within an economy of reason, whereas the sibylline prophetic utterance signals an "otherness" that is incommensurable with this rational order. Her inspiration is figured as a sexual invasion, inspiring the mediation between mortal and divine. Her being is *entheos*, filled with the god, further situating the Sibyl as a liminal figure.

Conclusion

A contemporary understanding of myth is one in which *muthos* is opposed to *logos*, which is often interpreted as the progression from mythic thinking to reason. To think without recourse to the binaries that oppose myth and *logos*, fiction and reality, would be a way of thinking myth that opens the possibility of myth's function in language and as a mode of thinking. The mythic presents us with the possibility of a thinking subversively, a thinking that is, among other things, otherwise. The realm of myth is the realm of the possible. Myth offers a potent and fertile ground, where alternate visions are raised. One such vision is that of the oracle, as Pythia, as Sibyl. The figure of this prophetess is a potent and liminal figure, an intermediary between the mortal and the divine, whose speech acts may be read as the production and transmission of a knowledge that is at once ambiguous and authoritative. A contemporary reception of the oracle can be read as disturbing the binary between myth and reason, myth and history. The oracle is at once a real and a mythic figure, inseparable from the stories told about her. Thus, the idea that persists of the prophetess in contemporary times is that of a mad, frenzied, incoherent woman possessed by the god Apollo. And yet she was considered an authoritative source of divine knowledge until the oracle was shut down by Justinian in 529 CE. In this way the real and the imaginary map onto each other, be it in the representation of the figure of the oracle, or in the role of Delphi itself as a real and imagined place, potent with the promise of a new understanding of the world provided in the predictions uttered there.[87] Traditional accounts that depict the oracle, such as in Aeschylus, Ovid, and Virgil, offer the possibility for an alternate reading, one that celebrates the oracle as a liminal figure, whose words engender a vision of the world that is inspiring. The mythical speech of the oracle is an act of power that offers access to regions unknown and unexplored. The ambiguity of her speech signals a multiplicity of truth that otherwise could not be represented through a symbolic language of dualisms and oppositions. The mythic speech of the oracle proliferates with meaning(s); it is a language of excess and intimately tied to the body, birthing form as prophetic vision, thus challenging the rational model of speech understood as exactitude or the search for the pure concept. In this way, truth(s) appear as multiple rather than as univocal, similar to the narratives and interpretations surrounding the oracle. The figure of this prophetess, including her predictions, refuses a straightforward economy of meaning. Her divinely inspired speech, in its suggestibility, engenders a futurity that is unknown and indeterminate and therefore offers the possibility of interpretation and re-interpretation.

Notes

1. Marina Warner, *From the Beast to the Blond: On Fairy Tales and Their Tellers* (New York: Vintage, 1995), 11. Adapted from Pausanias: "Here I am, the plain-speaking Sibyl of Phoebus, Hidden beneath this stone tomb. A maiden once gifted with voice, but now for ever voiceless, By hard fate doomed to this fetter. But I am buried near the nymphs and this Hermes, Enjoying in the world below a part of the kingdom I had then."In *Description of Greece*, trans. W. H. S. Jones (Cambridge: Harvard University Press, 1965), 10.12.6.

2. The "work" of myth will throughout be discussed primarily as mythic language, particularly in connection to the figure of the Sibyl/Pythia.

3. Roberto Calasso, *Literature and the Gods*, trans. Tim Barks (New York: Vintage, 2001), 185.

4. Jacques Derrida, "*Khōra*," in *On the Name*, ed. Thomas Dutoit (Stanford: Stanford University Press, 1995), 90.

5. Derrida, "*Khōra*," 117.

6. "Material written about priestesses is largely mythological since it stems from prehistoric religious rites and rituals . . . The myth links us to an otherwise lost past when priestesses officiated in rituals . . . Thus the ancient

world is recoverable." See Norma Lorre Goodrich, *Priestesses* (New York: Harper Perennial, 1989), 8–9.

7. Jean-Pierre Vernant, *Myth and Society in Ancient Greece*, trans. Janet Lloyd (Brooklyn: Zone Books, 1980), 204.

8. Vernant, *Myth and Society*, 212.

9. Vernant, 206.

10. Vernant, 205.

11. Vernant, 207.

12. Vernant, 205–6.

13. Vernant, 207–8. The advent of writing opens up a commonality of the *logos* similar in effect to the vernacular translation of the Bible: no longer does the associated power and privilege belong exclusively to one class or hierarchy of people.

14. Vernant, 207.

15. Vernant, 211.

16. Vernant, 221. Vernant's definition, in focusing on the demonstrative function of philosophy, excludes other philosophical techniques such as aphorism or irony, which do not proceed via argument and logic.

17. Friedrich Nietzsche, *The Birth of Tragedy*, trans. Douglas Smith (Oxford: Oxford University Press, 2000), 97.

18. Vernant, *Myth and Society*, 210.

19. Vernant, 223–24.

20. Socrates: "It was then fitting for us to send it away from the city on account of its character" (*Rep.*, 607a). "We are, at all events, aware that such poetry mustn't be taken seriously as a serious thing laying hold of truth, but that the man who hears it must be careful, fearing for the regime in himself" (608b). Finally, "Thus we should at last be justified in not admitting him into a city that is going to be under good laws, because he awakens this part of the soul and nourishes it, and, by making it strong, destroys the calculating part . . . Similarly, we shall say the imitative poet produces a bad regime in the soul of each private man by making phantoms that are very far removed from the truth and by gratifying the soul's foolish part" (605b–c).

21. Derrida, "*Khōra*," 117.

22. Nietzsche, *The Birth of Tragedy*, 97.

23. Vernant, *Myth and Society*, 203. Importantly, Plato is himself a mythmaker. See *Rep.* (359d–60b), (414b–15d), (614a–21d), (621b8), for instances where the myths of Gyges, the Noble Lie, and Er are inextricably woven into the philosophical text. Here, his ideal city is a fabric woven of both mythology and philosophy. See also *Laws*, *Cri.*, *Grg.*, *Phd.*, *Phdr.*, *Symp.*, *Tim.* Each of these texts involve characters, typically Socrates himself, who deride *muthos* as nonserious, playful, irrational, imaginary, yet recount myths to illustrate deeply

philosophical claims. In such a way, Plato disturbs the very *muthos-logos* binary that he posits.

24. Vernant, *Myth and Society*, 211.

25. Vernant, 220.

26. Stephen David Ross, *The Gift of Beauty* (New York: SUNY Press, 1996), 33.

27. Ross, *The Gift of Beauty*, 28.

28. Ross, 29.

29. Ross, 31.

30. On *technē*, see Martin Heidegger, *Nietzsche: Vol. I, The Will to Power as Art*, trans. David Farrell Krell (New York: Harper and Row, 1968).

31. Ross, 29.

32. Ross, 32.

33. Ross, 66.

34. Ross, 37.

35. Ross, 39, 46.

36. Ross, 66.

37. Derrida, "*Khōra*," 147.

38. William Wians continues the line of thinking raised by Vernant in pointing out that, "Significantly, like many of their philosophical contemporaries, [poets] gave sustained attention to the complexities and ambiguities of language and persuasion that seemed calculated to draw attention to language's limits. . . . The continued deployment of myth by the poets was a decision arrived at rationally, not an unreflective perpetuation of a primitive mentality. It reflected in a profound way a playwright's considered attitude toward the world and the best means to communicate essential lessons about it." In *Logos and Muthos: Philosophical Essays in Greek Literature*, ed. William Wians, New York: SUNY Press, 2009, 4.

39. Vernant, 250.

40. Derrida, 90.

41. Derrida, 92–93.

42. Ross, 61.

43. Ross, 65–66.

44. On *alētheia*, see Heidegger, *Nietzsche: Vol. I, The Will to Power as Art*. To this end, Drew Hyland emphasizes the orientation of the human experience as both "necessarily complex and ambiguous," "in the middle" between nature and the divine, mastery (*logos/technē*), and humility in the face of finitude. "If we are different from the divine, different from nature, what is the nature of that access which we must already have to them which enables us to recognize that difference?" See Drew Hyland, *The Origins of Philosophy* (New York: Capricorn Books, 1973), 31.

45. Prophetic madness is, in Plato's *Phaedrus*, distinguished from ritual madness, poetic madness, and erotic madness, though all are god-sent. Peculiar to prophetic madness is that Apollo is the patron god. Furthermore, as Plato states, "The people who designed our language in the old days never thought of madness as something to be ashamed of or worthy of blame; otherwise they would not have used the word 'manic' for the finest experts of all—*the ones who tell the future*—thereby weaving insanity into prophecy" (Plato, *Phdr*. 244c; emphasis mine). In this regard, the madness of the Sibyl is distinctively mantic/manic—her utterances speak of an unknown futurity, which is different in kind from the cathartic element of ritual madness, which seeks to purge the individual of irrational impulses, as well as from poetic madness, where the gift of the Muses is "the power of true speech." However, this transmission of knowledge is twice-removed: The poet interprets the Muse, but is not herself possessed. See E. R. Dodds, *The Greeks and the Irrational* (Berkeley: California University Press, 1951), 64–82.

46. See Goodrich, *Priestesses*, 202; Fontenrose, *The Delphic Oracle, Its Responses and Operations, with a Catalogue of Responses* (Berkeley: University of California Press, 1978); Latte, "The Coming of the Pythia," *Harvard Theological Review* 33, no. 1 (1940). Dodds offers an alternative reading on the meaning of divine madness as indicating the presence of divinity.

47. See Fontenrose, *The Delphic Oracle*, 204.

48. See Julia Kindt, *Revisiting Delphi: Religion and Storytelling in Ancient Greece* (Cambridge: Cambridge University Press, 2016), 13.

49. See Plato, *Phdr*. 229c–30a.

50. See *Alcibiades I*, *Ch*., *Laws*, *Phil*., *Prot*.

51. It is, as Wians emphasizes, "The experience of events remembered and meditated on by the poets that have the power to teach. . . . *Muthoi* (such as those provided by the playwright) trace patterns and purposes of what was previously experienced without full comprehension. Poetic *muthoi* supplement the limited vision of ordinary human beings who inevitably are immersed in the immediate." Wians, *Logos and Muthos*, 193.

52. While the primary focus of this analysis concerns the literary records surrounding Delphi and the Delphic Oracle, archeological records support the claims made by Dodds, Goodrich, and Latte. See, for instance, James Whitley, *The Archeology of Ancient Greece* (Cambridge: Cambridge University Press, 2001).

53. See Goodrich, *Priestesses*, 195.

54. Goodrich, 201, 9.

55. See Latte, "The Coming of the Pythia," 16.

56. Latte, 10.

57. As Fontenrose indicates, only Lucan presents a frenzied Pythia, which has produced this "modern understanding," and Lucian is influenced by Virgil's *Aenead*, Book VI. See Fontenrose, *The Delphic Oracle*, 208–11.

58. See Dodds, *The Greeks and the Irrational*, 73. See also H. W. Parke, *A History of the Delphic Oracle* (Oxford: Blackwell, 1939). In *Priestesses*, Goodrich indicates that archaeological findings reveal "not the slightest proof concerning this 'tripod,'" but that during prophecy, the Pythia rested her hand on the omphalos, or tomb of Pytho (200).

59. Dodds, 69.

60. See Otto, *Dionysus, Myth and Cult* (Bloomington: Indiana University Press, 1965), 135.

61. See Dodds, 1.

62. See Goodrich, 199.

63. "The Sibyl . . . fulfils a certain function in thinking about forbidden, forgotten, buried, even secret matters." See Marina Warner, *From the Beast to the Blond*, 11.

64. See Goodrich's *Priestesses* and Lisa Maurizio's "The Voice at the Center of the World: The Pythia's Ambiguity and Authority," in *Making Silence Speak*, eds. André Lardinois and Laura McClure (Princeton: Princeton University Press, 2001).

65. "To search for a wooden dog that bites or a rock who will rule is to recognize that reality and language are not commensurate or transparent." See Maurizio "The Voice at the Center of the World," 43–44, 52.

66. Maurizio, 44.

67. Much discussion has focused on the presence of mephitic vapors in the inner sanctum of the temple, over which the Pythia conducted her service. Dodds claims the vapors are a Hellenistic invention, an attempt at rationalizing what cannot be rationalized—the trance state of the Pythia (73).

68. See Fontenrose, *The Delphic Oracle*, 238.

69. To this point, see Andrew Gregory's previous essay in this volume, "Was Circe a Witch?" Gregory's claim, that "the conception of a witch is not something ahistorical and given. It is something that has been constructed and there are many variations on that construction," speaks to the care of reception that is needed in order to avoid a contextualization, particularly of female figures such as Circe or the various oracles.

70. See Aeschlyus, *Agamemnon*, in *The Oresteian Trilogy*, trans. Philip Vellacott (London: Penguin, 1959), 1049–69.

71. See Goodrich, 201–2.

72. See Aeschylus, *Ag.* 1178–84.

73. See Helen Geyer-Ryan, "The Castration of Cassandra," in *Fables of Desire: Studies in the Ethics of Art and Gender* (Cambridge: Polity, 1994). Significantly, women writers of the nineteenth century repeatedly turned to the figure of the prophetess, or "madwoman," to revise patriarchal accounts of history, by rewriting and revisioning Greek mythology from a feminine perspective. Writers such as H.D., and Christa Wolf, for example, turned to subversive mythic figures,

such as Cassandra, to delineate struggles that have taken place and continue to take place, under different names and forms, as well as to articulate a modern vision of feminine creativity, artistic authority, and ontological authenticity. Also see Sandra Gilbert and Susan Gubar, *The Madwoman in the Attic* (London: Yale University Press, 1979).

74. See Ovid, *The Metamorphoses*, trans. Arthur Golding (London: Penguin, 2002), 115–19.

75. Ovid, *Met.*, Book XIV, 136–39.

76. Ovid, *Met.*, Book XIV, 146–54.

77. Birthing imagery often accompanies oracular responses to colonization. For example, when questioned on setting out to found a colony, the Pythia responds: "when he sees rain falling from a clear sky, he should acquire the land and found a city" (Fontenrose, 280–81). Similarly, on a proposed colony: "Ortygia lies in the sea on Trinakria, where Alpheios gushes forth mingling with the spring Arethusa" (278). Some who visited Delphi because of infertility were told to found a colony: "Labda conceives and will bear a rolling stone, which will fall among monarchs and will set Corinth right," and "Apollo loves you and will give you children. But first he commands you to settle great Croton among fair fields" (278). See also Maurizio, "The Voice at the Center of the World," 48–49.

78. See Maurizio, 46. Latte also notes that "the most important oracle of Apollo in [Anatolia] . . . was in the Lycian Patara. There during the period when oracles were given, the priestess was shut in every night in the temple . . . the god was supposed to visit his temple during the night and to have intercourse with the mortal woman. She was held to be his concubine," Latte, 13.

79. Maurizio, 48.

80. See Virgil, *The Aeneid*, trans. C. Day Lewis (Oxford: Oxford University Press, 1986), Book III, 476, 487.

81. Virgil, *Aen.*, Book III, 578–79.

82. Virgil, *Aen.*, Book III, 588.

83. Virgil, *Aen.*, Book VI, 67–72.

84. Virgil, *Aen.*, Book VI, 109–13.

85. Virgil, *Aen.*, Book VI, 114–15.

86. Virgil, *Aen.*, Book VI, 142–45.

87. See Kindt, *Revisiting Delphi*, 14–15.

Bibliography

Aeschylus. *The Oresteian Trilogy*. Translated by Philip Vellacott. London: Penguin, 1959.

Bachofen, J. J. *Myths, Religion, and Mother Right* Translated by Ralph Manheim. Princeton, NJ: Princeton University Press, 1973.

Biers, William R. *The Archaeology of Greece*. Ithaca, NY: Cornell University Press, 1980.

Briffault, Robert. *The Mothers*. London: George Allen & Unwin, 1927.

Calasso, Roberto. *Literature and the Gods*. Translated by Tim Barks. New York: Vintage, 2001.

Chesler, Phyllis. *Women and Madness*. London: Avon, 1983.

Cixous, Hélène, and Catherine Clement. *The Newly Born Woman*. Translated by Betsy Wing. Minneapolis: University of Minnesota Press, 1986.

Diner, Helen. *Mothers and Amazons*. Translated by John Lundin. New York: Julian Press, 1965.

Dodds, E. R. *The Greeks and the Irrational*. Berkeley: University of California Press, 1951.

Doherty, Lillian. *Gender and the Interpretation of Classical Myth*. London: Duckworth, 2001.

Effrossini, Spentzou, and Don Fowler. *Cultivating the Muse*. Oxford, UK: Oxford University Press, 2002.

Fontenrose, Joseph Eddy. *The Delphic Oracle, Its Responses and Operations, with a Catalogue of Responses*. Berkeley: University of California Press, 1979.

Frazer, Sir James George. *The Golden Bough: A Study in Magic and Religion, Vol. 1*. London: Macmillan, 1957.

Geyer-Ryan, Helen. "The Castration of Cassandra." In *Fables of Desire: Studies in the Ethics of Art and Gender*. Cambridge, UK: Polity, 1994.

Gilbert, Sandra, and Susan Gubar. *The Madwoman in the Attic*. London: Yale University Press, 1979.

Goodrich, Norma Lorre. *Priestesses*. New York: Harper Perennial, 1989.

Gordon, Jill. *Turning Toward Philosophy*. University Park: Penn State University Press, 1999.

Graves, Robert. *The Greek Myths*. London: Penguin Books, 1960.

Greer, Germaine. *Slip-Shod Sibyls*. London: Penguin Books, 1996.

Heidegger, Martin. *Nietzsche: Vol. 1, The Will to Power as Art*. Translated by David Farrell Krell. New York: Harper and Row, 1979.

———. *What Is Called Thinking?* Translated by J. Glenn Gray. New York: Harper Perennial, 1976.

Halperin, David M. "Why Is Diotima a Woman?" In *One Hundred Years of Homosexuality and Other Essays on Greek Love*. London: Routledge, 1990.

Hesiod. *Theogony and Works and Days*. Translated by M. L. West. Oxford: Oxford University Press, 1988.

Hyland, Drew. *The Origins of Philosophy: Its Rise in Myth and the Pre-Socratics*. New York: Capricorn Books, 1989.

Irigaray, Luce. *An Ethics of Sexual Difference*. Translated by Carolyn Burke and Gillian Gill. London: Athlone, 1993a.

———. *Sexes and Genealogies*. Translated by Gillian Gill. New York: Columbia University Press, 1993b.

———. *Speculum of the Other Woman*. Translated by Gillian Gill. Ithaca, NY: Cornell University Press, 1985.

Kindt, Julia. *Revisiting Delphi: Religion and Storytelling in Ancient Greece*. Cambridge, UK: Cambridge University Press, 2016.

King, Karen L. *Women and Goddess Traditions*. Minneapolis, MN: Fortress, 1988.

Latte, Kurt. "The Coming of the Pythia." *The Harvard Theological Review* 33, no. 1, 1940. http://www.jstor.org/stable/1507961.

Lipsey, Roger. *Have You Been to Delphi?* Albany: State University of New York Press, 2001.

Maurizio, Lisa. "The Voice at the Center of the World: The Pythia's Ambiguity and Authority," In *Making Silence Speak*, edited by André Lardinois and Laura McClure. Princeton, NJ: Princeton University Press, 2001.

Neumann, Erich. *The Great Mother*. Translated by Ralph Manheim. Princeton, NJ: Princeton University Press, 1972.

Nietzsche, Fredrich. *The Birth of Tragedy*. Translated by Douglas Smith. Oxford, UK: Oxford University Press, 2000.

Nightingale, Florence. "Cassandra and Other Selections." In *Suggestions for Thought*, edited by Mary Poovey. New York: New York University, 1993.

Otto, Walter. *Dionysus, Myth and Cult*. Bloomington: Indiana University Press, 1965.

Ovid. *The Metamorphoses*. Translated by Arthur Golding. London: Penguin, 2002.

Parke, H. W. *A History of the Delphic Oracle*. Oxford, UK: Blackwell, 1939.

Pausanias. *Description of Greece*. Translated by W. H. S. Jones. Cambridge, MA: Harvard University Press, 1965.

Plato. *Phaedrus*. Translated by Alexander Nehamas and Paul Woodruff. In *Plato: Complete Works*, edited by John M. Cooper. Indianapolis, IN: Hackett, 1997.

———. *The Republic*. Translated by Alan Bloom. New York: Basic Books, 1991.

Ross, Stephen David. *The Gift of Beauty*. Albany: State University of New York Press, 1996.

Seznec, Jean. *The Survival of the Pagan Gods*. Princeton, NJ: Princeton University Press, 1981.

Showalter, Elaine. *The Female Malady*. London: Vertigo, 1987.

———. *Hystories: Hysterical Epidemics and Modern Culture*. London: Picador, 1997.

Struck, Peter. *The Birth of the Symbol: Ancient Readers at the Limits of Their Texts*. Princeton, NJ: Princeton University Press, 2004.

Trzaskoma, Stephen M., Stephen Brunet, Thomas G. Palaima, and R. Scott Smith (eds.). *Anthology of Classical Myth*. Indianapolis, IN: Hackett, 2004.

Ussher, Jane. *Women's Madness: Misogyny or Mental Illness?* London: Harvester Wheatsheaf, 1991.

Vernant, Jean-Pierre. *Myth and Society in Ancient Greece.* Translated by Janet Lloyd. Brooklyn, NY: Zone Books, 1980.

Virgil. *The Aeneid.* Translated by C. Day Lewis. Oxford, UK: Oxford University Press, 1986.

Warner, Marina. *From the Beast to the Blond: On Fairy Tales and Their Tellers.* New York: Vintage, 1995.

Whitley, James. *The Archeology of Ancient Greece.* Cambridge, UK: Cambridge University Press, 2001.

Wolf, Christa. *Cassandra.* Translated by Jan Van Heurck. New York: Noonday, 1984.

Wians, William, ed. *Logos and Mythos: Philosophical Essays in Greek Literature.* Albany: State University of New York Press, 2009.

Zajko, Vanda, and Leonard, Miriam, eds. *Laughing with Medusa: Classical Myth and Feminist Thought.* Oxford, UK: Oxford University Press, 2006.

Chapter Three

The Roots of Life and Death in the Homeric Hymns and Presocratic Philosophy

Jessica Elbert Decker

Binary pairs frequently appear in Presocratic texts, but their relation is not the rigid dualism that Cartesian models later produce; instead, they are generative and, significantly, they appear as models of motion. In the major Homeric hymns, the ubiquitous binary pairing is mortal and immortal, or more simply, life and death. The emphasis on this theme is echoed in the fragments of Heraclitus, Parmenides, and Empedocles. Because these Presocratic texts are undoubtedly philosophical in their themes and explorations, they have often been read through the lens of later philosophical paradigms that are foreign to their genesis and method. However, it is not an accident that Heraclitus, Parmenides, or Empedocles created poetic texts. The poetic language of these texts and their Homeric context are inextricable from their philosophical significance, and commentators who approach the texts as such have discovered an abundance of associations and meanings invisible to the rationalistic philosopher who disregards the poetic tradition with which these Presocratic thinkers engage. Sensitivity to the nuances and breadth of the concept of *poeisis*—as artful making, creating, doing—is necessary in orienting oneself to the subtle art of language in these texts.

Charles Kahn's reading of Heraclitus in *The Art and Thought of Heraclitus* is innovative because of its attention to poetic and linguistic techniques in the fragments; the work of Serge Mouraviev on Heraclitus' text demonstrates that the fragments are even denser than expected.[1] Alexander Mourelatos, in *The Route of Parmenides*, approaches the text with acuity to its poetic character, and he discovers irony and doublespeak in the goddess's delivery of the *doxa* that radically shifts the meaning of the poem.[2] Peter Kingsley has demonstrated the manner in which both Parmenides and Empedocles strategically make use of Homeric formulas in their texts; this procedure can produce a wealth of associations in the listener through the subtle repetition of a Homeric phrase.[3] These poetic devices reveal a depth to Presocratic texts; they open up dimensions of the texts that would not be visible without their poetic context. The poetic features of the text create its living, active character—they are not still words printed on a page, but quick mechanisms that operate perfectly when catalyzed, like seeds lying dormant underground. This practice continues subtly in Plato, although he does not write in formal poetic speech: Alcibiades poetically describes Socrates as a Silenus statue in elaborate, charming, and seductive detail when he speaks in *Symposium*. Of course, the drunken Alcibiades, famous for spilling the secrets of the mysteries, gives us the real goods on Socrates, showing us the beauty hidden inside.

The rationalistic model of philosophy, as it came to be practiced later, is anachronistic and clumsy when contrasted with the ambiguous, acrobatic, and multifaceted poetic tradition of Homer, Sappho, and many Presocratic thinkers. This project is an attempt to hear the poetic texts of Heraclitus, Parmenides, and Empedocles in the context of the major Homeric Hymns that structured patterns of thought and imagination in the Ancient Greek world. As they were confronting the paradoxes that erupt between opposites—life and death, day and night, mortal and immortal—the Homeric hymns are not just amusing narratives but also a recording of the associations and symbolic resonances that were current in that time. It is also important to remember that the speech of the poet, in the Ancient Greek world, is not received in a manner familiar to our secular culture; it has a unique cultural function, as Detienne explains,

> The poet's speech never solicits agreement from its listeners or assent from a social group, no more than does a king of justice: it is deployed with all the majesty of oracular speech. It does not attempt to establish a chain of words in real time that would gather force from human approval or disagreement.

> To the extent that magicoreligious speech transcends human time, it also transcends human beings. It is not the manifestation of an individual's will or thought, nor does it constitute the expression of any particular agent or individual. It is the attribute and privilege of a social function.[4]

When Presocratic thinkers adopt the poetic voice as the instrument of their communication, as Heraclitus, Parmenides, and Empedocles do, they are expressly doing so within a culture where poetic speech has this social function and these magico-religious qualities; as Detienne argues, poetic speech is living and active, it *realizes* (*kranei*) and manifests real effects.[5] Analyzing these Presocratic texts in search of rational argumentation, in the tradition of Aristotle and those who followed, is an untenable approach given the cultural and religious context of the texts; besides which, our contemporary notion of rationality had not even begun to be developed before Plato. The poetic language of these Presocratic texts is living and active; it moves *kata physin*, or according to nature, as the texts themselves verify through their efficacious transmission.

Life and death seem to be the binary pair most emphasized in the major Homeric hymns, but it is crucial to remember that death is part of the process of life; it is inextricable from it.[6] Sexual difference and generation are also strikingly apparent themes in the hymns, closely associated with life and death, which necessitates their inclusion in any cosmic or metaphysical considerations. This approach to reading the Presocratic texts in their poetic context reveals a different manner of thinking the binary as a liminal and generative model of motion, in contrast to the Aristotelian and Cartesian models of logic where no paradox is possible. As we explore the natural world in the various disciplines of science as they are practiced in Western culture, our empirical knowledge continues to show us that this kind of radical ambiguity is real in the physical world, for example, in the challenges that quantum physics raises for our understanding of the relation between matter and energy, or even more paradoxically, their definitions with regard to one another. The model of motion between binaries suggested by these ancient texts offers a corresponding metaphysical structure that can harmonize with our contemporary models of the physical world.

The major Homeric hymns composed in honor of Apollo, Hermes, Demeter, and Aphrodite demonstrate the manner in which the cosmic structure is imagined and reinforced. The distinction between mortality and immortality is a key theme that is present in all of the major hymns; as Prier has noted, "The Homeric Hymns are the natural place to turn in any investigation of men and gods because they deal directly both in language and in content with the relationship between the two."[7] This binary opposition is thematized throughout the structure of the hymns, and in the hymns to Aphrodite and to Demeter, it is explored in the explicit context of sexuality and generation. Following Irigaray, I maintain that sexual difference is deeply encoded in these binary relations, and our careful exploration of these symbolic constellations is necessary in order to reveal the latent structures of Western patriarchy.[8]

The rationalistic, hierarchical structures of canonical Western philosophy are not simply reflective of these ancient texts as models or copies; they resulted from a particular orientation and method, from a specific arrangement of epistemological and ontological categories—for example, many of these Presocratic ideas were taken out of their own contexts and placed into a very different, Aristotelian method of ordering and then through the repetition of habit, became solidified as rationalistic principles (*logos* as "reason," for example). This poetic reading of the Presocratic texts alongside the Homeric hymns emphasizes the themes of motion, eros, memory, and the poetic voice. Motion is essential to Homeric cosmological structures, as we will see in the figure of Hermes, and motion is also significant in the narrative structures of poetic texts, particularly because poetry was usually sung in the Ancient Greek world. Memory is the bedrock of the poetic tradition, as Mnemosyne (Memory) is the mother of all the Muses and forgetting is akin to death. Most significantly in reading these texts otherwise than the binary, the erotic character of the cosmological narratives in both the Homeric and Presocratic texts will be emphasized. Reading the major Homeric Hymns with this emphasis demonstrates the crucial role that sexual difference plays in Ancient Greek cosmological narratives and reveals latent possibilities for reading these narratives in a different light—a reading sensitive to the liminality of borders and the permeability of apparent oppositions.

The Tension of the Lyre: The Ambiguous, Living *Logos* of Apollo and Hermes

In Heraclitus' fragments, the image of the bow is a recurrent and densely significant reference to the god Apollo, particularly in light of DK 93's explicit mention of the oracular method.[9] Characterized by Plato as the philosopher of flux, Heraclitus' claim that the world is one of ceaseless motion and change has been his most enduring legacy. However, this characterization is misleading, because it omits the paradoxical quality of Heraclitus' teaching and focuses only on one side of a complicated opposition: flux and stasis, or motion and stillness. This misreading is often responsible for pitting him against Parmenides, though both thinkers are exploring this paradox.[10] Throughout his fragments, Heraclitus presents opposites as a tension; the image of the bow is emblematic of this expression.

> DK 51: They do not comprehend how a thing agrees with itself [*homologeei*] while being drawn apart [*diapheromenon*] a backward-stretched [*palintropos*] harmony like that of the bow or the lyre.[11]

In contemporary philosophical terms, Heraclitus is making a radical claim about identity and difference: each thing is both identical to itself and simultaneously *not* identical to itself. In the Western philosophical canon, identity and difference are usually cast in opposition: a thing is identical only with itself and it is different from all other things. This is the basis of Aristotelian logic, where a thing cannot be both A and not-A simultaneously. In contrast to this binary model of identity, the kind of identity that Heraclitus describes is a *dynamic* identity: a thing's identity is constituted through its motion, as in DK 125's *kykeon* that "separates if it is not stirred" or DK 12's same rivers and "other and other waters."[12] Dynamic identity need not *appear* to be moving, as the *kykeon* and the river do; it can also appear as still—the image of the bow is dynamic identity as tension and stillness, as in DK 48: "The name of the bow [*bios*] is life; its work is death." This model of dynamic identity is significantly linked to the god Apollo, who embodies this tension in oracular language.

> DK 93: The Lord whose oracle is at Delphi neither declares nor conceals but gives a sign.

> DK 54: The hidden harmony is better than the obvious one.

The tension of DK 93 is between declaring and concealing, the ambiguous language of the oracle that does both at once. Heraclitus declares Apollo through the epithet "the Lord whose oracle is at Delphi," and he conceals Apollo in two ways, one obvious and one hidden: first, by omitting his name (the obvious) and, second, by cloaking the meaning of DK 93 in ambiguous words (the hidden). The really tricky move is where we see that the method of working through this riddle, in revealing the obvious and the hidden, reveals another hidden element that gives symmetry to this fragment. Just as Heraclitus conceals Apollo in two ways, he declares Apollo in two ways. The obvious is the epithet "the Lord whose oracle is at Delphi," and the hidden is this experience of understanding the tensions in the fragments as they are demonstrated by the *logos*, by Heraclitus' words: they *invoke* Apollo. This hidden concealing and declaration of Apollo, which are experiential in nature, are examples of the works that Heraclitus refers to in his programmatic DK 1, where he identifies his "words *and* works." In oracular speech, which is a species of what Detienne calls "magico-religious speech," speech and action are inseparable; words are acts.[13] With Heraclitus' strategic use of Apollo in mind, an examination of the *Homeric Hymn to Apollo* will identify his liminal role in the Olympian cosmos as mediator between the divine and mortal world.

Apollo is described as a powerful and dangerous force, even to the gods. In the *Homeric Hymn to Apollo*, the three areas of honor (*timai*) associated with Apollo are the bow, the lyre, and oracular speech.[14] In the Homeric hymns, "The goal of each poem is to characterize and to convey fully the essence of its chosen divinity both in speech and in action."[15] The hymns identify both words and works, acting and speaking; just as Heraclitus identifies his own "words and works" in his programmatic DK 1.[16] Jenny Strauss Clay analyzes Apollo's arrival on Olympus, as dramatized in the *Homeric Hymn to Apollo*: "[T]he hymn opens with a violent and dramatic scene that vividly portrays the terrifying power of Apollo through his effect on the gods assembled. They tremble at his approach, then leap up from their chairs, not so much from respect, but rather out of uncontrollable fear at the sight of the god brandishing his bow."[17] Clay notes the attempts made by scholars to soften the effect of this scene, and explain away the panic of the gods at Apollo's approach.[18] She points out that this destructive and terrible portrayal of the god is repeated in the dialogue between Leto, Apollo's mother in her labor pangs, and the island of Delos, which Leto hopes will welcome the birth of the god.

The speaking island of Delos explains her reticence by citing a rumor that the god Apollo will be *atasthalos*; as Clay explains, "No single

English term can convey the full range of this Greek word. 'Overbearing,' 'violent,' 'reckless,' or 'lawless' offer only partial translations for this highly charged term. In Homer, it is frequently linked with a form of *hybris*."[19] This threatening aspect of Apollo is defused in the opening scene of the hymn, when his mother Leto calmly unstrings the bow and closes the quiver, and leads him to his appointed seat, where Zeus welcomes his son with nectar in a golden cup.[20] While, "for the moment, the awesome potential for destructive violence remains unrealized," Apollo remains an ambiguous threat to Zeus's ordered cosmos.[21] This tension between the bow, instrument of death, and the lyre, instrument of movement and life, is manifest in Apollo himself, like DK 48's bow whose name is life but whose work is death and is figured in the epithet *atasthalos*.[22]

This liminal status of Apollo is significant because of his oracular power; oracular words are double-edged and ambiguous, like Apollo himself, capable of causing great joy or terrible destruction. As the threshold to the Delphic oracle warned "Know thyself," Heraclitus repeats this injunction in DK 116: "It belongs to all human beings to know themselves and to think soundly." Apollo's function as the oracle is a mediating function; he communicates the will of Zeus. Apollo signifies, then, a "cosmic innovation" where Apollo will serve as "a mediator between his father and mankind."[23] This mediating function is crucial in both separating and joining the divine world and the world of human beings; it is a tension between these worlds that is bridged through a particular kind of speech—cryptic, oracular, prophetic *logos*. Heraclitus' use of Apollo in his *logos* indicates not only its oracular character, but also its prophetic function. This withholding of the name of the god brings us to Heraclitus' DK 32, which Serge Mouraviev tells us, after studying the linguistic structure of Heraclitus' fragments, "is incidentally the central fragment of Heraclitus' whole doctrine."[24]

> DK 32: The wise is one alone, both willing and unwilling to be spoken of by the name *Zenos*.

In DK 32 Heraclitus chooses to use the archaic reference to Zeus, "Zenos," which refers to *life*. As he claims in DK 1, Heraclitus' *logos* will speak *kata physin*, or according to nature—this *logos* is one that is driven, very literally, by life itself. Throughout the fragments, the figure of Zeus appears as the driving force characterized as "knowing the plan by which it steers all things through all" (DK 41) and as the "thunderbolt [that] pilots all things" (DK 64). This returns us to the prophetic character of Heraclitus' *logos*: if this *logos* speaks *kata physin*, then it is the voice of life itself. In the structure of Heraclitus' text, DK 32's centrality is not simply intellectual, but physical. As Mouraviev has demonstrated, the text itself does this in its syllabic and syntactic ways; it moves and does multiple things at once.[25] It is an embodiment of its particular *physis*; in this case, DK 32 acts as a lightning rod, identifying a center where many rhyming spokes and repeating spirals can turn the wheels.

The tension of the bow and the lyre is expressed in the Homeric hymns as the relationship between the brothers Apollo, patron of the lyre, and Hermes, its inventor. Hermes is the last of the Olympian gods, and the Homeric hymn in his honor dramatizes his scheme for obtaining the *timai* of a divinity. Since the Olympian order seems already complete when Hermes shows up on the scene, his function and prerogatives are special: his presence initiates motion into the Olympian cosmos. As Clay explains, "To find his place on Olympus, Hermes must discover his particular sphere of activity—the traversing of boundaries—and, appropriately, he must wrest his privileges from the god whose business it is to ensure those boundaries [Apollo]. Hermes, then, introduces dynamic movement and vitality into what might otherwise be a beautifully ordered but static cosmos."[26] Clay identifies Hermes with *metis*, the cunning resourcefulness that is able to find a path through any impossible situation. His weapon, contrasted with the force (*bia*) of Apollo—as Apollo threatens to throw him into Tartarus—is persuasion and *metis*.[27]

Hermes has another function relevant to our themes, as his actions are repeatedly identified with fire in the Homeric hymn in his name: "Hermes it was who first delivered up the firesticks and fire."[28] Later in the hymn, when Hermes binds the cows Zeus commanded him to return to Apollo, Hermes "surveyed the area with his eyes darting fire."[29] Since fire plays an important role in Heraclitus' thought, it is worth noting the traditional associations between fire and divinity. As Prier writes, "Fire occupies a symbolic realm," and, citing examples from the Homeric hymns, "divine splendor is immediately connected with light—light that is no material concept, but a direct, affective, and symbolic representation of the archaic mentality."[30] In the *Homeric Hymn to Hermes*, the cows that Hermes cooks on the fire are for naught, as he realizes his divinity—he cannot eat meat. In the *Homeric Hymn to Demeter*, the goddess Demeter, disguising herself as an old woman, tries to make the infant boy she nurses immortal; "Each night she would hide him away in the burning fire."[31]

Fire is an appropriate vehicle for Heraclitus' meaning because, unlike the other elements, it is *always* in a state of motion. Earth, air, and water (the other three elements) by contrast, can be either in motion or at rest, while fire is by its own nature always in motion.

The *kosmos*, literally, beautiful arrangement or ordering, that Heraclitus describes is characterized by the movement between opposites—a kind of oscillation that, when it appears as static, looks like the tension of the bow or the lyre. In DK 30, Heraclitus explicitly identifies *kosmos* as everliving fire.

> *Kosmos*: the same for all, no man nor god has made, but it ever was and ever will be fire everliving, kindled in measures and in measures extinguished.

Kosmos is identified as a process rather than a static being, though it is eternal (*aei*), or more literally, immortal or everliving. This aspect of Heraclitus' thought is easily overlooked if one accepts Plato's schematic, where the eternal must also be unchanging.

In the *Homeric Hymn to Hermes*, fire is implicated in another act of transformation: the young god invents the lyre by killing a tortoise and using its shell. On the morning of his birth, Hermes wanders out of the cave and comes across a chance find (called a *hermaion*), a tortoise, out of which he constructs the first lyre. Hermes kills the tortoise in a quick and smooth action, by penetrating its life away. As the *Homeric Hymn to Hermes* recounts, "And as when a sudden notion passes through the breast of a man who is constantly visited by thoughts, or when sparkling glances spin from someone's eyes, so glorious Hermes made his action as quick as his word."[32] The swift and fiery action of Hermes in killing the tortoise through penetration is a symbolic expression of his function—at the end of the hymn, Zeus proclaims that Hermes will have "the exclusive right to penetrate into the underworld and carry messages to Hades."[33] Hermes is the only Olympian god with the ability to breach the border between the living and the dead, a liminal duty for the god who initiates motion into the cosmos.

This ability of Hermes to transgress boundaries also ties him to Apollo, whose epithet is "far shooter" and whose will is able to traverse space seemingly without time. This is especially interesting in light of Kingsley's work in *A Story Waiting to Pierce You*, on the hyperborean origins of Apollo as "skywalker"—a being capable of action at a distance, bilocation, and having the ability to travel seemingly impossible distances in a short time through ecstatic trance.[34] Apollo's epithet "far shooter" is *hekatos*, which invites attention to his possible connection, at least in his function, with the goddess Hekate and her role as psychopompous, as she is the only god before Hermes who has the ability to traverse the boundaries of the living and the dead. While Hekate is described at some length in Hesiod's *Theogony*, she also plays a crucial role as mediator in the *Homeric Hymn to Demeter*.

Generative Liminality: Demeter, Persephone, and Aphrodite

As Demeter and Persephone are the main protagonists in the *Homeric Hymn to Demeter*, the essential presence and liminal function of Hekate in the hymn is often overlooked. Hekate first aids Demeter in her search, then later becomes the attendant and escort of Persephone in her travels between worlds. This tripartite structure is necessary for movement between worlds to take place; as Clay points out, the hymn spatially "embraces the three domains of the cosmos: Olympus, the earth, and the underworld. It explores the relations between these three realms as well as the possibilities of movement and communication between them."[35] Just so, the narrative of the hymn introduces Hekate after Persephone's abduction, and Hekate returns when Persephone is restored to her mother. As a liminal goddess and *psychopompous*, Hekate's domain is the borderland between worlds: she both separates and unites these realms as she traverses their limits.

To better understand the function of Hekate in the poetic tradition, her appearance in Hesiod's *Theogony* is illuminating. As Jenny Strauss Clay has pointed out, the seeming digression where Hekate is praised in *Theogony* is so striking and unusual that many commentators attempted to explain it away by claiming that perhaps Hesiod himself had familial, cultic reasons for this effusive veneration of Hekate.[36] In addressing this "Hymn to Hekate," Clay argues that "the lengthy treatment of Hecate at a pivotal moment in the *Theogony* attests not to a personal whim of Hesiod's, but to the poet's understanding of her critical mediating function. Hecate mediates not only between the old and the new order, the Titans and the Olympians: her powers bridge the three spheres of the *cosmos*, and she forms the crucial intermediary between gods and men."[37]

When Zeus asserts his Olympian reign, he divides it between himself and his brothers, Poseidon and Hades: Poseidon rules over the sea, Hades over the underworld, and Zeus over the sky. In bestowing *time* (honor) on Hekate, Zeus is said to give her "splendid gifts—to have a share of the earth and of the barren sea, and from the starry sky as well she has a share in honor, and is honored most of all by the immortal gods."[38] While the underworld is not explicitly mentioned in the honors that Zeus names for Hekate, her function as a chthonic goddess is undeniable.[39] Hekate's domain, then, is not limited—in presiding over all three realms, she unites them without contravening Zeus's division of them between himself and his brothers. This liminal function of Hekate is crucial in identifying a primary theme of the hymn: negotiating borderland spaces, especially those of life and death.

In the opening scene of the hymn, Persephone is playing, plucking flowers; and she herself is called flower-faced, signaling her maturity and mirroring the narcissus she discovers.[40] The narcissus is the catalyst to her abduction and serves as a harbinger of her journey to the Underworld; as Helene Foley points out, "The root *nark-* in *narkissos* suggests torpor and death."[41] But the narcissus is not only death, it is a wonder to behold (*thauma*) and described as a toy or plaything (*athurma*), a thing of delight and joy. This marriage of delight and death is a startlingly precise metaphor for sexuality and demonstrates the manner in which these themes are bound together in the imagery of the myth. The maiden Persephone reaches out for this impossible hundred-headed flower and the earth yawns open. The narcissus is grown as a snare (*dolon*) by Gaia, but this is done, according to the hymn, "to gratify Zeus' design to the Host-to-Many."[42]

Persephone is in a meadow (*leimones*), a word euphemistically associated with female sexuality, as Empedocles implies when he mentions the "divided meadows of Aphrodite."[43] Persephone is accompanied by the Okeanidai, the daughters of Okeanos; these water nymphs are *kourotrophoi*, or nurses of the young, in keeping with the hymn's theme of childbearing and child raising.[44] As in the *Hymn to Aphrodite*, where nymphs will raise the half-immortal child Aeneas, the presence of these nymphs signals at once the liminal borderland of mortality and immortality, and the liminal movement from childhood to adulthood. The Okeanidai are also water nymphs, and Persephone herself, in her chthonic aspect, is associated with water; Empedocles names her as one of the four roots: "Nestis, who moistens with tears the spring of mortals."[45] Just as fire was a crucial symbolic element in the hymn to Hermes, water is an emblem of Persephone and the underworld with its dark rivers.

In Heraclitus' fragments, water is consistently associated with death and forgetting. DK 1's use of two cognates of *lethe* bring the river of the underworld to flow in its other and other waters. Reading several fragments on this theme together, there are patterns and reversals; points of contact between opposites become liminal places where they seem to blend together: waking/sleeping, death/birth, immortal/mortal, up/down.

> DK 1: But other human beings are oblivious [*lanthanei*] of what they do awake just as what they do asleep escapes [*epilanthanontai*] them.
>
> DK 36: For souls it is to die to become/be born water, for water it is to die to become/be born earth; out of earth water is born/arises, out of water soul.[46]
>
> DK 62: Immortals are mortal mortals immortal living the others' death dead in the others' life.
>
> DK 60: The way up and down is one and the same.

In DK 1, Heraclitus says that forgetting, like water, like death, permeates mortal existence despite the reversals of waking and sleeping. Reading Heraclitus in the poetic tradition, we may remember that Mnemosyne, whose name means *memory*, is the mother of all the Muses. The way down is for souls to die in the river of forgetting; the way up is of memory that, like fire, is everliving. Leaving aside the cosmological debates, the significance of these fragments for *psyche* in Heraclitus is clear: forgetting is oblivion, and memory is life. This makes plain the prophetic and oracular function of Heraclitus' text: it is a gymnasium for the memory, as any serious student of Heraclitus' fragments can attest.

The underworld of Persephone is a place of reversal and inversion: she is a newly wedded daughter and she is in the land of the dead. Just at that point in her life when she would become most alive—a maiden picking flowers—and she herself, symbolically, ripe to be picked, she is carried away by Hades, lord of death. The outright reversal in this narrative is stunning; as her mother, goddess of fertility, causes all the fruits to wither on the vine above.[47] What saves Zeus's Olympian cosmos from catastrophe is a pomegranate seed: Hades places the seed in Persephone's mouth so that she might return; the seed is like a remembrance, and of course, a consummation of her marriage with Hades. Then the Eleusinian Mysteries, whatever their content, are done in memory of this mysterious descent and ascent. As Peter Kingsley points out, "the underworld is a place of paradox and inversion. In particular it is the place where polar opposites coexist and merge, and especially the place where the paradox of destructive force being converted into creative power is realized at its greatest intensity."[48] The richness of the underworld cannot be managed in mortal money; divine guidance is required. This brings us to the gates of Parmenides' poem, the gates of Night and Day where opposites meet.

The goddess of Parmenides' poem is unnamed, but her greeting to the *kouros* immediately assures him that he is not dead; "It was no hard fate that sent you traveling this road." This is a polite and hospitable thing to mention to someone who has just mysteriously arrived in the underworld, as "hard fate" is a euphemism for death.[49] While the proem to Parmenides poem is replete with strategic ambiguity, as Mitchell Miller has persuasively demonstrated, the evidence of the proem noted by Kingsley strongly suggests that the unnamed goddess is Persephone.[50] This identity is of course ambiguated when the *doxa* portion of the poem describes a goddess of mixing; this same goddess seems to be described as Aphrodite in Empedocles' fragments.[51] This ambiguity between Persephone and Aphrodite is essential, as the pomegranate seed is an impossible sign of fertility and life in the land of the dead.[52] The pomegranate seed mirrors the impossible hundred-headed narcissus at the beginning of the story, as a fascinating condensation of seemingly opposite powers: death and sexuality. Persephone and Aphrodite are intertwined in this dance of life and death.

Just as Empedocles will later do in his teaching, the speaking goddess of Parmenides' poem tells a double tale. The poem includes two sections, referred to in scholarship as the "way of truth" and the "*doxa*." As Peter Kingsley suggests, "the two halves of Parmenides' poem are the two faces of a dual goddess: life in death, death in life."[53] The goddess tells the *kouros* that he must learn "all things, both the unshaken heart of persuasive truth and the opinions of mortals in which nothing can truthfully be trusted" and goes on to offer two possible paths, ambiguated again to three in the "third way" of mortals whose path "keeps turning backwards on itself (*palintropos*)."[54] This use of *palintropos* is significant because of Heraclitus' DK 51, where the bow and the lyre are *palintropos*, backward-stretched. Scholars have often read this as a polemic against Heraclitean flux, but in both Parmenides and Heraclitus it is used to indicate the appearance of motion that is simultaneously stillness. In Parmenides, the human beings on this backward-stretched path are going nowhere, shuffling in place impossibly like an M. C. Escher drawing. It is when they recognize their immobility (*amechania*, as the goddess dubs it) that they are able to experience eternity, reality, "the way of truth."[55] Thus, in Parmenides stillness is the core. In Heraclitus, the core is motion: the *palintropos* bow may appear to be still but it is aiming its arrow with dynamic strings.

Receptivity to paradox and ambiguity is essential for any reading of these Presocratic texts, and the unnamed goddess in Parmenides' poem does not disappoint in her use of sly puns and witty neologisms, especially when describing the opinions of mortals. The path of not-being is quickly dismissed since nothing can be said of it; the only true path is that of what *is*. But then human beings have gotten it into their "twin heads" to double everything, as the speech of the *doxa* makes plain in persistent syntactic ambiguity. Mourelatos carefully examines the goddess's speech in the *doxa* and identifies irony and double speak; an emblematic example occurs at B8.53, which he translates as "perceptible forms, accordingly, they laid down two notions to name."[56] Mourelatos argues that there is a strategic tension between two renderings of this phrase: "The first says 'they decided'; the second the exact opposite, 'they did *not* decide, they were of *two* minds, they vacillated.'"[57] He recognizes a double audience for the goddess's proclamation of the *doxa*: There are the uninitiated mortals who take the *doxa* at face value, then there is the divine perspective, shared by the *kouros* in his privileged access, who recognize the irony of the mortal position when it is spoken from the mouth of a goddess. This doublespeak proliferates in the *doxa* portion of the poem, as well as in the description the goddess gives of the so-called third way that mortals create, attempting to think both being and nonbeing in a confused and helpless manner.[58] Doublespeak as a divine voice is crucial to understanding Parmenides, and it appears in full force in the words of the goddess Aphrodite, in the Homeric hymn in her name.

The *Homeric Hymn to Aphrodite* seems peculiar among the Homeric Hymns because it appears to blame rather than praise the goddess it invokes. As Clay has noted, "Whereas the other hymns seem to end with the triumph of the god celebrated, *Aphrodite* moves from triumph to defeat or, at least, to a partial diminution of the power of the goddess."[59] I will demonstrate that the hymn is *not* in fact a defeat nor a diminution of her power, instead, the text—like all the other Homeric Hymns—is an exhibition of the goddesses' works and methods. Clay expresses the commonly accepted reading of the hymn succinctly: "[N]o longer insubordinate to her father, Aphrodite has become a true daughter of Zeus."[60] This interpretation is misleading and inconsistent with what we know to be the purpose of the hymn because it makes the *Hymn to Aphrodite* an impossible exception to the rule: All the Homeric Hymns express, in performative narratives, the function and domain of the gods and goddesses invoked. To assume that the *Hymn to Aphrodite* somehow does the opposite, namely, strips the goddess of her powers and shows her renouncing those works in which she delights, is a strange and somewhat alarming conclusion.

Aphrodite is not only guilty, from Zeus's perspective, of sullying his immortal status by causing him to couple with mortal women; she threatens the distinction between mortal and immortal at its core by producing hybrid offspring that have mortal and immortal parents. As Peter Smith writes, "We learn that what she [Aphrodite] has been doing to the gods is an embarrassment to them not because it shows them unable to resist the power of desire but because it has involved them in a kind of miscegenation, a painful contact with mortality, and so with death."[61] The "epoch-making moment" of the hymn, to use Clay's parlance, is the supposed end of mortal and immortal couplings, an end to the age of heroes, mortal-immortal hybrid children.[62] In this reading, focusing on the ambiguous language of Aphrodite, I will argue that the epoch-making shift has more to do with Aphrodite's methods than the outcomes of her works.

The hymn begins by identifying Aphrodite's domain: all of the gods, mortals, and animals are subject to her powerful sway; only three goddesses remain immune to Aphrodite's devices. Athena, Artemis, and Hestia are virgin goddesses not subject to Aphrodite's works, but no one else escapes, even Zeus himself, whom Aphrodite "led astray" and "easily coupled him with mortal women."[63] The dramatic action of the hymn is framed as Zeus's vengeful plan to turn Aphrodite's weapons of seduction against her, but no explanation is offered as to how Zeus is suddenly capable of wielding those weapons. As Clay comments, "It is intriguing to realize that Zeus can avail himself of Aphrodite's methods when necessary to pursue his own ends."[64] This convenient device is one of many ploys on the part of Zeus when it comes to feminine-coded powers; after all, he "gives birth" to Athena after swallowing his first wife Metis and takes credit for the birth of *all* mortal women in his creation of Pandora.[65] Here again, Zeus claims to have possession of Aphrodite's power; "he cast into her heart a sweet longing for Anchises," as the hymn recounts.[66] Aphrodite is the source of sweet longings, the cause and queen of desire; of course, therefore, she herself can also experience her works. In fact, we are often told in Homeric texts that she *delights* in them. Olympian logic dictates that everything happens in accordance with the plan of Zeus; therefore, Aphrodite desires Anchises by divine necessity. The desire itself, however, remains her own. Zeus cannot simply turn Aphrodite's weapons against her, as readings of the narrative assume, because Aphrodite *is* the weapon. Aphrodite cannot be lacking in *eros;* she embodies it.

Patriarchal plot devices aside, what are we to make of Aphrodite's role in this narrative—is she an "unwitting tool" of Zeus, as Clay has it?[67] Or could Aphrodite have some devices of her own at work in the narrative? In fact, why would a hymn in her honor be anything but a display of her wiles and authority? Scholars appear to be unanimous in identifying Aphrodite's humiliation at the hands of Zeus, but there are some possible alternatives to this reading. When Aphrodite speaks, it is generally unwise to assume naivety; the goddess of seduction and sexuality is famous for her whispered words and charming enchantments. And yet, shockingly, all of her speech in the hymn seems to be read as simply what it appears to be: Aphrodite is merely disguised as a mortal maiden in her predictable seduction of Anchises. Perhaps this remarkable fact is a testament to her magical efficacy; nevertheless, Empedocles warns, "Gaze on her with your understanding and do not sit with stunned eyes."[68] Like the deceptive words of the god Hermes, Aphrodite's speech is replete with ambiguity and innuendo.[69] Just as the goddess in Parmenides' poem used doublespeak in her message to the mortal *kouros*, Aphrodite uses doublespeak throughout the hymn.

Aphrodite disguises herself as a mortal maiden and presents herself to the dubious Anchises, who immediately recognizes her as a goddess: He offers to build her an altar and make sacrifices, and asks for a long life, good fortune, and healthy offspring. Aphrodite responds with charming words and lies mixed with truth, as the Muses claim to do; she denies her divinity and invents her mortal genealogy. Then, significantly, she tells Anchises that she knows his language as well as her own, explaining that a Trojan nurse raised her; this is the earliest mention of bilingualism in extant Greek literature.[70] Aphrodite states her bilingual ability twice for emphasis: "I know your language as well as ours, because a Trojan nurse nursed me at home and reared me throughout my childhood, taking me over from my dear mother; so I am well acquainted with your language."[71] If we believe Anchises when he says he recognizes her as a goddess, then Aphrodite's response takes on a different meaning: She is acknowledging his recognition in a subtle manner. Aphrodite is telling him, on the surface, that she can speak his Trojan tongue, but underneath, she is assuring him that she knows how to speak both the language of the divine and that of mortals, a different kind of bilingualism that appears throughout Ancient Greek texts as doublespeak.[72]

Just as Aphrodite repeated her bilingual ability twice, she repeats her mention of Hermes and his role in her alleged abduction (as a mortal maiden). "Twice Aphrodite mentions that Hermes snatched her away from the dance of Artemis, the traditional locus of rape or abduction."[73] Clay argues that perhaps this repetition is meant to "titillate and inspire Anchises."[74] While Aphrodite is certainly titillating to Anchises, her repeated invocation of Hermes has a deeper meaning. Hermes is the border-crossing god, just as Aphrodite is transgressing the borders of mortal and immortal by causing hybrid offspring to be born. Aphrodite elaborates on her contact with Hermes with these words: "[A]fter showing me the way and pointing you out, the mighty Argus-slayer went off to rejoin the families of the immortals, while I have come to you forced by necessity."[75] Once again, if we read her speech as ambiguous, as lies mixed with truth, her words take on a different meaning: What if what she says is true, and Hermes did "show her the way," seeing as she had to love Anchises by necessity, in this case, the will of Zeus?[76] Aphrodite has no choice but to desire Anchises, however, she need not give up any of her power in doing so—she must *appear* to be humiliated, and allow Zeus to believe he has triumphed. But her love for Anchises is not a repudiation of her power; it is a testament to its force.

Clay argues that Aphrodite is at first unaware of Zeus's intervention, but after she falls into his trap, she realizes that she was duped. "By saying that she "fell" into Anchises' bed, Aphrodite indirectly acknowledges herself to have been pushed."[77] This indirect reference is unconvincing; it is not Zeus who pushed her into Anchises' bed, but eros—the force of desire over which Aphrodite is queen. Furthermore, Clay argues: "It may be objected that Aphrodite's recognition of Zeus' role in her discomfiture is not explicitly stated. It must, however, be postulated on the grounds of both dramatic and narrative logic. As we have seen, her implicit recognition at the moment of her epiphany corresponds to Anchises' recognition of her divinity."[78] However, if Aphrodite is slyly playing along, her epiphany is only apparent; it is part of her performance. On the grounds of dramatic and narrative logic, the hymn is not a tale of Aphrodite's shame, but a demonstration of the power of her deception and subtlety.

The speech that Aphrodite makes to Anchises after they go to bed is the evidence usually offered by readers who perceive Aphrodite's humiliation at Zeus's hands, so this part of the text requires careful scrutiny. Aphrodite begins by emphasizing *fear* and reassuring Anchises not to be afraid—three times in fact: "Anchises, most glorious of mortal men, be of good courage, and let your heart not be too afraid. You need have no fear of suffering any harm from me or the other blessed ones."[79] This is to be expected, as Anchises has reason to fear a goddess, but as we shall see later, it is significant to her whole proclamation. In her speech to Anchises, Aphrodite brings up three seemingly tangential narratives, and Prier demonstrates that each of these expresses a blurring of the boundary between mortal and immortal: Zeus's rape of Ganymede, Eos' rape of Tithonus, and Aphrodite's proclamation that Aeneas will be raised by nymphs. Prier argues that "All three tales suggest or indeed define a third area derived directly from the initial underlying opposition between [mortal and immortal]."[80] Aphrodite's choice of these liminal tales is expressive of her function as the goddess of sexuality and seduction, where things different from one another mix in generativity (male/female, mortal/immortal). Finally, we come to the passage that is read as Aphrodite's denunciation of her works. What she actually says to Anchises follows:

> I shall suffer great reproach among the gods evermore on your account. Formerly they used to be afraid of my whisperings and wiles, with which at one time or another I have coupled all the immortals with mortal women, for my will would overcome them all. But now my mouth will no longer open wide enough to mention [*exonomenai*] this among the immortals, since I have been led very far astray, awfully and unutterably [*onomaston*] gone out of my mind, and got a child under my girdle after going to bed with a mortal.[81]

Once again, she begins with *fear*. The gods used to be afraid of her, she says. Certainly, none of the traditional and commonplace notions of Aphrodite that we entertain now, and project onto the texts, invoke fear; we imagine smiling cherubs shooting heart arrows and so forth. This could not be further from the truth of Aphrodite, who is awesome and terrible and capable of causing *ainon akhos*, the dreadful sorrow that she expresses when she names her mortal son Aeneas. Aphrodite is not going to cease in her works, and certainly not in a hymn in her honor; the hymn is a demonstration of how the terrible and terrifying Aphrodite became the goddess we know—persuasive, seductive, seemingly unthreatening. Aphrodite does not renounce her works or say that she will no longer delight in them; what she says instead is that she will not *name* them. Just as she repeated her ability to speak bilingually, and she repeats her invocations of Hermes, Aphrodite says this twice: she will no longer proclaim her works; they will go on in secret (she will no longer "mention," "unutterably"). This reading is further supported by a significant detail of her speech: she warns Anchises to keep silent about their affair.

Commentators are puzzled about this piece—why should Aphrodite invoke secrecy if everyone knows that Aeneas is her son?[82] Why should Aphrodite care that mortals know of her indiscretion in sleeping with a mortal man? Because, as Aphrodite has already hinted, she has adopted deceptive speech like that of Hermes. She did not promise to cease in her works, of drawing mortal to immortal lovers, she simply promised not to mention this to the gods. The new epoch that she is enjoining is one of subtlety and ambiguity; Aphrodite will operate invisibly. So goddesses may appear as maidens, and secret whispers take the place of proclamations; words and beings can be two things at once: true and false, mortal and immortal, the liminal goddess at her apex.

Aphrodite is appearing (to the readers) as a powerful goddess set to seduce Anchises while simultaneously appearing to Anchises as a helpless maiden for him to seduce. She is, in fact, the stronger in this game, yet appears the weaker. Clay notes this aspect of Aphrodite's approach to Anchises; "seduction, we should note, in which the weaker overcomes the stronger, is the polar opposite of forcible rape. Throughout, Aphrodite has made herself appear the weaker."[83] Just so, Aphrodite may appear to be falling into Zeus's trap, while playing him all along. She once again plays the part of the weaker—she appears humiliated, disgraced, and remorseful of her actions. It's a lucky thing that her daddy Zeus came along and saved her from herself. The irony of the situation is cutting and fiercely comical, a fitting tribute to the goddess who delights in laughter.

The Aphrodite of Empedocles' fragments is not the sweet daughter who learned her lesson from Zeus; she is a seductive and overwhelming force of mixture and *metis* that ceaselessly devises the illusory world of mortals in arrangements simultaneously beautiful and terrible. Empedocles tells his student Pausanias: "[B]ut as for you: because you have come aside here, you will learn. Mortal *metis* can manage no more."[84] Aphrodite is responsible for the *amechania*, the helplessness, in which the hapless mortals on the "third way" of Parmenides' poem are trapped. She is queen of the mortal world of mixture, and Empedocles is outing her, blowing her cover, to the initiated.

> Just like when painters work on intricately ornamented pictures—professionals, well skilled in their craft through *metis*, who take special paints of various colors in their hands and mix them with either greater harmony or less to produce shapes and forms resembling anything and everything, creating trees and men and women and animals and birds and water-nourished fish and long-lived gods who have the highest of dignity and honors—just so, don't let deception overthrow the seat of your awareness and make you believe that whatever you see, all those countless numbers of mortal beings around you, has any other source. But know this, and know it clearly, once you have heard these words spoken by a god.[85]

Empedocles says that the blood around the heart is the most perfect mixture possible; it is the height of Aphrodite's devices. Mortal thinking is done *through* her; we are not thinking our own thoughts, we are thinking the thoughts of love—and the world around us is becoming increasingly violent and barbaric as the four roots that Empedocles names are able to exert their own will and return like to like, "placing trust in mad Strife."[86] One way we might approach this oncoming strife is to remember that, as Heraclitus tells us in DK 60, "The way up and down is one and the same," and that sometimes to be torn apart, or to die, is to be born and reemerge a different kind of thing, as Empedocles so plainly tells us that death is transformation. To do this with awareness, with an understanding of how the binary functions, as well as its limits, is essential in bringing the memories across to the other shore.

The poetic voice is eternal in this way: As individual human beings fade away and die, the poet's words live on for aeons and wait to be activated again and do their work. This is the voice of prophecy that knows no time and listening to this voice is a distinctly erotic practice, as it means always leaning toward something beautiful that can't quite be possessed or owned, hoping for future glimmers that might sign the path, like tendrils ever seeking for something that is just out of reach, just around the bend in the dark woods, just over the next green hill. This kind of traveling and way of being—where motion is accepted as a constant but eternity is an ever-flooding shadow, always there and same and still—this kind of awareness is not to be found in rigid structures and rationalistic concepts that build walls where no walls ever were. The poetic voice is erotic because it reaches beyond the limits: the limits of time, space, logic, death. In Plato's works, as Jill Gordon has persuasively demonstrated, eros is the primary motivating element that allows human beings a chance of experiencing the divine; Diotima's ladder of love is not wrought with heartless logic, but with desire and beauty.[87] The tradition of philosophy as practice for dying, as Plato names it in *Phaedo*, is not a sad affair of tears, but a welcoming of transformation, as his many dialogues perform the desires and play of lovers.[88] As Gordon suggests, "Eros is coextensive with the individuation of souls and thus with their alienation from divine being. Alienation entails a forgetting of our origins, but recollection tethers the forgetful human soul to its origins."[89] For Plato, memory is an erotic activity. *Anamnesis* is a return to something already familiar. Perhaps Freud would find it uncanny; it is a homecoming like the famed Odysseus who remembered his home and his wife Penelope, despite all of the attempts to make his memory slip away. In Empedocles, the four roots have their own homecoming in that madness of strife that sets them free from the bonds of mixture. This return is not a return to the same, as some idyllic past, but a return with difference.

In Zeus's Olympian pantheon, Hermes is the last-born god and completes the cosmos by bringing motion into it: the structure without motion was inert. The tension signified by the bow and the lyre is like the tension of the poetic voice, uniting past and present, mortal and immortal through song. The joining together and drawing apart are not just the province of the bow but also signify sexuality and reproduction, the dance of life and death and the shifting seasons. In this way, binary distinctions are revealed as permeable borders traversed and patterned by the oscillation between them, rather than rigid categories that sit in isolation from one another. In the opening of the cosmological dialogue *Timaeus*, Socrates asks if anything has been left out, if anything is lacking, from the model of the proper state that has been recalled from the previous day's discourse, and expresses his dissatisfaction with the discursive approximation in the following way:

> I may compare my feeling to something of this kind: suppose, for instance, that on seeing beautiful creatures, whether works of art or actually alive but in repose, a man should *be moved with desire to behold them in motion* and vigorously engaged in some such exercise as seemed suitable to their physique; well, that is the very feeling I have regarding the State we have described.[90]

Just as Zeus's cosmos is not complete without motion added to it via Hermes, the idyllic state constructed in speech is, according to Socrates, also lacking—and he uses the language of desire here: he says, "Or are we still yearning [*pothos*] for something further in what was said, my dear Timaeus, something that's being left out?"[91] Plato explicitly links eros with motion in this passage, before he begins his cosmology—a cosmology that uses the model of the family and sexual reproduction as its paradigm, and also emphasizes motion, particularly the strange motion of the third kind, *khora*.[92]

To return to where we began, to remember the origin of this journey, we arrive again at Heraclitus' bow and lyre.

> DK 51: They do not comprehend how a thing agrees with itself [*homologeei*] while being drawn apart [*diapheromenon*] a backward-stretched [*palintropos*] harmony like that of the bow or the lyre.

To think otherwise than the binary is to recognize that there can be no static identity, no perfectly defined thing that cannot slip away from its designated place. All things are in process, a process of return that is "turning backward on itself" (*palintropos*) and consists in ceaseless change and difference. The cosmos is not one of chaotic flux, however, as Heraclitus demonstrates, *logos* is the patterning of this movement and *logos* repeats its own everliving motions of oscillation and return. No greater damage could be done to the understanding of Heraclitus' *logos* than to imagine that it is a principle of rationality, in our contemporary sense of the word. This is troubling, as traditional interpretations tend toward statements like this, from A. A. Long: "No one, I presume, needs to be persuaded that Heraclitus' *logos* involves rationality in some sense or senses of that word."[93] Canonical western philosophy has devised a very specific notion of rationality, one that has historically excluded women, people of color, non-European cultures and any ways of thinking that do not strictly adhere to the arbitrary regimen of laws encoded by men like Aristotle who deem themselves the highest authority, despite other traditions that challenge the assumptions and first principles of its construction.

The path that Western metaphysics and science has taken since Aristotle is a very specific one, and not the only possible path: our contemporary models of rationality imagine mastery and control over the natural world, order created through a wise Father, or some benevolent demiurge. This fantasy is at the heart of the human motivation to dominate the natural world through science, and it has led us to the brink of extinction. The order of the cosmos arises *kata physin*, according to nature; it is not driven by any authority or individual will. However, this does not mean that each thing is auto-poetic, self-making, because all things live in association and immersion with other things; the idea that each thing could, through its own power, make itself is a dangerous fantasy of mastery and autonomy. Rational models of the cosmos often neglect or dismiss the essential presence of *chance*. As Emanuela Bianchi has demonstrated in *The Feminine Symptom*, Aristotle's teleological metaphysics of mastery is undone by the aleatory motions of matter, the unpredictable movements of chance.[94] Aristotle's hierarchical, binary system of thought cannot account for chance, and his concept of matter is as far from panpsychism as is possible, so the workings of chance end up coded as evil, as against nature.[95]

Chance is an enemy to any rational model that relies on mastery. Unfortunately for these outdated models, chance is a significant force in our contemporary understanding of Darwinian systems and the physical world. As Elizabeth Grosz has argued, Darwin's theory outlines "a marvelous machine of the production of the new," precisely because of the role of chance in evolutionary processes.[96] This paradigm, of constant change and dynamic identity, strikingly resembles Heraclitus' model of constant change with difference. This is also the model presented by contemporary thinkers of the physical world who recognize the permeability of boundaries; Donna Haraway suggests a model of *sympoiesis*, making-together, and demonstrates the ways in which this language is a more accurate description of empirical observations of biological systems.[97] Haraway identifies our old paradigms, such as our belief that there can be an isolated, individual, autonomous organism, and demonstrates that what we have instead is often an "assemblage." For example, our human bodies contain various microorganisms that are necessary for our continued life and healthy functioning. The cosmos is not a neat row of separate souls awaiting enlightenment—it is much more like the hot compost piles that Donna Haraway sees; none of us exist without the whole biosphere in which we live: "In polytemporal, polyspatial knottings, holobionts hold together contingently and dynamically, engaging other holobionts in complex patternings."[98] The practice of poetic language, and of thinking, is an erotic practice because it reaches beyond the limits of the words and does not aim to capture and freeze things into a static concept or state; boundaries are permeable and fluid. Rather than trapping things in the bonds of their words, capturing them like frozen specimens to dissect, poetic language expresses the world in motion, like the beautiful creatures that Socrates so longs to behold in the *Timaeus*, engaged in some activity, as they move and live *kata physin*.

Our understanding of binaries like life and death, mortal and immortal, and sexual difference are completely dependent on a linguistic and metaphysical system that arbitrarily freezes and isolates things according to our habitual conceptual structures. Like the living physical world around us, our ways of thinking must also learn to move. The methods and teachings of these ancient poetic texts are not antiquated and archaic modes of thought but living, working devices that can assist us in creating different practices and new kinds of awareness that do not depend on the violence of rigid binary divisions. To return again to these poetic texts, to breathe and speak their words with our voices, to enliven the dormant seeds that lie waiting to be born in the deep darkness of our time, this is what the living world around us needs to hear: new songs, new voices, beautiful new patternings that have never been before.

Notes

1. See Charles Kahn. *The Art and Thought of Heraclitus* (Cambridge: Cambridge University Press, 1979); see Serge Mouraviev, "The Hidden Patterns of the Logos: Poetic Form and Philosophical Content in Heraclitus," in *The Philosophy of Logos, Vol. I*, ed. K. I. Boudouris (Athens, 1996).

2. See Alexander Mourelatos (New Haven: Yale University Press, 1970).

3. See Peter Kingsley, *Reality* (Inverness: Golden Sufi Press, 2003).

4. Marcel Detienne, *The Masters of Truth in Archaic Greece* (New York: Zone Books, 1996), 75.

5. Detienne, *Masters*, 69–88. In poetic speech acts, words have an immediate effect and become reality. For example, in our contemporary Western culture: "I now pronounce you married."

6. A limitation in Freud's psychoanalytic theory as well, where in *Beyond the Pleasure Principle* he sets the death instinct *against* eros, and then is puzzled when he realizes that the death instinct also seems to work toward the same ends as eros.

7. Raymond Adolph Prier, *Archaic Logic: Symbol and Structure in Heraclitus, Parmenides, and Empedocles* (Paris: Mouton, 1976), 29.

8. Luce Irigaray, *Speculum of the Other Woman* (Ithaca: Cornell University Press, 1995); Irigaray demonstrates the crucial significance of sexual difference in the metaphysical systems of the ancient world.

9. DK 93: "The Lord whose oracle is at Delphi neither declares nor conceals but signs." Before diving into the Homeric hymns in honor of Apollo and Hermes, it is crucial to note that the Pythagorean table of opposites placed the male in the column of the limited, numerically the odd as opposed to the even, which is unlimited and female.

10. While Heraclitus emphasizes motion, Parmenides emphasizes stillness; neither of them attempt to eradicate the reality of the other.

11. My translation. *Homologeei* resonates with DK 50; *diapheromenon* resonates with DK 10.

12. The *kykeon*, a drink made of wine, barley, and cheese, must be stirred before drinking or it would separate back into its separate components. DK 12: As they step into the same rivers, other and still other waters flow on them.

13. See Detienne, *Masters of Truth*. See Elbert Decker, "How to Speak Kata Physin: Magicoreligious Speech in Heraclitus," *Epoche: A Journal for the History of Philosophy*, 23, no. 2 (Spring 2019): 263–74 for a detailed discussion of this aspect of Heraclitus' text.

14. Jenny Strauss Clay, *The Politics of Olympus: Form and Meaning in the Major Homeric Hymns* (Princeton: Princeton University Press, 1989), 19: "at his birth, Apollo proclaims three areas of influence as his own: the bow, the lyre,

and the oracular power. Only at the end of the hymn has the god come into possession of these three *timai*."

15. Clay, *Politics*, 17.

16. DK 1: "Although this *logos* holds forever human beings are forever uncomprehending (*axynetoi*) . . . human beings seem like the unexperienced when they try such words and works as I set forth, distinguishing each thing *kata physin* and saying how it is."

17. Clay, *Politics*, 19–20.

18. See Clay's discussion of the scholarship on this theme, *Politics*, 20–27.

19. Clay, *Politics*, 36. *Atasthalos* is used in the *Odyssey* and the *Iliad* to indicate depthless anger; in the *Iliad* it is said of Achilles, after he has killed Hector (*Il.* 22.418), and in the *Odyssey*, it is used to describe Odysseus' angry glance when he is taunted about not "appearing athletic" when he chooses not to compete in the races of the Phaeacians because he is overcome with sorrow (*Od.* 8.166). In both of these contexts, it is interesting to note that violence is not imminently used to follow up the rage; it is contained, just as it is in the *Hymn to Apollo*.

20. All of this action occurs at *Homeric Hymn to Apollo*, 1–13.

21. Clay, *Politics*, 21.

22. Once again, the opposites are at work: Apollo as *atasthalos* is unlimited, uncontained threat, but coded as male and limited, Apollo withholds this threat and instead creates a dynamic tension. The epithet of Apollo as destroyer, Apollo *Oulios*, is significant in this regard; see Kingsley, *Reality*, 38–43.

23. Clay, *Politics*, 44.

24. Serge Mouraviev, "The Hidden Patterns of the Logos," 204.

25. The syntactic ambiguity is so dense that Mouraviev has identified eighteen different possible translations and articulated the manner in which the movement occurs in the fragment:"it means that the words 'One,' 'Wise,' 'Sole' or their referents, taken together or separately, on one pole, and the word combination 'the name of Zeus' on the other are torn apart by opposite tendencies which incite them to repulse each other, but also to attract each other, and that these mutual repulsions and attractions act both inside the first pole and between it and the second pole. These attractions and repulsions seem to concern first and foremost the relation between the name and what is named." Mouraviev, "The Hidden Patterns of the Logos," 162–63.

26. Clay, *Politics*, 102.

27. Apollo uses force when he threatens Hermes: "I shall take you and hurl you into misty Tartarus, into the dismal darkness past help," *Hymn to Hermes*, 255–56.

28. *Homeric Hymn to Hermes*, 110–11.

29. *Homeric Hymn to Hermes*, 415.

30. Prier, *Archaic*, 28: "Here at last we move into the symbolic realm of light, an area of unusual perception, that finds expression at important junctures in the Homeric Hymns. This is especially true in terms of fire—a symbol employed directly by Heraclitus, Parmenides, and Empedocles." Prier goes on to identify scenes in the Homeric hymns to Demeter, Hermes, and Apollo that demonstrate this concept.

31. *Homeric Hymn to Demeter*, 239.

32. *Homeric Hymn to Hermes*, 43–45.

33. Clay, *Politics*, 148–49.

34. See Peter Kingsley, *A Story Waiting to Pierce You* (Inverness: Golden Sufi Press, 2010). It is especially important to note that the Hyperborean Apollo is fully incarnate—he is a physical human being, not a mirage or phantom, and these feats of travel are done with a physical body.

35. Clay, *Politics*, 208.

36. Jenny Strauss Clay, in "The Hecate of the Theogony," *Greek, Roman and Byzantine Studies* 25, no. 1 (1984) discusses the scholarly interpretation of Hekate's role in *Theogony* in great detail.

37. Clay, *Politics*, 37.

38. *Theogony*, 411–15.

39. For a thorough and illuminating study of the figure and function of Hekate, see Sarah Iles Johnston, *Hekate Soteira: A Study of Hekate's Roles in the Chaldean Oracles and Related Literature* (Atlanta: Scholars Press, 1990). See also Koch's essay in this volume for insightful discussion of Hekate's liminal function.

40. At line 8 of the *Homeric Hymn to Demeter*, Persephone is described as *kalukaupidi*, flower-faced.

41. Helene P. Foley, *The Homeric Hymn to Demeter: Translation, Commentary, and Interpretive Essays* (Princeton: Princeton University Press, 1994), 34.

42. *Homeric Hymn to Demeter*, line 9, Foley's translation.

43. Fragment 69.

44. As Foley points out in discussing Persephone's companions in the opening scene, "in Persephone's later version of the story in this poem (417–24), the powerful virgin goddesses Pallas (Athena) and Artemis are also present at the abduction," and Aphrodite is present in Orphic fragment 49.40ff and Euripides' *Helen* 131444, 33. Also the liminal nature of the Okeanidai is relevant here, as they are neither mortal nor divine.

45. Empedocles DK 31.

46. Gábor Betegh, "On the Physical Aspect of Heraclitus' Psychology: With New Appendices," in *Doctrine and Doxography: Studies on Heraclitus and Pythagoras*, ed. David Sider and Dirk Obbink (Berlin: De Gruyter, 2013), 228. Betegh persuasively argues that that "the focus is on the changes, and not merely

on the states" and that the Greek word "*thanatos*" refers "not the state of being dead, but to the event of dying."

47. This is an aspect of the hymn that makes the bond between mother and daughter viscerally felt, as Demeter physically mirrors her daughter's plight first through causing all the vegetation to die, then by disguising herself as an old woman beyond childbearing years.

48. Peter Kingsley, *Ancient Philosophy, Mystery and Magic: Empedocles and the Pythagorean Tradition* (London: Oxford University Press, 1995), 77.

49. See Peter Kingsley, *Reality*, 27 for "no hard fate" as a euphemism for death.

50. See Miller (2006) for discussion of strategic ambiguities in the proem and their function; on the unnamed goddess as Persephone see Kingsley, *Reality*.

51. Plato cites a line from Parmenides' *doxa* in *Symposium* at 178b, in the speech of Phaedrus: "first she contrived Eros." This strongly indicates that Aphrodite is the goddess implicated.

52. See Kingsley, *Reality*, on Persephone-Aphrodite polarity: 206–20, 578.

53. Kingsley, *Reality*, 219.

54. DK 6.

55. *Amechania* is a very significant term: Sappho identifies *eros* as producing *amechania* in Fragment 130, and in the *Doxa* portion of Parmenides' poem we encounter the line, cited in Plato's *Symposium*: "First of all the gods she contrived *eros*," DK 13.

56. Mourelatos, *Route*, 228.

57. Mourelatos, *Route*, 229.

58. As Kingsley has demonstrated, the ambiguity in this section is dense and witty: "Twin heads, knowing nothing, for helplessness [*amechania*] in their chests is what steers their wandering minds as they are carried along in a daze, deaf and blind at the same time. Indistinguishable undistinguishing crowds [*akrita phula*] who reckon that being and non-being are the same but not the same. And, for all of them, the route they follow is a path that keeps turning backwards on itself [*palintropos*]." See Kingsley for discussion of strategic ambiguities and humor in the "third way" in *Reality*, 83–110, 565.

59. Clay, *Politics*, 155.

60. Clay, *Politics*, 200.

61. Peter Smith, *Nursling of Mortality: A Study of the Homeric Hymn to Aphrodite* (Frankfurt: Verlag Peter D. Lang, 1981), 40.

62. Clay, *Politics*, 154.

63. *Homeric Hymn to Aphrodite*, 35–38.

64. Clay, *Politics*, 164–65.

65. See Elbert Decker, "Manufacturing the Mother: Technical Appropriations of Birth in Ancient Greek Thought," in *Bearing the Weight of the World: Exploring Maternal Embodiment*, ed. Alys Einion and Jen Rinaldi (Demeter Press, 2018) for the catalog of Zeus's appropriation of female generativity. In the dis-

cussion of the *Homeric Hymn to Demeter*, above, the same situation occurs when Zeus seems to make the narcissus that fascinates Persephone grow.

66. *Homeric Hymn to Aphrodite*, 53–55.

67. Clay, *Politics*, 180: supports Aphrodite's ignorance of Zeus' trap: "Anchises' human ignorance of his divine bedfellow is matched by Aphrodite's ignorance of the will of the gods. Unwitting tools of Zeus, both the goddess and her mortal lover are united in their ignorance of his plan."

68. Empedocles, Fragment 25, line 21.

69. Detienne suggests this connection between Aphrodite and Hermes, *Masters*, 79: "The counterpart to the *Apate* of Aphrodite is another Deceit, a child of night, a negative power who is the sister of *Lethe* and of words of deceit (*logoi pseudeis*). These words of deceit, the flip side of 'whispered endearments,' are under the patronage of the nocturnal Hermes, the master of the *Peitho* of 'cunning' (*dolia*), the negative aspect of Aphrodite's "*Peitho*."

70. *Homeric Hymn to Aphrodite*, ed. Martin L. West (Cambridge: Harvard University Press, 2003), n46.

71. *Homeric Hymn to Aphrodite*, 113–16.

72. A classic example is when Odysseus tells the Cyclops his name is No One; in the *Odyssey*, Athena is frequently responsible for Odysseus' use of *metis*. See Elbert Decker, "I Will Tell a Double Tale: Double Speak in the Ancient Greek Poetic Tradition," *Epoche: A Journal for the History of Philosophy* 25, no. 2 (Spring 2021): 237–48.

73. Clay, *Politics*, 176.

74. Clay, *Politics*, 177.

75. *Homeric Hymn to Aphrodite*, 128–30.

76. The word Aphrodite uses, translated as "show," is *deixe*, which means to demonstrate. Liddel Scott Greek-English Lexicon, 375.

77. Clay, *Politics*, 184.

78. Clay, *Politics*, 190–91.

79. *Homeric Hymn to Aphrodite*, 192–95.

80. Prier, *Archaic*, 31.

81. *Homeric Hymn to Aphrodite*, 246–55.

82. Clay, *Politics*, 198, writes, "At long last, Aphrodite reveals her identity, but at the same time she enjoins secrecy on her lover. The injunction is puzzling."

83. Clay, *Politics*, 177.

84. Empedocles DK 2; Kingsley's translation in *Reality*, 326.

85. Empedocles, DK 23; Kingsley's translation in *Reality*, 384–85.

86. DK 10, line 14, Kingsley, *Reality*, 396–99.

87. See Jill Gordon, *Plato's Erotic World: From Cosmic Origins to Human Death* (Cambridge: Cambridge University Press, 2012).

88. Socrates explains philosophy as practice for dying at *Phaedo* 64a.

89. Gordon, *Plato's Erotic World*, 2.

90. Plato, *Timaeus*, trans. R. G. Bury (Cambridge, Harvard University Press, 1929), 19b. *Italics mine*.

91. Plato, *Timaeus*, trans. Peter Kalkavage (Indianapolis: Hackett Publishing, 2016), 19a.

92. See Elbert Decker, "Borderland Spaces of the Third Kind: Erotic Agency in Plato and Octavia Butler" in *Borderlands and Liminal Subjects: Transgressing the Limits in Philosophy and Literature*, ed. Jessica Elbert Decker and Dylan Winchock (London: Palgrave, 2017), for a detailed analysis of the erotic character of Plato's cosmology in *Timaeus*.

93. Anthony A. Long, "Heraclitus on Measure and the Explicit Emergence of Rationality," in *Doctrine and Doxography: Studies on Heraclitus and Pythagoras*, ed. David Sider and Dirk Obbink (Berlin: De Gruyter, 2013), 201.

94. See Emanuela Bianchi, *The Feminine Symptom: Aleatory Matter in the Aristotelian Cosmos* (New York: Fordham University Press, 2014).

95. Like those "monsters," female children, who are simultaneously born in accordance with nature and against nature; see Bianchi, *Symptom*, 26–50.

96. Elizabeth Grosz, "Darwin and Feminism: Some Preliminary Considerations." *Australian Feminist Studies* 14, no. 29 (1999): 4.

97. Donna J Haraway, *Staying with the Trouble: Making Kin in the Chthulucene* (Durham: Duke University Press, 2016), 59. Haraway challenges the traditional paradigm of the individual organism, and argues that instead, we are "holobionts": "critters interpenetrate each other, loop around and through one another, eat each other, get indigestion, and partially digest and partially assimilate one another, and thereby establish sympoetic arrangements that are otherwise known as cells, organisms, and ecological assemblages."

98. Haraway, *Trouble*, 60.

Bibliography

Alderink, Larry J. "Mythical and Cosmological Structure in the Homeric Hymn to Demeter." *Numen* 29, no. 1 (July 1982): 1–16.

Beck, Deborah. "Direct and Indirect Speech in the Homeric Hymn to Demeter." *Transactions of the American Philological Association* 131 (2001): 53–74.

Betegh, Gábor. "On the Physical Aspect of Heraclitus' Psychology: With New Appendices." In *Doctrine and Doxography: Studies on Heraclitus and Pythagoras*, edited by David Sider and Dirk Obbink, 225–61. Berlin, Germany: De Gruyter, 2013.

Bianchi, Emanuela. *The Feminine Symptom: Aleatory Matter in the Aristotelian Cosmos*. New York: Fordham University Press, 2014.

Brann, Eva. *The Logos of Heraclitus*. Philadelphia, PA: Paul Dry Books, 2011.

Breitenberger, Barbara. *Aphrodite and Eros: The Development of Erotic Mythology in Early Greek Poetry and Cult*. New York: Routledge, 2007.

Bungard, Christopher. "Lies, Lyres, and Laughter: Surplus Potential in the *Homeric Hymn to Hermes*." *Arethusa* 44, no. 2 (Spring 2011): 143–65.

Calame, Claude. *The Poetics of Eros in Ancient Greece*. Trans. Janet Lloyd. Princeton, NJ: Princeton University Press, 1999.

Clay, Jenny Strauss. *The Politics of Olympus: Form and Meaning in the Major Homeric Hymns*. Princeton, NJ: Princeton University Press, 1989.

———. "The Hecate of the Theogony." *Greek, Roman and Byzantine Studies* 25, no. 1 (1984): 27–38.

Detienne, Marcel, and Jean Pierre Vernant. *Cunning Intelligence in Greek Culture and Society*. Chicago, IL: University of Chicago Press, 1991.

———. *The Masters of Truth in Archaic Greece*. Trans. Janet Lloyd. New York: Zone Books, 1996.

Dilcher, Roman. *Studies in Heraclitus*. Hildesheim, Germany: Verlag, 1995.

———. "How Not to Conceive of Heraclitean Harmony." In *Doctrine and Doxography: Studies on Heraclitus and Pythagoras*, edited by David Sider and Dirk Obbink, 263–80. Berlin, Germany: De Gruyter, 2013.

Dodds, E. R. *The Greeks and the Irrational*. Berkeley: University of California Press, 1951.

Eliot, T. S. *The Complete Poems and Plays 1909–1950*. New York: Harcourt Brace Jovanovich, 1971.

Elbert Decker, Jessica. "Everliving Fire: The Synaptic Motion of Life in Heraclitus," *Epoche: A Journal for the History of Philosophy* 19, no. 2 (Spring 2015): 173–80.

———. "How to Speak Kata Physin: Magicoreligious Speech in Heraclitus," *Epoche: A Journal for the History of Philosophy* 23, no. 2 (Spring 2019): 263–74.

———. "*I Will Tell a Double Tale*: Double Speak in the Ancient Greek Poetic Tradition," *Epoche: a journal for the history of philosophy* 25, no. 2 (Spring 2021): 237–48.

———. "Manufacturing the Mother: Technical Appropriations of Birth in Ancient Greek Thought." In *Bearing the Weight of the World: Exploring Maternal Embodiment*, edited by Alys Einion and Jen Rinaldi, 83–98. Ontario: Demeter Press, 2018.

———. "Borderland Spaces of the Third Kind: Erotic Agency in Plato and Octavia Butler." In *Borderlands and Liminal Subjects: Transgressing the Limits in Philosophy and Literature*, edited by Jessica Elbert Decker and Dylan Winchock, 187–211. Cham, Switzerland: Palgrave, 2017.

Finkelberg, Aryeh. "Heraclitus, the Rival of Pythagoras." In *Doctrine and Doxography: Studies on Heraclitus and Pythagoras*, edited by David Sider and Dirk Obbink, 225–61. Berlin, Germany: De Gruyter, 2013.

Fletcher, Judith. "A Trickster's Oaths in the Homeric Hymn to Hermes." *American Journal of Philology* 129, no. 1 (Spring 2008): 19–46.

Foley, Helene P. *The Homeric Hymn to Demeter: Translation, Commentary, and Interpretive Essays*. Princeton, NJ: Princeton University Press, 1994.

Freud, Sigmund. *Beyond the Pleasure Principle*. New York: W. W. Norton, 1990.

Friedrich, Paul. *The Meaning of Aphrodite*. Chicago, IL: University of Chicago Press, 1978.

Granger, Herbert. "Early Natural Theology: The Purification of the Divine Nature." In *Doctrine and Doxography: Studies on Heraclitus and Pythagoras*, edited by David Sider and Dirk Obbink, 163–200. Berlin, Germany: De Gruyter, 2013.

Gera, Deborah Levine. *Ancient Greek Ideas on Speech, Language, and Civilization*. London: Oxford University Press, 2003.

Gordon, Jill. *Plato's Erotic World: From Cosmic Origins to Human Death*. Cambridge, UK: Cambridge University Press, 2012.

Graham, Daniel. *Explaining the Cosmos: The Ionian Tradition of Scientific Philosophy*. Princeton, NJ: Princeton University Press, 2006.

Grosz, Elizabeth. "Darwin and Feminism: Some Preliminary Considerations." *Australian Feminist Studies* 14, no. 29 (1999): 23–51.

Haraway, Donna J. *Staying with the Trouble: Making Kin in the Chthulucene*. Durham, NC: Duke University Press, 2016.

Holmes, Brooke. *Gender: Antiquity and Its Legacy*. New York: Oxford University Press, 2012.

Hölscher, Uvo. "Paradox, Simile, and Gnomic Utterance in Heraclitus." In *The Presocratics*, edited by Alexander P. D. Mourelatos, 229–38. New York: Anchor Books, 1974.

Huffman, Carl. "Philolaus' Critique of Heraclitus." In *Doctrine and Doxography: Studies on Heraclitus and Pythagoras*, edited by David Sider and Dirk Obbink, 121–44. Berlin, Germany: De Gruyter, 2013.

Hülsz, Enrique. "Heraclitus on Logos: Language, Rationality, and the Real." In *Doctrine and Doxography: Studies on Heraclitus and Pythagoras*, edited by David Sider and Dirk Obbink, 281–301. Berlin, Germany: De Gruyter, 2013.

Hussey, Edward. *The Presocratics*. Indianapolis. IN: Hackett, 1983.

Inwood, Brad. *The Poem of Empedocles: A Text and Translation*. Toronto, ON: University of Toronto Press, 2001.

Irigaray, Luce. *Speculum of the Other Woman*. Ithaca, NY: Cornell University Press, 1995.

Johnston, Sarah Iles. *Hekate Soteira: A Study of Hekate's Roles in the Chaldean Oracles and Related Literature*. Atlanta, GA: Scholars Press, 1990.

Kahn, Charles. *The Art and Thought of Heraclitus: An Edition of the Fragments with Translation and Commentary*. Cambridge. UK: Cambridge University Press, 1979.

Kalkavadge, Peter. *Plato's Timaeus: Translation, Glossary, Appendices and Introductory Essay*. Newburyport, MA: Focus Publishing, 2001.

Kingsley, Peter. *Ancient Philosophy, Mystery and Magic: Empedocles and the Pythagorean Tradition*. London: Oxford University Press, 1995.

———. *Reality*. Inverness, CA: Golden Sufi Press, 2003.

———. *A Story Waiting to Pierce You*. Inverness, CA: Golden Sufi Press, 2010.

Kirk, G. S., J. E. Raven, and M. Schofield. *The Presocratic Philosophers*. Cambridge, UK: Cambridge University Press, 1983.

Liddell, H. G., and R. Scott. *Greek-English Lexicon with a Revised Supplement*. Oxford, UK. 1996.

Long, Anthony A. "Heraclitus on Measure and the Explicit Emergence of Rationality." In *Doctrine and Doxography: Studies on Heraclitus and Pythagoras*, edited by David Sider and Dirk Obbink, 201–23. Berlin, Germany: De Gruyter, 2013.

Lord, Mary Louise. "Withdrawal and Return: An Epic Story Pattern in the Homeric Hymn to Demeter and in the Homeric Poems." *Classical Journal* 62, no. 6 (March 1967): 241–48.

Marciano, Laura Gemelli. "Images and Experience: At the Roots of Parmenides' *Aletheia*." *Ancient Philosophy* 28 (2008): 21–48.

Miller, Mitchell. "Ambiguity and Transport: Reflections on the Proem to Parmenides' Poem." *Oxford Studies in Ancient Philosophy* 30 (2006): 1–47.

Mourelatos, Alexander P. D. *The Route of Parmenides*. New Haven, CT: Yale University Press, 1970.

Mouraviev, Serge. "The Hidden Patterns of the Logos: Poetic Form and Philosophical Content in Heraclitus." In *The Philosophy of Logos, Vol. I*, edited by K. I. Boudouris. Athens, Greece, 1996.

Olson, S. Douglas. *The Homeric Hymn to Aphrodite and Related Texts*. Berlin, Germany: De Gruyter, 2012.

Onians, R. B. *The Origins of European Thought: About the Body, the Mind, the Soul, the World, Time, and Fate*. Cambridge, UK: Cambridge University Press, 1951.

Plato. *Symposium*. Translated by W. R. M. Lamb. Cambridge, MA: Harvard University Press, 1925.

———. *Timaeus*. Translated by R. G. Bury. Cambridge, MA: Harvard University Press, 1929.

———. *Phaedo*. Translated by Harold North Fowler. Cambridge, MA: Harvard University Press, 1914.

Prier, Raymond Adolph. *Archaic Logic: Symbol and Structure in Heraclitus, Parmenides, and Empedocles*. Paris: Mouton, 1976.

Robinson, T. M. *Heraclitus: Fragments, a Text and Translation*. Toronto, ON: University of Toronto Press, 1987.

Rowett, Catherine. "Philosophy's Numerical Turn: Why the Pythagoreans' Interest in Numbers Is Truly Awesome." *Doctrine and Doxography: Studies on*

Heraclitus and Pythagoras. Edited by David Sider and Dirk Obbink, 3–31. Berlin, Germany: De Gruyter, 2013.

Rubin, Nancy Felson, and Harriet M. Deal. "Some Functions of the Demophon Episode in the Homeric Hymn to Demeter." *Quaderni Urbinati di Cultura Classica* 5 (1980): 7–21.

Smith, Peter. *Nursling of Mortality: A Study of the Homeric Hymn to Aphrodite*. Frankfurt, Germany: Verlag Peter D. Lang, 1981.

Sowa, Cora Angier. *Traditional Themes in the Homeric Hymns*. Chicago, IL: Bolchazy-Carducci Publishers, 1984.

Stokes, Michael C. *One and Many in Presocratic Philosophy*. Cambridge, MA: Harvard University Press, 1971.

Struck, Peter. *The Birth of the Symbol*. Princeton, NJ: Princeton University Press, 2004.

Suter, Ann. *The Narcissus and the Pomegranate: An Archeaology of the Homeric Hymn to Demeter*. Ann Arbor: University of Michigan Press, 2002.

Vernant, Jean-Pierre. *Mortals and Immortals*, edited by Froma Zeitlin. Princeton, NJ: Princeton University Press, 1991.

Zeitlin, Froma, David Halperin, and John Winkler, eds. *Before Sexuality: The Construction of Erotic Experience in the Greek World*. Princeton, NJ: Princeton University Press, 1990.

Chapter Four

The Intelligibility of Difference

Anaxagoras' and Lugones' Ontologies of Separation

Holly Moore

Introduction

Although the traditional interpretation of Parmenides has been rightly debated in recent scholarship, there is surely no more strident a statement of ontological binarism in Presocratic Greek thought than that of Parmenides' goddess, who instructs the journeying youth in "the only ways of enquiry there are to be thought of. The one, that [it] is and that it is impossible for [it] not to be, is the path of Persuasion (for she attends upon Truth); the other, that [it] is not and that it is needful that [it] not be, that I declare to you is an altogether indiscernible track: for you could not know what is not—that cannot be done—nor indicate it" (DK 28 B 2).[1] Whether or not this claim is attenuated by the goddess' account of the *doxa* of humans,[2] the prohibition against inquiring into what is not and the attendant affirmation of the static, finite oneness of being posed a serious challenge to philosophers and cosmologists, such as Anaxagoras, who sought to recognize and to think the metaphysical basis of difference, change, and multiplicity. Parmenidean monism is thus ironically tied to binarism: the affirmation of the oneness of being supported by the unintelligibility of multiplicity, a position drawn out dialectically in Zeno's paradoxes. This logic of purity, then, stands as the Parmenidean inheritance of Anaxagoras and other so-called pluralists.

Because of his depiction as an arch pluralist (an identification made nearly unquestionable given its origin in Aristotle's doxography), until relatively recently Anaxagoras has been cast as an opponent of the Eleatic school, this both because of the logical binarism that subtends the orthodox reading of Parmenidean monism but also because of the way Anaxagoras was construed as antagonistic to Parmenidean monism. For example, in their highly influential English translation of the canonical Presocratic philosophers, G. S. Kirk, J. E. Raven, and M. Schofield assert, regarding the reputed opening lines of Anaxagoras' work: "It shows at the outset how extreme was the reaction of Anaxagoras against the Eleatic monism."[3] However, just as Rose Cherubin and others[4] have unsettled the stark account of Parmenidean monism, Patricia Curd[5] and Daniel Graham[6] have convincingly rejected the premise that Anaxagoras was anti-Eleatic, arguing that the evidence of antagonism is missing, and that given the fragments' explicit sympathy for key doctrines of Eleatic thought, it is inaccurate to describe his reaction as "extreme." On the "standard interpretation,"[7] Anaxagoras' antagonism to Eleatic thought is evidenced by his emphasis on pluralism. But this functions as evidence only if it is presupposed that pluralism is incompatible with holism; the argument of the standard interpretation is at best trivial, and at worst, circular. In addition to the reappraisal of Parmenides' monism itself, recent commentators[8] have stressed that far from defying monism, Anaxagoras' pluralism is holistic (an infinitely multiplicitous plenum, rather than a mechanistic infinitude achieved through division into parts), and seeks to maintain not only Parmenides' goddess's ban on not-being by rejecting the notion of a "smallest" and that of a "largest" but also to assert the oneness of being, of "the one *kosmos*" (B 8).[9]

Nevertheless, the same scholars who have defended Anaxagoras (and Parmenides) against the portrayal of physical pluralism as necessarily antagonistic to monistic ontology have saddled his account of *nous* with a kind of dualism. In response, I argue that *nous* names the intelligibility of difference, thereby retaining a holistic reading of Anaxagoras' metaphysics while also reframing Anaxagoras' account of *nous* as a theory of immanent difference. This view has the additional benefit of requiring us to address interpreters' reliance on modern chemical models in the reconstruction of Anaxagoras' physics of mixture and separation. Drawing on feminist political philosopher María Lugones's theory of "curdled-separation," I suggest instead the model of a curdled emulsion as a way of conceptualizing Anaxagoras' complex account. Leveraging modern political ontology for interpreting an ancient physical theory also suggests there is political significance in interpreting Anaxagoras' pluralism as resistant to theoretical purity.

Anaxagoras' Holistic Pluralism

Few could dispute Anaxagoras' Eleatic allegiance to the doctrine that not-being cannot be. First, there is B 17, where Anaxagoras critiques the view that coming into being and perishing are not absolute: "The Greeks do not think correctly about coming-to-be and passing-away; for no thing comes to be nor passes away, but is mixed together and dissociated from the things that are. And thus they would be correct to call coming-to-be mixing-together and passing-away dissociating." In this way Anaxagoras resembles Anaximenes—not in terms of the material of the *kosmos* but in terms of the claim that generation and destruction are reformulations of already given things. Anaxagoras, however, is also more sensitive to the notion of increase and decrease to the totality of the *kosmos*; despite dissociation ". . . all things are in no way less or more (for it is impossible that they be more than all), but all things are always equal" (B 5). His argument for the nature of this totality, in fact, derives from this very prohibition on absolute increase or diminution, both of which entail the affirmation of not-being.

Although this reasoning strongly suggests Parmenides' poem, an even more explicit denial of not-being is the central premise of Anaxagoras' reasoning for the claim that "all things are in all things" and provides us the strongest evidence of his Eleaticism. The following fragments together comprise this argument:

> B 3: Nor of the small is there a smallest, but always a smaller (*for what-is cannot not be*)—but also of the large there is always a larger. And [the large] is equal to the small in extent [*plēthos*], but in relation to itself, each thing is both large and small. (Author's emphasis)
>
> B 6: Since the shares of the large and the small are equal in number, in this way too, all things will be in everything; nor

> is it possible that [anything] be separate, but all things have a share of everything. *Since it is not possible that there is a least, it would not be possible that [anything] be separated, nor come to be by itself, but just as in the beginning, now too all things are together.* In all things there are many things present, equal in number, both in the greater and in the lesser of the things being separated off. (Author's emphasis)

There must always be a smaller, for, as the atomists indeed go on to contend, to find some "smallest" is also to assert the existence of void and not-being. If there is always a smaller, then there is no way to fully separate anything from anything else and no final item or kind is ultimately divisible from any other. Thus, Anaxagoras repeats over and over that "all things are in all things" because all things are ultimately inseparable.[10]

Following the line of argumentation regarding the "smallest," several scholars[11] have argued that Anaxagoras is signaling in these fragments a relatively direct response to Zeno's paradoxes of pluralism. That is, rather than seeing infinite divisibility as the destruction of the pluralist position, Anaxagoras boldly embraces infinite divisibility not simply as the basis for his pluralism but also as a way of preserving the Eleatic doctrine that not-being cannot be.

Despite agreement regarding Anaxagoras' faithfulness to the Eleatic rejection of not-being, Anaxagoras is, however, also traditionally read as departing from Parmenides because of his pluralism. Largely due to the outsized influence of Aristotle's doxography, Anaxagoras is identified as first and foremost a pluralist and, thus, construed as antagonistic to Parmenides' ontological monism. Certainly, the opening to Anaxagoras' book is a testament to the centrality of multiplicity to his account of the *kosmos*.

> All things were together, unlimited [*apeira*] both in amount and in smallness, for the small, too, was unlimited [*apeiron*]. And because all things were together, nothing was evident on account of smallness; for air and aether covered all things, both being unlimited, for these are the greatest among all things, both in amount and in largeness. (B 1)

Note that Anaxagoras begins with a double claim regarding the quantitatively *apeiron* nature of all things: all things are limitless in their quantity (which may be construed in terms of kinds or individuals), as well as in their divisibility. Thus, limitlessness not only qualifies "all things" but also specifies the way in which they were "all together." *Apeira* is in the plural not simply because boundlessness applies to the nature of each but also because the boundless and indefinite nature applies to their plurality—they have an unlimited number of ways of being mixed with each other. However, Anaxagoras is not necessarily thereby attributing limitlessness to the whole (which was perhaps Anaximander's claim) but to all things, which make up the whole. If this is the case, there is no prima facie incompatibility between Anaxagoras' pluralism and Parmenides' claim that the one is finite, and this situates Anaxagoras' pluralism as holistic from the start.[12] Moreover, even if we take B 1's claim that there is always a larger to be saying that the *kosmos* is itself infinite, we must balance this against Anaxagoras' emphasis on the inclusive parity that follows from the fact that all things are in all things: "In all things there are many things present, equal in number" (B 6).[13] That is, the infinitude of the *kosmos* would entail the infinitude of each thing, itself a *kosmos* of all things.

If we retain a holistic view of Anaxagoras' pluralism, we find not only that this is consistent with Parmenides' monism regardless of whether the one is construed as infinite or finite, but we also have a more generous way of interpreting the otherwise baffling and extravagant claims of B 4a.

> Since these things are so, it is right to think [*khrē dokein*] that there are many different things present in everything that is being combined, and seeds of all things, having all sorts of forms, colours, and flavours, and that humans and also the other animals were compounded, as many as have soul. Also that there are cities that have been constructed by humans and works made, just as with us, and that there are a sun and a moon and other heavenly bodies for them, just as with us, and the earth grows many different things for them, the most valuable of which they gather together into their household and use. I have said this about the separation off, because there would be separation off not only for us but also elsewhere.

Anaxagoras is not merely speculating that there might be other worlds just like ours, tucked inside and enveloping our own—he claims that this follows *necessarily* (*khrē*) from what he has already established. Although we cannot be certain of the referent of "Since these things are so," it is clear that the premises of "all things in all things" and "infinite division" ("separation off") together force the conclusion that there are infinitely many *kosmoi* resembling our own. Not knowing where this fragment appears in the complete text, it is nevertheless reasonable to draw on the reputed first fragment as one basis for the premises. "All things in all things" is clearly connected (if not the same as) the claim of B 1 that "all things were together," and the necessity of infinite division too derives from "the small was unlimited." As I have discussed above, for the small to be unlimited requires that there is no end to division, the smaller producing always another still smaller.[14] As John Sisko contends, "Anaxagoras not only argues for a world of plurality within a Parmenidean framework, he argues for a plurality of worlds within this selfsame framework . . . it is a cosmology of worlds within worlds within the One."[15]

In arguing for a holistic reading of Anaxagoras, I concur with scholars who take seriously his Eleatic inheritance, while making sense of the nature of his pluralism. Although he does not reject Parmenides' one, he does appear to reject the binary opposition of one and many (or, perhaps, to embrace their mutual determination), seeking to elaborate the manyness within the plenum of being. Anaxagoras retained the insight regarding not-being that derived from the binary logic of Parmenides' goddess but used it to deduce the necessity for infinite divisibility and, thus, infinitely nested *kosmoi*. In spite of these interpretive advantages of a holistic account, this perspective has not been put to the purpose of providing insight into Anaxagoras' invocation of *nous*. Such an account is important because most interpreters fall back on substance dualism and appeals to efficient cause in order to explain the function of *nous* in Anaxagoras' account, both of which are in tension with the very pluralism outlined above. Furthermore, leaving *nous* untouched by Anaxagoras' pluralism risks reinstating the very binaries his account seems determined to unsettle. In what follows, I offer a phenomenalist rendering of *nous*, such that the plurality and difference that pervades Anaxagoras' account of the *kosmos* might be understood as intelligible, while not thereby becoming determined and thus limited.

Nous and the Problem of Dualism

Many scholars who provide a robustly pluralist account of Anaxagoras' physics nevertheless ultimately treat Anaxagoras' ontology as dualist.

This is because *nous* is introduced as an unmixed cause of separation, both cosmic as well as local, instigating the manifestation of phenomenal differences. Most take Anaxagoras' physics as absolutely pluralist, with matter being both qualitatively and quantitatively boundless, but then construe his ontology as dualist, marking mind and matter as different substances.[16] The only alternative offered is the appeal to reductive materialism, whereby *nous* becomes nothing more than the physical mechanism (another thing) by which motion or natural laws are introduced into the system. Seeking an account of *nous* that corresponds to the phenomenal pluralism sketched above, I will use Sisko's argument that Anaxagoras' cosmology does not describe a temporal sequence of events to argue that *nous* functions as descriptive of the order immanent to, though not initially manifested by, the original mixed whole. In this way, *nous* remains inherent to the *kosmos*, rather than a being external or ontologically distinct, while not sharing in the mixing of all things.

Nous and the Two Moments of Cosmogenesis

While Anaxagoras is unequivocal regarding the boundless intermixing of "all things," in the same breath, he carves out space in his account for *nous* as pure and unmixed, and yet present to some things: "in everything there is a share of everything except *Nous*, but there are some things in which *Nous*, too, is present" (B 11).[17] *Nous* receives extended treatment in fragment 12, where it is described as "boundless [*apeiron*],"[18] "self-ruling [*autokrates*]," "mixed with no thing," and "alone itself by itself."[19] These last two traits are said to be necessary for its ability to control (*kratein*), because if it were mixed with anything, "it would partake [*metetxen*][20] of all things," given Anaxagoras' earlier claim[21] that all things are mixed with all things. *Nous* is then also described as the "finest" and "purest" as well as the strongest, having "discernment [*gnōmē*] about everything" (B 12).

The activity of *nous* is given special attention: Its control extends over all things that have soul, "both the larger and the smaller," a phrase that echoes the depiction of internal multiplicity within all things in B 6. The rule of *nous* is manifest not simply locally in those things with soul but also more broadly as controlling "the whole revolution, so that it started to revolve in the beginning," first from a small area and growing more over time. Anaxagoras thereupon returns to *nous*' activity of knowing, connecting it to the act of separation: "And *Nous* knew [*egnō*][22] them all: the things that are being mixed together, the things that are being separated off, and the things that are being dissociated." Although there are many separations occasioned by *nous*, "nothing is completely separated off or dissociated one from the other except *Nous*." And, whereas nothing is like anything else, and everything is what it manifests "most," *nous* is, on the other hand, all alike, "both the greater and the smaller" (B 12).

Although Anaxagoras' introduction of *nous* provides an explanation of the mechanism by which differences become manifest, the theoretical coherence of the account appears to be threatened by the suggestion that there are two stages of cosmogenesis—before (see B 4) and after what he terms "the separating off" (see also B 5 and B 6). A critical interpretive problem arises in light of the two-stage model of cosmogenesis: If *nous* is the cause of the "separating off," and thus precedes it, how does it escape the primal mixture of "all things in all things"?

The view of Anaxagoras as an ontological dualist provides one response to this problem: *nous* is immaterial; "all things in all things" applies only to material entities. However, as we have seen, the claim "all things in all things" is not driven by dogmatic pluralism but by a philosophical justification that must apply to *nous* as much as to anything else: "all things in all things" provides a stable basis for maintaining the Eleatic principle that "not being must not be." Since *nous* must be subject to this primary tenet, *nous* too must be subject somehow to "all things in all things." Indeed, for all its differences from all the other things of the *kosmos*, *nous* is nevertheless also characterized as *aperion*.[23] And if the *apeiron* nature of things necessitates their infinite divisibility, *nous* too must be subject to these requirements. But Anaxagoras asserts that *nous* does not mix with anything and is "alone itself by itself"—and yet, it is also present to some things. This is the paradox that arises in light of the dualist view.[24]

Another option is to treat *nous* as material, but matter of a special kind, as Graham does in the following suggestion: "Here, as is often noticed, *nous* acquires special properties that distinguish it from ordinary stuffs. But it is still treated as a physical entity with extension."[25] Graham makes this claim without any specific evidence, drawing from seemingly anachronistic assumptions about the nature of *nous*'s causation—namely, that it is first and foremost an efficient cause.[26] Simply put, there is nothing explicit within B 12 that requires *nous* be either a physical entity or that it be "extended," a Cartesian term that imports a modern mechanistic and spatial order highly anachronistic to Anaxagoras' thought. More importantly, even if we take *nous* as either ontologically or merely physically distinct from the "all," introducing *nous* begs the question of how *nous*' agency produces the "separating off."

Atemporal Cosmology

Behind the difficulties with the status of *nous* and accounting for its causal power, lies the broader basis of these problems: the temporality of Anaxagoras' cosmogony. It is natural, in light of the use of the past tense and his invocation of "*archē*," to impute a temporal cosmogenesis to Anaxagoras' account. But if we are to take seriously his Parmenidean heritage, temporality remains a phenomenal appearance and therefore cannot characterize the cause of that phenomenal order. That is, since his ontological claims that "all things are in all things" and "there can be no least" are not temporally contingent and apply no matter what might become manifest, we might also have to understand the claims about *nous* not as primarily concerning temporal causation but instead as constitutive of the nature of any "separating off." If "all things in all things" is an absolute, then the activity of separating off, though different in each manifestation of separation, is nevertheless an ongoing condition of the *kosmos* for which *nous* is the cause. As John Sisko has suggested, we might do better to refigure the stages of Anaxagoras' cosmogony as an ontological account of the relationship between given manifestations of separation.

Now, Anaxagoras does appear to follow in the tracks of someone like Anaximander, who suggests that there is a primary state of the *kosmos*, a state of infinite indeterminacy, which is subsequently transformed through concatenating separations. Not only does Anaxagoras use the language of "before" and "after" (B 4b) and the imperfect tense (B 1), he also hypostatizes separation in one fragment, referring to "the separating off" (B 4a). These appear to be the basis on which interpreters assert Anaxagoras conceives of some first, cosmic event and, thus, impute to *nous* the nature of an efficient, temporal cause. However, I argue that no such initial event is required—moreover, that it is barred by his view of divisibility. I will now show how each of these aspects of his account may be adequately explained without recourse to the frame of temporal causation.

First, Anaxagoras' use of the imperfect tense is notable in that it suggests ongoing rather than completed action. In addition, the use of "before" and "after" in B 4a also need not entail a temporal but merely a logical order. Moreover, I do not here mean to argue that there is *no* temporality in Anaxagoras' account, only that there is no "first" separation; thus, there may be a state prior to a given separation and a state following it, without there thereby being some initial state before *any* separation. Finally, the hypostatization of "the separation off," which appears in only one fragment, notably occurs when Anaxagoras explicitly claims that there are indeed *multiple* such separations, thereby denying that there is any one, first separation, but instead affirming the infinite multiplication of "scenes" of separation: "I have said this about the separation off, because there would be separation off not only for us but also elsewhere" (B 4a).

In sum, there is no reason to think Anaxagoras asserts there is a beginning of separation. In fact, when he does refer to the *archē* (which is not determinately temporal), he refers to mixture as a constant state, "but just as in the beginning [*hōposper archēn*], now too all things are together" (B 6). Importantly, the rationale for this conclusion relies on his principled rejection of "a least": "Since it is not possible that there is a least, it would not be possible that [anything] be separated, nor come to be by itself" (B 6). The purported "original" state of the *kosmos*, then, is the same before as after: mixed and infinitely differentiated, and just as there is no final separation, there is also no first.[27] Further, if Anaxagoras embraces the infinite division of things, there is no reason to impute to him anything other than an infinite division of time as well; that is, if he denies one version of Zeno's paradox, we wouldn't rightly expect him not to deny the other.

Similarly, the *kosmos* is never described as fixed or immobile in a time prior to the introduction of the rotational motion of *nous*. Readers deduce retroactively that this first state is static once Anaxagoras offers an account of *nous*, which is named as the cause of "separating off." Instead, we might take *nous* not as an external, first cause of motion but as simply a regional and ongoing one. This makes sense of the otherwise strange claims that *nous* is "even now where all the other things also are, in the surrounding multitude, and in the things that were joined together and in the things that have been separated off" (B 14).

If there is no first causation, if *nous* is an ongoing and immanent cause, as I suggest, what might this look like? Let's say that here, in a particular place at a particular time, an eddy or whorl within the flow of the intermingling of all things is touched off by some prior differential, such that *this* cold comes to be separated off here and now from *this* hot. It is the localization of *nous*'s influence that produces the relative differential. Was that difference created by *nous*? Surely not; this difference *must* have already been present; what *nous* names is the various ways that aggregations take form and manifest the differences already present but obscured by other manifestations due to their relative concentration in a given region. *Nous* is responsible for local concentrations that aggregate within the *kosmos*, revealing a difference *present but latent*.[28] Indeed, this is effectively how *nous* itself is characterized: It is what is not mixed yet present to some things. *Nous* is the principle by which difference becomes manifest, becomes present. When difference becomes manifest, it does so for one in whom *nous* is present. But the apprehension of the manifestation of difference has a correlate in what becomes manifest: the difference that shows itself. And this, too, is the sign of *nous*, of its power of separation.

Ultimately, this reading again brings us to the problem of dualism. If, instead of an immanent, ontological cause of differentiation, *nous* is instead construed as an efficient agent of motion, is it not therefore "outside" the one *kosmos*? If so, how does it "initiate" motion without bringing something into being that was not before, thereby violating the Eleatic principle that not-being come into existence? Indeed, if *nous* is construed as an efficient cause, acting as an agent separate from that which it causes, we cannot avoid dualism.

We are forced to admit instead that there *cannot* be a time before separation, nor a time before *nous*; there can only be a time before (and after) particular separations, which reveal the order of *nous*. And this means that *nous*, and the differences it makes manifest *precede* separating off(s). This requires that we reconceive the temporality of Anaxagoras' claims. Sisko argues that the language of "before" and "after" indicates two relative stages rather than two temporal events. He claims that Anaxagoras' Eleatic holism is incompatible with a temporally two-stage model. As Sisko concludes, "there is, for Anaxagoras, no *first event*."[29] Thus, *nous* is the cause of motion but not in the sense of being an external cause, but rather as an eternal, ongoing cause. I take this to be compatible with the suggestion that Anaxagoras is not offering *nous* as an efficient cause (an agent separable from the moved) but instead as an immanent cause, the motion inherent to the whole in its self-relation as infinitely multiplicitous. For, the interrelation of differences is, as any Eleatic would admit, a form of motion.

After the "separating off," the nature of things has not changed; what has changed is simply their arrangement, aggregation and manifestation. Manifestation is of course coordinate with *nous*, for there is no manifestation without one for whom the manifest becomes manifest. This can operate at any level of analysis, but there will be a time before manifestation and a time after manifestation, and each of these is a movement of *nous*, a movement somehow with and without an agent, both and neither active or passive. The middle passive character of manifesting (*phainesthai*) and becoming (*gignomenai*) are perhaps a clue to Anaxagoras' attempt to integrate and thereby undermine the binary of subject and object, agent and patient. The two moments of cosmogenesis are the two moments implicit in every moment of the world's appearance, from each possible vantage point. This interpretation, again, complements Anaxagoras' understanding of innumerable worlds. The *kosmos* is reborn in every instant as the infinite *kosmoi* of an infinite number of perspectives; *nous* is simply the name for the reality of all these possibilities, that is, for the intelligibility of difference.

The alternative is, as I've suggested, to view *nous* as the original and ongoing cause of all motions/separations, but as a cause that is immanent to that system. Even if there is a time prior to *any given separation*, there is no time before *all* motion (for there is not a time before *nous* nor a time before what *nous* moves). *Nous* is neither a member of that system nor an agent separate from it; *nous* is the name of that system's self-differentiation, its latent patterns/concentrations, and its "logic" of separations. Again, B 6 reminds us of the explanatory value of the fact that "all things in all things" applies *both before and after the separating off*; the purpose of this claim is to show that all possible separations (of an infinite variety) are already present within the whole and that the agency of *nous* resides in its producing emergences of recognizable ("manifest") difference. *Nous* is, then, simply the name for *difference becoming manifest. Nous* is not something other than what is always already present to the whole. The value of this interpretation comes in the way it makes sense of Anaxagoras' appeal to the *intelligibility* of difference; this reading provides a basis for understanding *nous* as not simply a cause but the principle of there being knowledge of difference, for where there is manifestation of difference, there is knowledge.

In addition to avoiding the difficulties that come from claiming that Anaxagoras is a physical pluralist and an ontological dualist, this view of *nous* reveals Anaxagoras' phenomenalist and relativistic account of difference and the immanent intelligibility of the order of the *kosmos*. In addition, however, this intelligibility is always provisional and subject to the affordances of vantage. That is, Anaxagoras fulfills the ontological promise of Parmenides' claim that being and knowing are one, while also providing a mechanism for explaining why, nevertheless, we are often unable to discern the truth of things: their intelligibility is not (yet) manifest. This is why he affirms both that "Owing to their [the senses'] feebleness, we are not able to determine the truth" (B 21), and "appearances are a sight of the unseen" (B 21a). Without *nous* as an immanent cause of the manifestation of difference, these two claims would be contradictory. This view of *nous* as the immanent cause of the manifestation of difference in the *kosmos* has one final advantage. Few interpreters account for the curious way that Anaxagoras bars *nous* from being mixed, while nevertheless claiming that it is "present." This holistic interpretation allows *nous* to be understood as a relational predication rather than an existential one: nous is present as the immanent relation of difference among the infinitely diverse. It, like all other natures, need not be *manifestly* present as concentrated in any given region, even though it is also in everything.

This antidualist view, however, requires an adequate alternative model for understanding the immanent order and differentiation depicted by Anaxagoras in his account of mixture and separation. I maintain in what follows that just such a model is available in the political ontology of contemporary political philosopher María Lugones's depiction of curdled separation. Moreover, this alternative model provides a stronger foundation for understanding the immanence of *nous* as the intelligibility of difference in Anaxagoras' cosmology.

Models for Separation and Mixture in Anaxagoras

Anaxagoras' holistic account of the interpenetrating mixture of all things, as well as his account of *nous*, reveals the centrality of a conceptualization of immanent difference to his ontology. While his holism expresses Anaxagoras' faithfulness to Parmenidean monism, his account of *nous* affords intelligibility and order to the manifold differentiation present within the whole. Although I have argued that *nous*' causal nature is formal rather than efficient and names immanent differences rather than introducing differentiation, Anaxagoras' account includes reference to many forms of what I have called above "aggregations," local separations[30] that manifest concentrations of differences already present within the original mixture but collected together. If *nous* is simply the manifestation of immanent difference, it is necessary to examine plausible models for depicting such separations, seeking consistency between the ontology of immanent difference and Anaxagoras' account of the various types of difference that become manifest.

Anaxagoras identifies several types of things included in the infinite plurality: "the small" (B 1, B 3) and "the large" (B 3); "air and aether" (B 1) and "earth" (B 4a); "seeds of all things," "all sorts of forms [*ideas*], colours and flavours [*hēdonas*]" (B 4a); as well as oppositional pairs.[31] Understanding how the mixture and separation of these might be figured seems necessary for any account of the operation of difference in Anaxagoras.[32] Scholars have proposed many models to conceive of the whole depicted by Anaxagoras, but, as I argue below, one way or another they all presuppose the discrete heterogeneity explicitly rejected by Anaxagoras in B 12, "nothing is dissociated or separated off one from another," and B 8, "The things in the one *kosmos* have not been separated from one another, nor hacked apart with an axe—neither the hot from the cold nor the cold from the hot." María Lugones's theory of "curdled separation" provides an alternative model for explaining the possibility of heterogeneous substances in Anaxagoras' mixture, while making sense of his claim that separation is "not with an axe." This view of separation as always incomplete stands in contrast with the account of *nous* as pure and unmixed, so I try also here to provide a sense of what this means for Anaxagoras' account more broadly but also to show the nonbinary and antiteleological nature of an account of difference that is always impure and incomplete. Indeed, this view of Anaxagoras' metaphysics as always underway yields an even firmer sense of the nature of *nous* as the immanent possibility of the appearance of difference within the whole.

From suspensions, pastes, and powders to seas, paints, and coffee,[33] a host of metaphors appear in the scholarly literature on Anaxagoras, all attempting to negotiate two features of Anaxagoras' account: that "everything is in everything" (B 1, B 3, B 6) and the existence of the heterogeneous things outlined above. I will focus here on Richard Sorabji's view, as it is based on a thorough survey of the scholarship on the subject, as well as on the critiques levied against such an account by Curd and Graham. Finally, I will assess Curd's and Graham's proposals, ultimately arguing that they, too, rely on a notion of discrete *archai*, which violate the principle of incomplete separation, articulated in fragments six and eight.

In his treatment of Anaxagoras in *Matter, Space and Motion*, Richard Sorabji assesses prior interpreters' models of mixture in Anaxagoras, and after critiquing liquid "blending" models for requiring that things be "homogeneous, rather than being, as we should think, composed of molecules or atoms," he defends his proposed model of an "infinitesimal powder."[34] He explains, "the powder model can be expressed in terms of the idea that elementary (non-compound) bone and honey [his running examples] exist in ordinary honey in infinitely small units. The units need to be sizeless . . . Although points are sizeless, it is less clear how units of matter can be."[35] Sorabji's reservations over the problems Anaxagoras' theory has, if construed in this way, are poignant. More importantly, however, the notion of a unit in Anaxagoras is entirely unattested; worse yet, the idea of an infinitesimally small unit contradicts the tenet that "there can be no smallest" (B 3, B 6). Further, units, if this were something Anaxagoras might admit, are entirely relative to that which is measured; there can be no ultimate unit, no limit to infinite divisibility. This appears to be what Sorabji is aiming for with the claim to "infinitesimal" units, but if so, the use of "unit," especially in Anaxagoras' physics, seems incoherent not only with his explicit claims but with the idea of a unit. Ultimately, the powder model relies on the notion of a unit, but the claim that there can be a "non-compound" element does not track with what Anaxagoras says about the condition of "everything in everything" and, thus, this particulate model fails to adequately represent Anaxagoras' theory.

In the commentary to her translation of Anaxagoras' fragments and testimonials, Patricia Curd assesses prior models of the Anaxagorean "mixture." Citing Malcolm Shofield's[36] and Colin Strang's[37] responses to Sorabji, Curd too argues against any "particulate" view[38] of Anaxagoras' mixture, stating, "the particulate version makes great difficulties for interpreting 'everything in everything' in a coherent way, for each particle must have unlimited particles of everything in it, and the same for each of the particles in each of the particles and so on."[39] In opposition to this, Curd proposes her own "blending" model (to use Sorabji's term).

> We can picture this by first imagining the ingredients as being like pastes or liquids; they are all mixed and smeared together such that all the ingredients are in every possible place in

> some concentration or other . . . at no time will there be pure or unmixed areas of any ingredient. Indeed, no matter how much a particular ingredient (flesh, fire, gold) may emerge from the background mix in a certain area . . . all the other ingredients will still be mixed in that ingredient in that area to some degree.[40]

I quote this at length because it is an extremely clear and persuasive account of what Anaxagoras might have been thinking, most importantly, the idea that discrete entities appear in virtue of a densification and concentration of similar kinds of things in a given area.[41] However, there is a problem in what Curd is offering here, residing in the appeal to the notion of "ingredients," which I think necessarily comes with all such models.

The term *ingredient* is first introduced in Curd's title gloss to fragment B 1 that begins her "Notes on the Fragments": "B1: The original state, before *Nous* initiates the rotation that causes the ingredients to separate off and recombine."[42] This is a very strong reading of B 1, which uses no term even remotely like *ingredient*. Ingredient appears to be a rendering based on the treatment of *aēr* and *aither* as primordial elements in the "original mixture." Above, I have argued, following Sisko, that Anaxagoras' invocations of temporal language should not be construed as chronological but instead as logical "moments" of the relationship between the manifestation of a phenomenally discrete entity and its immersion in the underlying (and overlaying) mixture. But even if you subscribe to a temporally two-stage cosmogenesis, as Curd does, there is no necessity to appeal to elements or "basic entities."

Let us return to the metaphor of pastes to assess how the notion of ingredient operates for Curd. She suggests that we imagine each ingredient is "mixed and smeared together such that all the ingredients are in every possible place in some concentration or other."[43] I submit that one cannot imagine that each ingredient is so mixed, however thoroughly, in such a way as to both maintain the "all things in all things" requirement and the genuine heterogeneity of the things within the multitudinous mixture. With such a model, one seems destined to postulate homogeneous, ultimate units (like Sorabji), which undermine the "all things in all things" requirement. Curd herself acknowledges these principles and their consequences, but somehow does not believe these to be violated by her model. She says, "there never were, are, or will be pure instances of any of the ingredients of the initial mix," emphasizing in a footnote that this is a *metaphysical* rather than physical impossibility.[44] And, again, "nothing that is basic (either stuff or opposite), in no matter how great a concentration or small an amount, can ever exist in a pure state, no matter how briefly," explaining that the doctrine that "the denial of a least entails that nothing can be completely separated or exist apart."[45] Nevertheless, her notion of "ingredients" suggests precisely such distinct and ultimately separated entities, which breaks with the demand in B8 that things "are not hacked apart with an axe."[46]

In addition to Curd's canvass of the more specific criticism of the "particulate" theories, Daniel Graham, like Curd, defends a view of Anaxagoras' mixture of things that presupposes that there are "ultimate realities" (even if he also identifies those as "identical with everyday realities").[47] Like Curd, Graham holds that pure entities cannot be discovered through physical mechanisms: "Extraction never removes all of one kind of matter, nor does what is extracted ever consist of one pure kind of stuff."[48] Graham also denies that Anaxagoras' view can be compared to modern chemical models since "it does not provide for the creation of compounds from elements."[49] However, he does claim that Anaxagoras' view

> has similarities to that part of chemical theory that deals with mixtures—with colloids, suspensions, and solutions. Molecules from one or more substances can mix with those of another, either in trace amounts so as to register no phenomenal properties, or in sufficient quantities to characterize the solution, e.g., the salty taste in salt water, or to dominate in the mixture, e.g., watery wine versus wine-flavored water. The boundless number of basic substances are elements in the sense of being basic building blocks of matter.[50]

So, Graham denies that the modern view of elements is suited to Anaxagoras' theory but asserts that molecules or "basic substances" function as elements. It seems clear that regardless of *what* precisely one *identifies* as elements, this has little to do with whether one is affirming an elemental model. The problem here is the same as with Curd: such changeless substances require a notion of purity and of limit that are specifically rejected by Anaxagoras' claim to the infinite diversity of "things"[51] as well as these interpreters' own rejection of any "one pure kind of stuff."

In addition to begging the question, the models of suspension or colloid, or even solution, all rely on the positing of *discrete entities*, which immediately violates the principle of all in all, and of infinite diversity (not just infinite divisibility). In fact, these models reveal that separation *is only ever phenomenal*; it depends on what level of analysis one takes how and where homogeneity and heterogeneity will operate. This is in fact the key, I think, to Anaxagoras' account, and Graham and Curd both appear to be sensing this in their emphasis on phenomenalism. But by treating *nous* as a separable agent, they court dualism or even idealism, which I do not believe to be necessary and, in fact, harmful for understanding Anaxagoras' account of the ontology of separation and mixture. All the other models offered, even those of the holists, appear to have the same problem: They are both chosen and interpreted on the basis of modern conceptualizations of mixtures, such as liquid suspensions and other colloids, which presuppose ultimate discreteness or homogeneity, thereby violating the requirement that "all things are in all things."

If we look more generally at the problem, we see that we need a model for similarity in difference and for the interpenetration of differences, which allows for change. *This*, I submit, is exactly what political philosopher María Lugones claims to be doing, and her model of a curdled emulsion produces an account of what she calls "curdled separation," which is far more consistent with Anaxagoras' claims about *both* combination and separation than the atomistic and mechanistic accounts that the above models are tied to.

In the next section, then, I outline Lugones's model of a curdled emulsion, and argue that it is not only more appropriate to Anaxagoras' heterogeneous pluralism but also allows for a deeper appreciation of the political consequences of Anaxagoras' account of the immanent intelligibility of difference I have argued for above. Nevertheless, I also seek to make clear the ideological difference between Lugones's political ontology and Anaxagoras' (meta)physics. Finally, I'll reflect on the stakes of the reading I've provided, in particular the practice of using the thinking of María Lugones, a contemporary Latina feminist philosopher, as the basis for reading a canonical figure against that canonical reception.

Curdled Emulsion: Lugones's Model of Difference without Split-Separation

In her 1994 essay, "Purity, Impurity and Separation," María Lugones develops the model of "curdled-separation" as an alternative conceptual basis for political resistance.[52] Appealing to the humble process of making mayonnaise, Lugones assesses the various forms of separation invoked as the yolk and oil are mixed, coalesce, and break. Lugones's purpose for developing such a model is to test "whether separation is always or necessarily an exercise in purity," for the logic of separation and its reliance on the opposition of "same" and "different" is deeply implicated in the ideological binaries that produce and sustain many forms of oppression.[53] Far from giving up on separation as a tool for political resistance, however, Lugones seeks a generative model for cultural and political pluralism.

To begin her analysis, Lugones invokes her own experience of cultural separation through language: "Much of the time, my very use of the word *separate* exhibits a form of cultural *mestizaje*."[54] Being multilingual, Lugones alludes to the fact that her use of the English term *separate* is also inflected by her understanding of the Spanish cognate *se separó* and its additional connotations, which mix into her use of *separate*. Rather than seeing this linguistic *mestizaje*[55] as a failure to assimilate to the dominant, monocultural linguistic regime, Lugones seeks an alternative conceptualization of her own separation from within[56] that regime such that it be construed neither as a failure of unity, nor as the utter rupture between two incommensurable kinds. Lugones thus aims to produce a robustly intelligible concept of plurality and difference, which does not simply reduce to the otherness of nonidentity, and she does this by attending to the multivalence of the verb *separate* in an analysis of the process of making mayonnaise, which involves multiple acts and states of separation.

Before turning to an account of emulsification itself, Lugones begins her analysis where the mayonnaise maker does: with the separation of an egg. This primary, transitive use of the verb *separate* is what Lugones calls "split-separation." Such separation effects a complete distinction between two things, and in so doing it does not create but, instead, locates a preexisting difference. In addition to the transitive sense of "separate" as "distinguish" or "pull apart," however, the verb may also be used intransitively to refer to an unsuccessful emulsion. That is, a semantic ambivalence is already involved in the term *separate*, which supports an alternative to the purity model invoked by "split-separation." A "broken" emulsion occurs when the comingled parts (for example, the oil and yolk) begin to separate from each other, coalescing around nodes of greater degrees of similarity. In the case of a broken emulsion, the separation is never completed and is only ever partial, such that there is an ongoing *degree* of distinctness, yet never a final separation. This is in notable contrast to the ultimate "resolution" implicit to the model of a colloid, where all suspensions in principle will eventually fall out.

This example helps to demonstrate the reason that the verb in this sense is intransitive in English and reflexive, "*se separar*," in Spanish. That is, when an emulsion breaks, the separation is immanent to the mixture itself: "it separates." This difference is not without significance. While the first sense of separation requires an exercise in control from without (viz., keeping the yolk out of the white and extracting the white from its envelopment of the yolk), the second separation is an expression of the inherent instability of the mixture itself. Notice, too, that this second sense of separation, as breaking or curdling, is not simply the inverse of the prior split-separation, which operates in the example as the purification of the yolk from the white. As Lugones explains,

> When an emulsion curdles, the ingredients become separate from each other. But that is not altogether an accurate description: rather, they coalesce toward oil or toward water, most of the water becomes separate from most of the oil—it is instead, a matter or different degrees of coalescence. The same with mayonnaise; when it separates, you are left with yolky oil and oily yolk.[57]

That is, the prior state of pure separation that preceded the emulsion is not regained through the self-separation that occurs when the emulsion curdles.

Coordinate with her analysis of these two forms of separation, Lugones goes on to examine two very different conceptualizations of plurality: fragmentation, which tracks with the structure of split-separation, and multiplicity, with curdled-separation. To characterize a plurality as fragmented is already to assert the logical domination of the whole from which the plurality is derived. As a result, according to this framework, plurality is construed as derivative of a prior unity and a deviation from an original commonality. Plurality as fragmentation accords to each part an absolute difference, describing an ultimate divide not simply from the original whole but also of each fragment from every other. This reflects the purity ideal of totalitarian monoculturalism and its limitation of communication and interaction, such that no solidarity (and collusion) might arise among those who diverge from the norm, whether for similar or different reasons. Plurality taken as multiplicity, on the other hand, is not construed as derivative, nor as the many deviations from a norm, but as constitutively heterogeneous, from which an equally multiplicitous range of mixtures might be formed spontaneously. Lugones's theory of separation provides a conceptual framework for recognizing difference *as* different but also as resistant to the logic of purity, and this, I believe, is the conceptual ground on which a useful comparison can be made between her theory and that of Anaxagoras.

Had Anaxagoras not included the agglomerations that mark each "separating off" in his account, his metaphysics might indeed be better described with reference to a suspension or even a solution—a mixture that is whole, seamless and consistent. But Anaxagoras' cosmology includes knots and whorls, aggregations within the mixture, and this is precisely the conceptualization that I assert Lugones describes as curdled-separation. There is difference and differentiation, but it is never pure, and remains always sticky, messy—broken. Although these aggregations are more than simply the "seeds" he discusses, seeds occupy an interesting (and contested) position in Anaxagoras' account, as they model not only aggregation and infinite divisibility, but also the generative power of impending separations.

Anaxagoras' appeal to seeds (*spermata*), then, appears to elucidate the nature of separation and manifestation. As Kirk, Raven, and Schofield have it, seeds, are "coagulated" from matter, which remains "infinitely divisible."[58] There is a great deal more that could be said about seeds, particularly with respect to the debates surrounding homoiomeries. However, even if seeds are ultimately taken to be different from other kinds of aggregations and limited to biological seeds, seeds are still paradigmatic of the incomplete separation suggested by the model of curdled emulsion for two reasons. First, they are themselves nonhomogenous, containing inchoate yet coherent differences. Second, they offer a relatively naturalistic kind of evidence for Anaxagoras' claim about nested *kosmoi*. That is, seeds acquire separation by means of there being an order internal to each one's infinitely many. Second, seeds show how such incomplete separation can nevertheless be ordered and productive. Seeds are evidence of *nous* as the principle of change, and yet again, they also already contain all things.

Key to Lugones's account, and something that importantly differentiates it from those I have critiqued before, is her attention to the *activity* involved in the production of separations; her analysis focuses on processes of separation rather than the states of relations of objects, which presupposes that *things are already implicitly separated.* This is the trouble with mechanistic, chemical models—what Thomas Paxson, Jr. identifies as an ontology founded on the conception of being understood as dependent on parts. Lugones, on the other hand, does not *presuppose* separation but represents it as an activity introduced into the matter that's given. For example, her beginning point is the separation of an egg. While the egg has internal differentiation, the egg *is not yet separated* until the mayonnaise maker introduces that separation through a process (one typically completed using the two halves of the cracked eggshell in a back and forth exchange of the yolk, as the white drops of its own weight from the yolk). In addition, there is no expectation that a separated yolk is in fact entirely pure; there is always some amount of the membrane of the white that will cling to the yolk. Even that which has been separated retains some of that from which it was separated. There is neither a pure origin nor a pure terminus, and the production of the supposedly "pure" state is itself artificial.

The value of this feature of the model of curdled-separation is twofold. First, it introduces to the model not simply an account of the things separated but a role for *nous* as that which produces separation. Second, it demonstrates the way the incomplete separation represented by broken emulsion presupposes a prior separation that is also impure in so far as it is *constructed by* nous. That is, *nous* names the introduction of intelligibility, which mirrors separation and difference. With this, Anaxagoras once more maintains his Eleatic heritage. His account of *nous* as the *archē* of separation is an expression of Parmenides' ontology of intelligibility expressed in DK 3: "For to think and to be is the same."

By getting a better understanding of Anaxagoras' view of separation, its nature under the influence of *nous*, we also come to understand the function of *nous* in his account and find that *nous* is not another substance, but marks the manifestation of difference, as motion takes place within the original plenum. To say that motion begins with *nous* is already simply to say that difference begins. So, *nous* is the source, cause, and rule of separation, but since difference was always already present (infinitely so), *nous* is the name for the already indwelling differentiation within all things. *Nous*' purity, then, must be read as the actualization of difference, nevertheless a contingent arising of manifestness, rather than itself a separate, enduring sameness. *Nous* becomes, under this reading, the intelligibility of change, given the infinite, embedded logic of difference of the *kosmos*.

Anaxagoras' contribution, then, resides in his recasting of plurality not as the brokenness of an original whole but as the very constitution of the whole as multiplicity rather than fragmentation. The mixed, then, becomes the basis of the possibility of the manifestation of differences. This immanent intelligibility must be marked as itself different from the mixture (i.e., *nous* is "pure," "unmixed," and "separate"), otherwise *nous* would not be able to control, would not be an *archē*; it would not be the name of the intelligibility of the manifestation of difference but that which becomes manifest. And, although *nous* is present to some things, it is nevertheless not itself manifest. It shows itself in and as the ordering nature of things. *Nous*, therefore, is far more of a logical than ontological principle, or, its logical role defines its ontological one.

Conclusion: The Politics of the Intelligibility of Difference

I have defended here a likely controversial view of Anaxagoras' *nous*. Following John Sisko, I argue that Anaxagoras is a Parmenidean holist, but I also depart from the prevailing view that Anaxagoras is in any way providing a physicalist, mechanistic, or genetic account of the *kosmos*. I assert, rather, that his cosmogony is also a metaphysical cosmology and *nous* is neither simply an efficient nor a final cause. *Nous* is an ontological principle, the name of immanent differences and their coming to be intelligible borne within the mixture of the *kosmos*. The contents of this mixture, then, need to be adequately represented as nonultimate, and separation as *always underway*. I have appealed to Lugones's model of curdled-separation as a model adequate to these conditions and maintain that this provides a stronger account of both the physics and the metaphysics underpinning Anaxagoras' account of difference. What remains to discuss are the political conditions and consequences of such a thinking of difference.

It is clear that Anaxagoras was no political theorist, but the fact that he did not theorize regarding politics certainly does not mean that his thinking did not have its own political context—after all, Anaxagoras, not Socrates, was the first philosopher of Athens accused of atheism on account of his unorthodox cosmological views.[59] From the fragmentary and doxographical evidence of Anaxagoras, however, there seems no doubt that he had little to say directly regarding matters political or ethical, and that most of his reflections were contributions to the metaphysical debates of his time—namely, questions about the causes, constitution, and nature of the *kosmos*.

Reflecting on the relationship between these two philosophers, between a contemporary political theorist and a Presocratic metaphysician, we find in both someone determined to think about a relational phenomenon in a novel way—in a way that frees them from the conceptual constraints of a dominant, binary theoretical order. In Lugones's case, she seeks to think separation other than through a framework that conceives of difference as fragmentation, so that she may investigate the possibility of harnessing curdled-separation as a tool that does not simply retrench a politics of purity. And, however Eleatic Anaxagoras may be, he mirrors Lugones in responding to the dominant model of metaphysical thinking of his own time, a model founded on a logic of purity and the one-and-many binary, which does not provide a robust account of the ontological grounds for the intelligibility of difference. Thus, these thinkers seem to share in common a resistance to accounts that presuppose the values of purity and homogeneity, and both seek to rehabilitate a notion of relationality as freed from the ultimate subjection to a sovereign measure.

In the end, this reveals the value of taking seriously the ontological structures that organize our thinking about difference. Whether an ontology is built to provide a foundation for political theory, it surely has political implications, particularly in its relationship to other frameworks. This reveals the artificiality of the distinction between political theory and metaphysics, a binary of significant contemporary relevance, which can be destabilized by reading for resonances such as that between Lugones and Anaxagoras. Reading the metaphysical canon against itself, listening to the resistances that are not simply those that participate in the given antagonisms, we might begin to undermine the view of intellectual history as a legacy of arguments rather than of a rich, unfolding discourse, and see it as a site not of completion but of construction and contestation.

Notes

1. G. S. Kirk, J. E. Raven, and M. Schofield, eds., *The Presocratic Philosophers*, 2nd ed. (Cambridge: Cambridge University Press, 1983), 245.

2. There is long-standing debate about whether the goddess presents two or, rather, three paths for inquiry (counting the "two-headed" way of humans, B 6, as its own) and how to reconcile the "*Doxa*" section (B 8 ln 50 ff) in light of the ban on pursuing "what is not." Regardless of where one comes down on this, the *logic* of DK B 2 clearly relies on a strict binarism. Although the reading of a third path significantly alters how *we* understand Parmenides' thinking, it would seem not to retroactively alter the inheritance of Parmenidean monism as grounded in binary opposition, nor of the problems of coherently accounting for a pluralistic world.

3. Kirk, Raven, Schofield, *Presocratic Philosophers*, 358.

4. Rose Cherubin, "Light, Night, and the Opinions of Mortals: Parmenides B8.51–61 and B9," *Ancient Philosophy* 25, no. 1 (2005): 1–23; Alexander Nehemas, "On Parmenides' Three Ways of Inquiry," *Deucalion* 33/34 (1981): 97–111; Patricia Curd, *The Legacy of Parmenides: Eleatic Monism and Later Presocratic Thought* (Princeton: Princeton University Press, 1997); John A. Palmer, *Parmenides and Presocratic Philosophy* (Oxford: Oxford University Press, 2009).

5. Curd, *Legacy of Parmenides*.

6. Daniel Graham, *Explaining the Cosmos: The Ionian Tradition of Scientific Philosophy* (Princeton: Princeton University Press, 2006), esp. 186–95.

7. See Graham, *Explaining the Cosmos*, 186–223.

8. Thomas D. Paxson, Jr., "The Holism of Anaxagoras," *Apeiron* 17, no. 2 (1983): 85–91; John Sisko, "Anaxagoras' Parmenidean Cosmology: Worlds within Worlds within the One." *Apeiron* 36, no. 2 (2003).

9. Unless otherwise noted, translations of all fragments cited here are those of Curd. Numbering of the fragments follows the Diels-Krantz edition.

10. Margaret Reesor succinctly summarizes the steps of the argument as follows. "Anaxagoras' principle of infinite degrees of more or less, which precluded a smallest or largest, was based on the Parmenidean concept 'that it is not possible for being not to be.' This concept required the hypothesis that a minimum presupposed the possible nonexistence of the quantity, quality or entity below the minimum. Anaxagoras argued that that which does not have a minimum is inseparable, and that consequently entities cannot be separated from entities, qualities from qualities and qualities from entities. In this way all things were in all" ("The Meaning of Anaxagoras," *Classical Philology* 55, no. 1 [1960]: 7).

11. O. Gigon, "Zu Anaxagoras," *Philologus* 91 (1936/7): 14–17; Reesor, "Meaning of Anaxagoras"; Kirk, Raven and Schofield, 360–62.

12. G. E. L. Owen argues to the contrary that the use of *peiras* in DK 28 B8 indicates only the consistency or stability of being, not its spatial finitude

("Eleatic Questions," *Logic, Science and Dialectic* [Ithaca, NY: Cornell University Press, 1986], 20). Nevertheless, infinite divisibility does not entail the infinitude of that which is divided. For instance, Sisko argues for a reading of Anaxagoras as a holistic monist, consistent with Parmenides, claiming they *both* maintain an infinite one ("Anaxagoras' Cosmology," 92–94). My interpretation does not, however, hinge on how one construes infinite division, nor whether the oneness of Anaxagoras' *kosmos* is itself limitless or discrete.

13. See also B 5, cited above.

14. In his defense of a holistic account of Anaxagoras, Paxson takes a different tack to argue for Anaxagoras' holism. Rather than viewing each whole (including the *kosmos*) as dependent on its parts, which would require Anaxagoras to maintain there are ultimate homogenous elements, Paxson observes, "parts seem to be conceived by Anaxagoras as being ontologically dependent on the wholes that comprise them" ("Holism of Anaxagoras," 86).

15. Sisko, 91.

16. This view is at least as old as Simplicius thanks to whom we have many of the extant fragments: "That he assumes a double world ordering, the first intelligible, the other perceptible, having come from the first, is clear from what has been said" (B 14).

17. Given how much is at stake in the interpretation of *nous* in Anaxagoras' work, it is surprising how persistent the practice of capitalization remains, since this is of course not part of the original text and significantly predetermines the reading of *nous* as reified or personified, paving the way for theological interpretations. Although I retain this when I quote Curd's translation, I will not capitalize *nous* in my own text, except to follow standard conventions of capitalization.

18. This is the only trait that *nous* appears to share with all the mixed things, suggesting it is not wholly other and it too is infinitely in magnitude and diversity.

19. "*Monos autos eph' heautou*," a phrasing that suggests Plato's framing of forms.

20. This, again, is the terminology employed by Plato to describe things' "participation" of forms.

21. The fragment itself refers to "earlier" claims: "just as I have said before."

22. There is some debate regarding the "cognitive" nature of *nous*, which is treated carefully by André Laks in "Mind's Crisis: On Anaxagoras' *NOUS*." *Southern Journal of Philosophy* 31, supplement (1993): 19–38. Laks rejects A. M. Silvestre's argument that mind is simply an efficient cause and that its cognitive activity is negligible ("Significato e Ruolo del *Nous* nella Filosofia di Anassagora," *Il Contributo* 12 [1988]: 29–52). He argues that because the cognitive activity of *nous* occurs by acts of *krisis* (judging, discerning), its knowing is the same as its role as a cause of separation. Curd also opts for "critical discernment" as the

activity of apprehension that *nous* performs and contends, "The plan that *Nous* may have and is carried out in great revolutions of the mass of ingredients is internal to and identical with those occurrences."

23. B 7 is relevant here: "so as not to know the extent of the things being separated off, either in word or in deed."

24. It cannot be a great surprise that Anaxagoras' thinking resides within such a paradox, given, as we've seen, his embrace of the paradox of the one and many.

25. Graham, 213.

26. The strongest piece of evidence that *nous* is a moving cause is the claim that it "started the rotation." If we take an example from meteorology, however, we see quickly the way that moving agency is in no way distinct from the phenomenon of change. We say that the tornado spun, but the tornado was not a tornado until it was already spinning—a tornado just is its spinning. This is of the same form as Nietzsche's critique of agency in *Genealogy of Morality* I.13, and perhaps why he championed Anaxagoras' antiteleological tendencies in *The Tragic Age of the Greeks* as well as why Socrates lamented the same in the *Phaedo*.

27. None of this requires us to deny the initial "scene" of separation described by Anaxagoras—an earlier (which does not entail there be a first) condition, in which *aither* and *aēr* dominate, suppressing the manifestation (only at *our* scale of phenomenal apprehension?) of the infinite differences present within the mixture.

28. This notion of presence aligns with the ambiguous claims Anaxagoras makes about *nous* as "present to" some things.

29. Sisko, 110.

30. It may seem ironic that when talking about aggregations, we might just as well be inclined to define these in terms of separation. This is because for Anaxagoras separation indicates both division as well as differentiation, such that the concentration of a certain plurality of similar things is at the same time their manifestational "separation." Separation, then, refers simultaneously to differentiation and manifestation. Curd recognizes something similar when she says, "What looks like separation from the mix will actually be more like a clumping together in the mix" (182).

31. Such as hot and cold (B 4a, B 4b [warm] B 12, B 15), wet and dry (B 4b, B 12, B 15), bright and dark (B 4b, B 12, B 15), light and heavy (B 10), and dense and rare (B 12, B 15).

32. I will not here address the so-called *homoiomerous* substances nor the account of the generation of organisms except to say that any suggestion of any concept of ultimately homogeneous things simply cannot be Anaxagoras' position in light of the unwavering commitment to "all things in all things," as Curd and others have convincingly established. G. B. Kerferd offers a notable

counterposition, affirming "There is no logical inconsistency between the principle of homoeomerity and the principle of mixture in this case" ("Anaxagoras and the Concept of Matter before Aristotle," *Bulletin of the John Rylands Library* 52 [1969]: 129–43).

33. Coffee: Kerferd, "Anaxagoras and Matter," 499; powder: Richard Sorabji, *Matter, Space and Motion* (London: Duckworth, 1988), 64; sea: Daniel Graham, "The Postulates of Anaxagoras," *Apeiron* 27 (1994): 102–4; paint: Jonathan Barnes, *The Presocratic Philosophers* (London: Routledge, 1996), 325; suspension: Sisko, 99–100; sea: Daniel Graham, "Was Anaxagoras a Reductionist?," *Ancient Philosophy* 24 (2004): 5; paste/liquid: Curd, 181.

34. Sorabji, *Matter, Space and Motion*, 63, 64.

35. Sorabji, 64.

36. Patricia Curd, *The Legacy of Parmenides: Eleatic Monism and Later Presocratic Thought* (Princeton: Princeton University Press, 1997).

37. Colin Strang, "The Physical Theory of Anaxagoras," *Archiv für Geschichte der Philosophie* 45 (1963): 101–18.

38. The modern account of the particulate theory is put forward by Paul Tannery ("La théorie de la matière d'Anaxagore." *Revue Philosophique* 22 (1886): 255–74). Among contemporary interpreters, Gregory Vlastos was an early defender ("The Physical Theory of Anaxagoras," *Philosophical Review* 59 [1950]: 31–57). See also: E. Lewis "Anaxagoras and the Seeds of a Physical Theory," *Apeiron* 33 (2000): 1–23.

39. Curd, 183n10.

40. Curd, 181–82.

41. There is, however, no reason that the aggregation of the same kinds of things is what is required in order for things to become manifest, except in the case of homoiomerous things; even in that case, we can follow Barnes: "the principle [of homoiomerity] says, not that every part of a lump of gold is 'gold and nothing else,' but that every part of a lump of gold has the same material constitution as the lump itself" (Barnes, *Presocratic Philosophers*, 326).

42. Curd, 33.

43. This view appears to be not substantially different from that of Barnes, who uses the example of paint to argue against a particulate account: "Any stuff contains every stuff; but the contained stuffs are not present by virtue of a mechanical juxtaposition of particles; they are present as items in a chemical union. . . . Artists may make a patch of their canvas seem green in either of two ways. First, and unusually, they may adopt a *pointilliste* technique, setting minute dots of blue next to minute dots of yellow: from a distance the effect is green; from close up we see adjacent spots of blue and yellow. Alternatively, they may mix masses of blue and yellow on their palette and apply the mixture to the canvas: the effect from a distance is green; and however closely we look at it, the effect is still green" (325–26). In contrast to Curd, however, Barnes

is also critical of the notion that the question of "elements" is of interest to Anaxagoras (327).

44. Curd, 179 and n2.

45. Curd, 180.

46. Paxson, again, offers a helpful alternative, when he points out that "Instead of wholes being ontologically dependent on their parts . . . parts seem to be conceived by Anaxagoras as being ontologically dependent on the wholes that comprise them" (86).

47. Graham (2004), 16.

48. Graham (2006), 198–99.

49. Graham (2006), 199.

50. Graham (2004), 199.

51. Graham contends, however, that the "*apeiros*" of B 1 does not commit Anaxagoras to an infinite diversity of kinds: "It is simply not clear that Anaxagoras is committed to an infinite number of substances, though he possibly might be" (2004, 198n26).

52. María Lugones "Purity, Impurity, and Separation," *Signs* 19:2 (Winter, 1994): 458–79.

53. Lugones, "Purity and Separation," 458.

54. Lugones, 459.

55. Drawn from the word *mestiza*, *mestizaje* is used of and by women of Mexican heritage to describe the multiplicity of racial, ethnic, and cultural histories inscribed on their bodies and minds, particularly women's, as a result of the ongoing legacies of settler colonialism and white cis-hetero-patriarchal US domination in the Americas. "*Mestizaje*" is richly elaborated by feminist poet, theorist, and activist, Gloria Anzaldúa, who uses the concept to examine the political and cultural resources of people who find themselves to be a border, pulled by multiple, often conflicting or even contradictory claims upon their identity and experience. See her *Borderlands/La Frontera: The New Mestiza* (San Francisco: Aunt Lute Books, 1987) and her editorial collaboration with Cherríe Moraga, *This Bridge Called My Back: Writings by Radical Women of Color* (Watertown, MA: Persephone Press, 1981).

56. Sina Kramer terms this condition "constitutive exclusion" (*Excluded Within: The (Un)Intelligibility of Radical Political Actors* (Oxford: Oxford University Press, 2017).

57. Lugones, 459.

58. Kirk, Raven, and Schofield, 368.

59. It seems that the charges against Anaxagoras, if there were any (it's not clear whether he fled because of the trial or threat of trial, or if he was banished as a result of one), were in fact different in the way Socrates claimed: namely, that Socrates was not being charged with atheism but with religious novelty, a fine point on the basis of which Socrates wages his refutation of Meletus. It is

generally accepted that Anaxagoras fled Athens, being caught up in some way with the anti-atheism proclamation of Diopeithes around 433 BCE. See Kirk, Raven, and Schofield's commentary (354).

Bibliography

Anzaldúa, Gloria, and Cherrié Moraga, eds. *This Bridge Called My Back: Writings by Radical Women of Color*. Watertown, MA: Persephone Press, 1981.

Anzaldúa, Gloria. *Borderlands*/La Frontera: *The New Mestiza*. San Francisco, CA: Aunt Lute Books, 1987.

Barnes, Jonathan. *The Presocratic Philosophers*. London: Routledge, 1996.

Cherubin, Rose. "Light, Night, and the Opinions of Mortals: Parmenides B8.51–61 and B9." *Ancient Philosophy* 25, no. 1 (2005): 1–23.

Curd, Patricia. *The Legacy of Parmenides: Eleatic Monism and Later Presocratic Thought*. Princeton, NJ: Princeton University Press, 1997.

———. *Anaxagoras of Clazomenae: Fragments and Testimonia: A Text and Translation with Notes and Essays*. Toronto, ON: University of Toronto Press, 2007

Gigon, O. "Zu Anaxagoras." *Philologus* 91 (1936/7): 1–41.

Graham, Daniel. "The Postulates of Anaxagoras," *Apeiron* 27 (1994): 77–121.

———. "Was Anaxagoras a Reductionist?" *Ancient Philosophy* 24 (2004): 1–18.

———. *Explaining the Cosmos: The Ionian Tradition of Scientific Philosophy*. Princeton, NJ: Princeton University Press, 2006.

Kerferd, G. B. "Anaxagoras and the Concept of Matter before Aristotle." *Bulletin of the John Rylands Library* 52 (1969): 129–43. Reprinted in *The Pre-Socratics: A Collection of Critical Essays*. Edited by Alexander P. D. Mourelatos. Princeton, NJ: Princeton University Press, 1993.

Kirk, G. S., J. E. Raven, and M. Schofield, eds. *The Presocratic Philosophers*. 2nd ed. Cambridge, UK: Cambridge University Press, 1983.

Kramer, Sina. *Excluded Within: The (Un)Intelligibility of Radical Political Actors*. Oxford, UK: Oxford University Press, 2017.

Laks, André. "Mind's Crisis: On Anaxagoras' *NOUS*." *Southern Journal of Philosophy* 31, supplement (1993): 19–38.

Lewis, E. "Anaxagoras and the Seeds of a Physical Theory." *Apeiron* 33 (2000): 1–23.

Lugones, María. "Purity, Impurity, and Separation." *Signs* 19:2 (Winter, 1994): 458–79.

Nehemas, Alexander. "On Parmenides' Three Ways of Inquiry." *Deucalion* 33/34 (1981): 97–111.

Owen, G. E. L. "Eleatic Questions." In *Logic, Science and Dialectic*, 3–26. Ithaca, NY: Cornell University Press, 1986.

Palmer, John A. *Parmenides and Presocratic Philosophy*. Oxford, UK: Oxford University Press, 2009.

Paxson, Jr., Thomas D. "The Holism of Anaxagoras." *Apeiron* 17, no. 2 (1983): 85–91.

Reesor, Margaret. "The Meaning of Anaxagoras." *Classical Philology* 55, no. 1 (1960): 1–8.

Silvestre, A. M. "Significato e Ruolo del *Nous* nella Filosofia di Anassagora." *Il Contributo* 12 (1988): 29–52.

Sisko, John E. "Anaxagoras' Parmenidean Cosmology: Worlds within Worlds within the One." *Apeiron* 36, no. 2 (2003), 87–114.

Sorabji, Richard. *Matter, Space and Motion*. London: Duckworth, 1988.

Strang, Colin. "The Physical Theory of Anaxagoras." *Archiv für Geschichte der Philosophie* 45 (1963): 101–18.

Tannery, Paul. "La théorie de la matière d'Anaxagore." *Revue Philosophique* 22 (1886): 255–74.

Vlastos, Gregory. "The Physical Theory of Anaxagoras." *Philosophical Review* 59 (1950): 31–57. Reprinted with expanded footnotes in *The Presocratics: A Collection of Critical Essays*, edited by Alexander P. D. Mourelatos, 459–88. Princeton, NJ: Princeton University Press, 1993.

Part Two

Platonic Transformations

Chapter Five

As Much Mixture as Will Suffice

Socrates' Embodied Intermediacy in Plato's *Phaedo* and *Symposium*

Hilary Yancey and Anne-Marie Schultz

> And he offered the cup to Socrates, who took it quite cheerfully, Echecrates, without a tremor or any change of feature or color, but looking at the man from under his eyebrows as was his wont, asked: "What do you say about pouring a libation from this drink? It is allowed?"—"We only mix as much as we believe will suffice," said the man.
>
> —*Phd.*, 117b2–6

> "But how would it be, in our view," she said, "if someone got to see the Beautiful itself, absolute, pure, unmixed, not polluted by human flesh or colors or any other great nonsense or mortality, but if he could see the divine Beauty itself in its one form?"
>
> —*Symp.*, 211c1–212a1

Scholars often read Plato's *Phaedo* as promoting an ascetically grounded dualism between the body and the soul.[1] Perhaps the most famous advocate of this view is the nineteenth-century philosopher Friedrich

Nietzsche. In *Twilight of the Idols*, Nietzsche argues that Socrates believed that death was the great healing and deliverance from the prison of the body: "Even Socrates said as he died: 'To live—that means to be a long time sick: I owe a cock to the savior Asclepius.' "[2] In *The Gay Science*, Nietzsche makes a similar point: "Whether it was death or the poison or piety or malice—something loosened his tongue at that moment and he said: 'O Crito, I owe Asclepius a rooster.' This ridiculous and terrible 'last word' means for those who have ears: 'O Crito, life is a disease.' "[3] If we accept Nietzsche's rather stark view of Socrates' last words, Asclepius—the god of healing—cures Socrates from the disease of embodiment through the *pharmakon* administered by the prison guard. In this view, Socrates' courage in the face of death is grounded in his understanding that bodily incarnation is bad for the soul, which is healed only by permanent separation.[4] Aside from Nietzsche's reading, numerous passages of the *Phaedo* suggest that any mixture of body and soul is itself bad. For example, Socrates remarks, "the soul of the philosopher most disdains the body, flees from it and seeks *to be by itself*,"[5] and later cautions, that until philosophy takes over, the "soul is a helpless prisoner, chained hand and foot in the body."[6]

This dualism between body and soul still pervades philosophical discussions of embodiment, including those in race, transgender, and disability studies. Common binaries in these discussions include those between genders or sexes, between gender and sex, and between impairment and disability (as found in social models of disability). In their article "Feminist Perspectives on the Body," Kathleen Lennon and Edward N. Zalta note that discussions of embodiment are starting to question said binaries: Models of disability seek to transcend the impairment/disability distinction, and discussions of transgender issues seek to understand the "complex interpellation of biological and cultural factors" involved in embodied experience. Plato may or may not figure directly into these contemporary discussions. Nonetheless, dualist interpretations *of* Plato can reinforce a binary view of the human being and undervalue robust discussions of human embodiment.[7] This dismissive view of embodiment has been linked to philosophical views that associate the mind with masculine identity and the body with feminine identity, something that many feminist scholars challenge. To mention two examples, Genevieve Lloyd's *The Man of Reason* and Susan Bordo's *The Flight to Objectivity* explore how a particular view of reason as masculine in turn shapes the view of women that has pervaded the history of philosophy so deeply that it is often difficult to think of philosophy outside of this context.[8]

Close examination of the *Phaedo* complicates the claim that Plato is a soul/body dualist. In a dialogue about the *end* of Socrates' bodily incarnation, Plato includes numerous details as to the bodily experiences of the characters gathered in prison on Socrates' final day—including their movements and physical expressions of emotion, pleasure, and pain. In this paper, we argue that the characters' bodies—their physiognomy—reveal something important about their respective journeys on the path of philosophy. Particularly, we suggest that the relevant difference between Socrates' embodiment and the embodiment of his companions is a difference in the *manner* of embodiment, rather than between someone who disdains the body (Socrates) and those who are still chained to it (his friends). We describe this as a difference between *intermediacy* and *mere mixture*, the former being a kind of appropriate or sufficient mixture of body and soul.

To better understand this notion of intermediacy or appropriate mixture, we place the *Phaedo* in conversation with both the *Symposium* and the larger mystery and "religious" context of the ancient Greek world.[9] In our view, the Socrates of the *Phaedo* experiences the same in-betweenness of Eros that Diotima describes in the *Symposium*. Diotima teaches a youthful Socrates that Eros (Love) is between beauty and ugliness, wisdom and ignorance, and morality and immortality. Resisting dichotomies of either/or, Eros "binds together" the two extremes and possesses qualities of both. As a great spirit, Eros "shuttle[s] back and forth between the two . . . [He] round[s] out the whole and bind[s] fast the all to all."[10] We analyze the multivalent portrait of Eros as depicted in Diotima's speech given the explicit references to the "rites of love" and "higher mysteries,"[11] and also in light of the explicit Empedoclean dimensions of Eryximachus' speech, which is appropriately situated in the median position of the first five speeches.[12] With this sense of erotic intermediacy in mind, we turn to the physical descriptions of Socrates and his companions in the *Phaedo*. We then contrast these descriptions, arguing that his friends fail to fully embody the intermediacy Socrates has achieved. The differences reveal how the practice of philosophy in fact depends on—and is realized in—embodiment to perform its transformative magic on the souls of those who undertake it.

We aim to illuminate not only the cross-dialogic resonances between the *Phaedo* and the *Symposium* but also Plato's relationship with Pythagoreanism, Empedocleanism, and strains of the "mystery" religions of the Greek world, particularly with respect to the value of mixture, intermediacy, and embodiment. We hope that our duly apportioned mixture provides support for an emerging view of Socrates in the secondary literature that is more positive with respect to the body and ontologically receptive of difference and flux than the secondary literature typically acknowledges.[13]

Magic, Mystery, and Mixture in the Ancient World

In 1995, Peter Kingsley wrote *Ancient Philosophy, Mystery, and Magic: Empedocles and Pythagorean Tradition*. It establishes the broader religious context within which many Presocratic philosophers worked. Kingsley's work helps us see that these ancient thinkers should not be regarded in terms of the relatively isolated fragments we have, but in terms of a larger exploration of the structure of the cosmos, a spiritual interest in the physicality of the regions of the earth, the human desire for connection with the divine, and even the attainment of immortality. The Presocratics' investigation into the nature of things was not simply metaphysical speculation but part of what we would today regard as religious or spiritual practice, or, as Plato puts it with respect to Pythagoras at *Republic* 600, a *bios*, a way of life.[14] While this view may not apply to all Presocratic thinkers (e.g., Anaxagoras), Kingsley calls our attention to the need to understand these thinkers in this broader context as we explore their connections and resonances with the *Phaedo* and the *Symposium*. Before returning to Plato, we will briefly discuss the concept of mixture in three Presocratic philosophers who are referred to in the *Phaedo*: Pythagoras, Empedocles, and Anaxagoras.

Pythagoras and Mixture

The concept of appropriate mixture pervades Pythagorean thinking. While there is abundant material from various Neopythagorean traditions, it is often difficult to discern which ideas were Pythagoras' own and which are developments of later Pythagoreanism. Nonetheless, we will discuss four points generally attributed to Pythagoras that help us understand the notion of an appropriate mixture. First, his view of number as the *arche* helps us see the interrelationality of the things that are. Number composes the universe and guides its composition. According to Carl Huffman, "Pythagoras is known for the *honor* he gives to number and for removing it from the practical realm of trade and instead pointing to correspondences between the behavior of number and the behavior of things.[15] Second, Pythagoras' belief in metempsychosis, transmigration of soul, can be regarded as an application of souls finding the appropriate mixture of bodies for their new incarnation; reincarnation as a mixing together of a new life or new reordering for the soul. Third, Pythagoras' notion of harmony, musical and otherwise, involves appropriate mixture of numeric relationships. Harmony arises through the interrelationship or the mixture of elements of sound. Finally, Pythagorean religious practices emphasize mixture. The Pythagorean concept of the mixing bowl, which was used in various rituals, is a concrete symbol of mixture. Appropriate mixture is a gateway for experiencing the divine. Additionally, the emphasis on the secrecy of Pythagorean teachings and also all of the *akusmata* (religious sayings associated with Pythagorean teaching) may be a way of guarding against inappropriate mixture both for individual Pythagoreans in their practice and also in terms of protecting the community.

Empedocles

Empedocles is widely regarded as having the first complete conceptualization of mixture as the basis for cosmological explanation, though it is important to realize that Empedocles himself exists in a line of Presocratic thinkers concerned with mixture. Aryeh Finkelberg traces the theory of cosmological mixture from Xenophanes to Empedocles. Finkelberg notes that though Xenophanes espouses a theory of "recurrent cosmogonical mixture of two primary bodies," he did not account for all phenomena in this way. Parmenides is the first, he argues, to make the theory of mixture the basis of all natural explanations, but not until Empedocles do we see "the theory came to final conceptualization as self-sufficient, and hence an alternative to αλλοιωσιζ . . . and was put to instrumental use in accounting for the distinctive identities of things" (16).[16]

Mixture in the Presocratic corpus is intimately connected with—and in the case of Empedocles, completes the explanation for—physical creation and destruction. Without these echoes in mind, it becomes too easy to read Plato as declaring that the soul's mixture with the body is counterproductive, a hindrance or a harm. For some mixture, on the Presocratic view, brings forth life and accounts for change, both creation and destruction.[17] More particularly, there is an *appropriate* amount and kind of mixture, as the attendant at Socrates' death suggests. Thus, we maintain that Plato follows the Presocratic philosophers and makes a distinction between a *thorough* mixture of body and soul, the kind where the two become indistinguishable from one another, and an *appropriate or sufficient* mixture, where body and soul are connected, perhaps even intertwined, but not indistinct. As Empedocles says, "Whenever they arrive in the Aither mixed so as to form a man or one of the wild beasts or bushes or birds, that is when [people] speak of coming into being; and whenever they are separated, that [is what they call] the ill-starred fate of death. They do not call it as is right, but I myself too assent to their convention" (B9).[18] Empedocles refers to Hera as "life-giving" (B6), which suggests his understanding that Hera, drawing things together into one cosmos (in one way, mixing things), produces life. Yet he also suggests that the separation caused by Strife is productive (see B17 and the Strasbourg Papyrus, ensemble a)—hence the "double story" of Love and Strife. We can see a hint of this endless cycle in Socrates' description of pleasure and pain as eternally following on one another, "like two creatures with one head,"[19] and we will see how this distionction also characterizes Eros in the *Symposium*—for "he springs to life when he gets his way; now he dies—all in the very same day."[20]

Anaxagoras

Patricia Curd notes that Anaxagoras is the philosophical heir of two main strains of the Presocratic tradition. On the one hand, he stands in the tradition of the Milesian material monists. On the other hand, he is clearly philosophizing in the wake of the Eleatic philosophers, particularly Parmenides. Anaxagoras' metaphysical speculations then proceed in light of the Eleatic consideration that change is ultimately illusory. What this means for any understanding of mixture is obviously a challenge.[21] However, if one were to find a single philosopher that articulates the importance of mixture, it would indeed be Anaxagoras. Curd notes, "Anaxagoras maintained that the original state of the cosmos was a mixture of all its ingredients (the basic realities of his system). The ingredients are thoroughly mixed, so that no individual ingredient as such is evident, but the mixture is not entirely uniform or homogeneous."[22] She offers an additional description: "The mixture begins to rotate around some small point within it, and as the whirling motion proceeds and expands through the mass, the ingredients in the mixture are shifted and separated out (in terms of relative density) and remixed with each other, ultimately producing the cosmos of apparently separate material masses and material objects, with differential properties, that we perceive."[23] The original state of the cosmos was an unlimited (*apeiron*) mixture of all the ingredients. The mixture of ingredients, all with all, exists eternally. Anaxagoras regards *nous* as the mechanism by which different manifestations of mixture occurs.

Differently put, Anaxagoras is using mixture to overcome a central problem with Greek philosophy prior to him. He writes, "The Greeks do not think correctly about coming-to-be and passing-away; for nothing comes to be or passes away, but is mixed together and dissociated from the things that are. And thus they would be correct to call coming-to-be being mixed together and passing-away being dissociated (DK 59 B17). Anaxagoras in fact uses mixture to further an Eleatic worldview about the impossibility of change, of things coming to be and passing away. Nothing changes. Everything is mixed: "There is a share of everything in all things."[24] Thus, there is good reason to think that Plato's understanding of the soul mixing with the body has strong roots in these three Presocratic predecessors. Further, each of these three figures appears in the *Phaedo*. The setting of the dialogue is the Pythagorean enclave in Phlius, and Simmias and Cebes are associated with Philolaus. There is direct mention of Anaxagoras in the first argument for the immortality of the soul and the famous autobiographical passage where Socrates runs across the books of Anaxagoras: "As I reflected on this subject I was glad to think that I had found in Anaxagoras a teacher about the cause of things after my own heart."[25] Kingsley explores the numerous Empedoclean allusions in the journey through the earth that the soul takes in the later sections of the *Phaedo*.[26] Plato galvanizes the importance of the Presocratic interest in mixture. Jill Gordon draws on the mixing bowl metaphor to explain her understanding of soul in the Platonic dialogues, with a specific focus on the *Timaeus*. She writes, "Soul is both an undifferentiated mass when in the mixing bowl, and something that can be divided into individual souls. Individual souls are themselves not divisible, and individuated souls, furthermore, still share a connection to the mixture of soul out of which they came."[27] Simply put, Plato's view of the soul mixing with the body is more complex than regarding it as an unfortunate and temporary hindrance. In fact, the most fertile, productive state might be one of appropriate mixture, what we call in this paper the *intermediate*. To better establish the nature of this intermediacy, we now turn to how Eros is characterized in the *Symposium*.

The Intermediacy of Eros in the *Symposium*

Plato's *Symposium* begins, as many of the dialogues do, in the *middle* of things. Apollodorus starts speaking, apparently in answer to a question posed by an unnamed friend: "In fact, your question does not find me unprepared. Just the other day, I was walking to Athens from my home in Phaeleron and a man I knew called me from behind."[28] As the intricately crafted narrative unfolds, we learn of the events of a party at Agathon's house where Socrates recounts the teachings on love that he learned from a "wise priestess of Mantinea."[29] Whether Diotima was an actual historical character or at least a character grounded in the historical existence of similar priestesses remains a vigorous topic of debate in the secondary literature. Andrea Nye argues that there is evidence of the historical existence of a Diotimean tradition presenting the exploration of Eros as spiritual mediation. However, for the time being, we will bracket this question and focus instead on the way in which Socrates characterizes her and her teachings in his autobiographical narrative that lies at the heart of the *Symposium*.

Diotima's speech has three main movements: the presentation of Eros as an intermediary force (202a–203b), the story of Eros' origin at Aphrodite's birthday party (203b–204b), and the ladder of love (204d and following). Diotima's account of love, recounted by Socrates in his speech, begins by outlining the possibility that Love is an intermediate. She admonishes Socrates, "Then don't force whatever is not beautiful to be ugly, or whatever is not good to be bad. It's the same with Love: when you agree he is neither good nor beautiful, you need not think he is ugly and bad; he could be something in between."[30] This picture of the intermediate does not include the intermediate possessing properties of either extreme: Love may have neither ugliness nor beauty in it. However, Diotima appears to be in a *corrective* mode at this point in her dialogue with Socrates. The corrective tone of her speech is not surprising because Socrates presents her as a specific response to Agathon's misconceptions about the nature of love. He explains that he "believed pretty much everything that you believed now Agathon,"[31] before Diotima corrected him. Socrates emphasizes the affinity between the youthful vision of himself and Agathon by casting himself as Diotima's interlocutor in the reported story. Diotima appears as Socrates' teacher, Socrates as the misguided student of love. Thus, within the narrative context of Diotima's conversation with Socrates, it seems that her primary purpose is to establish that such a concept of the intermediate exists. The young Socrates, like Agathon, makes a metaphysical mistake by suggesting that if Love is not beautiful, he must be ugly.[32] Diotima then gives Socrates a positive understanding of Eros' character. "He's like what we mentioned before," she said. "He is in between mortal and immortal." Stuck in his binary, oppositional way of thinking, Socrates is somewhat incredulous. He asks his teacher for clarification, "What do you mean, Diotima?"[33] Diotima explains, "He's a great spirit, Socrates."[34] Diotima describes the intermediate aspect of Eros as playing the role of a *messenger* between gods and humans: "They are messengers who shuttle back and forth between the two"[35] and a *binding force*. "Being in the middle of the two, they round out the whole and bind fast the all to all."[36] The intermediate, on this description, completes the whole: The two extremes alone are insufficient to capture the full picture of mortality and immortality, beauty and ugliness, or even wisdom and ignorance. The intermediate adds something to the concepts that would otherwise be missing. The intermediate also *connects* the two extremes. Diotima claims that the gods do not deal directly with mortals, but instead rely on the intermediaries, the spirits or *daimons*, to complete their interactions, conveying prayers, sacrifices, commands, and gifts.[37] The intermediate is not a mere absence of either extreme; it has its own positive identity and role, a role that encompasses both extremes. Working within the context of Irigaray's engagement with the *Symposium*, Paul Miller offers a promising reassessment of Diotima's teaching. He writes, "to the extent that Diotima's speech presents a scenario that transcends the binarism of a strictly phallic eroticism, and offers the vision of an erotics and ethics of sexual difference, even within the highly charged male homoerotic context of a traditional Greek symposium, it does so because Plato wrote it that way, that is, because the text is structured in that way."[38] Hyland also engages Irigaray's treatment of Diotima's speech, emphasizing that "Irigaray correctly notes that the young Socrates, and presumably Plato's Greek readers, has considerable trouble comprehending this intermediary status as between, this interruption of the binary oppositions that constitute so much of our discursive understanding."[39]

Interestingly, Berg observes that of all the prior speeches, only Eryximachus concedes to the existence of the in-between "in admitting that the human good in order to be real, that is, if it were not to collapse into the merely apparent good or the beautiful, had to be a mixture of the 'good' and the bad and that the good of this mix to consist in a similar mixture, namely, of pleasure and pain."[40] But even Eryximachus' concept of the intermediate as a mixture of the contraries does not do justice, in Berg's view, to the unique nature of the in-between as *neither* one extreme nor the other.[41] Though the first part of Diotima's speech suggests that the in-between is not merely an aggregate of the two, the second part of her speech, we argue, suggests that the extremes come together in an important way.

Eryximachus misrepresents Heraclitus with respect to the discordant and the harmonious. He argues, "Naturally, it is patently absurd to claim that an attunement of a harmony is in itself discordant or that its elements are still in discord with one another. Heraclitus probably meant that an expert musician creates a harmony by resolving the prior discord between high and low notes."[42] Heraclitus is famous for his understanding of discord as *necessary* to harmony (harmony cannot exist without it), so Eryximachus seems to be deliberately misreading Heraclitus on this point. That Plato gives Eryximachus this misrepresentation of Heraclitus, compared with how Diotima describes Eros' intermediacy later, serves to link Plato and Heraclitus more closely in the *Symposium*.[43]

This intermediate view of Eros unfolds further in the second main part of Diotima's speech, the story of Poros and Penia (*Symp.* 203b) and the origin of Eros. In response to another query by the young Socrates, "Who are its mother and father?"[44] Diotima describes Eros as born from the scheming of Penia, who begs at the gates of the gods' celebration that honors Aphrodite: "Then Penia schemed up a plan to relieve her lack of resources: she would get a child from Poros. So she lay beside him and got pregnant with Love."[45] Eros' birth from this union of opposites begets important characteristics in Eros itself: elements of *both* his mother and father.

Diotima explains this dual origin to Socrates: "As the son of Poros and Penia, his lot in life is set to be like theirs. In the first place, he is always poor, and he's far from being delicate and beautiful (as ordinary people think he is); instead, he is tough and shriveled and shoeless and homeless, always lying on the dirt without a bed, sleeping at people's doorsteps and in roadsides under the sky, having his mother's nature, always living with Need."[46] The characteristics Eros has inherited from his mother establish him as a seeker of the Beautiful, for, as we learned from Diotima earlier, Eros is in between beauty and ugliness and therefore needs the Beautiful. This should remind us of the philosopher's own search for the Beautiful. (As Meno so rightly put it, we do not search for what we already know.)[47] The philosopher, like Eros, is always living with Need. There are also practical resemblances between Eros and Socrates as well, for we learn from Alcibiades' speech about Socrates' toughness and ability to live shoeless and in the cold without a cloak.[48] At the opening to the *Symposium*, Socrates lingers on the porch—the doorstep—of the neighbor's house;[49] Socrates' penchant for doing philosophy on the road resembles Eros' inheritance from Penia. Diotima continues: "But on his father's side he is a schemer after the beautiful and the good; he is brave, impetuous, and intense, an awesome hunter, always weaving snares, resourceful in his pursuit of intelligence, a lover of wisdom through all his life, a genius with enchantments, potions, and clever pleadings."[50]

Eros is not helpless in his need. Instead, he is described as resourceful, clever, and a lover of wisdom. The philosopher, too, is a lover of wisdom. Berg helpfully points out when discussing this section that in fact it is *Penia* who is the resourceful philosopher, given how she schemes to beget Eros by lying with Poros.[51] Berg argues that Diotima separates the characteristics of Eros into characteristics of his parents, "the better to perceive the structure of that whole for what it is."[52] This philosophical side of Eros also echoes descriptions of Socrates as a kind of enchanter, and Socrates' own description of himself as such in the *Phaedo*[53] and the *Charmides*,[54] as well as how he is described negatively. Indeed, as Schindler notes, "as commentators have pointed out through the ages, the likeness between Socrates and Eros extends even to the physical appearance; Socrates' description of the barefooted and somewhat ugly Eros appears to be a description of Socrates himself."[55] Schindler continues, "Socrates dramatically becomes love by seeking what love seeks, which lies in a crucial respect beyond what he (Socrates /Eros) is. There is a mirroring of self and other in both cases, but the order of the reflection is fundamentally different."[56] The philosopher has a scheming nature, though this is not negative; the scheming is after the beautiful and the good, the highest things we can seek. Eros described this way seems to aptly characterize Socrates' own nature and particularly his nature as we encounter him in Plato's dialogues in his pursuit of intelligence and wisdom. As Berg notes, Socrates makes it clear that Eros is self-conscious of its need for the beautiful: "Eros, therefore, has self-reflection and self-knowledge built into its very existence and this self-reflection seems, in and of itself, to be detached from shame."[57]

Thus described, Eros' own nature binds the two extremes together. In Eros, opposites are joined while remaining distinct. Love is not a mere mixture of life and death (in which both are dissolved into something altogether different), but rather he at once "springs to life when he gets his way," and then "dies—all in the very same day."[58] There is an appropriate mixture of life and death that creates something new—Eros himself—and yet retains distinct elements of his parentage. While Eros in some sense is "in between" beauty and ugliness while possessing the qualities of neither, in other ways he is "in between" insofar as his nature contains elements of both poverty and resource, death and life. As Diotima explains, "but then anything he finds his way to always slips away, and for this reason Love is never completely without resources, nor is he ever rich."[59] As Lamascus observes, "it is certainly not the case that Eros is in between the natures of his parents in this sense [of not possessing characteristics of either extreme], for Diotima describes Eros as sharing in the qualities of his parents and inheriting the characteristics of both. In some curious fashion, Eros is able to be poor, but never without resource."[60]

Thus, we have at least a sketch of the concept of the intermediate. The intermediate or "in between" embraces and binds fast the extremes, and its nature combines qualities of both, while *being* neither. Diotima claims that people who love wisdom resemble Eros, having this intermediate nature: "Those who love wisdom fall in between those two extremes. And Love is one of them, because he is in love with what is beautiful, and wisdom is extremely beautiful."[61] Lamascus notes furthermore that as we follow Love, we become more like him: "As Eros is himself a daimon, the soul that follows Eros will become like the daimon himself."[62] One plausible aim of Diotima's speech to Socrates is to demonstrate the relationship between the philosopher (a lover of wisdom) and Love itself. One who loves wisdom, she argues, is between extremes, loving the beautiful but in an important way being without it, just as Eros is always in Need and nonetheless a resourceful "schemer after the beautiful and good."[63] As we have seen above, Socrates resembles Eros' intermediacy; he is the model philosopher. As we will show in the next section, the *Phaedo* shows that his physical self has characteristics of intermediacy.[64]

Socrates' Embodiment of Intermediacy in the *Phaedo*

Like the *Symposium*, the *Phaedo* begins in the middle of things. In the opening frame conversation, set in Phlius after Socrates' death, we hear Echecrates asking Phaedo if he was present himself at the events of Socrates' death.[65] After some conversation with Echecrates, Phaedo begins his own account of that day. His narrative also starts in the middle of things. Phaedo presents his auditors with an initial vision of Socrates. Socrates has recently been released from his bonds, "Socrates sat up on the bed, bent his leg and rubbed it with his hand." Phaedo tells us that as Socrates rubbed his leg, he offers his friends a detailed physical description of the experience of pain and pleasure.[66] "What a strange thing that which men call pleasure seems to be, and how astonishing the relation it has with what is thought to be its opposite, namely pain! A man cannot have both at the same time. Yet if he pursues and catches the one, he is almost always bound to catch the other also, like two creatures with one head."[67]

Socrates' metaphor of pleasure and pain is unlike Diotima's of Eros: It is neither a detailed exploration of intermediacy nor a mythic account of a divine offspring. But the notion of "two creatures with one head" is reminiscent of the dynamic description of Eros as a single creature containing both poverty and resource and as both springing to life and dying in the same day.[68] This description—and Socrates' telling of a fable—also resembles Aristophanes' speech in the *Symposium* in which he describes love in terms of the two halves seeking completion. While we lack adequate space to explicitly compare Diotima's description of Eros with that of Aristophanes, it is worth noting here that Socrates' comments echo both speeches. There may also be echoes of Pausanias' speech (where he contrasts Common Aphrodite and love that attaches to "women no less than boys, to the body more than to the soul" with Heavenly Aphrodite, and the love that is "attracted to the male" only and to what is more virtuous and intelligent) and his distinction between body and soul.[69] Socrates is clear that we are mistaken if we believe that pleasure and pain are opposed, when they are actually joined together in an "astonishing relation."[70]

Socrates then suggests a possible myth about physical pleasure and pain: "I think that if Aesop had noted this he would have composed a fable that a god wished to reconcile their opposition but could not do so, so he joined their two heads together, and therefore when a man has the one, the other follows later. This seems to be happening to me. My bonds caused pain in my leg, and now pleasure seems to be following."[71] Socrates' companions do not take up a philosophical conversation about the content of this fable; they focus on his comment as an opportunity to change the subject to poetry. But Socrates' description is revealing;

he experiences physical sensations in the manner of intermediacy. In one sense there is no reconciliation of the two, yet in another sense they exist as a single, complex phenomenon. This ought to draw our attention back to the intermediacy of Eros. Just as Eros' need anticipates and calls forth his resourcefulness, so the pleasure and pain in Socrates' physical body anticipate and call forth one another.

In fact, Diotima describes the whole of bodily existence as a complex phenomenon of coming to be and passing away: "Even while each living thing is said to be alive and to be the same—as a person is said to be the same from childhood till he turns into an old man—even then he never consists of the same things, though he is called the same, but he is always being renewed and in other respects passing away, in his hair and flesh and bones and blood and his entire body."[72]

One might argue that Socrates' embodied experience of pleasure and pain is irrelevant to his soul. Indeed, Socrates seems to disdain this very bodily experience when he says that "there is likely to be something such as a path to guide us out of our confusion, because as long as we have a body and our soul is fused with such an evil, we shall never adequately attain what we desire, which we affirm to be the truth."[73] The fusion of body and soul is an impediment to *fully* attaining truth. Yet Socrates affirms a path out of the confusion (the life of the philosopher) while embodied. If anything, to be on the path of Eros, to be in the process of becoming more like the *daimon*, seems to require in itself that we have not yet achieved our desire. Eros is by definition in the intermediate state, not yet achieving the beautiful that it desires. In his bodily life, Socrates experiences the intermediate in every way, even physically: He is on the path to the Beautiful but has not yet attained it.

In fact, the philosopher's task appears to be one of transforming the person from being one that is thoroughly *mixed* or "polluted"[74] with the body to one that at most experiences an intermediary state, the state of Eros on the path to the Beautiful. "The lovers of learning know that when philosophy gets hold of their soul, it is imprisoned in and clinging to the body . . . Philosophy sees that the worst feature of this imprisonment is that it is due to desires."[75] Socrates suggests that philosophy, in this life, "gently encourages" the soul and persuades it to withdraw from the senses, not altogether, but "in so far as it is not compelled to use them."[76] The philosopher lives in an intermediate state. As such, he achieves "a calm from such emotions."[77]

If we recall Diotima's "ladder of love," we will note that the body itself plays a vital role in launching the philosopher on the journey to this intermediate and calm or undisturbed state. She notes: "A lover who goes about this matter correctly must begin in his youth to devote himself to beautiful bodies."[78] Diotima describes this beginning as a necessity, the first rite in the "final and highest mystery."[79] While it is true that as the philosopher—the lover—progresses *beyond* that love for bodies to the "more valuable" love for souls, it does not require that the philosopher come to positively *hate* the body, as might be thought on a cursory reading of the "evil" language used in the *Phaedo*. Rather, the philosophers must be able to properly order thier love for the body. Diotima explains, "so that if someone is decent in his soul, even though he is scarcely blooming in his body," he can "be content to love and care for him and to seek to give birth to such ideas as will make young men better."[80] Thus, while Socrates is careful not to overvalue the body, this does not require that he live as one who is disembodied. Rather, it seems to be that when one is appropriately focused on the more valuable thing—the soul—one's body achieves a certain harmony or "calm."

This calm in the body seems reflected in Socrates at the beginning of the philosophical discussion of the *Phaedo*. Cebes reports that his friend Evenus was asking him about Socrates' decision to write poetry in his final days. Socrates explains that he was not trying to rival Evenus' own poetry. Rather, Socrates explains that he has reconsidered his lifelong view that philosophy was the highest art one could practice. He chose to set some of Aesop's fables to verse. This new practice seems to help Socrates be even more firmly settled in his decision to greet his death with equanimity. Socrates tells Cebes to share this story with Evenus and "tell him, if he is wise, to follow me as soon possible. I am leaving today, it seems, as the Athenians so order it."[81] Simmias seems somewhat incredulous and asks, "What kind of advice is this you are giving to Evenus, Socrates? I have met him many times, and from my observation he is not at all likely to follow it."[82] Socrates asks Simmias if Evenus is a philosopher and concludes, "Then Evenus will be willing, like every man who partakes worthily of philosophy. Yet perhaps he will not take his own life, for that, they say, is not right."[83] At this point, Phaedo's narrative voice interjects, "As he said this, Socrates put his feet on the ground and remained in this position during the rest of the conversation."[84] While it might seem a small detail, Socrates' shifted physical posture is an important clue to how the body can be drawn up into the work of philosophizing. His physical posture is connected to the earth and active; Socrates is poised to rise and walk around, much as he practiced philosophy before his imprisonment. Rather than being overly distracted by his bodily pain or pleasure, Socrates' shift of posture signals his readiness to undertake philosophical dialogue and more specifically to examine how the philosopher—through his philosophizing—is poised to embrace death. Given how his bodily posture changes just before he begins to do philosophy, it seems that Socrates' body is *responsive* to his philosophizing. Rather than continuing to imprison him either through painful sensations or by inertia, Socrates' body is shown to be one that undertakes philosophy with him.

The intermediacy expressed in Socrates' body is perhaps most clear in the moments surrounding his actual death. Earlier in the day, Crito had raised a concern for Socrates about his "heated" condition before drinking the poison. Phaedo tells us that Crito warns: "what the man who is to give you the poison has been telling me for some time, that I should warn you to talk as little as possible. People get heated when they talk, he says, and one should not be heated when taking the poison, as those who do must sometimes drink it two or three times."[85] Crito himself seems to be stuck in a metaphysical point of view that depends on not mixing extremes—like the extremes of hot and cold. Socrates cannot introduce a contrary element (that of heating) into himself lest that mixture interfere with the efficacy of the poison. But of course, as we see throughout Socrates' interaction with the poison, his concern is not with an intrabodily mixture but with the appropriate mixture of body and *soul*, and with preserving the hierarchy that such appropriate mixture permits. Thus, Socrates asks the attendant about pouring a libation from the cup and seems unfazed by the prospect of mixing his body with the poison: Socrates tells Crito that he should take no notice of the attendant and "only let him be prepared to administer it twice or, if necessary, three times." Crito tells Socrates that "I was rather sure you would say that but he has been bothering me for some time."[86] The danger of mixing heat and hemlock is simply irrelevant to Socrates, focused as he is on the task of doing philosophy. It is his friends who have an inappropriate concern for bodily mixtures and an exaggerated worry about keeping extremes within the body separated. Perhaps this helps illuminate the further ways in which Socrates' friends lag behind him on the philosophical journey—they are both too thoroughly mixed and too concerned for keeping extremes separate.

His embrace of intermediacy is reinforced by the manner in which Socrates takes the poison. When Socrates is offered the cup, Phaedo tells Echecrates that he "took it quite cheerfully, without a tremor or any change of feature or color, but looking at the man from under his eyebrows as was his wont, asked: 'What do you say about pouring a libation from this drink? It is allowed?'—'We only mix as much as we believe will suffice,' said the man."[87] Socrates then drains the cup "calmly and easily" and, following the instructions of the guard, begins to walk around. At this point in the dialogue Socrates is literally between life and death—he has taken the poison that will kill him but is not yet dead. Phaedo describes, "He walked around, and when he said his legs were heavy he lay on his back as he had been told to do, and the man who had given him the poison touched his body, and after a while tested his feet and legs, pressed hard upon his foot and asked him if he felt this, and Socrates said no."[88] Socrates' body thus experiences elements of both life and death—and even as his body is in the process of dying, his soul is, in Socrates' view, springing to life. The manner of his death is in this way an embodiment both of the nature of the path toward truth (the path of Eros) and what Socrates himself has described death to be: the springing to life that comes from its opposite. Socrates himself seems to notice this in-between character of his death, for Phaedo notes: "As his belly was getting cold, Socrates uncovered his head—he had covered it—and said . . ."[89] Socrates can feel his death approaching. His final words about the cock being owed to Asclepius suggests that death is a cure for the ills of this life, and his admonishment to his friend not to forget[90] seems to suggest that Socrates takes his death to demonstrate to them how their time with him—this concrete, embodied experience—should be a reminder of how both to live in the body and how to welcome death.[91]

Socrates' Friends: Distinguishing Mixture and Intermediacy

Having seen how Socrates embodies intermediacy, we now want to turn to a brief comparison between this embodiment and the embodiment of Socrates' friends. In contrast to Socrates' comments about how pleasure and pain follow one another, Phaedo tells Echecrates that he—and the others gathered—felt a more thorough *mixture* of pleasure and pain. "That is why I had no feeling of pity, such as would seem natural in my sorrow, nor indeed of pleasure, as we engaged in philosophical discussion as we were accustomed to do—for our arguments were of that sort—but I had a strange feeling, an unaccustomed mixture of pleasure and pain at the same time as I reflected that he was just about to die."[92] At the same time Phaedo goes on, "All of us present were affected in much the same way, sometimes laughing, then weeping; especially one of us, Apollodorus—you know the man and his ways."[93] This suggests that Socrates' friends experience some aspects of intermediacy (laughing and weeping occurring at different times), but they still seem to be alternating between extremes or they experience the mixture "as unaccustomed,"[94] with both pleasure and pain present but (apparently) less distinct than in Socrates' self-description at 60b. They are, perhaps, on the way to understanding and embodying the Socratic approach, but behind Socrates himself.

Phaedo's inclusion of not just himself but all of those present in his account also attests to some understanding of mixture. Their experience is collective or mixed together with each other's, rather than distinct and separate for each one of them. However, it seems fair to say that Phaedo and the others present experience intermediacy far less completely that Socrates. One key difference to observe is that Socrates' intermediacy results in a calm among his emotions, whereas his friends' mixture results still in their being overcome by their bodily reactions to their friend's death. Intermediacy does not entail that Socrates feels nothing in the face of his death, indeed he admits that he is in danger of not having a "philosophical attitude about [it],"[95] but that he is capable of distinguishing between and perhaps anticipating the shifts within his emotional state and thus can maintain the calm that comes from continuing to properly order attention to the body and the soul. His friends are so mixed that they are overcome by one emotion and another, unable to anticipate how one feeling—pleasure—can follow another—pain. This captures one way that intermediacy is distinct from a more chaotic mixture: Intermediacy seems compatible with a soul that is "pure when it leaves the body,"[96] in contrast with those whose soul is "permeated by the physical" and "ingrained in it."[97] Socrates' friends are overcome by their physical reactions, and in this way, they have not achieved the appropriate purity that can indeed characterize even an embodied soul before its ultimate purity in death. Differently put, his reason for rejecting misology has to do with the fact that he is facing "death itself,"[98] contrasted with his friends' need to do so "for the sake of your whole life still to come." Thus, while the immediate conversation here is not about Socrates' attitude toward his death directly, it nonetheless suggests that he experiences temptation to abandon the "philosophical attitude" about the life of philosophy, which is itself essential for a proper perspective on death.

Consider, too, how Phaedo describes the group's final moments with Socrates. "Most of us had been able to hold back our tears reasonably well up till then, but when we saw him drinking it and after he drank it, we could hold them back no longer; my own tears came in floods against my will."[99] Phaedo desires to achieve the calm from his emotions Socrates described earlier, but is unable. Crito, too, cannot restrain his tears and Apollodorus, who we are told "had not ceased from weeping before," makes everyone break down except Socrates.[100] Socrates embraces this as a moment to further teach and admonish his friends, " 'What is this,' he said, 'you strange fellows. It is mainly for this reason that I sent the women away, to avoid such unseemliness, for I am told one should die in good omened silence. So keep quiet and control yourselves.' "[101] Phaedo notes that these words make Socrates' friends feel ashamed, and they check their tears.[102] Socrates' bodily disposition with respect to his impending death exemplifies the path of lovers of wisdom—the path of philosophers. Achieving the calm with respect to the body that the philosopher has requires becoming more like the intermediate. His admonishment suggests that his friends need more encouragement to follow his example and advance from the "strange mixture" of pleasure and pain to the intermediacy that characterizes lovers of wisdom.

Concluding Thoughts: Where Do We Go from Here?

Much remains to be explored in how the characters' physical embodiment reveals more about their souls in Plato's dialogues. One particular area for further exploration is the relationship between the intermediate as we have characterized it here and Empedocles' (and perhaps to some extent, Parmenides') cosmogony. Empedocles focuses on "rational mixtures," and this might have analogues to the intermediacy of Eros as Diotima describes it.[103] In this chapter, we have drawn together the particular descriptions found in the *Phaedo* with the intermediacy of Eros in the *Symposium*, arguing that Socrates embodies the kind of intermediacy that characterizes a true philosopher. This intermediate bodily experience can harmonize with Socrates' account of the relationship between body and soul in the *Phaedo*, where we need not see a philosopher as disdaining embodiment per se but instead cautioning against an inappropriate mixture of body and soul that disorders their importance. Finally, drawing on Phaedo's description of Socrates' friends, we can see how these friends fail to fully embody intermediacy and are instead still "thoroughly mixed"—which helps explain their inability to achieve the calm Socrates feels about his death. Our embodiment, while not part of our ultimate purity after death, might not be a mere hindrance to philosophy. Perhaps our souls and bodies can both experience the intermediacy of Eros in productive ways.

We have focused in this paper on the specific cross-dialogic resonances between the *Symposium* and the *Phaedo*; however, we must also note the rich possibilities for extending this discussion of intermediacy and embodiment in other dialogues. We will briefly mention three: the *Charmides*, the *Apology*, and the *Timaeus*. In the *Charmides*, Socrates suggests that Charmides' physical ailment (his headache) is in fact rooted in a problem of his soul, namely, his intemperance. The "certain leaf" that Socrates claims can cure his headache can only work on the body when the "charm" of philosophy has reestablished the soul as the proper arbiter of harmony in the human being.[104] According to Socrates (who credits it to Zalmoxis), the real problem with Athenian medicine is that Athenian doctors and patients fail to see the *true* whole of the human being as the body and the soul together (opting instead to only treat the body). This is similar to the mistake made by Socrates' friends in the *Phaedo*, who are overcome by what is happening to Socrates' body and are, perhaps, too thoroughly mixed with their bodies to still see the true relation between body and soul. The cure for Charmides' headache will come, not from *ignoring* the body, but from resituating it within the whole human being.

This is how Socrates admonishes the men of Athens in the *Apology*: "Good Sir, you are an Athenian . . . are you not ashamed of your eagerness to possess as much wealth, reputation and honors as possible, while you do not care for nor give thought to wisdom or truth, or the best possible state of your soul?"[105] The problem is not being embodied, but being so mixed in with the body that one loses sight of the source of true health and wholeness, which is the care for one's soul. Thus he tells the jurors, "when my sons grow up, avenge yourselves by causing them the same kind of grief that I caused you, if you think they care for money or anything else more than they care for virtue, or if they think they are somebody when they are nobody."[106] The body is a problem when it distracts from care of the soul; but there is a possibility here, as in the *Phaedo*, that the intermediate approach of philosophy can avoid this error.

Finally, the *Timaeus* presents clear challenges to the dualist interpretation of Plato on body and soul. In fact, as Monica Vilhauer argues in this volume, the *Timaeus* may challenge even the hierarchical ordering of body and soul that we have noted in these other dialogues. She writes, "So what is the remedy for these sicknesses in the human being that arise from a lack of harmony between body and soul? Timaeus shows us, once again, that the solution is not to ignore or disengage from the body and to care only for the soul (as we might have heard in the *Phaedo*).[107] It is to cultivate both soul and body so that the animal is strong, proportional, and balanced as a whole." The coming to be of the cosmos as described in the *Timaeus* is a complex, dynamic interaction between the soul and the body (or that which has material, bodily existence) that requires both elements for the existence of the whole.

In *Plato's Erotic World*, Jill Gordon argues that *eros* is perhaps the most crucial element in Plato's teaching and acts as an intermediary between mortal experience and the divine throughout the dialogues.[108] Gordon traces these erotic themes in dialogues not usually considered "erotic" and shows that eros is essential to all of Plato's corpus. In future work, we hope to show that this new understanding of soul/body intermediacy might helpfully influence contemporary discussions of embodiment, particularly in discussions where Plato has been cited as espousing a soul/body dualism. Given the ways in which the binary still dictates the terms of many philosophical discussions of transgender, race, and disability, showing how a founder of the Western philosophical tradition has himself embraced intermediacy can help reframe conversations about embodiment. We hope that mixture and mediation will provide insights that would enhance the inclusivity of multiple modes of embodiment. More broadly, we hope that this work will contribute to a sustained feminist reassessment of the place of ancient thinkers like Plato in contemporary philosophical debates. Intersectionality will no doubt play a larger role in future studies involving feminist and ancient philosophy, and new methods of investigating these ancient texts will continue to emerge as well. Our hope is that the abundant riches of Plato's philosophy will continue to provide resources for the reexamination of the role of women in philosophy by rethinking embodiment through the lenses of intermediacy and mixture.

Notes

1. There is a long interpretive tradition going back to the Neoplatonists that regards the dialogues in these terms. For a survey of various views, see Colleen Zoller, *Plato and the Body: Reconsidering Socratic Asceticism* (Albany: State University of New York Press, 2018). Andrea Nye, *Socrates and Diotima: Sexuality, Religion and the Nature of Divinity* (New York: Palgrave Macmillan, 2015) also provides a good summary of how this dualistic view of Plato has shaped our received understanding of Plato in philosophically pernicious ways. See also Drew Hyland, *Finitude and Transcendence in the Platonic Dialogues* (Albany: State University of New York Press, 1995) and Drew Hyland, *Questioning Platonism* (Albany: State University of New York Press, 2004).

2. Friedrich Wilhelm Nietzsche, *Twilight of the Idols; and the Anti-Christ* (London: Penguin Books, 1990), 39.

3. Friedrich Wilhelm Nietzsche, *The Gay Science*, trans. Walter Kaufmann (New York: Vintage Books, 1974).

4. See Laurel A. Carson, "Have We Been Careless with Socrates' Last Words?," *Journal of the History of Philosophy* 40, no. 4 (2002): 421–36.

5. Plato, *Phd.* 65d.

6. *Phd.* 82e–83a.

7. Many scholars are engaged in reassessments of Plato's apparent dismissiveness of the body. See Sarah Brill, *Plato and the Limits of Human Life* (Bloomington, IN: Indiana University Press, 2013) and Zoller, *Plato and the Body*. Schultz's *Plato's Socrates as Narrator: A Philosophical Muse* (Lanham, MD: Lexington Books, 2013) work on narrative and emotions also problematizes a rigid dualistic reading of Plato, though her focus is more on the binary of reason and emotion rather than body and soul. See also Hyland, *Finitude and Transcendence*. Much of the rigid dualism that some scholars attribute to Plato himself would be better attributed to how Plato's dialogues were received in the subsequent intellectual tradition as they came to be associated with Platonism. Hyland notes, "A fascinating and worthwhile study could be made of the history of Platonism, of how the dialogues came to be (mis)interpreted by subsequent philosophers as espousing Platonism," *Finitude and Transcendence*, 15. Hyland's chapter on Derrida in *Questioning Platonism* (85–122) is an excellent example of the importance of distinguishing critiques of the dualism of Platonism from Plato's own more complex and multivalent views.

8. See Genevieve Lloyd, *The Man of Reason* (New York: Routledge, 1984) and Susan Bordo, *The Flight to Objectivity* (Albany: State University of New York

Press, 1987). Significant feminist philosophical engagements with the ancients started in the 1970s. Groundbreaking articles by Arlene W. Saxonhouse, "The Philosopher and the Female in the Political Thought of Plato," *Political Theory* 4, no. 2 (1976): 195–212, https://doi.org/10.1177/009059177600400206; Christine Garside Allen, "Plato on Women," *Feminist Studies* 2, no. 2/3 (1975): 131–38, https://doi.org/10.2307/3177773; Susan Moller Okin, "Philosopher Queens and Private Wives: Plato on Women and the Family," *Philosophy & Public Affairs* 6, no. 4 (1977): 345–69; Julia Annas, "Plato's *Republic* and Feminism," *Philosophy* 51, no. 197 (1976): 307–21; and others set the stage for a rich feminist engagement with Plato's dialogues. Important anthologies in the 1990s provide a range of ways that feminists engage Plato. See Bat-Ami Bar On, *Engendering Origins: Critical Feminist Readings in Plato and Aristotle* (Albany: State University of New York Press, 1993), Nancy Tuana, ed., *Feminist Interpretations of Plato*, Re-Reading the Canon (University Park: Penn State University Press, 1994). See Paul Miller, *Diotima at the Barricades: French Feminists Read Plato* (Oxford: Oxford University Press, 2016) for a helpful assessment of French feminist engagements with Plato. See also Gregory Vlastos, "Was Plato a Feminist?," *Times Literary Supplement* 4, no. 485 (1989): 276–89; Page DuBois, *Sowing the Body: Psychoanalysis and Ancient Representations of Women* (Chicago: University of Chicago Press, 1988); and Brooke Holmes, *Gender: Antiquity and Its Legacies (Ancients and Moderns)* (Cambridge: Cambridge University Press, 2012).

9. "Religious" is a problematic term to apply to the ancient Greek context. For an excellent discussion of this issue, see Carlin A. Barton and Daniel Boyarin, *Imagine No Religion: How Modern Abstractions Hide Ancient Realities* (New York: Fordham University Press, 2016).

10. Plato, *Symp.* 202e3, 202e6.

11. *Symp.* 210a.

12. *Symp.* 185a–189d. We draw upon Peter Kingsley, *Ancient Philosophy, Mystery, and Magic: Empedocles and Pythagorean Tradition* (Oxford: Oxford University Press, 1995). We also rely on Simon Trepanier, *Empedocles: An Interpretation* (New York: Routledge, 2004) with respect to the Empedoclean dimensions of the *Phaedo*.

13. See Brill, *Plato and the Limits*; Schultz, *Socrates as Narrator*; and Zoller, *Plato and the Body*.

14. Plato, "Republic," in *Plato: Complete Works*, ed. John M. Cooper, trans. G. M. A. Grube and C. D. C. Reeve (Indianapolis: Hackett, 1997), 971–1223.

15. Carl Huffman, "Pythagoras," in *The Stanford Encyclopedia of Philosophy*, ed. Edward N. Zalta, Summer 2014, https://plato.stanford.edu/archives/sum2014/entries/pythagoras/. Several recent books greatly enhance our understanding of Pythagoras, Pythagoreanism, and the communities that arose after the death of Pythagoras. See G. Cornelli, *In Search of Pythagoreanism* (Berlin: De Gruyter, 2013); G. Cornelli, R. McKirahan, and C. Macris, eds., *On Pythagoreanism* (Berlin:

De Gruyter, 2013); Carl A. Huffman, *A History of Pythagoreanism* (Cambridge: Cambridge University Press, 2014); Leonard Zhmud, *Pythagoras and the Early Pythagoreans* (Oxford: Oxford University Press, 2012).

16. Aryeh Finkelberg, "Xenophanes' Physics, Parmenides' Doxa and Empedocles' Theory of Cosmological Mixture," *Hermes* 125, no. 1 (1997): 16.

17. As Monica Vilhauer discusses in chapter 7 of this volume, Plato's own account of the creation of all things in the *Timaeus* involves mixture, and, as she further argues, the mixing we see in the *Timaeus* is *not* counterproductive but necessary for things to be truly whole.

18. Patricia Curd, ed., *A Presocratics Reader: Selected Fragments and Testimonia* (Indianapolis: Hackett, 2011), 82.

19. *Phd.* 60b6.

20. *Symp.* 203e2.

21. See Holly Moore's chapter in this volume. Regarding Fragment B1, she helpfully observes, "*Apeira* is in the plural not simply because boundlessness applies to the nature of each but also because the boundless and indefinite nature applies to their plurality—they have an unlimited number of ways of being mixed with each other."

22. Patricia Curd, "Anaxagoras," *The Stanford Encyclopedia of Philosophy* (Winter 2015 Edition), Edward N. Zalta (ed.), URL = https://plato.stanford.edu/archives/win2015/entries/anaxagoras/.

23. Curd, "Anaxagoras."

24. Anna Marmodoro, *Everything in Everything: Anaxagoras' Metaphysics* (Oxford: Oxford University Press, 2017).

25. *Phd.* 97e1.

26. See Kingsley, *Ancient Philosophy*. See also Trepanier, *Empedocles: An Interpretation*.

27. Jill Gordon, *Plato's Erotic World: From Cosmic Origins to Human Death* (Cambridge: Cambridge University Press, 2012), 40.

28. *Symp.* 172a.

29. *Symp.* 201d.

30. *Symp.* 202b3.

31. *Symp.* 201e3.

32. *Symp.* 202a1.

33. *Symp.* 202d.

34. *Symp.* 202e1.

35. *Symp.* 202e3.

36. *Symp.* 202e5.

37. See *Symp.* 202e.

38. Miller, *Diotima at the Barricades*, 108.

39. Hyland, "Questioning Platonism, 142.

40. Steven Berg, *Eros and the Intoxications of Enlightenment: On Plato's* Symposium (Albany: State University of New York Press, 2010), 102–3.

41. Berg, *Eros and the Intoxications*, 103.

42. *Symp*. 187ab.

43. See Jessica Decker, "Borderland Spaces of the Third Kind: Erotic Agency in Plato and Octavia Butler," in *Borderlands and Liminal Subjects: Transgressing the Limits in Philosophy and Literature*, ed. Jessica Elbert Decker and Dylan Winchock (New York: Palgrave Macmillan, 2017), 187–211.

44. *Symp*. 203b1.

45. *Symp*. 203c1.

46. *Symp*. 203c–d.

47. *Meno* 80d3.

48. *Symp*. 220a.

49. *Symp*. 175a.

50. *Symp*. 203c6–d8.

51. Berg, *Eros and the Intoxications*, 107.

52. Berg, *Eros and the Intoxications*, 108.

53. *Phd*. 77e–78a.

54. *Ch*. 155e.

55. D. C. Schindler, "Plato and the Problem of Love: On the Nature of Eros in the *Symposium*," *Apeiron: A Journal for Ancient Philosophy and Science* 40, no. 3 (2007): 209.

56. Schindler, "Problem of Love," 209.

57. Berg, *Eros and the Intoxications*, 100.

58. *Symp*. 203e1.

59. *Symp*. 203e3.

60. Lorelle D. Lamascus, *The Poverty of Eros in Plato's* Symposium (London: Bloomsbury Academic, 2016), 88.

61. *Symp*. 204b2–4.

62. Lamascus, *Poverty of Eros*, 78.

63. See *Symp*. 203d, as quoted above.

64. There is, of course, a need for further exploration of how Socrates embodies this intermediacy in other dialogues, most notably in the *Symposium* itself. Alcibiades' description of Socrates that Socrates is able to enjoy a feast while being able to withstand hunger, and can drink without being overcome with drunkenness, and even withstand cold even in bare feet (220a–223d).

65. *Phd*. 57a.

66. His first words in the *Phaedo*, notably, are to Crito, asking that Xanthippe be led away (260a).

67. *Phd*. 60b1–6.

68. Our thanks to Jessica Decker for suggesting this additional resonance within the *Symposium*.

69. *Symp*. 181b.

70. *Phd*. 60b. Again, see Vilhauer in this volume, who notes that "Plato's *Timaeus* . . . offers a picture of life—on the large scale of the cosmos, as well as

the small scale of the human being—as a psychosomatic whole, in which intelligence and sensation are intertwined." The notion of intertwinement seems at play here in Socrates' image of two creatures with one head. See Plato, *Phd.* 60b.

71. *Phd.* 60c.

72. *Symp.* 207d5–e1.

73. *Phd.* 66b2–5.

74. See *Phd.* 81b.

75. *Phd.* 82a1–3.

76. *Phd.* 83a6.

77. *Phd.* 84a5.

78. *Symp.* 210a6–7.

79. *Symp.* 210a2.

80. *Symp.* 210c1–2.

81. *Phd.* 61b.

82. *Phd.* 61c.

83. *Phd.* 61c.

84. *Phd.* 61d2.

85. *Phd.* 63d5–e1.

86. *Phd.* 63d5–e4.

87. *Phd.* 117b2–6.

88. *Phd.* 117e2–5.

89. *Phd.* 118a1.

90. *Phd.* 118a3.

91. See *Ap.* 39e–42a, for another formulation of Socrates' preparedness for death.

92. *Phd.* 59a2–4.

93. *Phd.* 59b1.

94. *Phd.* 59a3.

95. *Phd.* 91a2.

96. *Phd.* 80e2.

97. *Phd.* 81c2–3.

98. *Phd.* 91a1.

99. *Phd.* 117c4–6.

100. *Phd.* 117d1–3.

101. *Phd.* 117e.

102. *Phd.* 117e.

103. On mixture in Empedocles, see Friedrich Solmsen, "Love and Strife in Empedocles' Cosmology Phronesis," *Phronesis* 10, no. 2 (1965): 109–48; Aryeh Finkelberg, "Xenophanes' Physics, Parmenides' Doxa, and Empedocles' Theory of Cosmological Mixture," *Hermes* 125, no. 1 (1997): 1–16; David Sedley, *Creationism and Its Critics in Antiquity* (Berkeley: University of California Press, 2007); and Denis O'Brien, "Hermann Diels on the Presocratics: Empedocles' Double Destruction of the Cosmos (Aetius ii 4.8)," *Phronesis* 45, no. 1 (2000): 1–18.

104. *Ch.* 155e1.
105. *Ap.* 29e.
106. *Ap.* 41d.
107. See Vilhauer p. 196 in this volume.
108. Gordon, *Plato's Erotic World.*

Bibliography

Allen, Christine Garside. "Plato on Women." *Feminist Studies* 2, no. 2/3 (1975): 131–38. https://doi.org/10.2307/3177773.

Annas, Julia. "Plato's *Republic* and Feminism." *Philosophy* 51, no. 197 (1976): 307–21.

Bar On, Bat-Ami. *Engendering Origins: Critical Feminist Readings in Plato and Aristotle*. Albany: State University of New York Press, 1993.

Barton, Carlin A., and Daniel Boyarin. *Imagine No Religion: How Modern Abstractions Hide Ancient Realities*. New York: Fordham University Press, 2016.

Berg, Steven. *Eros and the Intoxications of Enlightenment: On Plato's* Symposium. Albany: State University of New York Press, 2010.

Bordo, Susan. *The Flight to Objectivity*. Albany: State University of New York Press, 1987.

Brill, Sarah. *Plato and the Limits of Human Life*. Bloomington, IN: Indiana University Press, 2013.

Carson, Laurel A. "Have We Been Careless with Socrates' Last Words?" *Journal of the History of Philosophy* 40, no. 4 (2002): 421–36.

Cornelli, G. *In Search of Pythagoreanism*. Berlin, Germany: De Gruyter, 2013.

Cornelli, G., R. McKirahan, and C. Macris, eds. *On Pythagoreanism*. Berlin, Germany: De Gruyter, 2013.

Curd, Patricia, ed. *A Presocratics Reader: Selected Fragments and Testimonia*. Indianapolis, IN: Hackett, 2011.

Curd, Patricia. "Anaxagoras." In *The Stanford Encyclopedia of Philosophy*, edited by Edward N. Zalta, Winter 2015. https://plato.stanford.edu/archives/win2015/entries/anaxagoras/.

Decker, Jessica. "Borderland Spaces of the Third Kind: Erotic Agency in Plato and Octavia Butler." In *Borderlands and Liminal Subjects: Transgressing the Limits in Philosophy and Literature*, edited by Jessica Elbert Decker and Dylan Winchock, 187–211. New York: Palgrave Macmillan, 2017.

DuBois, Page. *Sowing the Body: Psychoanalysis and Ancient Representations of Women*. Chicago, IL: University of Chicago Press, 1988.

Finkelberg, Aryeh. "Xenophanes' Physics, Parmenides' Doxa and Empedocles' Theory of Cosmological Mixture." *Hermes* 125, no. 1 (1997): 1–16.

Gordon, Jill. *Plato's Erotic World: From Cosmic Origins to Human Death*. Cambridge, UK: Cambridge University Press, 2012.

Holmes, Brooke. *Gender: Antiquity and Its Legacies (Ancients and Moderns)*. Cambridge, UK: Cambridge University Press, 2012.

Huffman, Carl. "Pythagoras." In *The Stanford Encyclopedia of Philosophy*, edited by Edward N. Zalta, Summer 2014. https://plato.stanford.edu/archives/sum2014/entries/pythagoras/.

Huffman, Carl A. *A History of Pythagoreanism*. Cambridge, UK: Cambridge University Press, 2014.

Hyland, Drew. *Finitude and Transcendence in the Platonic Dialogues*. Albany: State University of New York Press, 1995.

———. *Questioning Platonism*. Albany: State University of New York Press, 2004.

Kingsley, Peter. *Ancient Philosophy, Mystery, and Magic: Empedocles and Pythagorean Tradition*. Oxford, UK: Oxford University Press, 1995.

Lamascus, Lorelle D. *The Poverty of Eros in Plato's* Symposium. London: Bloomsbury Academic, 2016.

Lennon, Kathleen, and Edward N. Zalta. "Feminist Perspectives on the Body." In *The Stanford Encyclopedia of Philosophy*, Fall 2014. https://plato.stanford.edu/archives/fall2014/entries/feminist-body/.

Marmodoro, Anna. *Everything in Everything: Anaxagoras' Metaphysics*. Oxford, UK: Oxford University Press, 2017.

Miller, Paul. *Diotima at the Barricades: French Feminists Read Plato*. Oxford, UK: Oxford University Press, 2016.

Nietzsche, Friedrich Wilhelm. *The Gay Science*. Translated by Walter Kaufmann. New York: Vintage Books, 1974.

———. *Twilight of the Idols; and the Anti-Christ*. London: Penguin Books, 1990.

Nye, Andrea. *Socrates and Diotima: Sexuality, Religion, and the Nature of Divinity*. New York: Palgrave Mcmillan, 2015.

O'Brien, Denis. "Hermann Diels on the Presocratics: Empedocles' Double Destruction of the Cosmos (Aetius ii 4.8)." *Phronesis* 45, no. 1 (2000): 1–18.

Okin, Susan Moller. "Philosopher Queens and Private Wives: Plato on Women and the Family." *Philosophy & Public Affairs* 6, no. 4 (1977): 345–69.

Plato. "Apology." In *Plato: Complete Works*, edited by John M. Cooper, translated by G. M. A. Grube, 17–36. Indianapolis, IN: Hackett, 1997.

———. "Charmides." In *Plato: Complete Works*, edited by John M. Cooper, translated by Rosamond Kent Sprague, 639–63. Indianapolis, IN: Hackett, 1997.

———. "Meno." In *Plato: Complete Works*, edited by John M. Cooper, translated by G. M. A. Grube, 870–97. Indianapolis, IN: Hackett, 1997.

———. "Phaedo." In *Plato: Complete Works*, edited by John M. Cooper, translated by G. M. A. Grube, 49–100. Indianapolis, IN: Hackett, 1997.

———. "Republic." In *Plato: Complete Works*, edited by John M. Cooper, translated by G. M. A. Grube and C. D. C. Reeve, 971–1223. Indianapolis, IN: Hackett, 1997.

———. "Symposium." In *Plato: Complete Works*, edited by John M. Cooper, translated by Alexander Nehamas and Paul Woodruff, 457–505. Indianapolis, IN: Hackett, 1997.

Saxonhouse, Arlene W. "The Philosopher and the Female in the Political Thought of Plato." *Political Theory* 4, no. 2 (1976): 195–212.

Schindler, D. C. "Plato and the Problem of Love: On the Nature of Eros in the *Symposium*." *Apeiron: A Journal for Ancient Philosophy and Science* 40, no. 3 (2007): 199–220.

Schultz, Anne-Marie. *Plato's Socrates as Narrator: A Philosophical Muse*. Lanham, MD: Lexington Books, 2013.

Sedley, David. *Creationism and Its Critics in Antiquity*. Berkeley: University of California Press, 2007.

Solmsen, Friedrich. "Love and Strife in Empedocles' Cosmology Phronesis." *Phronesis* 10, no. 2 (1965): 109–48.

Trepanier, Simon. *Empedocles: An Interpretation*. New York: Routledge, 2004.

Tuana, Nancy, ed. *Feminist Interpretations of Plato*. Re-Reading the Canon. University Park: Penn State University Press, 1994.

Vlastos, Gregory. "Was Plato a Feminist?" *Times Literary Supplement* 4, no. 485 (1989): 276–89.

Zhmud, Leonard. *Pythagoras and the Early Pythagoreans*. Oxford, UK: Oxford University Press, 2012.

Zoller, Colleen. *Plato and the Body: Reconsidering Socratic Asceticism*. Albany: State University of New York Press, 2018.

Chapter Six

Overturning Soul-Body Dualism in Plato's *Timaeus*

Monica Vilhauer

In Plato's *Phaedo*, we hear a story about human life that casts the body—the seat of sensation and all the affections—as an "evil" that contaminates us, infects us, and acts as an obstacle to knowledge.[1] The philosopher must treat the sickness of the body by "purifying himself." He must despise and disassociate from his body as much as possible and allow his best self, his intellectual soul, to pursue truth unhindered. The "healthy" good life, here, is depicted as the one that practices for dying and is, as much as possible, disembodied.[2] These broad strokes have been incredibly influential in the way our Western philosophical tradition (1) has defined the human being as soul or mind, as opposed to body; (2) has separated the "rational" human from "unintelligent" nature; and (3) has envisioned ethics as a project to control the body, its sensations, and its desires.[3] Feminists have spent considerable effort showing the way in which the hierarchical soul-body dualism is itself gendered and closely associated with the hierarchical masculine feminine dualism (or gender binary) that systematically operates to denigrate women. Elizabeth Spelman argues, in her essay "Woman as Body: Ancient and Contemporary Views,"[4] that though we may find occasional attempts by Plato to suggest that women are capable of the same range of talents as men (as in Book V of the *Republic*), it is in his soul-body dualism that we find Plato's underlying misogyny. She tells us that the lesson from Plato is: "To have more concern for your body than your soul is to act just like a woman."[5] In matters of wisdom, courage, self-control, love, and the overall "good life," one should not follow the example of women, who remain slaves to their bodies. She points out: "It is true that Plato chastises certain kinds of men: sophist, tyrants, and cowards, for example. But he frequently puts them in their place by comparing them to women!"[6] If individuals do not learn to overcome and control their bodies, they will become womanly and consequently fail in their attempts to achieve full humanity, health, and happiness. With convincing evidence from a wide range of Plato's dialogues, she argues that Plato continually conceives of woman as body and, thus, he associates women with the very thing that he believes drags down and enslaves the best part of the human being. Though I agree with Spelman that Plato regularly presses the hierarchical distinction between soul and body and associates women with body, I aim to show that there are also resources within Plato's own writings for overturning the very soul-body dualism that he spends so much time carving out—resources that should prove helpful for undoing the gender binary. To do this, I will turn in this chapter to Plato's *Timaeus*, which offers a picture of life—on the large scale of the cosmos, as well as the small scale of the human being—as a psychosomatic whole in which intelligence and sensation are intertwined. I aim to show that the *Timaeus* provides us with a picture of the good life that is achieved by emphasizing, rather than severing, the deep connections between soul and body, and that the dialogue offers a prescription for living as a harmonious whole. Such a picture and prescription should prove helpful for reenvisioning traditional gender identities or gender traits as intertwined aspects of a whole person, whose cooperation brings about harmony in the human being.

Cosmic Life

Timaeus begins his speech by telling us a "likely story" of the birth of the cosmos.[7] He asserts that the cosmos is the sort of thing that has "come to be," as it is visible, touchable, and has a body. All things that come to be, Timaeus says, must have some cause, which he initially posits as "the craftsman" (*dêmiourgos*) and later expands on to include two things: intellect (*nous*), associated with the craftsman, and necessity (*anankê*), associated with bodies. The cosmos can only come to be by the "standing-together" (*systasis*) of necessity and intellect.[8] We soon see that the cosmos itself is a great living animal in which intellect and necessity, and in which soul (*psyche*) and body (*soma*), are completely interwoven.

Timaeus tells us that since our cosmos is beautiful, and so our craftsman good,[9] the craftsman must have ordered "the all" by looking to a self-same model grasped by intellect for guidance. For, it is because of intellect and proportion that things are beautiful. He continues that the good craftsman took up all that was visible, but which moved unmusically, and "brought it into order from disorder."[10] The craftsman realized that in order for "the all" to be beautiful it needed intellect. And, because "it's impossible for intellect apart from soul to become present in anything," the craftsman constructed intellect within soul and soul within body and "joined them with one another by bringing them together center to center."[11] Thus, he gave birth to a great visible and intelligent living animal (*zôon*) that was constructed of the four elements—fire, earth, water, and air—combined according to proportion.

We have here a first lesson that soul and body are intimately intertwined in all that lives. They are joined together to produce life.[12] But in our next lesson, we discover that the intertwining goes so deep that our ability to distinguish soul from body, even conceptually, is questionable. When Timaeus tries to break down the construction of the cosmos into steps, and tries to describe the construction of the cosmic body, we learn that soul is already at work, not only in the proportional combination of the four elements, but in the very constitution of those elements. The physical "stuff" that exists before it is brought together with soul is disorderly, without ratio and measure, and is not yet even in the forms of fire, air, earth, and water, or what we might call the forms of the simplest bodies. Before the craftsman gets involved, there are only "traces" of fire, air, water, and earth, but they are not yet fully articulated as such. Timaeus says:

> Now on the one hand, before that time [before the all was ordered], all these things were in a condition that was without ratio and measure; and when the attempt was made to array the all, at first fire, and water and earth and air—although they had certain traces of themselves—were yet altogether disposed as is likely for everything to be whenever god is absent from anything; and since this was their nature at the

> time, god first of all thoroughly configured them by means of forms and numbers.[13]

The four elemental bodies are configured geometrically out of triangles by the intellect of the craftsman. That's how the craftsman makes the "traces" orderly and intelligent. Now, we remember "it's impossible for intellect apart from soul to become present in anything." So, it seems that the simplest elemental bodies actually become identifiable bodies (with form and geometric order) by becoming ensouled. Bodies can't even be bodies without soul.

When Timaeus turns to the construction of the cosmic soul, his story further calls into question any hard dualism in which body and soul are totally different kinds of things. Whereas the Socrates of the *Phaedo* tells us the body is visible, composite, always changes, and can scatter and die, while the soul is invisible, intelligible, one, always the same, and cannot disintegrate;[14] Timaeus tells us, first, that cosmic soul is itself a blend of Being and Becoming (Being, which is self-same and nonpartitioned, and Becoming, which changes, is partitioned, and comes to be in the realm of bodies).[15] The cosmic soul includes not just what Timaeus calls the nature of the Same, but also the nature of the Other within it. Soul has, thus, a most fundamental thing in common with body: the nature of the Other is in both. But we learn that soul has even further things in common with body in Timaeus' story. Timaeus tells us, second, that both soul and body "come to be" and are generated (whereas, for Socrates in the *Phaedo*, only bodies are generated). He tells us, third, that the cosmic soul moves in circuits, which suggests it is spatial like a body. After the craftsman blended together Being and Becoming, Timaeus explains, he cut up his mixture into strips that he formed into two circles, and set them into motion.[16] If cosmic soul is to move around in a circle, it must have some physical properties, even if they are not visible to the human eye, just like bodies. Timaeus proclaims, fourth, that nothing exists outside of the cosmos, which is perfect, complete, and self-sufficient (and which, we remember, is touchable and has a body). Thus, there seems to be no real possibility of disembodied soul in Timaeus' story, as there is for Socrates in the *Phaedo*, who argues for souls that live on, separate from their bodies, after their bodies die. For Timaeus, any soul that exists must be within the cosmos, and since the cosmos is itself a bodily entity, we can infer that all soul must be embodied. (This casts an interesting doubt on whether even the craftsman exists outside of, or separate from, the cosmos he is making.) In the *Timaeus*, any hard dualism between soul and body is already called into question on the macrocosmic level of "the all."[17]

Next, Timaeus' story of the way in which the cosmos comes to give a silent account of itself emphasizes not only the importance of intellect but also that of sensation for achieving self-knowledge. Once again, the dualistic thinking of Socrates in the *Phaedo*, which attempts to hold apart soul and body and emphasize intellection alone as the path to knowledge, is called into question. Timaeus describes the way in which the cosmos, once constructed, begins her life, connects with herself, and informs herself about herself. The cosmos comes into contact with herself by perceiving all the particulars within herself—by touching on and being touched by each thing. Timaeus says the following of the cosmos:

> [W]henever she touches on something that has its Being dispersed or, again, something whose Being is non-partitioned, she is moved throughout her whole self and tells what that thing is the same as and what it's other than, and in what exact relation and where and how and when it turns out that particular things *are* and are affected, both for what comes to be and for what's always in the same condition.[18]

Timaeus depicts the cosmos as "giving an account" to herself that is quite similar to the description given by Socrates in the *Republic* (which the listeners supposedly heard the day before) of the activity of the philosopher who has knowledge.[19] The great psychosomatic animal seems to philosophize, even if silently, by giving an account to herself of all her inner pieces. She is able to "give an account" because of both her intellect, which understands that within herself that has the nature of the Same, and because of her ability to touch on and perceive all of the physical aspects of herself, which have the nature of the Other. On the level of the cosmic whole, physical sensation, thus, is presented as an aid to knowledge, not an obstacle. There seems in the *Timaeus*, thus, to be a rethinking of the value of the body in the process of knowledge and a holding together of intellect and sensation as cooperative partners in this process. The body and its power of sensation is not treated as an inferior element in the universe to be denied or suppressed. It is essential for self-knowledge on a cosmic scale.

Mortal Life

What we hear about the relationship between soul and body and the role of sensation for knowledge on the macrocosmic level of the living whole is imitated on the microcosmic level of the human animal. Timaeus' story of the way in which the immortal and mortal parts of the soul are woven together with the body in the human being emphasizes their interconnection and their cooperation for maximum functioning.

Timaeus tells us that the immortal part of the soul with its divine circuits was placed in the head, perched on top in a position of rule. The face was placed around the divine part in order to offer "organs for all the forethought of the soul."[20] This suggests that human beings can only properly be guided by a partnership between soul and physical organs. The mouth, in particular, is a site of cooperation—fulfilling the soul's needs for intelligent speech, and the body's needs for nutrients—as it is formed to be "the entrance for things that are necessary but an exit for things that are best."[21] The spirited part of the soul was placed in the chest near the physical heart, so that once it "boils up" it affects that organ which sends signals (pumps blood) to the rest of the body, and makes it jump into action. The desiring part of the soul that's connected with physical needs was placed near the belly, farthest from the rational part, so as not to disturb it. Since this desiring part does not understand reason, but "falls readily under the spell of images and phantasms,"[22] the liver, which reflects intellectual thoughts as if in a mirror, was placed near it either to frighten it and forbid it when appropriate, or to provide divine inspiration that might touch on truth and soothe it when needed.[23] Finally, the gods who designed us knew the sort of gluttony that would be in us because of our desire for food and drink, and they knew that we "would use much more than was temperate and necessary. So in order that quick destruction through diseases might not arise . . . they put in place the 'lower belly,' as it is named, as a receptacle for the holding of superfluous food and drink."[24] It is not the case, then, that only the soul regulates the body, as we've been told by the Socrates of the *Phaedo*. Our bodies have been fashioned in such a way as to regulate their own potential for excessiveness. The body is presented here as a partner working in cooperation with the soul for our good, rather than as a disease.

So far, Timaeus has shown us the way in which the human being is akin to the rest of nature, made of the same "stuff," and woven together as a psychosomatic whole whose parts operate together in friendship. Now, in spite of all of its commonality with the cosmos, the human being—because it is a finite, individuated being—experiences its own condition in a striking and unique way. What is it like to be an individual entity who is not self-sufficient and who is "subject to inflow and outflow"[25] in the midst of a world larger than itself? Timaeus tells us that living as a human being is much like attempting to swim in a rushing river, undergoing all sorts of collisions with other bodies that rattle and disrupt the divine cosmic circuits within us to their very core. Timaeus says of our human experience,

> And these circuits, as though bound within a prodigious river, neither mastered it nor were mastered, but were forcibly swept along and also did sweep, so that the whole animal was moved—moved, however, in whatever disorderly way it might happen to progress . . . as prodigious as was that food-supplying wave that washed over it and then flowed away, still greater was the uproar that the affections of the bodies produced by attacking each of them whenever a body of one of them would collide with fire, having met up with it as something alien from the outside, or also with a solid chunk of earth or with the liquid glidings of waters, or when it would be overtaken by a blast of wind-swept air, and when the motions swept through the body by all these properties would attack the soul—which is also the very reason why all these motions were then called "sensings" and are still called now.[26]

Our human condition, here, is likened to a state of seasickness. The sensations that the human being undergoes severely "shake up" and "attack" the soul, producing an "uproar of affections" that can overwhelm us, disorient us, and cause our souls to "become unintelligent."[27]

Living as an individuated, sensing being, no doubt, comes with some big challenges, a story that sounds familiar to us from the *Phaedo*. However, Timaeus believes that the answer for how to deal with the uproar of sensation and affection is not to ignore or despise our bodies. The way to deal with the onslaught of sensation and affection is to learn how to use them to reorient ourselves and find stability. Timaeus tells us how we can enlist the help of sensation to get us back in touch with the cosmic circuits that course in our souls and throughout "the all." It is especially with sight—by raising our gaze to the motions of the heavenly bodies in the sky—that we remember the stable order within us. He says that god gave us vision so that we might observe the circuits of intellect in heaven and imitate them to stabilize the orbits of thinking within ourselves. Timaeus declares,

> [L]et it be said that this is the cause and these the reasons for which god discovered vision and gave it to us as a gift: in order that, by observing the circuits of intellect in heaven, we might use them for the orbits of the thinking within us, which are akin to those, the disturbed to the undisturbed; and, by having thoroughly learned them and partaken of the natural correctness in their calculations, thus imitating the utterly unwandering circuits of the god, we might stabilize the wander-stricken circuits in ourselves.[28]

Timaeus tells us that it is, in fact, because of our sensation of the movement of the heavenly bodies and our recognition of night and day and their return that we are able to count, grasp anything on a mathematical level, inquire into cosmic order, and develop a philosophical account of it. Timaeus emphasizes that we need not only sight but hearing as well in order to maintain healthy order within ourselves. Hearing is needed to access both speech and music, according to which we might attune our souls. Sensation is not something, then, we should attempt to ignore. It is not simply a disrupter. It is essential for bringing back order and balance to our mortal lives.[29] If we direct it in the right way, it can help us cope with and overcome the "seasickness" we feel when we're overwhelmed by external stimuli.[30] Futhermore, we need it to pursue our highest philosophic activities as human beings. Unlike other Platonic texts, the *Timaeus* does not prescribe that we divide ourselves against ourselves to remedy our problems. It doesn't portray one part of ourselves (the body, or the power of sensation) as a simple problem-causer that needs to somehow be disarmed, silenced, or cut out. In an antidualist move, it repeatedly treats both soul and body as essential for maximum functioning, and it emphasizes the importance of their intertwined cooperation for the highest states of health.

Now that we've seen the broad theme at work in the *Timaeus* of what sorts of sicknesses humans suffer and how we are to remedy them, let's look at the more focused story Timaeus tells of our peculiar human diseases near the end of his speech, and what sort of prescription he offers for "the treatment of our bodies and thought-processes."[31] Timaeus reminds us that if an animal is to be good, it is to be beautiful, which means it must have proportion, most importantly between soul and body.[32] The cause of the greatest human diseases, he tells us, is an imbalance between body and soul. The first case of such an imbalance is when the soul is stronger than its body. In such a situation, when the soul becomes enraged, strenuously studies, or vigorously debates, she "shakes it [the body] all up from the inside and fills it with diseases."[33] The second case is when a body is stronger than its soul. When the body's desire for food outweighs or overwhelms the soul's desire for prudence, the body becomes too big and the soul becomes "dull, slow to learn and forgetful, thereby producing the greatest of diseases—stupidity."[34] So what is the remedy for these sicknesses in the human being that arise from a lack of harmony between body and soul? Timaeus shows us, once again, that the solution is not to ignore or disengage from the body and to care only for the soul (as we might have heard in the *Phaedo*). It is to cultivate both soul and body so that the animal is strong, proportional, and balanced as a whole. Timaeus says: "The one safeguard from both these conditions is this: never to set the soul in motion without body nor body without soul, so that both of them, by defending themselves, may become equally balanced and thereby healthy."[35] Mathematicians must be sure to also cultivate their bodies by attending to gymnastics, and athletes must apply themselves "to the liberal arts and all philosophy"[36] if they are to become healthy, beautiful, and good. It is by keeping both our bodies and souls in motion so that they do not become idle, weak, or totally mastered by outside forces, and by attending to them by nourishing and exercising them in the ways appropriate for each, that we treat sicknesses of disproportion. It is by keeping our bodies and souls in motion *together* that we also maintain and strengthen their unity as an integrated whole.

By now we have seen that the integrated cooperation of balanced parts is central to the health of a living organism in the story of the *Timaeus*, and that creating or maintaining health (whether on a macro or microcosmic scale) is in large part about bringing about a state of balanced wholeness. Just like the good, creative activity of the craftsman, the good, creative activity of a human being involves blending, mixing, balancing, making beautiful proportion, making harmonious friendships between parts, and making whole. Unlike some other Platonic texts, the thrust of the *Timaeus* is far more holist than dualist. It stresses integration and intermixing, not division and opposition, in both its way of understanding living systems and its recommendations for remedying sickness and bringing about health in our own lives. If the soul and body represent masculine and feminine sides of life in Plato's works, as many feminists have argued, then the lesson of the *Timaeus* is that we must mix and balance these masculine and feminine sides of life within ourselves in order to bring about our healthiest and most beautiful state of harmonious wholeness. The lesson is not to exorcise the feminine. The *Timaeus*, thus, is one of those resources within Plato's corpus that overturns the hierarchical soul-body dualism and associated gender binary that ground other Platonic dialogues.

Chôra: The Excluded Feminine?

But what if the *Timaeus* is a strange tale in which soul and body do not represent masculine and feminine sides of life at all, as in other Platonic texts. What if it is a tale in which soul and body both represent the masculine, while the feminine is relegated to someplace that is beyond both soul and body? What if the thing feminized in the *Timaeus* is not the body at all but, rather, a far more ambiguous, difficult to identify, "something" that precedes the birth of all bodies: the "place" or formless "space" where bodies are born? What might this mean for femininity? Is the feminine excluded in the *Timaeus* from active participation in the generation of the cosmos, and from the cosmos itself?

In his third "new beginning" of his cosmology, Timaeus suggests that his prior stories of the most basic metaphysical "kinds" were too simple. There are not just two metaphysical kinds, but three: "that which comes to be, that *in which* it comes to be, and that *from which* what comes to be sprouts as something copied."[37] That *from which* things come to be is the intelligible, invisible, unsensed, and stable model. It is the eternal forms. It is Being. That which comes to be is the visible, sensed, unstable imitation or copy of the form. It is born, grows, decays, and dies. It is the manifold and ever-changing world of "informed" bodies. It is Becoming. But there is a third kind—that *in which* things come to be—which he had forgotten.

Timaeus struggles to name this "*in which*," this "third kind," for it lacks any shape or form that would make it identifiable, distinguishable, and nameable. It is invisible and indestructible, like Being, but it shape-shifts along with whatever forms enter it, "appear[ing] different at different times,"[38] and it is ever-changing like Becoming. Lacking form, it is unbalanced, disorderly, and unmusical. Timaeus calls it "difficult and obscure."[39] We cannot grasp it with knowledge or opinion. We can only approach it with a dreamlike "bastard reasoning."[40] It seems to be beyond *logos*, and yet Timaeus has quite a lot to say about it.[41]

He first tries to name the third kind by calling it a "receptacle" (*hypodochê*), a receiving place offering enclosure and hospitality. Later he expands on this by calling it a place or "space" (*chôra*), "providing a seat for all that has birth . . . [for] it's necessary somehow for everything that *is* to be in some region and occupy some space."[42] It is the space where all of Becoming is born. And finally, he calls it a "molding stuff" (*ekmageion*) that temporarily takes on the various shapes it receives, but never has any stable shape of its own, and is itself totally neutral, receptive, and malleable. Timaeus explains that in order for it to take on the imprints of other shapes well, it must itself be shapeless and pure. He declares the following:

> If the imprints are going to be sufficiently various with every variety to be seen, then that in which the imprints are fixed wouldn't be prepared well unless it's shapeless with respect to all those looks that it might be going to receive from elsewhere. For if it should be similar to any of the things that come on the scene, on receiving what was contrary to itself or of an altogether different nature, whenever these things arrive, it would copy them badly by projecting its own visage alongside the thing copied. And that's why that which is to take up all kinds within itself would be outside of all forms.[43]

What is remarkable about this story is the way in which the three metaphysical "kinds" are decisively gendered by Timaeus. Being is the father. Space/receptacle/molding stuff (which, remember, is supposed to be completely neutral and without shape) is the mother and wet nurse of becoming. And Becoming is the offspring and (presumably male) imitation of the father's form. In their most basic manifestations, the masculine is associated with eternal forms; the feminine is associated with ambiguous and unnameable space (or perhaps matter, as Aristotle took it); and the product/child is an embodied imitation of the father's form.[44]

What does all of this mean for the role of femininity in the universe? The insinuation might be, first, that the feminine lacks any identity of her own, because she lacks form (either as original or as imitation). She is unidentifiable and unintelligible. She is no-thing. Second, it might mean that the feminine element of reality is just "there," but doesn't do anything. She is completely passive. She plays no contributing role in the masculine self-reproduction of all things in the cosmos—in which fathers beget sons, in which models beget copies, in which forms beget bodies—beyond providing a place where the masculine drama can play out. Even if a child begotten is, so to speak, a "girl," she would, strictly speaking, still be a masculine entity, in so far as she participates in any form, and therefore shares a likeness to the father. An embodied, living feminine creature is erased from the story. Femininity is cast out and lives somewhere in exile—beyond Being and Becoming, soul and body, original and imitation—for femininity is beyond (or more properly before) all forms, all distinctions, and all language. The feminine is, thus, excluded from any active role in all that lives. Some contemporary feminists read just this message in the *Timaeus* and declare that the feminine is denied all agency in Plato.

Luce Irigaray, in her essay Plato's *Hystera*, highlights Plato's relegation of the feminine to "the beyond" of all that is intelligible and his exclusion of her from active participation in generative processes. She shows how the feminine in Plato's metaphysics is actually not portrayed as the inferior and problematic participating member of the pairs man/woman, soul/body, and form/matter, as earlier feminists might have thought. Rather, the feminine is exiled to some nonparticipatory "space" that is beyond all binaries.

In her essay, Irigaray takes up the status of the space/receptacle/molding stuff of the *Timaeus* in the context of Plato's cave. She sees the cave—in the famous, central metaphor of Plato's *Republic*—to be a womb (*hystera*) (which she also refers to as mother, receptacle, mold, and matter) in which the eternal forms are physically manifested. The cave/womb, in Irigaray's reading, is a reproductive space in which reflections, copies, or shadows of originals are born. She explains that the cave must be pure and "virgin," without any character or activity of its own, in order to reflect originals clearly and not contaminate the "likenesses" of the forms that dance around insider her.

Irigaray sees the cave/womb as a matrix in which all representation occurs and in which all distinctions are produced, like the distinctions between light and dark, intelligible and sensible, original and imitation, father and child, truth and fantasy, good and evil, the one and many, and life and death. But, she argues, this matrix itself is never represented in Plato's metaphysical stories, never identified, and never even noticed. It disappears, like a mirror behind all of the images that dance on its surface. It is "that unrepresentable origin of all forms and all morphology."[45]

The cave/womb, as Irigaray sees it, is the feminine ground (or, even better, the virgin soil) of a masculine system of reality crafted by Plato. The feminine ground makes possible everything that matters in an economy that only counts original forms (the father) and their likenesses (his offspring), but it is a ground that is itself excluded and placed "outside" of that economy. For Irigaray, femininity is relegated by Plato to an "indefinite beyond." It is a "remainder," a "surplus," an "excess" that cannot be accounted for within the patriarchal economy of Being and Becoming. From Irigaray's perspective, it is not just forgotten but "willfully unnoticed."[46] This is because it is a threat to the father's power. The mother must be erased in order for the father to claim his reign as the singular source of all that is. It is the "[e]clipse of the mother, of the place (of) becoming, whose non-representation or even disavowal upholds the absolute being attributed to the father."[47]

As Judith Butler puts it, the feminine for Irigaray is an "inscriptional site" and "unthematizable materiality" within a phallogocentric economy,[48] and it must be excluded for the posturing of an all-masculine reproductive system in the universe to maintain internal coherence. Butler declares of Irigaray's work: "Her reading establishes the cosmogony of the Forms in the *Timaeus* as a phallic phantasy of a fully self-constituted patrilineality, and this fantasy of autogenesis or self-constitution is effected through a denial and cooptation of the female capacity for reproduction."[49] Irigaray shows that what is excluded from the Platonic "phallic phantasy" is already inside it and "calls into question its systematic closure and its pretension to be self-grounding."[50] In other words, Irigaray shows that the Platonic patrilineal system is completely dependent on the feminine, which it needs as its support, even as it desperately tries to exclude it.

Now, Butler's own concern is that Irigaray's identification of "the excluded" with "the feminine" in Plato's work misses the fact that (a) other things are excluded from Plato's economy besides women, like slaves and animals, and (b) the excluded woman is a particular kind of woman—a heterosexual mother-woman—which means all other kinds of women are excluded from the exclusion (doubly excluded). So, there is a worry that there are not only types of misogyny at work in Plato's metaphysics, but also types of racism, deep anthropocentrism, and heterosexism that need to be addressed, which Irigaray misses.[51] But both Irigaray and Butler, in their reading of the space/receptacle/molding stuff of the *Timaeus*, focus on the insinuation that femininity is something unintelligible and passive. They emphasize what we might call Timaeus' "rules" about the feminine in the guise of *chôra*. The formless, shapeless feminine cannot be identified, comprehended, or even named. The feminine must never resemble the father's original form, nor the child's imitative form. She is different from them both, but has no designation of her own. The feminine is totally receptive. She can be penetrated, but can never penetrate. She can be affected, but can never affect. She can never contribute something of her own to the offspring. Let's pause here and ask: Is this really what the *Timaeus* has made of femininity? A noncontributing, passive, no-thing? Does the *Timaeus* really cast the mother of Becoming as totally lacking in agency? Is there another story we could tell?

Retrieving Feminine Movement

I'm not sure that Irigaray's and Butler's emphasis on Timaues' "rules" about *chôra* reveals a complete picture of the third metaphysical kind, or the "cosmic feminine" that she represents. Timaeus' account of *chôra* includes not just a set of rules about her, but fascinating descriptions that directly contradict those rules. What I find missing from Irigaray's and Butler's analysis is one of the most interesting parts of Timaeus' story about *chôra*—her movement.

Timaeus might suggest at first that *chôra* is a rather characterless and neutral "space." But then he goes on to describe her in rather dynamic terms. She moves and shakes in unique ways. Timaeus says that when different shapes enter the mother's space,

> she herself is shaken by those kinds [traces of earth, water, air, fire] and, being moved, in turn shakes them back; and the kinds, in being moved, are always swept along this way and that and are dispersed—just like the particles shaken and winnowed out by sieves and other instruments used for purifying grain: the dense and heavy are swept to one site and

> settle, the porous and light to another. So too, when the four kinds are shaken by the recipient, who, being herself moved, is like an instrument that produces shaking, she separates farthest from each other the kinds that are most dissimilar, while pushing together as close as possible those that are most similar—which is exactly why these different kinds also held a different place even before the all was arrayed and came to be out of them.[52]

Granted, *chôra* "is shaken," and so there is a passive side to her movement. But she is not a strictly passive entity. She actively shakes back, and her shaking back has an interesting function. It organizes the "four kinds" that enter her by putting like with like. The new state she generates, as particles leave her space, is one of little communities or coagulations of like with like, each in their own place and distinguished from each other. Her activity of organizing kinds offers the craftsman some already distinguished content that he can further order with ratio and number. She, thus, plays an active and productive role in the creation of Becoming even before the father gets involved.

Her passive-active shaking movement not only introduces a kind of organizing activity into the universe, different from the father's, it also introduces the specific kind of movement experienced by a mortal animal—a simultaneously sensitive and responsive movement of interrelation with what is other than oneself. Timaeus tells us that *chôra* is moved by "being liquefied and ignited and receiving the shapes of earth and air, and suffering all the other affections that follow along with these."[53] But, as we saw, she also moves back, and affects these shapes as they exit her. She is in an interactive relationship with what is other than herself. She is acted on and acts back. She receives and she responds. She is transformed and she transforms. And, because of this double-movement, this ambiguously passive-active way of being, "she sways irregularly in every direction."[54] Similarly, the mortal animal experiences "an uproar of the affections" whenever it "would collide with fire . . . with a solid chunk of earth, or with the liquid glidings of waters, or when it would be overtaken by a blast of wind-swept air."[55] The mortal animal, like *chôra*, is moved and affected, but also moves and affects. Timaeus tells us that due to the inflow and outflow of the elements, the mortal animal's circuits "were forcibly swept along and also did sweep" and in the process "the whole animal was moved . . . in whatever disorderly way it might happen to progress . . . forwards and backwards, and again to the right and to the left, both down and up, wandering every which way down all six regions."[56] This ambiguous, passive-active, disorderly movement, which seems to mimic *chôra*'s, is a movement that is essential for individuated creatures to make contact with their world. It is the movement in which the double experience of sensation—of simultaneously touching and being touched—occurs. It is an essential movement for a being that is not self-sufficient, but that must interact with other beings in interdependent systems of perpetual change to live. In other words, it is essential to the mode of being that is Becoming; and it is the "mother" of Becoming that contributes it to the universe.

In the Timaeus, as Sara Brill notes, "the way something moves is treated as essential to what it is."[57] Perhaps the "mother of Becoming" is not a neutral, character-less "no-thing" after all. Perhaps her ambiguous double-movement is the key to what she is. Perhaps, granted, she is still so variable and fluid that she is beyond all binaries in her passive-active way of being (still an interesting idea worth pursuing, and yet another possible site of resistance against the gender binary from within Plato). But she's not lacking in agency, and she's not lacking in a contributing role in the genesis of the cosmos, as Irigaray and Butler interpreted her to be. Perhaps the mother's movement, as Timaeus continually emphasizes, is unbalanced, unmusical, disorderly, and wandering. Perhaps, as Emanuela Bianchi poetically puts it, this movement of the mother marks "the feminine as errant, striking cacophonous, arrhythmic notes in an assuredly masculine harmony as immeasurable disorderly motion."[58] But as we've seen (and as Bianchi also argues) this arrhythmic movement has a positive and productive force. It's indeterminate and wandering character offers the freedom necessary for creative contact with what is other than oneself. Such a contact involves spontaneity and the chance of unanticipated results. Such a contact is significant for both parties, in that it involves mutual transformation. And such a contact produces new connections and communities between beings. This free movement—perhaps a sort of playing or dancing like no one is watching[59]—is essential to the life of Becoming, and it is a movement that cannot be found in "the father." The father, to be sure, also contributes a kind of motion in which mortal beings participate—the circular motion of the so-called circuits of the soul, and the blending and balancing movements we spent so much time on in the first half of this chapter. But the father's movements alone are not sufficient for mortal life. Again, we see in the story of the *Timaeus* that a healthy whole—in this case the whole of a mortal creature that must live in interactive relationships with other beings—involves a combination and cooperation of masculine and feminine elements.

When we focus on Timaeus' descriptions of the different *movements* that the masculine and feminine metaphysical kinds introduce into the universe, we see that they are not opposed to each other, or related to each other as master/slave, superior/inferior, or active/passive. Both actively contribute necessary elements to the dynamics of their offspring's life. Timaeus may try to deny *chôra* or "the feminine" agency when he calls her "all-receptive," but he fails in the face of his own descriptions of her movement. Once again, we find in the *Timaeus* a story in which the feminine (whether cast as body, or sensation, or *chôra*) is crucial for the functioning of the whole. The feminine, in her different possible guises, is not ignored or suppressed, but balanced in collaboration with the masculine. The hierarchical, dualistic systems of soul/body, intellect/sensation, active/passive, master/slave, human/nature, being/space, form/matter—and their associated gender binary of masculine/feminine—just do not hold up in the bulk of the *Timaeus*. They are repeatedly overturned in favor of holistic systems.

A Final Tale about Women

And yet, one cannot ignore a familiar tale that pops up twice in the dialogue. If you don't do a good job living the ideal human life, you will become unjust and "womanly." If you fail to live well, you will be reborn a woman. Fail again, and you will become a beast.[60] But something is different this time when we hear the old tale in which women and nonhuman animals are demoted in the hierarchy of living beings. It is not rooted in its usual set of analogies, associations, or "reasons" that support it. One can't say this time, without massive contradiction with the rest of the dialogue, that living badly (and so "like a woman") means that you can't figure out how to silence your body and make it the soul's slave. One can't say this time that living badly means that you let sensation have its way and can't figure out how to deny and ignore it. Such claims do not fit with the rest of the dialogue in which, as we've shown, the healthy/good life is *not* a matter of the soul's suppression of the body, nor a matter of a masculine life principle ruling over a feminine life principle. It is, rather, about their cooperation and creation of an integrated whole. So, what is going on here? Why the slip back into the traditional denigration of women, as those who are unable to play the master, at the end of an account in which creating master-slave relationships is not the goal, and human health is characterized in terms of balance and perhaps even an androgynous ideal? I admit that this is incredibly frustrating. I think that it reminds us that misogyny runs much deeper than theoretical associations or systems of binary thinking.[61] Feminists will meet a limit to what they can do to resist misogyny if they restrict themselves to the analysis and critique of theory. The theoretical associations and dualistic systems of thinking that usually prop up the gender binary and the demotion of women are, more often than not, replaced with holistic frameworks in the *Timaeus*. And yet misogyny is still present. What can we surmise from this? I can't help but conclude that philosophical thinking always remains situated in cultural biases, even when it attempts to do something radical and break free of them. Reason is surrounded by unreason, as if by bookends. We will have to find ways to affect the bookends.

Conclusion

In the *Timaeus* we find a story about human life that disrupts the strict dualism of the *Phaedo*, which has been handed down to us as representative of the Platonic theory that systematically divides soul and body, and privileges what is "one and the same" and intellectual over what is changing and physical. We've seen that in some parts of the *Timaeus*, the soul-body dualism is so fundamentally disrupted that the conceptual distinction cannot be maintained. In other places, where the conceptual distinction is still upheld, the relationship between the two aspects of life is portrayed as a close-knit partnership. In the *Timaeus* we find a story that does not prescribe a divorce from our bodies in order to overcome our human ills, but encourages us to integrate and harmonize soul and body so that they establish a balanced friendship. If body represents the feminine in the *Timaeus*, as in other dialogues, then the message is not to suppress or ignore the feminine, but to strengthen it and partner it with the masculine to create a healthy whole.

In the part of the *Timaeus* where a new formulation of a gendered dualism might potentially open up—between (on the one hand) masculine Being and Becoming, and (on the other) feminine *chôra*—we find disruption at work again. Though Timaeus may make some attempts to cast *chôra*/the feminine as the passive, inessential element in the family drama of the cosmos, the project fails as soon as he starts to describe her active and creative movement. Both masculinized and feminized metaphysical elements, as we saw, turn out to be essential participants in the creation of Becoming as a whole. Dualism is overturned in favor of holism again.

The *Timaeus* offers a useful remedy for overly dualistic philosophical thinking and overly dualistic ways of living. It can aid feminists in the project of overcoming the gender binary by helping them to reconceive masculine and feminine as interactive elements that exist and operate together within a given organism. Such masculine and feminine elements relate to each other, not as opponents, but as cooperative partners to create a balanced whole. From this perspective, the "project of life" might be conceived, not in terms of developing only one side of the gender binary within ourselves, and then finding our place as master or slave in society and the larger natural ecosystem. Instead, it might be conceived in terms of developing both the masculine and feminine elements within ourselves, combining them in inwardly cooperative relationships, and then developing outwardly cooperative relationships with other creatures (human and nonhuman), with whom we share our world. In this way we might find our proper place as microcosm within the larger cosmic order of interdependent systems.

Notes

1. *Phd.* 66b, 67a.

2. Socrates famously says in the *Phaedo*: "[T]he one aim of those who practice philosophy in the proper manner is to practice for dying and death" (64a)—that time when we might finally be relieved of all the problems brought on by our attachments to the body and the physical world, and we might finally attain the wisdom and happiness we have been seeking. Friedrich Nietzsche reads Socrates' attitude toward death to be one that is antilife and connected to the notion that physical life is itself a sickness (for which death is the only cure). This is an attitude, according to Nietzsche, that is a symptom of Socrates' own

decay. Friedrich Nietzsche, "The Problem of Socrates," in *Twilight of the Idols*, trans. Richard Polt (Indianapolis: Hackett, 1997), 12–17. Pierre Hadot, on the other hand, sees Socrates' attitude toward death to be part of a spiritual practice—learning to die—in which individuals mature. Living in such a way that one is learning to die involves rising beyond one's partial and individual point of view to a more universal, objective point of view. Pierre Hadot, *Philosophy as a Way of Life*, trans. Michael Chase (Oxford: Blackwell, 1995), 93–101. So, for Hadot, the practice is not one of decline but cultivation in which we learn to see and connect ourselves to the whole of humanity and nature. As attractive as Hadot's reading is, the body is still cast as a problem (in this case, the problem of our individuation and partial perspective) that needs to be overcome as much as possible.

3. For interpretive work that disrupts this traditional interpretation of the *Phaedo*, see the chapter by Hilary Yancey and Anne-Marie Schultz in this volume. They develop ways in which the dualistic reading of the *Phaedo*, so influential for the history of Western metaphysics and ethics, might be overturned with resources from within the *Phaedo* itself.

4. Elizabeth Spelman, "Woman as Body: Ancient and Contemporary Views," *Feminist Studies* 9, no. 1 (Spring 1982): 109–31.

5. Spelman, "Women as Body," 115.

6. Spelman, 118.

7. Timaeus suggests at the outset that different subject matters allow for different types of speech that are appropriate to them. While speech about unchanging Being can be expected to be a precise, logical, and truthful philosophical account (*logos*); speech about changing Becoming, which is itself just a likeness of Being, can only be expected to be a "likely story" (*mythos*), associated with opinion (Plato, *Tim.* 29b–d). Interestingly, Socrates signals that the speech Timaeus is about to give is of a third kind: Socrates calls it "*nomos*," which is translated as *song*. This seems to be a kind of foreshadowing for the metaphysical "third kind" that will be introduced later as *chôra*, which is neither Being nor Becoming and which may need its own kind of speech appropriate to it—one that is beyond (and before) *logos* or *mythos*. So, not only will the *Timaeus* be working beyond metaphysical binaries, it will be working beyond binaries of speech as well.

8. *Tim.* 48a.

9. Already in Timaeus' story, sensation has a key role. It is because we sense that "the cosmos is the most beautiful of things born" (Plato, *Tim.* 29a) that we are led to understand that our craftsman was good, and that the model used was most perfect, stable, unchanging, and complete. Sensation, thus, leads to philosophical thinking, rather than hindering it (as the Socrates of the *Phaedo* suggests).

10. *Tim.* 30a.

11. *Tim.* 30b, 36e.

12. To learn how Timaeus' discussion of creation as a fertile and productive mixing of the four elements with soul is rooted in a line of Presocratic thinkers (Pythagoras, Empedocles, and Anaxagoras), see the chapter in this volume by Hilary Yancey and Anne-Marie Schultz. Dive further into Anaxagoras' way of understanding separation within a mixture, or immanent difference, in Holly Moore's chapter in this volume.

13. *Tim.* 53ab.

14. *Phd.* 78–80.

15. The craftsman constructed the cosmic soul out of a process of blending. First, he took Being (which is self-same and nonpartitioned) and Becoming (which changes, is partitioned, and applies to bodies), and blended them together to make a third form of being. He then takes these three things—(1) Being (which has the nature of the Same), (2) Becoming (which has the nature of the Other), and his (3) intermediate blended third type of being—and blends all three together, having to force the Same and Other together, since "the Other was loathe to mix" (Plato, *Timaeus*, 35a).

16. Timaeus says that after the blending of the cosmic soul, he then cut up his mixture into portions (according to a Pythagorean musical scale) and split the whole structure down its length into two strips, crossed the two strips like an X, and bent each of them into a circle. The outer circle he designated to move in the course of the Same (which is the course on which the so-called fixed stars that we perceive will lie), and the inner circle he designated to move in the course of the Other (which is the course on which the sun and planets we perceive will move).

17. See Gabriela Roxana Carone, "Mind and Body in Late Plato," *Archiv fuer Geschichte der Philosophie* 87, no. 3 (2005): 235–46 on this point. She argues that in Timaeus' story, body necessitates soul and intelligent organization, and that soul necessitates body and space.

18. *Tim.* 37b.

19. The philosopher, the one who has knowledge, is portrayed in the *Republic* as having the ability to give an account of what a thing is and how it is different from what it is not. The philosopher also knows the difference between that which always is, and that which changes, can grasp both kinds of things for what they are, and can explain the relationship between the changing thing and the stable Form in which it participates. See Plato, *The Republic of Plato*, trans. Allan Bloom (New York: Basic Books, 1968), 476d.

20. *Tim.* 45b.

21. *Tim.* 75e.

22. *Tim.* 71b.

23. Divination, which has such an important role in the *Phaedrus* for the philosopher (who is overcome by divine inspiration in love and led by it toward

wisdom) is able to take place because of a partnership between one of our body parts, which reflects images, and thought, which interprets their meaning.

24. *Tim.* 72e.

25. *Tim.* 43a.

26. *Tim.* 43b–c.

27. *Tim.* 43c, 44b.

28. *Tim.* 47b.

29. There's an interesting commonality between the shaking/sweeping movement of sensation, and the shaking/sweeping movement of what Timaeus will call the "receptacle of becoming," or "Space" (*chôra*), which we'll be getting to below. I'm saying here that the movement of sensation is not simply a disruptive force that jumbles up or disorients. It is also a force that can create order and balance. Later I will suggest that the movement of sensation imitates the movement of *chôra*. Although *chôra* is shaken up when outside shapes enter her, she also shakes back, and in the process she produces the first moments of order and organization in the cosmos.

30. This is experientially true of actual motion sickness. When one feels swept around by external stimuli in a car or boat, the remedy for the nausea is directing one's eyes to a faraway stable spot, like the horizon, to reorient and rebalance.

31. *Tim.* 87c.

32. *Tim.* 88d.

33. *Tim.* 88a.

34. *Tim.* 88b.

35. *Tim.* 88b. Note that Timaeus suggests that to keep our bodies in motion we should imitate the motion of what he calls the "receptacle of becoming," or "Space" (*chôra*). Timaeus tells us that *chôra* is shaken as the elements enter her and she receives their shapes, but that she also shakes back, and in the process begins to organize physical particles (52e). If we imitate this motion, if we "shake back" we will guard against battles being fought within us between foes, and "produce health" (88e). We'll come back to the connection between *chôra*'s movement and mortal animals below.

36. *Tim.* 88c. We can't help but hear echoes of Socrates' holistic educational program in the *Republic* of music, gymnastics, and philosophy, which Timaeus presumably heard the day before.

37. *Tim.* 50c.

38. *Tim.* 50c.

39. *Tim.* 49a.

40. *Tim.* 52b.

41. In his essay *Khōra*, Jacques Derrida initiates thinking about what kind of speech is appropriate for the metaphysical third kind. As *chôra* is neither

Being nor Becoming, he calls into question whether the appropriate speech can be either *logos* or *mythos*, and suggests that it must somehow be beyond them both, defying all binaries. The appropriate speech for *chôra* is some third genre that, like *chôra*, situates binaries, or offers the place in which binaries are born, without itself being subject to the law of binaries. But what kind of speech is that? He notes that the "dream-like" reasoning needed to speak *chôra* "could just as well deprive it [that speech] of lucidity as confer upon it a power of divination" (Jacques Derrida, "*Khōra*," in *On the Name*, trans. David Wood (Stanford: Stanford University Press, 1995), 90. Could it be that the speech appropriate to *chôra* is divinely inspired? More like that obscure speech of an oracle than that of a madman? And could that oracular speech be the kind that situates and gives place and distinction to *logos* and *mythos*?

42. *Tim.* 52b.

43. *Tim.* 50d–e.

44. An interesting study could be done comparing the metaphysical "third kind" in Plato's *Timaeus* with another feminine figure in ancient Greece—the oracle. Sasha Biro, in her chapter in this volume, develops the way in which the oracle is depicted as a kind of virginal vessel, without status or character of her own, possessed by the god who impregnates her with his divine truth, which she births in a kind of speech that is indeterminate, cryptic, and lends itself to multiple meanings. She and her utterances cannot fit into the usual rational order. Yet they are authoritative and communicate ambiguous and paradoxical truths, which the usual rational order, bound to binary thinking, cannot. There seems to be a strong parallel between the way in which *chôra* is inundated with forms that shake her until she produces an initial kind of indeterminate order that gets further organized in a variety of ways later on, and the way the oracle is inundated with divine knowledge from the god Apollo, which shakes her until she produces a prophetic kind of riddle that will further be interpreted in a variety of ways. As Biro tries to revive the importance of the oracular speech as expressing a significant mode of reasoning and truth beyond the *logos*/*mythos* binary that would exile it to the sphere of madness, I try to revive the importance of *chora*'s unusual movement as a significant and unique contribution to the birth of the cosmos beyond the active/passive and intelligible/unintelligible binaries that would deny her all agency and distinction.

45. Luce Irigaray, "Plato's Hystera," in *Speculum of the Other Woman*, trans. Gillian C. Gill (Ithaca: Cornell University Press, 1985), 253.

46. Irigaray, "Plato's Hystera," 301.

47. Irigaray, "Plato's Hystera," 307.

48. Judith Butler, *Bodies that Matter* (New York: Routledge, 1993), 38.

49. Butler, *Bodies that Matter*, 43.

50. Butler, *Bodies that Matter*, 45.

51. Butler, *Bodies that Matter*, 48–49.

52. *Tim.* 52e.

53. *Tim.* 52d.

54. *Tim.* 52e.

55. *Tim.* 43c.

56. *Tim.* 43b.

57. Sara Brill, "Animality and Sexual Difference in the *Timaeus*," in *Plato's Animals*, eds. Jeremy Bell and Michael Naas (Bloomington: Indiana University Press, 2015), 165.

58. Emanuela Bianchi, "Receptacle/Chōra: Figuring the Errant Feminine in Plato's *Timaeus*," *Hypatia* 21, no. 4 (Autumn 2006): 135.

59. Julia Kristeva likens *chôra*'s rhythmic movement to gestural and vocal "play" that produces provisional order and articulation. Julia Kristeva, *Revolution in Poetic Language*, trans. Margaret Waller (New York: Columbia University Press, 1984), 25–27.

60. *Tim.* 42c, 90e.

61. Gregory Vlastos tried to reconcile Plato's derogatory remarks about women with his feminist political program in the *Republic* in his article, "Was Plato a Feminist?" He argues that when Plato disparages women by saying they can't control the impulses of their bodies, lower appetites, or emotions, he is making an observation about the way the common women of Athenian society behaved in his time, not a comment about women's nature, capacity, or what they could become if the best among them were to get proper education in an ideal city. Vlastos thinks if we distinguish Plato's not-so-flattering descriptions of women's cultural situation, from his political ideal in which he grants the best women equal education and ruling privileges alongside the best men, then we will see that Plato's derogatory remarks about women are not inconsistent with (and don't take away from) his feminist political program in the *Republic*. Vlastos even says it is a "triumph of imaginative impartiality" that Plato could separate his everyday feelings about women in his own society from his theory of social justice. Gregory Vlastos, "Was Plato a Feminist?," in *Feminist Interpretations of Plato*, ed. Nancy Tuana (University Park: Pennsylvania State Press, 1994), 23. Elizabeth Spelman, in her "Hairy Cobblers and Philosopher-Queens" gives the brilliant comeback: "Misogyny has always been compatible with having high regard for "exceptional" (and surely for imaginary) women," suggesting that Plato's praiseworthy comments about a few exceptional (or imaginary) women is not enough to make him a feminist. Elizabeth Spelman, "Hairy Cobblers and Philosopher-Queens," in *Feminist Interpretations of Plato*, ed. Nancy Tuana (University Park: Pennsylvania State Press, 1994), 99. Spelman calls into question whether any feminism can really be found in a political philosophy that treats the majority of women, even the majority of women in his ideal city (in the lower craftsman class), as inferior and fit to be ruled.

Bibliography

Bianchi, Emanuela. "Receptacle/Chōra: Figuring the Errant Feminine in Plato's *Timaeus*." *Hypatia* 21, no. 4 (Autumn 2006): 124–46.

Brill, Sara. "Animality and Sexual Difference in the *Timaeus*." In *Plato's Animals*, edited by Jeremy Bell and Michael Naas. Bloomington: Indiana University Press, 2015.

Butler, Judith. *Bodies That Matter*. New York: Routledge, 1993.

Carone, Gabriela Roxana. "Mind and Body in Late Plato." *Archiv fuer Geschichte der Philosophie* 87, no. 3 (2005): 227–69.

De Beauvoir, Simone. *The Second Sex*, translated by H. M. Parshley. New York: Vintage Books, 1989.

Derrida, Jacques. "*Khōra*." In *On the Name*, translated by David Wood. Stanford, CA: Stanford University Press, 1995.

Gadamer, Hans Georg. "Idea and Reality in Plato's Timaeus." In *Dialogue and Dialectic: Eight Hermeneutical Studies on Plato*, translated by P. Christopher Smith. New Haven, CT: Yale University Press, 1980.

Hadot, Pierre. *Philosophy as a Way of Life*, translated by Michael Chase. Oxford, UK: Blackwell Publishers, 1995.

Irigaray, Luce. "Plato's Hystera." In *Speculum of the Other Woman*, translated by Gillian C. Gill. Ithaca, NY: Cornell University Press, 1985.

Johansen, Thomas. "Body, Soul, and Tripartition in Plato's *Timaeus*." *Oxford Studies in Ancient Philosophy* XIX (2000): 87–111.

Kristeva, Julia. *Revolution in Poetic Language*, translated by Margaret Waller. New York: Columbia University Press, 1984.

Nietzsche, Friedrich. "The Problem of Socrates." In *Twilight of the Idols*, translated by Richard Polt. Indianapolis, IN: Hackett, 1997.

Plato. *Plato's Timaeus*, translated by Peter Kalkavage. Newsburyport, MA: Focus Publishing, 2001.

———. *Phaedo* in *Five Dialogues: Euthyphro, Apology, Crito, Meno, Phaedo*, translated by G. M. A. Grube. Indianapolis, IN: Hackett, 1981.

———. *The Republic of Plato*, translated by Allan Bloom. New York: Basic Books, 1968.

Sallis, John. *Chorology: On Beginning in Plato's Timaeus*. Bloomington: Indiana University Press, 1999.

Spelman, Elizabeth. "Woman as Body: Ancient and Contemporary Views." *Feminist Studies* 9, no. 1 (Spring 1982): 109–31.

———. "Hairy Cobblers and Philosopher Queens." In *Feminist Interpretations of Plato*, edited by Nancy Tuana, 87–107. University Park: Pennsylvania State Press, 1994.

Tuana, Nancy (ed.). *Feminist Interpretations of Plato*. University Park: Pennsylvania State University Press, 1994.

Vlastos, Gregory, "Was Plato a Feminist?" In *Feminist Interpretations of Plato*, edited by Nancy Tuana, 11–23. University Park: Pennsylvania State Press, 1994.

Chapter Seven

The Argument of Socrates' Action in *Republic* V

Mary Townsend

Plato composed not one but two separate attempts to solve the conundrum of the woman question: that is, what to do about the role of women in civil society? The most famous, of course, is Socrates' attempt in the *Republic*, where he anoints the women of the ruling class as philosopher-queens, albeit as weaker in some respects than the men. But while Socrates does his best to avoid discussing the woman question at all, his counterpart, the Athenian Stranger of the *Laws*, is forthright about the pressing nature of the problem: The customary practice of leaving women unarranged (ἀκοσμήτως) by law, without public standing and so with no public stake in public well-being, is a serious case of neglect.[1] The Stranger's own solution is relatively moderate, though often ignored by *Republic* commentators; he proposes a partial share in the rulership for women, and some shared education.[2] But while Socrates' solution to the woman question pleases hardly any reader ever, it remains the more vivid and even appealing of the two, perhaps equally in its scope and limitations; and so it tends to be thought of as Plato's answer simply. But the majority of attempts to understand what Socrates in particular is saying about the woman question lift his words out of the fabric of the *Republic*'s conversational back-and-forth, reducing a highly tense moment to an unsatisfying formula of "what Plato said" in general. In doing so, they fall short of a serious attempt to understand the force of Socrates' idiosyncratic plans.

To make matters worse, Socratic irony volatizes our relation to the drama: to what extent do we even know what Socrates is ultimately proposing for women? And while, as Kierkegaard notes, the opposite of what is said is the weakest form of irony, there still remains this problem: the very real possibility that by his strange plans, Socrates might be pointing to serious problems with the attempt to rearrange the position of women in the polis.[3] Because of this, much of the scholarship that takes Socratic drama and Socratic irony seriously tends to consider that instead of suggesting women rule as philosopher-queens, Socrates intends the opposite: to laugh and scorn at any alteration in the customary place of women. But this treats the woman question as separate from the immediately following proposal of philosopher-kings, sinking the women while letting the ironic reversal go lightly on philosophy's own foibles. I propose to show the link in dramatic action between Socrates' proposals for women and for philosophy, and to speak to the dramatic reason for the emphasis on women's relative weakness. Socrates' response to the woman question is much richer and more aporetic than is generally imagined.

One brief note: Another aspect of the woman question takes the form of "what is it?" and this is the more difficult question to ask in good faith. For instance, in reading Irigaray's *Speculum of the Other Woman*, one is struck by her sheer frustration when she addresses Freud's thinking on woman, wherein he attempts to explain that women are, in their nature, a sort of conundrum: that they *are* a question.[4] (Whereas the joke is, they are a conundrum to *him*.) And yet there's an irony that this particular "what is it?" question, more than most, so often takes place via the larger context of the search for perfect justice and the ideal polity. Fortunately, it's precisely this that Plato's work can help us with. As a lover of Plato at heart, to me it seems that to let all the questions of women be called into question for us is a human good. The problem remains, however, that it's a peculiarly difficult question over which to find one's self in real and thorough *aporia*; the search for a thing's thinghood distorts the search for justice, and vice versa. In the hope that the *Republic* can help us with this difficult human task—since after all, the novelty of the philosopher-kings is that they would get to the bottom of both—the inquiry is begun.

The Female Drama

The project of the conversation of Plato's *Republic* is to describe a city in speech, in order to behold perfect justice, without regard for consequences, writ large in its details, thus offering hope for a final end to human miseries. In the midst of a large number of educational provisions, Socrates notes in passing that in their city, women and children will be held in common—dropping that in, as though the details will be easy to arrange.[5] But fortunately, his audience is on to him, and before he can change the subject entirely to the question of the less-than-perfect polities, he's asked for more detail.

Instead of immediately addressing the demand of his audience, however, Socrates insists that the city-building must start again from the beginning: An adequate address to the woman question will require thorough measures. Socrates begins his attempt with three proposals, known by scholars as the Three Waves, due to the waves of laughter Socrates foresees his notions will inevitably provoke in those who hear them. Socrates' First Wave is that women should share in all the pursuits of the men of the guardian class, doing all in common with them. Socrates complicates this by adding that they will also exercise naked together. The Second Wave is much stranger; the guardians will be bred together via the pretext of a lottery, which will be rigged, and subsequent children will be raised by the whole community, with neither parents nor children knowing whose is whose. Finally, still under the guise of answering the woman question, Socrates institutes the civic arrangements he is most famous for, which he fears will provoke not only laughter but death threats as well: the Third Wave announces the rule of philosophers as the final authority in the city, with all the new provisions for their philosophic education in Books V–VII to follow. The kingship of philosophers is his final attempt to describe a city that is most perfectly just, for their rule will guarantee it, and as much as possible, make such a city possible to be.

But again, while many find the comedy of the first two waves to be enough to dismiss the substance of their proposals as undesirable and impossible, the comedy of the Third Wave is neglected.[6] Leo Strauss, for instance, finds no essential reason why the philosopher couldn't rule the city well; rather, it's the attempt to enact perfect justice on women and the family that shows the undesirability of justice without consequences.[7]

But this reading artificially separates the first two waves from the third, and again, softens the irony for the non-female-related of the trio alone.[8] After all, any city that, in the name of philosopher-kings, calmly disposes of everyone over the age of ten to begin anew is not without its architectonic problems.[9]

In contrast to this interpretive separation, consider Socrates' many descriptions of the connections between the parts of this argument. First, before embarking on the trio of proposals in Book V, Socrates pauses a moment to express several caveats and hesitations. Notably, he observes that "perhaps presently it would be right, since the manly [ἀνδρεῖον] drama of the preceding conversation has completely come to an end, to accomplish the womanly [γυναικεῖον] drama anew."[10] Socrates is presenting an analysis of the tenor of the conversation that has come before: the manly drama is what makes up the education of the ruling, "guardian" class in music and gymnastic, where justice is seen as each class of the city and of the soul minding their own business. Yet there is a rightness (ὀρθῶς) to proceed now in a different manner, and this new manner is the manner of the *gynaikeion* drama. Now, *gynaikeion* can imply a variety of things, and many of them involve not properly speaking "right"; often there is a sense of "womanish" or "effeminate" as less-than-lovely qualities, although a more neutral, even benign English translation would reasonably be something like "womanly" or perhaps "ladylike."[11] It is precisely this new womanish sequence, which Socrates notes as part of the same observation, that the questions of his interlocutors have called forth (προκαλῄ).

Later on in Book VI, Socrates presents another analysis of the structural movement at work, contending that the series of arguments that begins with the First Wave and is completed by the newly philosophical version of the guardian's education, is a conversational entity that might not have been spoken of otherwise at all. In fact, he remarks that it would "have slipped past us, as if covered round in a veil," imagining the argument as though it were wearing the clothes of a woman.[12] To think this moment through, consider the ire of the magistrate in *Lysistrata* who remarks, "Me be silent for you, damnable woman, you with a veil around your head?"[13] Here in *Republic* V, the veiledness of the argument proves to be not enough to let it slip by entirely, however, or to keep Socrates from giving it weight. Although Socrates' comparisons of his arguments to womanly things are unexpected, they are consistent. In some sense, therefore, it seems that for Socrates, the whole of the discussion of the next few books, starting from Book V and completed in Book VI, is this womanish drama, and not simply the parts that explicitly deal with women.[14] In his imaginative language, Socrates lumps together the woman question and the rule of philosophy as a single *gynaikeion* argument.

To further explore the parallels Socrates is invoking here, it is worth considering other moments in the Platonic dialogues where Socrates explicitly calls on the notion of "drama." There are two other places where Socrates makes interestingly similar contrasts. In the *Apology*, Socrates ridicules the sort of court defendant who supposes they will suffer something terrible if they receive the death penalty, as though they were otherwise immortal without such a sentence. Such men, Socrates remarks, are no different from women, and such pitiable dramas ought not to be allowed.[15] In the *Theaetetus*, Socrates compares the art of midwifery as favorable to that of the go-between, but reserves a still greater place for his own art, that is nevertheless analogous to the midwife's, namely, his famous midwifery of souls. Socrates' own drama is better or larger on these grounds, despite the remaining difficulty that unlike those who help women give birth, Socrates' dramatics often involve the introduction of false children, that is, false images.[16]

But how to contrast each of these instances of drama? In the lines from the *Apology*, Socrates uses the classical rhetorical trope of calling out ordinary human behavior, namely, fear of death penalties and indeed fear of death, as shamefully other than what men would, heaven forbid, ever find themselves experiencing. In this case, there is no question of Socrates' actions being other than those of perfect manhood; indeed on these grounds, Socrates would be the first and only man to have lived. In the lines from the *Theaetetus*, by contrast, Socrates is approving of the *gynaikeion* variety, but is still aggrandizing his own competing version; here, however, the contrast is not to cast one side as nothing or as unlawful, but to build on the genealogical ground of his midwife mother, Phaenarete, by completing what she began in the direction of soul, not without greater difficulty and danger. It's worth noting, however, that while Socrates claims that his version deals with men, he does not claim that the art itself is the manly sort.

The passage from the *Republic*, however, is the most complex and interesting of this trio of comparisons. Consider: Socrates casts the manly drama as "completely finished" (παντελῶς διαπερανθὲν), but that the womanly drama will be "accomplished anew" (αὖ περαίνειν), echoing his line at 450a that the discussion will have to start over "as if from the beginning" (ὥσπερ ἐξ ἀρχῆς). Now, this analysis of the structure of the *Republic* is slightly specious, even on metaphorical grounds, since Books V–VII retain an interest in warfare, and Books II–IV in musical gracefulness. But notably, whatever can be said about the putative womanish quality of Books V–VII, they do most certainly contain remarkably beautiful images and arguments concerning the task and scope of philosophy and philosophers, some of the most entrancing in Plato's corpus. Unlike in the *Apology* and *Theaetetus*, therefore, Socrates is giving greater weight to the womanly drama than to the manly, and for once the womanly drama must now be brought fully into accomplishment by himself; and the accomplishment involves a discussion of Socrates' own characteristic pursuits.[17]

But beyond the temptation to analogize, what concretely is dramatized by the *gynaikeion* drama in Books V–VII? In a startling moment in Book VI, where Socrates allows himself to consider not just philosophy in the city in speech, but philosophy under all regimes, Socrates calls on the sympathies of his audience in a way that offers them a concrete direction for their feelings toward philosophy. When attempting to explain how souls who otherwise might have taken up philosophy become distracted by other pursuits, Socrates converts philosophy in the abstract into a single human figure by means of an image, raising the problem past error to pathos. Since the real suitors of philosophy have become ensnared elsewhere, philosophy is left alone as though she were an unwed virgin, with all her family dead, and so at the mercy of a multitude of unworthy suitors that she is powerless to rebuff.[18] Now, it's no surprise that Socrates himself has fellow-feeling for the plight of philosophy; it's striking however that his rhetorical strategy in the face of a possibly hostile audience is to raise sympathy for philosophy by assuming a prior, natural sympathy for a maiden in distress, presumably to make it that much easier for his listeners to sympathize over philosophy's plight in turn—again, the opposite strategy from the *Apology* and *Theaetetus*.

It's worth noting that Socrates' image does not turn on some amorphous "feminine" quality, but on the awkward political plight of the citizen-wife, whose desires remain unconsidered and overlooked by the customs that surround her, putting her even in physical danger from the desires of others—later, Socrates even speaks of a philosophy spattered in mud.[19] This draws out a remarkable aspect of philosophy's analogous political difficulty: just as was the case for women in the Greek world at large, whether wife, prostitute, or enslaved, philosophy does not get to pick its lovers under customary arrangements, and is left, dangerously, to be pursued and/or captured by those who neither love it or nor consult its loves. Both women and philosophy, it seems, have a political problem on the structural order, and with this image, Socrates draws out a sympathy for both at once, almost with a sort of chivalry, the better to lay the ground for his proposed revolutions.[20]

The Action of the Argument

But this sort of pathos is only the most obvious kind of dramatic result. "Drama" in the Greek is also more simply an "act" or "deed."[21] What is the action of Socrates' argument, with respect to women?[22] Again, the notion that women would share in all the tasks of the guardians as partners is very far from the early-childhood arrangements requested by his audience; and likewise it is very far from Book IV's "women in common" that seems to imply someone's amorous daydream. No one asked for rule-sharing; it wasn't on anyone's mind. Socrates introduced it out of the blue on his own authority. While Socrates includes separate arrangements for marriage and children as the act of the Second Wave, the practical upshot of the First affects women in their own right: the best of the women will be educated and share in the rule.

While shared education is explicit in the First Wave, we're left to deduce from the final statement that since they will "share in war and all the rest of the guardianship connected with the city," they will also rule.[23] Since rule is the reason for the guardians' education, the deduction seems not unreasonable. Fortunately, later passages make this explicit. At the end of the discussion of the philosophic education, Socrates adds that everything previous will apply to "ruling women" (τὰς ἀρχούσας) as well.[24] The act of Socrates can be stated thus: he has drawn the best of the women out of the dangers of their customarily private state, right into the center of public civic life, and has secured for them rule and education. This is his deed, what his argument accomplishes.

But as it happens, this is precisely what Socrates also does for philosophy. Just as in the case of women, there was no request from the audience for talk about philosophers. Rather, completely on his own authority, Socrates introduces the subject of the rule of philosopher-kings out of nowhere, from his own private considerations. It's this act alone that justifies a new discussion of education and allows for the images of the Cave, Divided Line, and the Good as Sun; Socrates has taken the shape of the argument into his hands in a big way. Likewise, this act allows him in happy result to tailor all the arrangements of the city for philosophy's good. Socrates offers the pick of the best students of either sex, and he imagines that his secret breeding project will perpetuate the traits he desires. The focus of the city is to make sure that the education of the guardians goes off perfectly.[25] Not only does Socrates liken the precariousness of the customary position of women to that of philosophers, his solution is the same: give them the best education, and put them in charge. In short, the action of Socrates' argument with respect to women and to philosophy is the same. Such action is not an analogy that stands outside the text as an alien comparison, alien poetics, but one that Socrates himself alludes to on several crucial occasions—and it's this very action that Socrates calls womanish. As in *Odyssey* XI.437, where the "womanly designs" of Clytemnestra, who ensnared her husband into death, are decried, such womanly scheming speaks to Socrates' cleverness in neatly introducing what was no one's priority but his own.

But, this said, what about the most controversial aspect of Socrates' plans for women, that in all the tasks the guardians do together, the men will be taken as stronger and women as weaker? This is the passage that loses the friendship of many current readers for the *Republic*; on the other hand, for many this aspect of the law seems to void the action into meaninglessness. Seth Benardete says, "that [women] are on the whole weaker than men should entail that in a sex-blind test for admission into the city, most would not pass."[26] Bloom goes further, remarking it is "highly improbable that any women will even be considered for membership in the higher classes."[27] The importance of these quotations is to show just how much is at stake in the First Wave of the *Republic*: not only whether there is some final solution to the woman question in general, but whether women are capable of the highest things—that is, of philosophy. Likewise, this reasoning seems to threaten to spoil the force of Socrates' double action that I've been building; for if women are simply weaker and incapable of philosophy, what can we gain from Socrates' comparison of their political position? And so we have to think through the ramifications of this principle carefully.

Glaucon's Principle of Weakness and Strength

The first, most crucial thing to notice from the drama of the passage is that the principle of men-as-stronger is initially Glaucon's idea. Socrates begins the wave by describing the partnership of men and women as a common hunt, noting how foolish it would be to leave the lady dogs inactive most of the year, as if they were incapacitated by giving birth to puppies; he recommends rather that they do all in common, and share all the hard work.[28] This being good sense to any dog breeder, Glaucon responds, "sure: except that we use the females as weaker, the males as stronger."[29] But Socrates ignores his statement, instead taking Glaucon through a different argument, concluding that men and women will have the same education, which Glaucon is happy enough to accede to (452a, "it's likely, from what you're saying"). He notes that shared naked exercise will raise some eyebrows, but gets a very strong agreement from Glaucon that customs change, and moves on.[30] But then things start to get rough: Socrates gets Glaucon to admit that he thinks women's natures differ from men, and then asks, but then, how on earth can we give the same education to people with different natures? Socrates points out at length that Glaucon has been contradicting himself: "Will you be able to make any defense against yourself, you amazing man?" Glaucon responds with a dignified request for help (453c, "but I ask you, in fact I am asking you, to be the interpreter of this argument"). Socrates shoots back that it will not be easy. It is as though, he says, they have fallen into a sea, and only a lucky rescue, perhaps from a passing dolphin, will save them now.[31]

It's not usually recognized that this is one of the most lively and heated arguments of the book. The comic interlude of naked exercise tends to garner the most attention, but the plot or dramatic structure of the section is the shaming of Glaucon, which he receives in this moment of *aporia* roughly at the center of the First Wave, and its subsequent resolution. Glaucon is willing to concede the same education for men and women, but not men's similarity in nature to women, and Socrates makes him pay for it.

Socrates points out that for any real discussion about the precise difference of men and women, eristic, or contentiousness, is to be avoided and dialectic sought—and then he reintroduces Glaucon's principle of the superior strength of men. He takes it far, claiming that in every pursuit men surpass that of women, giving as his examples of men's superiority, weaving and baking. Glaucon happily agrees.[32] Two points: Socrates' examples are obviously absurd; he picked two things women customarily excel at and thus would be activities in which men would be quite out of practice, and he leaves out the most absurdly obvious counterexample, namely, childbirth, at which it is impossible that men should excel.[33] The contentiousness of his examples shows Socrates' awareness of the weakness of Glaucon's principle of weakness. But once this initial caveat to common partnership is granted, Glaucon is at peace, offering the magnanimous statement that of course many women exceed many men at many things—though on the whole, it is as Socrates says.[34] After this peak of the argument, Glaucon is happy to go along with Socrates, offering women full participation in all the duties of the male guardians, agreeing that the best women and men are obviously best for the city, and even conceding that some women have souls that are philosophic.[35] And so, after all, Socrates manages to get his way, the very thing he attempted to set up in his opening statement: all education in common and a chance at some share in the rule between men and women. Rather than destroying the action of the wave, Socrates' adoption of Glaucon's principle of weakness is precisely what makes the action possible: by means of this concession, rule and education for the best of the women remains on the books. This is a *gynaikeion* act of scheming indeed.

It's important to notice that Glaucon is not upset at the threat of women's rule on behalf of such a measure's threat to the common good. Others, such as Adeimantus and Polemarchus, would be worried about what women as rulers would do to traditional arrangements for children; it's their concern that prompts Socrates to return to the question of marriage and child rearing in the first place.[36] Rather, Glaucon's own clannish wish is to reserve the highest place for his *genos*, from natural pride of place—a clannishness, I will note, that is not limited to either sex in particular. But Glaucon's strongest concern is this caveat, that men still basically win out in the end; granted this, he is content.[37] Glaucon's principle *is* the dolphin rescue, the one Socrates insisted was their only hope. Rather than showing Socrates' secret commitment to leaving women out of the realms of the best, such a rescue shows Socrates' last-ditch attempt to get the women in, even at a cost. Fortunately, this desired rescue is described not as final but as aporetic (ἄπορον σωτηρίαν, 453d); and despite Glaucon's relieved certainty, the audience is under no obligation to be so easily soothed. Yet Socrates' careful drawing out of Glaucon's hesitations is a display of an important barrier to a public place for women: *thumos*, the spirited part of the soul, already up in arms with its fellow male rivals, is even more irritated when a whole other swathe of competitors arrives on the scene. Socrates remarks in Book VI that he hesitated to raise the subject of the Three Waves, because the topics are invidious (ἐπιφθονός): that is, likely to cause jealousy. Such jealousy is not the familiar sort of jealousy *over* a woman, as in the case of Helen of Troy, or *from* a woman, as in the case of poor Hera at Zeus's loves, but jealousy, I would suggest, at women's possession of rule, and indeed, of philosophy, in their own right.[38]

Final Thoughts

The dramatic link between Socrates' proposals for women and philosophy is the necessary framework to understand the irony involved in Socrates' attempt to ameliorate the problems of the customary position of each. But there's much left unresolved, and given that the problem and the solution are the same, we might ask if there's a shared tragic flaw within the shared solution. One possibility: why *does* Socrates introduce philosophy as ruler into the argument? And why is he willing to raze the fabric of ordinary human life, family attachments, marriages, and so on, hunting down all the female students to be found, in order to give philosophy all the good things that public political pride of place can offer? Perhaps Socrates is trying to dramatize himself, indulging in his private wish to save philosophy from its customary dishonor by giving it the highest honors—while also showing us, by the comedy that ensues from his action, that such a city is inevitably troubling, despite our perennial wish to hand over the human problem of justice to the wise.[39]

Yet Socrates' willingness to similarly attempt to rescue the best of the women, while announcing this action as womanly, rings as an invitation to the contemplation of philosopher-queens and philosophy as womanly, beyond the specific peculiarities of the city in speech. As in Socrates' final word on the best city at 592b, said to be a pattern laid up in heaven for us to follow in our own soul if we can, readers, no matter what regime they inhabit, are invited to consider the study of philosophy by individual women themselves as part of that pattern, no matter how repugnant the idea remains within any given broader or existing regime.

As for the harder what-is-it? question, the way in which men and women partake in the forms of same and difference among each other, the dolphin rescue that saved the evening's argument for women philosophizing ultimately does not lay to rest our doubts about female human nature at all, and in fact inflames them. It's fitting that such a rescue be described as aporetic, for it leaves us without an immediate way forward, only a sense that what has been said is clearly insufficient. Indeed, all readers must make a compromise; men, that women are present among the city's best rulers and are excellent learners at all; and women, that their presence required a certain unflattering weakness to be temporarily conceded. That no sex rests easy with the text ought to give us pause.[40] Although the woman question arose because of the wish for ideal arrangements within the city, it ends with us wondering what this question would look like outside of the context of the ideal state, and outside of the desire to rule and to be preeminent. It would also be further complicated by the possession of private property, which Socrates temporarily shelves by having his male and female guardians remain without, focusing his attention only on this propertyless class. Among Plato's various attempts to write a dramatic solution, Socrates' version is, as we ought to have expected, the most universally infuriating and, therefore, the one most capable of stinging its hearers into further philosophical action.[41]

But for now, if we are persuaded that the invitation to dialectic is written into the structure of his argument, Socrates' lawgiving achievement and the sort of scurrilous rhetoric that was required to get it ratified does offer us a way of moving past a particularly frustrating either/or: the very common felt need to either attempt to forgive Plato his sins with regard to women in order to continue to admire his philosophy, or needing to indict him in the last analysis.[42] For instead of offering us a straightforward account of the woman question, with all his foibles as a thinker immediately on the line, Plato offers us the sight of a very difficult yet also humorous wrangle on the subject, imagined between some of the all-too-human men in his life—his occasionally feckless elder brother Glaucon, and the idol of his youth, Socrates.[43] In this way, we're invited to see what it would take to convince a specimen of Athenian youthful manhood that women be given *some* public place in the polity and even, in the end, philosophy itself. And, so, the reader is enabled to witness the precise nature of what such success is built on, not to mention its human cost.

Beauvoir observes in *The Second Sex* the inevitable unease that human men often feel when faced with a direct confrontation with the capacity of women for excellence, and the reactionary tendency this unease ignites, that can push them into even more extreme views.[44] Socrates' *gunaikeion* actions, by contrast, avoid the full brunt of such ire, since while some readers of the *Republic* can comfortably picture themselves the stronger generally, others might yet hope to triumph in individual tests of intellectual strength that Socrates promises will reveal the real mettle of his guardians.[45] That Plato shows his awareness of this specific difficulty means for us that instead of needing to consider Glaucon's attachment to the principle of relative weakness as something Socrates, let alone Plato, necessarily agreed with, we can engage Plato's help in uncovering some of the flaws human beings inevitably display when they approach the woman question.

After their initial argument on women's education and nature capsizes, Socrates points out to Glaucon they've been pursuing the argument not only too contentiously but too manfully (454b): Plato is actively dramatizing the problems of manliness for the benefit of his readers in this very moment, and he is alive to the notion that the reasoning capacity itself can be swayed and even distorted by one's attachment to their sex. It should not be argued, therefore, that *Republic* V of itself, at least, is evidence that Plato saw women as second-class citizens. Given that we are bound to consider philosophy and philosophers as one of the central concerns of the work, once we've seen the link that Socrates makes between such concerns and the political place of women themselves, it's harder to consider the woman question as *less* central to the work. Therefore, it should be considered no less relevant to our interpreting activities for the whole.

But Socrates' actions are only one step in the project of seeing Plato's thought on the woman question as a whole; we have to consider not merely Socrates but also his lawgiving counterpart the Athenian Stranger, as well as the Eleatic Stranger and the infamous astronomer Timaeus, each of whom have their own particular characteristic philosophic attachments, and their own view of justice. Here we can only deal with Socrates, but there remains much future work to be done to realize the fundamentally idiosyncratic philosophizing of each of Plato's fictionalized characters. After all, Plato's Socrates is just that: Plato's own version of the eminently rewritable historical original, and each further Platonic character deserves no less care and attention than we give to Socrates, so that we can draw out the philosophical peculiarities, successes, and failures of each. But while Socrates' pedagogical style is not perhaps always the most successful, as an interlocutor he does offer the solid benefits of being absolutely committed to the cause of philosophy, willingness to think about the woman question directly and in a structurally political light, and the awareness and honesty peculiar to him about his own shortcomings with respect to wisdom. When Socrates lapses into actual anger, he does so on behalf of philosophy, rather than, say, the male sex (536c).[46]

Now, Socrates himself is no woman, which for him is inescapable; and yet, as Plato writes him, he is something other than a man's man. While in the *Republic* he makes a note of the *gunaikeion* qualities of his deeds, in the *Gorgias* it's his arguments that strike him as potentially the sort of thing that old women might say.[47] Now, it's often argued that Socrates' adoption of such womanish qualities is a kind of con-artist act, stealing away the desirable aspects of customary female habits of soul in order that male philosophers may be rather better at their task, and help to sustain their own hegemony.[48] But in the *Republic*, at least, we see this adoption of womanish qualities enacted not at the service of rounding out the souls of young men alone, but in order to recommend a regime much to the benefit of young women, one in which the hegemony is shared. Socrates' valorization of the guardians as a limited class invites all readers to consider whether they would be able to make the cut, and potentially, to desire to deserve it. In the *Republic* at least, Socrates argues that human women should share in the rule, not simply that rulership should be tempered by the female in the abstract, and he does so not without a certain courage in the face of anticipated contention.[49] (Oddly enough, that philosophy should see itself as female in some way is far less contentious than that women themselves should study it.) In this way, Socrates, who in his relation to philosophy attempts to employ womanish words and deeds despite his manly limitations, is able to argue not only that philosophy will be handed over to women, but in a sense, *back* to them as well. Although these troubled questions are not capable of complete resolution, perhaps one of the reasons why the paired subjects of women and philosophy spring to Socrates' mind as one with such force, when ideal conditions become available, is bound up in some otherwise lost prior intention to do just this, to hand something once given to him back.[50]

Now, while in the *Theaetetus*, a dialogue that takes place close to the time of Socrates' trial and thus in active anticipation of the possibility of his death, Socrates is very definite that his peculiar *elenchus*—his skill at bringing one into the consciousness of one's ignorance—is practiced on men and not women, in the *Apology*, by contrast, one of the pleasures he anticipates in the afterlife is that of examining both men and women.[51] In the *Republic*, where Socrates takes great pleasure in imagining philosophy as happily free from the need of his peculiar art, it makes a certain sense that his ideal city would prefigure the sort of Isle of the Blessed at which he would prefer one day to arrive.[52] In this way, Socrates' plans for women, for philosophy, and for himself are all attempts to transcend his own human one-sidedness, and as such form a legitimate part of his vision of the Good.[53]

Notes

1. *Laws* 780e–781d, and especially 781a: "Through a slackness towards [the female sex] many things have flown past you, which might have been better by far than things are at present, if they had fallen in with laws." All translations are my own.

2. For commentators that do make this comparison, see Elena Duvergès Blair, *Plato's Dialectic on Woman* (London: Routledge, 2012), 117–18, 151–86; Michael Kochin, *Gender and Rhetoric in Plato's Thought* (Cambridge, UK: Cambridge University Press, 2002), 87–111; and also Adela Adam, *Plato: Moral and Political Ideals* (Cambridge, UK: Cambridge University Press, 1913), 124–42.

3. Søren Kierkegaard calls the opposite of what is said "finite" irony (Søren Kierkegaard, *The Concept of Irony with Continual Reference to Socrates*, in *Kierkegaard's Writings*, trans. Howard V. Hong and Edna H. Hong, vol. 2 [Princeton: Princeton University Press, 1989], 248), while claiming that Socrates' irony, by contrast, is infinite (127).

4. Luce Irigaray, *Speculum of the Other Woman*, trans. Gillian C. Gill (Ithaca: Cornell University Press, 1985), 13–17.

5. 424a.

6. Bloom's account is not the highest regarded among those scholars influenced by Strauss, but is perhaps one of the most read, given that it accompanies his still popular translation; and he is quite explicit about the comedy of the First Wave and its dismissive nature (Allan Bloom, "Interpretive Essay," in *The* Republic *of Plato*, trans. Allan Bloom (New York: Basic Books, 1968), 381–84). Strauss's contribution to taking the Greeks on their own terms is the

more intelligible in the light of Strauss's history as Heidegger's student, and as one who took the problem of tyranny seriously; see Richard Velkey, *Heidegger, Strauss and the Premises of Philosophy: On Original Forgetting*. Chicago: University of Chicago Press, 2014.

7. Strauss remarks: "The just city is against nature because the equality of the sexes and absolute communism is against nature" ("On Plato's *Republic*" in *The City and Man* [Chicago: Rand McNally, 1964], 127).

8. Notably, Stanley Rosen argues that philosophy is satirized here too; yet for him, the satire of women's limitations is more just and all encompassing, whereas only one aspect of philosophy is justly on the chopping block, its mathematical, quasi-analytic side (*Plato's* Republic: A *Study* [New Haven: Yale University Press, 2005], 178, 229).

9. 451c. See Stanley Rosen, "Plato, Strauss, and Political Philosophy: An Interview with Stanley Rosen," *Diotima* II, no. 1 (Spring 2001).

10. 451c. Some readers have heard here a reference to the mimes of Sophron, which were divided, most likely by the author himself, into males and female "mimes" (μίμοι). These mimes were short, comedic, and occasionally lewd prose dialogues depicting ordinary life in Sophron's Sicily. The temptation to see a reference here is strengthened by the tradition of Plato's admiration for Sophron's writings, first referenced by Duris (ca. 340–260 BCE) and then taken up by Diogenes Laertius (3.18). The problem is that although both wrote prose dialogues and so in one sense in the same mimetic genre, as Aristotle briefly remarks in the *Poetics* (I.1447b10), so little remains of the *content* of Sophron's mimes, it's not really possible to speculate much further on what reflections on the specifics of Plato's dramatics might entail (although see fragments 4a and 4b on a women's festival). Hordern points out that simple mimetic performances were a staple of Greek popular culture (J. H. Hordern, *Sophron's Mimes: Text, Translation, and Commentary* [Oxford: Oxford University Press, 2004], 7), and posits that the *Republic* reference may be to the usual sorts of performances of the magodists, who would take both males and female roles, similar to maskers or mummers, acting out simple visual jokes like stealing fruit or burlesquing a foreigner (Hordern, 8). Another possibility is Socrates may simply be referencing the division of male and female choruses, as in Aristophanes' *Thesmophoriazusae* 151–54 (see Rolando Ferri, Review of *Sophron's Mimes: Text, Translation, and Commentary* for *Bryn Mawr Classical Review* [Oxford: Oxford University Press], August 2, 2005, accessed August 20, 2021, and Hordern, 26). In any case, it seems that the practice of dividing up dramatic actions, characters, or texts into portions dubbed manly or womanly, male or female, is a loose precedent, ripe for Socratic poetical innovation. For Socrates as the author of such innovations in the *Republic* in contrast to the sort he criticizes, see Jill Frank, *Poetic Justice: Rereading Plato's* "Republic" (Chicago: Chicago University Press, 2018), 31.

11. In the *Republic*, for the negative usage of *gunaikeion* there is the infamous, somehow womanly stripping of the bodies (469d), and for the good or neutral, the womanly task of woolwork in *Alcibiades I*, 1126e.

12. 503a, παρακαλυπτομένου; Liddell-Scott (s.v. παρακαλύπτω, 1996) note that for Plato, this verb in the middle voice implies the covering of the face. For women's use of a *himation* to veil the face, see Mireille M. Lee, *Body, Dress, and Identity in Ancient Greece* (Cambridge: Cambridge University Press, 2015), 116, 154ff. See also *Phaedrus* 237a, where Socrates speaks of covering his own face (ἐνκαλυψάμενος).

13. *Lys*. 530, translation my own.

14. It's worth noting that for those who read this as a reference to Sophron, this would entail that *both* the male and female drama are comedic, and not merely the female, in the sense that Sophron is the "father of comedy" (*Theaetetus* 152dff) in both the male and female modes. Book V–VII is no more a comedy of errors than Books II–IV.

15. *Ap*. 35b, "οὗτοι γυναικῶν οὐδὲν διφέρουσιν."

16. *Tht*. 150a: literally, the midwives' drama is "shorter" or perhaps "more shrimpy," "ἔλαττον δὲ τοῦ έμοῦ δράματος"; ἔλαττον is from ἐλαχύς, but used as the comparative of σμικρός.

17. Hordern notes that Sophron's womanly mimes contained male roles as supporting characters, and female supporting characters for the manly ones (*Sophron's Mimes*, 4); Socrates' innovation is to present this passage of his argument as womanly, where nevertheless a partnership between male and female is imagined.

18. 495c.

19. 536c.

20. Irigaray, by contrast, of course, finds in the *Republic*'s treatment of women the beginning and the end of Western metaphysics. But the *Republic* itself is a conscious attempt to show the appeal and the flaws of a very specific aspect of philosophizing; while psychoanalysis is a helpful and attractive way of thinking about the limits of Socrates' vision, working with Plato's own poetics provides much that is of interest as well.

21. See Aristotle, *Poetics* 1448a29. Recently, Jill Frank has argued that in the *Republic* Plato practices "representational" mimesis, which helps "bring to appearance what is not visible to the seeing eye" (*Poetic Justice*, 37). This difficulty of sight seems to be at work in the way that Socrates' actions are often initially invisible or hard to see. Socrates narrates to us the story, as though he were making everything he said or did easy to see, but often the story or plot of any given dialogue only becomes visible after the readers allows themselves to retell or reframe the narrative arc of the whole. For more on Socrates as self-narrator, see Anne-Marie Schultz, *Plato's Socrates as Narrator: A Philosophical Muse* (Lanham: Lexington Press, 2013).

22. For the importance of the action of the argument to Plato, see Seth Benardete, *Encounters and Reflections*, Ronna Burger, ed. (Chicago: University of Chicago Press, 2010), 124–28.

23. 457a.

24. This inclusion is often overlooked, but Socrates can't be more explicit: "'And ruling women (τὰς ἀρχούσας), too, Glaucon,' I said. 'Don't suppose that what I have said applies any more to men than to women, all those who are born among them with sufficient natures'" (540c). See also 543a. Whatever the final status of the city in speech, whether it itself is possible and under what conditions, the law for women that is promulgated is their rule and education in philosophy.

25. Strauss, 125, and Bloom, 468.

26. Bloom, 383.

27. Seth Benardete, *Socrates' Second Sailing: On Plato's* Republic (Chicago: University of Chicago Press, 1989), 113.

28. 451d.

29. 451e.

30. 452e, "παντάπασι μέν οὖν," "assuredly so."

31. 453c.

32. 455d, "πάνυ γε," "by all means."

33. Many readers notice this oddity; I would add that since Socrates refers to women's ability to bear at 454e, the suggestion stands as absurd even within the logic of this section.

34. 455d.

35. 456e.

36. 449b. See Carl Page, "The Truth about Lies in Plato's *Republic*," *Ancient Philosophy* 11, no. 1 (1991): 26.

37. Worth noting in connection with this impulse is Jacob Howland's argument that Glaucon fought for the cause of the Thirty Tyrants in *Glaucon's Fate* (Philadelphia, PA: Paul Dry Books, 2018).

38. 503a. I will note that the possibility of onlookers' laughter at common naked exercise doesn't alter Socrates' action either: He raises it initially as a problem, quickly obtains Glaucon's firm support that it won't be troublesome and anyway we should not regard it as such. And as a last word he offers specific measures that he insists will solve it; the female guardians will be covered with robes of virtue. These measures might still be problematic, and offer a clue to the whole, but they don't change the action, nor are they the substance of the action. For more, see Mary Townsend, *The Woman Question in Plato's* Republic (Lanham: Lexington Books, 2017), 89–104, 137–49.

39. For more on the flaws of the philosopher-king and its relation to the woman question, as well as the distinction between Socratic philosophizing and the philosophy Socrates describes in the *Republic*, see Townsend, 153–71,

and Frank, 141–53; my view is also indebted to Stanley Rosen's work in *Plato's* Republic: A *Study*. New Haven: Yale University Press, 2005.

40. Natalie Bluestone Harris recounts the remarkable history of male scholars who attempt to reinterpret this portion of the text or even rewrite it, in order to cut women out of Socrates' plans (*Women and the Ideal Society: Plato's* Republic *and Modern Myths of Gender* [Amherst: University of Massachusetts Press, 1987]). Nor has the text fared much better among writers in the feminist tradition, since the question of whether Plato can be said to be a feminist is so quickly mooted (see Elizabeth V. Spelman, "Hairy Cobblers and Philosopher-Queens," in *Feminist Interpretations of Plato*, Nancy Tuana, ed. (Philadelphia: University of Pennsylvania Press, 1994), 86–107. The text is designed to raise the ire of *any* reader.

41. For more consideration of the Athenian Stranger's moderate and at times even soporific strategies, see Townsend, 9–10, 110–30.

42. For instance, one common response to *Republic* V would be to note that Plato's preference in general for soul over body opens up room for female philosophizing over and above questions of bodily strength, since the soul is genderless, and has a practically positive effect (see Crystal Addey, "Plato's Women Readers," in *Brill's Companion to the Reception of Plato in Antiquity*, Harold Tarrant, Danielle A. Layne, Dirk Baltzly, and François Renaud, eds. (Leiden-Boston: Brill, 2018), 417. But, on the other hand, bodies are of human importance, in general, and bodies also remain important to the status of the guardians in the *Republic* as a whole. Socrates speaks of the body as helper to philosophy at 498b, and remarks that the guardians are better off if their body matches their soul at 494b; at the end of the *Republic*, in the Myth of Er (520b), he describes souls choosing a different sort of gendered body than the kind they had before, the better to prosecute their aims in the next life.

43. For an intriguing argument that tries to uncover Glaucon's personal history, including the troubling influence Critias may have had on him, see Howland.

44. Beauvoir, 11–14.

45. See for instance 413d, 537d, 543a. It seems crucial that Socrates' reminder that women too will participate in the philosophical and governing roles of the guardian class comes at the end of his long description of the various tests the guardians will receive at each age.

46. Yancey and Schultz's argument earlier in this volume that Socrates in the *Phaedo* is not engaging in a dualistic, immediate abandonment of the body in favor of the soul, but that he recommends a life that strives to be an intermediary on the way to death, lends support to this sense of Socrates as an interlocutor offering peculiar benefits to the reader.

47. *Gorgias*, 527c.

48. Another frequent variation is that the presence of women in *Republic* V is a sign of the needed yet concealed *eros* that true philosophy possesses, while

women remain but the impotent model for male activity, the difference being whether they see it as a negative or positive development; see Bloom, 384; Rosen, *Plato's* Republic, 167; Benardete, *Socrates' Second Sailing*, 114; David Halperin, "Why Is Diotima a Woman?," in *100 Years of Homosexuality: And Other Essays on Greek Love*, 118–211 (Oxford: Routledge, 2010), 118–211; Page DuBois, "The Platonic Appropriation of Reproduction" in *Feminist Interpretations of Plato*, Nancy Tuana ed. (Philadelphia: University of Pennsylvania Press, 1994), 67–85; and Arlene Saxonhouse, "The Philosopher and the Female in the Political Thought of Plato," in *Feminist Interpretations of Plato*, 139–55. My argument, by contrast, begins by identifying the similarity in political position, rather than internal quality of soul; and acknowledges that a womanly act brings not the ideal feminine but women themselves into the official study of philosophy.

49. Crucially, when Socrates lapses into contentiousness himself, it's on behalf of philosophy, not on behalf of men (536c).

50. The notion that Diotima, whom Socrates claims to learn from, is based on a historical figure known to the historical Socrates (as *well* as Aspasia) makes this speculation the more plausible; see Debra Nails, "Bad Luck to Take a Woman Aboard," in *Second Sailing: Alternative Perspectives on Plato*, Debra Nails and Harold Tarrant eds. (Helsinki: Societas Scientiarum Fennica, 2005), 73–90. As Crystal Addey argues, even Plato's Diotima provides a direct model for women in antiquity to put into context their own philosophizing ("Plato's Women Readers").

51. *Theaetetus* 310c, *Apology* 41c.

52. If, as Eva Brann argues, the *Republic*'s ring structure can be seen as analogous to Odysseus' journey to the underworld and back, then Book V, standing as it does in the center of the work and so the journey, could indeed partake of an afterworld sensibility ("The Music of the Republic in *The Music of the Republic: Essays on Socrates' Conversations and Plato's Writings* (Philadelphia: Paul Dry Books, 2004), 108–245.

53. As Ramelli points out later in this collection, certain Christian Platonists saw in individual humans and even or especially in Christ a humanity that transcended the one-sidedness of gender. She quotes Eriugena: "If God's *Logos* took up humanity, it took up not a part of it—which would be nothing—but all of it, together." In this way, Socrates' own reaching out toward a humanity that embraces both male and female is the authentic progenitor of Christian-Platonic theology.

Bibliography

Addey, Crystal. "Plato's Women Readers." In *Brill's Companion to the Reception of Plato in Antiquity*, edited by Harold Tarrant, Danielle A. Layne, Dirk

Baltzly, and François Renaud, 411–32. Leiden, the Netherlands, and Boston, MA: Brill, 2018.

Berg, Stephen. "The 'Woman Drama' of *Republic* Book V." In *Nature, Woman and the Art of Politics*, edited by Eduardo A. Velásquez, 53–72. Lanham, MD: Rowman & Littlefield, 2000.

Blair, Elena Duvergès. *Plato's Dialectic on Woman*. London: Routledge, 2012.

Bloom, Allan. "Interpretive Essay." In *The* Republic *of Plato*, translated by Allan Bloom. New York: Basic Books, 1968.

Benardete, Seth. *Socrates' Second Sailing: On Plato's* Republic. Chicago, IL: University of Chicago Press, 1989.

Benardete, Seth. *Encounters and Reflections*, edited by Ronna Burger. Chicago, IL: University of Chicago Press, 2010.

Brann, Eva. *The Music of the Republic: Essays on Socrates' Conversations and Plato's Writings*. Philadelphia, PA: Paul Dry Books, 2004.

de Beauvoir, Simone. *The Second Sex*, translated by Constance Borde, and Sheila Malovany-Chevallier. New York: Alfred Knopf, 2010.

Frank, Jill. *Poetic Justice: Rereading Plato's* "Republic." Chicago, IL: Chicago University Press, 2018.

Dubois, Page. "The Platonic Appropriation of Reproduction." In *Feminist Interpretations of Plato*, edited by Nancy Tuana, 67–85. Philadelphia: University of Pennsylvania Press, 1994.

Dubois, Page. *Sowing the Body: Psychoanalysis and Ancient Representationsof Women*. Chicago, IL: University of Chicago Press, 1988.

Ferri, Rolando. Review of *Sophron's Mimes: Text, Translation, and Commentary* for *Bryn Mawr Classical Review*, August 2, 2005.

Bluestone, Natalie Harris. *Women and the Ideal Society: Plato's Republic and Modern Myths of Gender*. Amherst: University of Massachusetts Press, 1987.

Halperin, David. "Why Is Diotima a Woman?" In *100 Years of Homosexuality. And Other Essays on Greek Love*, 118–211. Oxford, UK: Routledge, 2010.

Howland, Jacob. *Glaucon's Fate*. Philadelphia, PA: Paul Dry Books, 2018.

Hordern, J. H. *Sophron's Mimes: Text, Translation, and Commentary*. Oxford, UK: Oxford University Press, 2004.

Irigaray, Luce. *Speculum of the Other Woman*, translated by Gillian C. Gill. Ithaca, NY: Cornell University Press, 1985.

Kierkegaard, Søren. *The Concept of Irony with Continual Reference to Socrates*. In *Kierkegaard's Writings*, translated and edited by Howard V. Hong and Edna H. Hong, vol. 2. Princeton, NJ: Princeton University Press, 1989.

Kochin, Michael. *Gender and Rhetoric in Plato's Thought*. Cambridge, UK: Cambridge University Press, 2002.

Lee, Mireille M. *Body, Dress, and Identity in Ancient Greece*. Cambridge, UK: Cambridge University Press, 2015.

Nails, Debra. "Bad Luck to Take a Woman Aboard." In *Second Sailing: Alternative Perspectives on Plato*, edited by Debra Nails and Harold Tarrant, 73–90. Helsinki, Finland: Societas Scientiarum Fennica, 2005.

Nichols, Mary. *Socrates and the Political Community: An Ancient Debate*. New York: State University of New York Press, 1987.

Page, Carl. "The Truth about Lies in Plato's *Republic*." *Ancient Philosophy* 11, no. 1 (1991): 1–33.

Plato. *Platonis Opera*. Edited by John Burnet. 5 vols. Oxford, UK: Clarendon Press, 1963.

———. *Platonis Republicam*. Edited by S. R. Slings. Oxford: Oxford University Press, 2003.

______. *Plato's Republic*, translated by Raymond Larson. Hoboken, NJ: Wiley-Blackwell, 1979.

———. *Plato's* Republic I, translated by Paul Shorey. Cambridge, MA: Harvard University Press, 2003.

Rosen, Stanley. *Plato's* Republic: *A Study*. New Haven, CT: Yale University Press, 2005.

Saxonhouse, Arlene. "The Philosopher and the Female in the Political Thought of Plato." In *Feminist Interpretations of Plato*, edited by Nancy Tuana, 67–85. Philadelphia: University of Pennsylvania Press, 1994.

Schultz, Anne-Marie. *Plato's Socrates as Narrator: A Philosophical Muse*. Lanham, MD: Lexington Press, 2013.

Spelman, Elizabeth V. "Hairy Cobblers and Philosopher-Queens." In *Feminist Interpretations of Plato*, edited by Nancy Tuana, 86–107. Philadelphia: University of Pennsylvania Press, 1994.

Strauss, Leo. "On Plato's *Republic*." In *The City and Man*, 50–138. Chicago, IL: Rand McNally, 1964.

Townsend, Mary. *The Woman Question in Plato's* Republic. Lanham, MD: Lexington Books, 2017.

Velkley, Richard. *Heidegger, Strauss and the Premises of Philosophy: On Original Forgetting*. Chicago, IL: University of Chicago Press, 2014.

Part Three

Late Antique Destabilizations

Chapter Eight

Divine Mothers

Plotinus' Erotic Productive Causes

DANIELLE A. LAYNE

Heavenly, smiling Aphrodite, praised in many hymns,
Sea-born, revered goddess of generation, you like the night-long revel,
And you couple lovers at night, O scheming mother of Necessity.
Everything comes from you; you have yoked the world and you
control all three realms.
You give birth to all, to everything in heaven, upon fruitful earth,
And in the depths of the sea, O venerable companion of Bacchos.
You delight in festivities, O bride-like mother of the Erotes,
O persuasion whose joy is in the bed of love, secretive giver of grace,
Visible and invisible, lovely-tressed daughter of a noble father.

—*Orphic Hymn to Aphrodite* (trans. Apostolos N. Athanassakis)

This invisible cannot be seized or understood. And this is probably the reason why it has been excluded from a culture that favours a rather inquisitive rationalism and naturalism and that has retained of touch above all the means of grasping and appropriating. But it does not correspond to the touch that constitutes the most intimate core of ourselves and is concerned with the god Eros, and our erotic life.

—Luce Irigaray, "Perhaps Cultivating Touch Can Still Save Us"

The Problem: Irigaray and Plotinus' Material Mother

In *Speculum of the Other Woman*, Luce Irigaray infamously targets Plotinus as a prime example of the Western tradition's consistent degradation of the feminine as that which is a "bastard image" of the masculine, a kind of fun-house mirror in which masculine prerogative can see itself as superior. She is a mere material receptacle wherein, without her contrary, she is, as if, nothing. Undeniably, "Une Mère de Glace," the title for Irigaray's chapter devoted to verbatim extracts of Plotinus' *Ennead* III 6, spotlights an interesting double entendre wherein "mère" is both "mother" but also "mer" or "sea," while "glace" can be both "mirror" or "ice."[1] In other words, Irigaray attempts to capitalize on the trope that "mother," the prototypical image of the feminine, is cold, like the sea, reflecting nothing but a refracted image of essential being, that is, the warmth of masculine reality over and against the icy feminine imaginary. In this binary, matter/mother is deemed speculum, refractor, and surface in opposition to the demiurgic father who is reality, intellect, and principle. While he imposes his order onto her, she is charged with reproducing reality but, ultimately, she is condemned to fail. In her role as material mother, she becomes the errant cause of images and illusions that tempt *man*kind into "the sea of despair," far from the loving embrace of the Good or One. Clearly, Irigaray seems to concentrate her attention on Plotinus' characterization of Plato's receptacle from the *Timaeus*, where Plotinus writes:

> "The things which enter and leave are imitations of Beings"[2] and images going into shapeless image, and because of matter's shapelessness they appear to be seen acting on it, though they do nothing . . . Since [matter] is indeed weak and a falsity and falling into falsity, as in a dream or water or a mirror, of necessity it leaves matter unaffected.[3]

Irigaray's "Une Mere de Glace" concentrates on passages like this where Plotinus vehemently insists that the material maternal receptacle is not even an errant cause.[4] She is impotent in herself. She is not a cause at all. As Plotinus emphasizes, she is like a wax tablet, impressed by something other but not truly affected. As receptacle, she is simply there, like a stone warmed by the power of the sun, a line unaffected by color.[5] Again, she is a mirror unchanged by what she reflects because if she were not this placid surface, she would not be the "all-receiver."[6] If she had her own qualities, they would obstruct the perfect reproduction of Being. She must be receptacle and *nurse* of becoming but, in herself, nothing concrete. She is an uncanny surface or seat without agency or substance.[7] Explicitly associating matter with the mother of Eros in Plato's *Symposium*, Poverty, Plotinus argues,

> [I]f a semblance is made in another, that other must exist and provide a seat for what does not come to it, whereas for its part it makes a violent attempt to seize it by its presence, audacity and a kind of begging and poverty, and is deceived by its failure to seize it so that its poverty may remain and it may forever beg. For since [matter] is established as something grasping, [Diotima's] myth makes it into a beggar in revealing its nature as bereft of goodness.[8]

In short, *she* has no share in the good, *she* is pure insatiable need, and even in her coupling with the demiurgic father, here associated with Diotima's Plenty,[9] she has done nothing, has contributed nothing. She is always a cold surface on which to be inscribed, mere inscriptional space for the phallic signifying act. In one of his most damning statements on the nature of the material receptacle, Plotinus speaks of the incongruence between the analogy of motherhood and the impotence of matter, emptying his feminine principle further.

> And so "receptacle" and "nurse" are more appropriate names for it, but "mother" is applied more loosely, for matter does not give birth to anything. But those people seem to call it "mother" who think that she only receives and contributes nothing to the formation of her offspring, since all that is body in the child is formed from the food. But if the mother does contribute something to her offspring, it is not in respect of matter but of form [to which she may] also [be likened], since only the form is productive while the matter is barren.[10]

In short, only masculine form is productive as the material mother is inversely emptied of all fecundity. A bit further, Plotinus appeals to mystic rites concerning the god Hermes.

> Hence, I think, the wise men, too, of long ago, speak enigmatically in their mystic rites when they make the ancient Hermes with his reproductive organ always ready to work, making clear that what generates the sensible is the intelligible expressed principle, but revealing through the eunuchs in attendance the barrenness of matter which remains identical. For they have made it the mother of everything, a name which they apply to it precisely because they take it in the sense of substrate.[11]

Matter is only mother qua substrate, qua support or reserve, yet in this Plotinus admits she is "no longer female" because, unlike mothers in the concrete world, the material mother is incapable of generation, a capacity "present only to what remains male."[12] As Irigaray is wont to point out, the binary that subordinates the feminine or woman by positioning her in the place of privation means that all generation, despite appearances, ultimately serves and is due to masculine prerogative.

Obviously, then, for many feminists this is a repressive picture of the feminine that dangerously reinforces oppressive categories, a symbolic order bent on making women the privation or "less than" to men, the inverse image and unlikeness. Nonetheless, insofar as one may argue that the Western patriarchal symbolic order arose from a violent theft and appropriation of the embodied and spiritual lives of women, we may still find remnants of a divine feminine order lurking from within masculinist authors, an echo of humble reverence in the face of that power that failed to be (de)formed by the paternal need to control and discipline, and to deplete and appropriate.[13] In this vein, the remainder of this essay will turn to Plotinus' other mother figures, both productive of Eros: the goddess Aphrodite and intelligible or essentialized Poverty, who is explicitly associated with the Loving Intellect (νοῦς ἐρῶν) and intelligible matter (ἡ νοητὴ ὕλη).[14] As expected, Plotinus will indeed characterize Aphrodite as "less than," juxtaposing her power to superior masculine figures, for example, Ouranous, Kronos, and Zeus, while again regulating both feminine powers to maternal roles; yet unlike matter qua matter, these two goddesses are productive. Consequently, we shall see that there is certain feminine and even queer power haunting the *Enneads*, insofar as Aphrodite and Poverty are explicitly identified with Soul, while their equiprimordial progeny becomes the very movement of desire that unites and connects all things. In fact, in tune with Irigaray,

Plotinus may offer a good that encompasses the physical, the immanent, as well as the eroticism of the beyond,[15] insofar as the divine erotic allows for transcendence in immanence, beauty in the flesh, and a feminine sexuality that touches all things from first to last.

To understand this, we will first discuss Plotinus' principal metaphysical commitments so as to assist readers unfamiliar with his system. Distinctions between the One/Good, Intellect, and Soul will be helpful for understanding the role desire plays throughout Plotinus' project. This section will emphasize the fundamental eroticism that runs throughout reality. Further, it will show that Plotinus attempts to maintain a kind of gender neutrality when it comes to sex and gender identity at the level of the embodied soul. Souls are sex indifferent, while sex and gender are consequences of bodily morphology, and genital sex is simply a necessity for reproduction. The next section will attempt to subvert this corporeal understanding of gender, sex, and sexuality so as to highlight that for Plotinus these realities are not simply corporeal phenomena. Via unpacking Plotinus' allegorical reading of both Diotima's speech in Plato's *Symposium* as well as Pausanius' distinction between two Aphrodites, it will become clear that all of these categories first exist originally at the highest levels of reality. The result of this section will ultimately unpack the centrality of the feminine erotic within Plotinus' metaphysical system, while further suggesting a radical queerness (vs. gender neutrality) at the heart of what it means to be human. Finally, the conclusion will focus on a unique form of sexual intimacy, a touching of the Good that constitutes the individual soul's decisive benefice, a touching that ultimately makes all sexual desire, whether incorporeal or corporeal, something beautiful.

Again, to reiterate at the outset, this paper does not hope to rescue or save Plotinus from his sexism. No amount of apologetics could sufficiently erase his repeated and consistent disparagement of that which is coded as feminine in his system, for example, the body, the indefinite, matter, weakness, and specular images that threaten to pervert the good life. Rather, this methodology takes its cue from Amelius, a student of Plotinus, who asked the famed philosopher to sit for a portrait. A simple request, to be sure. Yet, the philosopher, noted by Porphyry, who gave "the impression of being embarrassed about having a body," refused.[16] Plotinus responded rather curtly: "Isn't it enough that I have to carry around the image that nature has clothed me with?"[17] In other words, Plotinus was horrified by the possibility of reproducing images of images, speculums of speculums, an abhorrence that was tacitly linked to his gendered metaphysical project. Nevertheless, devoted as he was to Plotinus, Amelius failed to follow his master's orders. Rebelliously, he devised a clever plan and snuck the famed Carterius into seminars, asking the artist to memorize Plotinus' features. The result was that, unbeknownst to the Neoplatonist, a likeness was produced, and so a specular image of Plotinus survives nonetheless.[18] Thus, like Amelius and Carterius, the following essay hopes to do work of which Plotinus would likely not approve, re-creating an image of his system that is only a mere likeness, perhaps even a bastard image, so as to think beyond his primary illustration of the feminine as mere speculum, rather transforming her into the erotic power constituting the Good of what it means to be and to become ourselves.

Plotinus' Metaphysical System and the Origins of Gender, Sex, and Sexuality

To understand the complexity of Plotinus' views of the assignment of sexed deities to specific realities in his system, we should take a moment to break down Plotinus' distinctions between the primary principles of the One (or the Good), Intellect, and Soul, while also unpacking Plotinus' psychology wherein there are fundamental distinctions between Soul, the World (or Cosmic) Soul, and, finally, individual souls. Throughout this exegesis our attention will be on the derivation of all things, even morphological sex, from erotic desire, a desire that connects and safeguards all things.[19]

First, as most are aware, the One (*hen*) is the absolute principle of all things that is itself no thing; in other words, the One is not an intelligible object but is that which is beyond being (*epekeina tes ousias*).[20] The One is unmixed with thinking or being insofar as it has neither predicates nor substantiality and can best be described as the vital and perfect cause of all things. Like Plato's Good beyond Being,[21] this fundamental principle is above all knowledge or truth, surpassing them in beauty and power. As absolute actuality, it is the cause of unity and plurality, limit and unlimitedness, sameness and difference, without itself being or participating in any of these terms. Everything, insofar as it is something, is generated from the One and, as a consequence, all things possess within themselves a seed or trace of divine beauty and goodness. In many ways, the One or the Good, within Plotinus' system, is a miraculous, ineffable surplus that wills itself and, in so doing, wills all of reality and life.[22] This has been described by some scholars as the One's own self-love.[23] As Plotinus confirms,

> And it is itself an object of love and love, that, is love of itself, inasmuch as it is only beautiful by reason if itself and in itself. . . . It is borne in a way inside itself, as loving itself, in the pure radiance, being itself that which it loved, that is, it has made itself exist, if indeed it is persisting activity and the most loved thing, like Intellect.[24]

In other words, the Good is the erotic principle par excellence and is, as such, the highest object of desire insofar as it is the final, perfective cause of existence. The Good is that which turns inward in a loving embrace of itself, a turn that stimulates the beauty and perfection of its own production of reality. To understand the loving embrace of the Good along different lines, it should be noted that Plotinus adheres to what has come to be called the Neoplatonic doctrine of cyclical creativity, wherein all things from Intellect to individual souls ultimately remain in (*moné*), proceed from (*prohodos*), and, finally, revert to (*epistrophē*) their causes and in such reversion or return become like their cause, in the highest case, the Good.[25] Specifically, the individual human soul, if it is to reach its constitutive good, must go beyond discursivity and intellectual thinking to reunite with the One. Interestingly, though, one must become like the One and love oneself; in other words, turn inward to that which always already loves itself, the Good that we all touch at the highest level of our soul. Plotinus describes this reunion as something likened to a singing and dancing chorus that must turn its attention to the chorus leader.

> We are like a chorus that, singing all the while, though relating to the chorus leader, may turn outwards from the spectacle, but when it does turn towards it, the chorus sings beautifully and does in truth relate to the chorus leader. So, too, we are always around it; when we aren't, then we will be completely dissolved, and will be no longer, but when we look towards it, that is "journey's end and rest" for us, and the end of discordance for us dancing round it a divinely inspired dance. And within the circling dance, behold the

> fount of Life, the fount of Intellect, the principle of Being, the cause of goodness, the root of Soul.[26]

Later we will discuss the sexual connotations that Plotinus uses to describe a soul's ecstatic connection with the One or the Good, but for now, it should be emphasized that the end of philosophical investigation, for Plotinus, is neither knowledge, reason, nor thought, but a spiritual union more accurately described by the corporeal revelry of singing and dancing. Ultimately, everything is euphorically drawn to this first principle and in that attraction all souls evidence their contact with the Good.

Before the production of soul, though, the primary procession of the Good is the Intellect. Keeping in mind that this production is not a temporal process but a description of the eternal unfolding of ontological priority at all levels of reality, be they intelligible or sensible, the Intellect is that which remains in a perfectly sated contact with the Good. Nonetheless, as a procession, Intellect is both like but also other than the Good and, so, the Intellect is both a one and a many. It is one insofar as it is the absolutely real and perfect being but many insofar as it is populated by a plurality of Forms. Intellect is that which thinks itself, and in thinking itself it thinks Forms.[27] As Plotinus writes,

> Each of them is Intellect and Being, that is, the totality consists of all Intellect and all Being—Intellect, insofar as it thinks, making Being come to exist, and Being, by its being thought, giving to Intellect its thinking, which is its existence. But the cause of thinking is something else, something which is also the cause of Being: in other words, the cause of both is something else. For those coexist simultaneously and do not abandon each other, but this one thing is nevertheless two. . . . For thinking could not occur if there was not Difference as well as Identity.[28]

Here, we have a remarkable conception of the nature of Intellect—that Difference is necessary to it, and, more importantly, a product of the Good helping constitute the possibility of Intellect's reversion to its own cause. Without the reality of Difference or Otherness, Being could not think itself, become an object for itself and, therefore could not actually be. Here, we should be clear that the first moment of procession from the One is, in fact, what has come to be called intelligible matter[29] or inchoate Being, since, primarily, Being is indeterminate otherness to the One. Plotinus elsewhere describes this aspect of Intellect with "Intellect Loving," a loving which is "drunk with nectar" (μεθυσθεὶς τοῦ νέκταρος).[30] This "drunk" Intellect or erotic Intellect will then become what it is via its love of the Good, a love reflected in its becoming like the Good. As other to the Good, though, it will be distinct from it but, again as we saw with soul, like or unified with the Good in loving itself, a love which is reflected in Intellect's thinking of itself. As Plotinus insists, "The Good has bestowed its trace upon Intellect to have by seeing it, so that even in Intellect there is desire and it both desires and attains forever."[31] This distinction between the loving or indeterminate Intellect and thinking Intellect helps clarify why Intellect is not absolute unity.[32]

So, Intellect is not simply two, namely, both the subject and object of thought, but there is a third, desire, that is inherent to the activity of Intellect. While Plotinus does not explicitly advance the later Neoplatonic triad of Being-Life-Intellect, it might be useful to appeal to Proclus' distinction between the Intelligible (Being), the Intelligible-Intellective (Life) and the Intellective (Intellect) within his understanding of the hypostasis Intellect insofar as it will assist us in understanding later Plotinus' mythological reading of this principle in the next section.[33] The Intelligible is the object of thought, the Intellective the subject of thought and the Intelligible-Intellective is the activity which joins them. Desire (or what Proclus deems Life)[34] will be associated with the principle of reversion and connection uniting all things that proceed from the One. In other words, that which unites the difference between Intellect and inchoate Being (as well as the difference surmounted between Intellect and the Good) is a certain absolute vitality, a productive desire that constitutes Intellect's reversion to itself and consequent perfection as that which is in absolute contact with the Good.

Intellect's desire to be like its cause, coupled with its own perfection, leads Intellect to proceed from itself, go outside itself and become other to itself in the same manner as the One's eroticism birthed something other to itself. This procession is Soul. Soul is best described as the image of the principle of Life or desire in the Intellect. It is that which desires to connect and join, to be attached. Soul is, as it were, the band of the universe. Yet, unlike the perfect desire of the Intellect, sated in itself via its absolute contact with the Good, Soul is outwardly directed and as such is the absolute principle of movement and animation. Soul in many respects is the middle term between the intelligible and the sensible, the eternal and the temporal, connecting and uniting the two. Like the Intellect that remains in the Good, Soul will remain in the intelligible world while also proceeding and therein constituting the sensible world, drawn by its own desire to be something separate and other to Intellect. Due to this, the World Soul or the Universal Soul of the cosmos comes into being and, by extension, individual souls as well. Here it must be stressed that while the World Soul and individual souls are separate or other than Intellect, there is a very real sense that for Plotinus there is a part that remains in Intellect and thus a part which is causally connected to the Good. Plotinus argues that "even our own soul does not descend in its entirety, but there is something of it always in the intelligible world."[35] In scholarship, this has come to be known as Plotinus' doctrine of the "undescended soul,"[36] whereby Soul, as a product of Intellect, has an essentiality or substantiality that is not lost even among embodied souls. Overall, Soul in all of its manifestations reflects the desire of Intellect, and itself becomes the vital erotic living principle of the world of becoming while simultaneously possessing a separate life constituting its transcendence, its intellectual life. As a consequence, both the World Soul and individual souls possess within themselves an intellectual soul that constitutes their perfection. Note the following chart:

Table 8.1

One	
Intellect	**Inchoate Being** (Erotic Intellect or Intelligible Matter/ Indefinite Dyad)
	Joining Principle (Active Desire)
	Intellect (Thought Thinking Itself, Plurality of Forms and the intellectual part of individual souls)
Soul	**Soul** (undescended, remaining in Intellect as *hypostasis*)
	World Soul (both undescended, remaining in Intellect due to its direct relation with Soul, and descended into embodiment, directly organizing the cosmos)
	Individual Souls (both undescended, remaining in Intellect due to its direct relation with Soul, and descended into embodiment)

So, with all this in mind, what are the origins of sex, gender, and sexuality in Plotinus' system?[37] Admittedly, Plotinus' views on these topics have not been thoroughly examined. This is probably because Plotinus does not seem, prima facie, to have much to say on the subject. Words like *gunaikos* (*woman*) or *anêr* (*man*) and their derivatives yield only seven instances of the former[38] and thirty-five of the latter in Plotinus' writings. This is far eclipsed by Plotinus' much more preferred—and more gender-neutral—term, *anthrôpos*, when speaking about the soul at both the embodied and disembodied level. Indeed, at first blush, it appears that Plotinus would argue for a fundamentally gender-neutral soul, whereby sex and gender differences would be a product of the World Soul in the creation and management of the sensible cosmos. For Plotinus, individual souls play no part in the constitution of their sex. As that principle which possesses the intelligible within, the World Soul looks to this principle directly and produces a cosmos ordered by natural laws and, breathtaking in its beauty, provides individual souls with body so as to allow them to become what they are—animating forces. At IV 3 9, 1–2, 20–34, a treatise devoted to the difficulties of the soul, Plotinus raises the problem.

> [W]e must also investigate how soul comes to be in body. What is the manner in which it does this? . . . The truth is like this: if there were no body, soul would not go forth, since there is no other place where it is its nature to be; but if it is going to go forth (προιέναι), it will give birth (γεννήσει) to a place for itself, so also a body. (trans. modified)

Notice that soul "generates," "gives birth to" (γεννήσει) body. It is not merely a neutral "production"; γεννήσει always retains a connotation of birth or growth. Also crucial is the deliberative, intentional preparation of the physical place and body on the part of soul. World Soul is body's "creator" (πεποιηκός) so as to provide beneficial care (ἐπιμέλεια ὠφελίμη), fitting individual souls to their appropriate embodiment. As Plotinus argues, soul

> comes from the intelligible world and gives it to the things below itself; to one kind of soul, always in the same way, to another in different ways at different times. . . . It does

> not always descend to the same extent, but sometimes does so more and sometimes less, even it is descending into the identical kind of [body]; each goes, in fact, to the body that is ready for it by its assimilation to the disposition [of the soul]. For each soul goes there to whatever destination to which it has been likened, one to a human being, another to another kind of being.[39]

Plotinus parallels *Timaeus* 41e–42c, where the disposition of the soul determines what form of life in which a particular soul will be placed. Nevertheless, unlike Plato, Plotinus does not suggest that moral vice leads a "vicious" male to inhabit a female body.[40] Rather, Plotinus states "[souls] become different either by variation of the bodies into which they are put, or by virtue of accidents of fortune or upbringing, or because they bring with them differences derived from themselves, or for all of these reasons, or certain of them."[41] Elsewhere, Plotinus advances a view of embodiment that parallels Plato's myth of Er. "Those who maintain their humanity will return again as human beings," Plotinus says, "While those who lived by sense-perception alone will return as animals. But if their sense-perceptions are accompanied by passions, they will return as wild beasts."[42] Like Plato, Plotinus is unburdened by any sense of contradiction that may arise in thinking about human souls entering into animal bodies, but Plotinus goes further than Plato, indicating that individuals who only pursue "a dim form of sense-perception" will even become trees and other plants.[43] Overall, Plotinus seems keen to recognize the flexibility of the soul's embodiment while also emphasizing that the body is not a product of merit, but each body is rather, in some sense, the equal when it comes to evidencing the soul's good. As Plotinus writes,

> What will then happen if the person who is virtuous happens to get a worthless body or the reverse? In fact, the characters of either kind of soul can form either kind of body to a greater or lesser degree.[44]

In sum, the soul is not responsible for its original bodily morphology and, moreover, regardless of one's bodily morphology one has an equivalent potentiality for virtue and ascent. Any apparent determinism on the choice of lives in, for instance, the Myth of Er, Plotinus allegorizes. When speaking of "choice" in the intelligible world, he says, it is really "an allegorical way of referring to the intention and disposition of the soul for life generally and everywhere."[45] While soul has a disposition (διάθεσις) for life, it has certain inclinations, which regularly, but not always, get exercised, and which are also not the only determining cause of the sort of life it will live. If this were the case, then it would not be possible for matter or any other cause to contribute, for good or ill, to the life of the individual embodied person. Nevertheless, material embodiment, as a secondary form of existence, insofar as the human being is primarily soul, means that the identity of the human being is not reducible to bodily morphology; what we are is something other than our sexed bodies.

So, again, it seems on the surface that for Plotinus, the human soul is sex indifferent. However, when we turn to Plotinus' account of Aphrodite, we shall see that Plotinus (perhaps despite himself) has not escaped sex difference—the Plotinian Soul is not gender neutral. Rather, as we shall discover in the next section, for Plotinus the two principles, Intellect and Soul, are gendered as divinely male and female, indicating that sex and gender for the Neoplatonist are not reducible to a particular form of life or appearance of the body. Insofar as all human beings identify with soul, Plotinus indicates that they partake of the divine feminine, and insofar as they possess within themselves an intellectual principle, they partake in the divine masculine. Yet, to be clear, neither of these terms, masculine or feminine, exist independently, free from mixture, as Aphrodite has a place in Intellect and Zeus a role in the Soul. As we shall see, the divine masculine and feminine are codetermining and always already becoming what they are through their interchange, desiring the same (*homo*-sexuality) while also desiring the other (*hetero*-sexuality). In short, there is a radical queerness or mixture of sex, gender, and sexuality at the very heart and height of what it means to be human and at the very core of reality and life. To understand this, we can now turn to Plotinus' mythologization of the relations between Intellect and Soul and their corresponding forms of desire.

Heavenly and Pandemic Aphrodite: The Birth of the Erotic Soul

In *Enneads* III, 5 "On Love," Plotinus seeks to resolve a textual and mythological conflict between competing conceptions of the birth of

Eros. Primarily, is Eros the son of Aphrodite or is he, as Plato's *Symposium* indicates, the progeny of Poverty and Plenty? As Plotinus begins to puzzle out the contradiction between the competing conceptions of the lineage of Eros, he begins with a few more questions, "Who is Aphrodite?" and "How was Eros born? From her or at the same time as her or could it happen in some way that he was born at the same time from her and at the same time as her?"[46] In short, Plotinus seems to be setting up the possibility that Eros and Aphrodite are equiprimordial principles that belong together, implying one another, where Aphrodite is both mother and a kind of twin sister to Eros. Following Pausanius' lead in the *Symposium*,[47] Plotinus first emphasizes the doubled-nature of the goddess, the Heavenly, born of the castration of Ouranous, and the Pandemic, born of Zeus and Dione. Beginning with the former, Plotinus emphasizes that Heavenly Aphrodite, while motherless, is a child of Kronos, presumably because she was born from his castration of Ouranous. Plotinus then identifies Kronos with the hypostasis Intellect while she is identified with the hypostasis Soul, which remains in the Intellect. As Plotinus writes,

> The heavenly Aphrodite . . . must be a most divine soul born pure directly from [Kronos] who is pure and remaining above, since she does not come into this world nor does she want to nor is she able to; it is not in her nature to come down to this world because she is a separate real existent and Substance and has no share in matter. This is the reason why they say enigmatically that she is "motherless."[48]

Notably, Plotinus reinforces his masculinist identification of maternal lower matter (that we saw in the introduction) in this passage, separating Aphrodite as far from the maternal stain as possible. Unlike maternal matter, who is impotent and the cause of the demise of being, Aphrodite is an intelligible reality whose power is absolute. One could say that if lower matter is to be characterized as completely dependent potency, which desperately desires the Good but is unable to obtain it, intelligible Aphrodite is her contrary; she is the lover whose love is immediately productive. Due to her love of Ouranous (the Good)[49] and Kronos (Intellect),[50] Aphrodite parthenogentically gives birth to Eros—intelligible perfect desire. As Plotinus writes,

> Actually, in pursuit of Kronos, then, or if you prefer, Heaven [Ouranous], the father of Kronos, [Aphrodite] turns her activity towards [Kronos], establishes an affinity to him, falls in love and brings forth Eros. And together with Eros she looks toward Kronos. And her activity has fashioned a *hypostasis*, that is, an *ousia*. And both of them look to the intelligible world. And the mother who gave him birth and beautiful Eros, who has come into being as a *hypostasis* that is always ranged towards another beauty, having its existence in this other beauty, in a sort of mid position between the one longing and the one longed for; he is the eye of the one longing and by means of its eye provides the lover with the sight of what is longed for, while Eros himself runs ahead with the vision before providing the lover with the power of seeing through the organ of visual perception. He is ahead, not like a person seeing by fixing his gaze on the object of his longing, but by himself plucking the fruit of the vision of beauty while it runs past him.[51] (trans. slightly modified)

This passage is remarkable for several reasons. First, since Heavenly Aphrodite is Soul residing within Intellect, we are invited to see Soul as an active component of Intellect's ability to see itself as an image or product of the Good or the One. Soul turns toward Intellect and gives birth to Eros, to desire, and it is this desire that bridges the gap between the lover and the beloved, between thought and the object of thought. In other words, Aphrodite, while only being explicitly allotted the role of Soul, also seems to act as the intelligible paradigm of the uniting principle between thought and the object of thought, while Eros is the vital principle that actualizes the desire for connection. In other words, Aphrodite actively produces the possibility of connection at the highest level of reality insofar as her progeny does not merely "fix his gaze" on the Good but actively "plucks the fruit" of that which they both desire. This seems descriptive of the form of desire constitutive of Intellect loving or intelligible matter—which, as we shall shortly see, will be allegorical represented by Penia—so that Aphrodite appears to mirror this more primal feminine within the hypostasis of Intellect. In other words, Aphrodite as Soul mirrors the productive cause of Intellect Loving, the premier feminine in Plotinus' system.

To be sure, Plotinus does not explicitly associate Heavenly Aphrodite with the uniting principle. It will be later Neoplatonists like Proclus who will associate the principle of Life or the intelligible-intellective with a feminine deity, in his case the goddess Night.[52] Yet, to be sure, we do seem to have a sense in which Plotinus either fails to be consistent, that is, desire is a product of Intellect in the production of Soul, or he fails to see that insofar as Intellect must desire the Good, Heavenly Aphrodite and Eros are that which unite thinking and being. Regardless of this possible discrepancy, Plotinus does, however, clearly link Heavenly Aphrodite and Heavenly Eros with the being and activity of Soul at the transcendent level, emphasizing their role as that which proceeds and constitutes the intellectual or higher aspect of the World Soul as well as individual souls.

> Now Eros of the higher soul would indeed be of the kind described; he would himself see above inasmuch as he is an attendant of the goddess and was born from and along with her and finds satisfaction in contemplating the gods. And since we say that soul which casts light over heaven in a primary way is separate, we will also make her Eros separate, however much we call the soul heavenly. For even if we say the best in us is in us, we will nevertheless make it separate, provided it is found only where the pure soul is.[53]

Here Plotinus is emphasizing that Soul and transcendent Eros are indeed part and parcel of the soul of the cosmos (World Soul) and individual human souls; they are the very core of their being, yet still something separate, something transcendent, something that requires the human soul to become a lover of that which resides within them. Individual souls must come to desire that which Heavenly Aphrodite desires so as to give birth to that which she births, Heavenly or perfectly sated Eros. Indeed, this is World Soul's and individual souls' constitutive task, communion with perfect desire (the higher soul in us) leading to contact with the Good.

So Heavenly Aphrodite and Eros reside at the level of the intelligible. Yet, again, for Plotinus, Aphrodite is, indeed, twofold as well as her progeny. There is also Pandemic Aphrodite and daemonic Eros. Yet, unlike Pausanius' account, this Pandemic Aphrodite and Eros are not sequestered to sexual bodily desire, but they are identified with World Soul and individual souls.

> And since there had also to be soul for the universe, the other Eros (heavenly) had to be with this soul (World Soul) from the beginning as its eye, born, too, through desire. And this Aphrodite who belongs to the universe and is not only soul nor simply soul (Pandemic Aphrodite) gave birth to the Love who is in this world and who from the start concerned himself with marriages and to the degree to which he is personally linked to the desire for what is above, moves the souls of the young and turns back the soul to which he is attached insofar as it is itself naturally disposed to recall the things above. For every soul desires the Good, both the mixed soul (embodied soul) and the soul of the individual (soul separate from being embodied), since it follows on from and is derived from the higher soul.[54]

Eager to emphasize that, in the end, Aphrodite and Eros are plural, Plotinus is careful to distinguish between universal Soul, universal Eros and individual souls with their individual erotic core.

> And we must think that there are many Aphrodites, too, in the universe, becoming daemons in it along with Love, all flowing from a universal Aphrodite, many partial Aphrodites depending on the universal Aphrodite along with their individual Eros, if indeed soul is the mother of Eros, and that Aphrodite is soul and Eros the activity of soul which strives for the Good. So, this individual Eros leads each soul to the nature of the Good; the Eros of the higher soul would be a god who always binds the soul to the Good, while that of the mixed soul would be a daemon.[55]

To clarify, within individual human beings there is both the trace of Soul itself, its higher aspect, and the soul that concerns itself with body. The higher soul is the erotic aspect that can come into contact with transcendent Eros, the god that remains above and in communion with the Good. Yet, even in the embodied soul there is daemonic Eros, which is limited and often misdirected insofar as it often looks to the outside world to satiate its desire, confusing its internal power with an external object of desire.

To explain this aspect of daemonic Eros, Plotinus turns to Diotima's account of Eros' secondary parentage, Poverty and Plenty. Contrasting this Eros with heavenly Eros that constitutes the perfection of all souls, Plotinus emphasizes that daemonic Eros is "neither a god nor self-sufficient, but for ever wanting."[56] As a child of Plenty, interpreted by Plotinus to be the intelligible principles within each individual soul, daemonic Eros is resourceful, but due to his maternal lineage, Poverty—the indefinite within the individual embodied soul—Eros is also at a loss, deficient and always wanting even in his fulfillment.

> And this is why he is said to be born from Plenty and Poverty in that deficiency and desire and the memory of the expressed (intelligible) principles come together and generate in soul the activity towards the Good and this activity is love. And his mother is Poverty because desire always belongs to what is in need. And Poverty is [intelligible] matter because [intelligible] matter is in need in every respect and *the indefinite aspect of the desire for the Good*—for there is neither form nor expressed principle in that which desires this—makes what desires even more akin to [intelligible] matter insofar as it desires. And what is turned towards itself is form alone remaining in itself. But if it desires to receive as well, it makes what is going to receive matter for what comes to it. And so then Eros is a material entity and he is a daemon born from soul insofar as soul lacks the Good but desires it.

Here, Plotinus seems to return to his disparagement of the material as that which infests or tempts the soul toward the indefinite, toward that which is merely receptive rather than active and productive. However, Plotinus is not identifying Poverty here with matter in its impotency (the Penia of Plato's receptacle) but with intelligible matter (inchoate Being that is drunk with love of the Good)—the reality of indefinite longing that belongs even to the life of the Intellect. In other words, the Soul's neediness arises from another mother figure in Plotinus' metaphysics, but a mother who is the source of Intellect's own drive toward itself and the Good. So, to take a speculative leap, even in this so-called lower or Pandemic Eros, in an Eros that cannot be sated, the individual soul actually takes on an essential indeterminacy, an essential insatiability. Yes, as most feminists would note, the Father (Kronos as Intellect realized or sober) may erase or sublimate intelligible matter, Penia, perfectly (as Intellect is fully sated desire), but the Soul and all its striving expresses the maternal principle of intelligible matter in its own joyous Becoming, making good even the reality of constant neediness in the souls of the cosmos and individuals.

> And so Eros has of necessity always existed as a result of Soul's desire to attain what is superior and good, and he was always there ever since Soul, too, existed. And he is a mixed thing sharing in deficiency, in that he wants to be filled, but not without a share in abundance insofar as he seeks what is missing from what he has. For that which is completely devoid of the good would actually never search for the Good.[57]

Again, emphasizing the identity of soul with the erotic, individuals have within themselves both the divine resources of heavenly Aphrodite and Eros, as well as an erotic element that is characterized by essential Penia, substantial indefiniteness, the drunk Intellect. In other words, and perhaps despite himself, Plotinus safeguards all forms of desire, even sensible, so-called vulgar desire, within the cosmos as, for him, even such wanton desire reflects, however misguided, the Good constituting the soul's erotic need.[58]

So, it appears that Plotinus' other mothers, Aphrodite and Penia (in Intellect), play a remarkably powerful role in his system. They are both principles of desire who birth the possibility of connection, Eros, without which nothing could return to the Good. Nonetheless, it behooves any honest author to note that Plotinus explicitly subordinates Aphrodites' power to Zeus, the Demiurge.[59] Shifting Aphrodite's object of love to him (rather than Kronos), Plotinus writes,

> [Zeus] will be at the level of Intellect, while Aphrodite, since she is from him and with him, will be placed at the level of Soul, having acquired the name Aphrodite because of her beauty, splendor, innocence, and delicacy of soul. For if we rank the male gods at the level of Intellect, while Aphrodite, since she belongs to him, is from him and with him, [and]

> will be placed at the level of Soul, having acquired the name of Aphrodite because of her beauty, splendor, innocence, and delicacy of soul. For . . . since a soul accompanies each intellect, in this way, too, Aphrodite will be the soul of Zeus, an interpretation witnessed by priests and theologians, who identify Hera and Aphrodite and assign the star of Aphrodite in the heavens to Hera.[60]

To be clear, this identification of Zeus with Intellect is not a discrepancy on Plotinus' account. In this passage, Zeus is not Intellect itself but is rather the intellectual part of Soul itself. In other words, since the Soul itself remains in Intellect, there is a real sense that even in the intelligible world, soul possess two aspects of itself, the intellectual and the vital. Consequently, despite feminizing the Soul throughout his treatise, Plotinus is in many senses queering it (where queer refers to a more fluid way of conceiving of the soul's identity). Soul itself will have both Zeus and Aphrodite within, insofar as she is the essentially vital or desiring side and he the intellectual. True, Plotinus is gender regulative, that is, *he* is intellectual while *she* is vital, but at the end of the day, the conclusion is the same. Individual souls are not gender indifferent but "both/and" insofar as both are necessary for the soul's good. No one person or individual soul is essentially feminine or masculine. Rather we are all both. To be sure, the feminine is that principle of love that gives birth to desire and it is by loving rather than merely gazing at the intellectual that the human soul ascends and comes into contact with the Good. Consequently, like many of the other classical authors explored in this volume, Plotinus in some sense recognizes that each individual soul is a radical mixture of the feminine and the masculine, wherein the feminine is a necessary and productive power of what it means to be human. She is not impotent; she is not a mere lying there. Rather, she is that part which allows all of us to turn toward and touch the good in all things, whether there or here.

Conclusion: Touching the Good

Returning to Irigaray's condemnation of Plotinus, it is true that his metaphysical system reduces the feminine, be it maternal matter but also the Soul qua Aphrodite, in all honesty, to a handmaiden to masculine prerogative. Yet, as we have seen, there is an important emphasis in the

Enneads on the soul itself being primarily feminine (regardless of one's bodily morphology) and secondarily queer (as a combination of masculine and feminine principles). This queerness/femininity is combined in such a way as to be in constant relation to one's own internal otherness and multiplicity that paradoxically allows for individuals to be more fully themselves. Yet, nevertheless, human eroticism, whether it be orientated to the world of things or toward the divine ideas, results from the mother of love (both as the Penia identified as intelligible matter but also as Heavenly Aphrodite), who continuously reproduces or births desire in all human beings regardless of their sex and gender. In fact, as Zeke Mazur has noted, Plotinus' entire system begins and ends in sexuality, again showing that sexuality for Plotinus is not reducible to corporeal life but belongs to the very structure of being.

> At each stage of Plotinus' system, then, one can discern parallel processes whose fundamental mechanism derives from the universal structure of sexual love. On the one hand, there is erotic desire, correlated with reversion towards the superior principles. On the other hand, there is biological reproduction, correlated with procession. Plotinus thus organizes the entire dialectical cycle according to a sexual model: that is, a model with both erotic and reproductive modalities. Moreover, the penultimate phase of the mystical ascent to the One recapitulates the first moment of procession. Therefore, just as in the natural world an act of sexual intercourse links erotic desire with reproduction, so also in Plotinian metaphysics, it is not surprising to find the two eternal motions, procession and reversion, naturally conjoined and mediated by a unitive act that is described in more or less explicitly sexual terms, an act which integrates the fulfilment of erotic desire with generation.[61]

Indeed, Plotinus' descriptions of the soul's contact with the One/Good are, indeed, highly sexualized. Consider the following:

> And when the soul has come to be with the One and, in a way, communed with it to a sufficient degree, then it should tell others of this intimate contact, if it can. It is, presumably, because he had such intercourse that Mino is famed as "Zeus familiar." And he was mindful of this intercourse when he

> framed the laws as images of it, since he had been impregnated by a grasp of the divine so as to make the laws.[62]

Several things are notable in this passage. First, the intimate contact or intercourse that Minos has with the One is productive; in his case it substantiates him as lawgiver. Second, intercourse is described in explicitly homoerotic terms, with Minos becoming impregnated by Zeus. Here, we may indeed have a masculine author appropriating women's generative power but, things are not so simple once we remember that the possibility for love and reproduction is caused by the feminine in Plotinus' system; she is that which allows for "intimate contact." One might also think of Irigaray's value for touch in her own system, whereby touch (over sight) constitutes the feminine divine and whereby touch does not subsume the one into the other but allows for a playful, intimate contact between disparate terms.[63] Indeed, likely against Plotinus' own self-awareness the philosopher ultimately offers something of this sort when he repeatedly and consistently frames the reunion of the individual soul with the Good in terms of a form of sexual touch that leads to the procreation of beauty in our lives. As he clearly writes,

> The truly beloved is in the intelligible world, who one can have intimate contact with by participating in him and relating to him truly, not just by enfolding him externally in our flesh . . . The result is that we hasten to exit from here, so we may, despite the vexation at being bound to the other side, enfold him with the whole of ourselves and contain no part with which we do not touch.[64]

In the end, while Plotinus may not have had much to say concerning corporeal sex, sexuality, and gender, these realities are inescapable aspects of his entire system, saturating his worldview and troubling a simple reading of the Neoplatonist as one who reduces the corporeal to the bedlam of existence. Rather, everything from first to last touches the One because everything in the material world is contacted to the Good via Soul's desire to touch the good in all things. As Plotinus writes himself and as we shall close on,

> The soul, impregnated with god, bears progeny, and this is the soul's beginning and end.[65]

Notes

1. See the translator's comment in Luce Irigaray, *Speculum of the Other Woman*, trans. G. Gill (Ithaca: Cornell University Press, 1985), 168.

2. Cf. Plato, *Tim.* 50c.

3. III 6 7, 27–44. All translations of the *Enneads* are Lloyd Gerson, *Plotinus, The Enneads* (Cambridge: Cambridge University Press, 2018). The editions utilized for the Greek derive from Paul Henry and Hans-Rudolph, *Plotini Opera* I–III (editio maior) (Paris: Desclée de Brouwer et Cie, 1951–1973). See Danielle A. Layne, "Feminine Power in Proclus' Commentary on Plato's Timaeus," *Hypatia: A Journal for Feminist Thought* 31, 1 (Winter 2021): 120–44, for a further feminist critique of this passage.

4. *Tim.* 48a.

5. III 6 9, 1–15. Cf. Aristotle, *On the Generation of Animals*, Loeb Classical Library (Boston: Harvard University Press, 1942), I 7.323b25.

6. III 6 10, 9. cf. *Tim.* 51a7.

7. III 6 13, 17. cf. *Tim.* 52a8–b1.

8. III 6 14, 7–12. cf. Plato, *Symp.* 203b4–c1.

9. *Symp.* 203b.

10. III 6 19, 17–25.

11. III 6 19, 27–32.

12. III 6 19, 37–40.

13. See Adriana Cavareo, *In Spite of Plato: A Feminist Rewriting of Ancient Philosophy*, trans. Serena Anderlini-D'Onofrio and Aine O'Healy (New York: Routledge, 1995), 5, where she writes: "Supposedly, the documented evidence of the existence of an original matriarchy, though abundant, does not add up to the kind of proof accepted by every scholar. But here documents and proofs are not the issue. In fact, my hermeneutical project consists of investigating the traces of the original act of erasure contained in the patriarchal order, the act upon which this order was first constructed and then continued to display itself." As Irigaray herself suggests: "[T]he speculum [the feminine produced by the masculine subject] is not necessarily a mirror. It may, quite simply be an instrument to dilate the lips, the orifices, the walls, so that the eye can penetrate the interior . . . Women, having been misinterpreted, forgotten, variously frozen in show-cases, rolled up in metaphors, buried beneath carefully stylized figures, raised up in different idealities, would now become the "object" to be investigated, to be explicitly granted consideration and thereby, by this deed of title, included in the theory. And if this center, which fixed and immobilized metaphysics in its closure, had often in the past been traced back to some divinity or other transcendence invisible as such, in the future its ultimate meaning will perhaps be discovered by tracking down what there is to be seen of female sexuality." Irigaray, *Speculum*, 145.

14. For Intellect in love see VI 7 35, 23–27. For intelligible matter see II 4 4, 6–9, II 5 3, 9, II 4 5, 13–38, II 4 15, 18–29, III 8 11, 4 and for its identification with Penia see III 5 6, 44. For more on erotic Intellect see A. Pigler, *Plotin, une métaphysique de l'amour* (Paris: Vrin, 2002), 75–130 and Alberto Bertozzi, *On Eros in Plotinus: Attempt at a Systematic Reconstruction (with a Preliminary Chapter on Plato)*, PhD diss. (Chicago: Loyola University Chicago, 2012), 224–25.

15. Luce Irigaray, *An Ethics of Sexual Difference* (New York: Cornell University Press, 1993).

16. Plotinus, "Porphyry's on Plotinus [= *Vita*]," in *Plotinus, Porphyry on Plotinus and Ennead I* (Boston: Harvard University Press, 1989), §1 2.

17. Porphyry, *Vita* §1 6–7.

18. Porphyry, *Vita* §1 11–17.

19. This is not a new thesis in Plotinion scholarship but one that I believe is still neglected at least in feminist engagement with the *Enneads*. See A. M. Wolters, *Plotinus on Eros: A Detailed Exegetical Study of Ennead*, III.5 (Toronto: Wedge Publishing Foundation, 1984); Pierre Hadot, *Plotinus on the Simplicity of Vision*, trans. M. Chase (Chicago: Chicago University Press, 1993); J. Lacrosse, *L'amour chez Plotin: érōs hénologique, érōs noétique, érōs psychique* (Brussels: Ousia, 1994); A. Pigler, *Plotin, une métaphysique de l'amour* (Paris: Vrin, 2002); José Carlos Baracat, "Soul's Desire and the Origin of Time in the Philosophy of Plotinus," in *Literary, Philosophical, and Religious Studies in the Platonic Tradition*, edited by J. Phillips and J. Finamore (Sankt Augustin: Akademic Verlag, 2013), 25–42; and, most importantly for this paper, Bertozzi, *On Eros*. For an explicitly feminist defense of Plotinus' metaphysics see E. Jane Cooper, "Escapism or Engagement? Plotinus and Feminism," *Journal for Feminist Studies in Religion* 23, no. 1 (Spring 2007): 73–93.

20. I 1 8, 9–10, V 3 13, 1–6.

21. Plato, *Rep.* 509b8–10.

22. VI 8 20, 32–33, VI 8 21 14–16. See further Lloyd Gerson, *Plotinus: The Arguments of the Philosophers* (New York: Routledge, 1994), 26–32, for a discussion of the freedom of the One.

23. See Bertozzi, 200.

24. VI.8 [39] 15.1–2 and 16.12–14. See Bertozzi, 200–209 where in his commentary on these two passages he connects this self-love to the questions of freedom in the One.

25. *Enneads* V, 2.1 and VI, 5–7. See Paulina Remes, *Plotinus on Self: The Philosophy of the 'We.'* Cambridge: Cambridge University Press, 2008), 51–53. Cf. Proclus, *Elements of Theology* §35.

26. VI 9 8, 35–VI 9 9, 2.

27. Cf. Aristotle, *Metaphysics Books 1–9* (Boston: Harvard University Press, 1968), 1072b19–21.

28. V 1 4, 27–35.

29. II 4 4, 6–9, II 5 3, 9. As we shall see later, this intelligible matter or the reality of indefiniteness even at the heart of Intellect, will be identified with Penia from Plato's *Symposium* 203b at III 5 7, 10–25.

30. VI 7 35, 23–27. Cf. Plato, *Sym.* 203b.

31. III 8 11, 23–25 (translation slightly modified). See also V 3 11, 11 and V 6 5, 9–10. See also Bertozzi, 197, whose description of the importance of both continuity/likeness and discontinuity/separatedness in all of Plotinus' fundamental realities is apt: "It entails discontinuity insofar as the hypostases are really distinct, independent, or separate from one another. But it also entails continuity to the extent that this separation is not to be understood spatially, but as a priority of being, or the ability of higher hypostases to subsist independently of the lower ones while leaving a 'trace' of themselves in their products. Now the *fil rouge* of both discontinuity and continuity, or this trace of the Principle in all that is derived from it, is *eros*. The self-love of the One, which is identical with its primary activity or activity of the essence, is at the source of all procession: it is the infinite power by which the One engenders all things. This *eros*, which in the One is perfect self-identity, is found in derivative form (that is, not as perfect self-identity, but as a love of the [the One] with different degrees of intensity depending on the level of unity of the thing possessing it) in everything else."

32. Bertozzi, 224–26.

33. See Proclus, *Elements of Theology, A Revised Text with Translation, Introduction and Commentary*, trans. E. R. Dodds (Oxford: Oxford University Press, 2004), §103.

34. Plotinus too deems this principle Life but the systematic role is clearer in the later Neoplatonist's metaphysics. See VI 7 17, 14–15, VI 7 17, 32–33, III 8 9, 33.

35. IV 8 8, 1–3. Cf. IV 9 9, 7–22, I 2 3, 23–33, and V 3 4, 29–31.

36. See A. H. Armstrong, "Plotinus" in *The Cambridge History of Later Greek and Early Medieval Philosophy* (Cambridge: Cambridge University Press, 1967), 195–268. For the classic arguments of the later Neoplatonic rejection of Plotinus' psychology, see Carlos Steel, *The Changing Self: A Study on the Soul in Later Neoplatonism* (Brussels: Palcis der Academien, 1978).

37. The following few pages on the origin of gender in Plotinus were written with the help of my esteemed colleague, Dr. Gary Gabor.

38. γυναῖκά II 3 2, 15, III 2 13, 15, IV 3 14, 6; γυναικός IV 3 32, 1; γυναικῶν III 1 3, 49, III 5 1, 57, V 8 2, 10.

39. IV 3 12, 33–39.

40. Plato, *Tim.* 41d8–42d2 and 90e6–a4. Cf. III 2 13 where Plotinus offers one instance of a gendered punitive measure insofar as men who sexually assault women will become women who are sexually assaulted.

41. IV 3 15, 7–10.

42. III 4 2, 16–18.

43. III 4 2, 16–24.
44. III 4 5, 10–13.
45. III 4 5, 2–4.
46. III 5 2, 12–15.
47. *Symp.* 180c–185c.
48. III 5 2, 19–25.
49. See V 8 13, 6 for a clearer confirmation of this identity.
50. III 5 2, 30–34.
51. III 5 2, 33–46.
52. See Layne, *Feminine Power* and Danielle A. Layne, "Otherwise than the Father: Night and the Maternal Causes in Proclus' Theological Metaphysics," in *Women and the Female in Neoplatonism*, ed. J. Schultz (Lieden: Brill, forthcoming).
53. III 5 3, 19–27.
54. III 5 3, 29–37.
55. III 5 4, 19–27.
56. III 5 5, 10.
57. III 5 9, 40–45.
58. See I 2 5, I 3 2, VI 7 31.
59. Again, to make sure we don't fail to note Plotinus' reinforcement of masculinist tropes, the Neoplatonist's characterization of the soul as feminine leads him to compare her to a prostitute, a rape victim, and/or a dutiful daughter. Consider VI 9 9, 25–39, where Plotinus describes the dual fate of Aphrodite: "The love which belongs naturally to the soul makes it evident that the Good is in the intelligible world. And in pictures and stories, Eros is yoked to souls. For since the soul is different from god, but comes from him, it loves him of necessity. And when it is in the intelligible world it possesses heavenly Eros, but becomes vulgar Eros in the sensible world. For in the intelligible world she is heavenly Aphrodite, and here she is vulgar, as if she had become a prostitute. For all soul is Aphrodite. This is expressed in riddling form by the story of the birth of Aphrodite, and of Eros coming to be with her. The natural state of soul, then, is to want to become unified with god, and this love is like that of a beautiful girl for her beautiful father. But when the soul comes into the world of becoming, she is, in a way deceived by her suitors, and, exchanging her love for another mortal love, is violated in her father's absence. She comes, then, to hate the violations in the sensible world, and, setting off for her father again, by having kept herself holy from things in the sensible world, she is in a state of contentment." VI 9 9, 25–39.
60. III 5 8, 13–22.
61. Zeke Mazur, "Having Sex with the One: Erotic Mysticism in Plotinus and the Problem of Metaphor," in *Late Antique Epistemology: Other Ways to Truth*, eds. P. Vassilopoulou and S. Clark (New York: Palgrave Macmillan, 2009), 73.
62. VI 9 7, 20–27.

63. See Luce Irigaray, "Perhaps Cultivating Touch Can Still Save Us," *Substance* 40, no. 3 (2011).

64. VI 9 9, 45–55. See also VI 9 7, 20–27.

65. VI 9 11, 21–22.

Bibliography

Aristotle. *On the Generation of Animals*. Boston, MA: Harvard University Press, 1942.

———. *Metaphysics Books, 1–9*. Boston, MA: Harvard University Press, 1968.

Armstrong, A. H. "Plotinus." In *The Cambridge History of Later Greek and Early Medieval Philosophy*, Cambridge, UK, Cambridge University Press, 195–268, 1967.

Baracat, José Carlos. "Soul's Desire and the Origin of Time in the Philosophy of Plotinus." In *Literary, Philosophical, and Religious Studies in the Platonic Tradition*, edited by J. Phillips and J. Finamore, 25–42. Sankt Augustin, Germany: Akademic Verlag, 2013.

Bertozzi, Alberto. *On Eros in Plotinus: Attempt at a Systematic Reconstruction (with a Preliminary Chapter on Plato)*. PhD Diss. Chicago, IL: Loyola University Chicago, 2012.

Cavareo, Adriana. *In Spite of Plato: A Feminist Rewriting of Ancient Philosophy*, translated by Serena Anderlini-D'Onofrio and Aine O'Healy. New York: Routledge, 1995.

Cooper, E. Jane. "Escapism or Engagement? Plotinus and Feminism." *Journal for Feminist Studies in Religion* 23, no. 1 (Spring 2007): 73–93.

Gerson, Lloyd. *Plotinus: The Arguments of the Philosophers*. New York: Routledge, 1994.

———. *Plotinus, The Enneads*. Cambridge, UK: Cambridge University Press, 2018.

Hadot, Pierre. *Plotin: Traité* 50 (III.5). *Introduction, traduction, commentaire et notes*. Paris: Les Éditions du Cerf, 1990.

———. *Plotinus on the Simplicity of Vision*. Translated by Michael Chase. Chicago, IL: Chicago University Press, 1993.

Henry, Paul, and Schwyzer, Hans-Rudolph. *Plotini Opera I–III* (editio maior). Paris: Desclée de Brouwer et Cie, 1951–1973.

Irigaray, Luce. *Speculum of the Other Woman*. Translated by G. Gill. Ithaca, NY: Cornell University Press, 1985.

Irigaray, Luce. *An Ethics of Sexual Difference*. Ithaca, NY: Cornell University Press, 1993.

Irigaray, Luce. "Perhaps Cultivating Touch Can Still Save Us." *Substance* 40, no. 3 (2011).

Lacrosse, J. 1994. *L'amour chez Plotin: érōs hénologique, érōs noétique, érōs psychique*. Brussels, Belgium: Ousia.

Layne, Danielle A. "Feminine Power in Proclus' Commentary on Plato's Timaeus." *Hypatia: A Journal for Feminist Thought* 31, 1 (Winter 2021): 120–44.

———. "Otherwise Than the Father: Night and the Maternal Causes in Proclus' Theological Metaphysics." In *Women and the Female in Neoplatonism*, edited by J. Schultz. Lieden, the Netherlands: Brill, forthcoming.

Mazur, Zeke. "Having Sex with the One: Erotic Mysticism in Plotinus and the Problem of Metaphor." In *Late Antique Epistemology: Other Ways to Truth*, edited by P. Vassilopoulou and S. Clark, New York: Palgrave Macmillan, 2009.

Perl, Eric. "The Togetherness of Thought and Being: A Phenomenological Reading of Plotinus' Doctrine 'That the Intelligibles Are Not Outside the Intellect.'" In *Proceedings of the Boston Area Colloquium in Ancient Philosophy* 22 (2006): 1–26.

Pigler, A. *Plotin, une métaphysique de l'amour*. Paris: Vrin, 2002.

Plato. *Republic, Volume I: Books I–5*. Loeb Classical Library. Boston, MA: Harvard University Press, 2013.

———. "Symposium." In *Lysis, Symposium and Gorgias*. Boston, MA: Harvard University Press, 1925.

———. "Timeaus." In *Timeaus, Critias, Cleitphon, Menexenus, Epistles*. Boston, MA: Harvard University Press, 1929.

Plotinus. "Porphyry's on Plotinus." In *Plotinus, Porphyry on Plotinus and Ennead I*. Boston, MA: Harvard University Press, 1989.

Proclus. *Elements of Theology, A Revised Text with Translation, Introduction and Commentary*. Translated by E. R. Dodds. Oxford, UK: Oxford University Press, 2004.

Remes, Paulina. *Plotinus on Self: The Philosophy of the 'We.'* Cambridge, UK: Cambridge University Press, 2008.

Steel, Carlos. *The Changing Self: A Study on the Soul in Later Neoplatonism*. Brussels, Belgium: Paleis der Academien, 1978.

Stern-Gillet, Suzanne. "Dual Selfhood and Self-Perfection in the Enneads." *Epoche: A Journal for the History of Philosophy* 13 (2009): 331–45.

Whitford, Margret. *Luce Irigaray: Philosophy in the Feminine*. New York: Routledge, 1991.

Wolters, A. M. Plotinus on Eros: A Detailed Exegetical Study of Ennead III.5. Toronto, ON: Wedge Publishing Foundation, 1984.

Chapter Nine

Beyond Maleness and Femaleness?

The Case of the Virgin Goddesses in Proclus' Metaphysics

JANA SCHULTZ

Virgin[1] goddesses are associated with a form of life that was off-limits for women in ancient Greece. Athena was worshiped as the goddess of war and wisdom and Artemis was associated with hunting. Thus, on the one hand, virgin goddesses appear as representations of possibilities of being female, which were suppressed by customs.[2] On the other hand, virgin goddesses were conceptualized as "unfemale," and thereby not as offering an alternative way of being female, but as representing a way of being male or at least of not being female despite having a female body.

The negative connotations of femaleness in ancient Greek culture—for example, the association of femaleness with irrationality and passions, with nature, body, or the sphere of becoming in general—were closely linked with women's sexuality and its bodily requirement. Virgins were regarded as being able to transcend femaleness (at least partly) by disengaging themselves from sexuality and procreation.[3] Thus, instead of providing a more "emancipated" picture of femaleness, the ideal of the virgin goddesses seems to contribute to the devaluation of "normal" women and to stabilize a system in which femaleness is despised in favor of maleness. This tension makes the virgin goddesses an interesting topic for the study of sex and gender in the ancient Greek world.

This chapter will examine the function of the virgin goddesses in the metaphysics of the Neoplatonic philosopher Proclus. I chose this example for two reasons. First, Proclus brings together different traditions into one philosophical system. His concepts of femaleness and virginity are informed by different philosophical schools—especially, of course, by Platonism, but also by Pythagoreanism, the Peripatetic school, and Stoicism—and by traditional myths and more recent theological texts as the *Chaldean Oracles*. Grasping the function of the virgin goddesses in his system should therefore help us to understand the function of virginity in the conceptualization of maleness and femaleness in ancient Greek culture in general. Second, Proclus was—according to Marinus' *Proclus or about Happiness*—deeply devoted to the goddess Athena (9, 6–8 and 30, 1–9). His devotion is mirrored in the importance he lays on the examination of this deity so that Proclus' works provide us with much material for an examination of the virgin goddesses.

I will focus on the question of whether the virgin goddesses fit into the classification of maleness or femaleness within Proclus' system or whether they undercut and transcend this distinction. Nevertheless, this question is connected to the concerns regarding the ideal of virginity and the devaluation of "normal" women. As we will see, Proclus regards the female deities and their contribution to (metaphysical) procreation as inferior in comparison to the male deities. Virgin goddesses—as not directly involved in procreation—are not affected by this devaluation, but this helps the "female side" only if virgin goddesses are regarded as female. Thus, the chapter will center on the question of which place the virgin goddesses occupy in Proclus' metaphysics, but the answer should ultimately shed light on the question of whether the virgin goddesses help to raise the value of femaleness.

I will first examine the distinction between maleness and femaleness in Proclus' metaphysics. It will be shown that Proclus determines maleness as being unifying and femaleness as being multiplying. These labels are not value-neutral. Being unifying means to be closer to the One, and that is, to the Good. In the second part, I will investigate the virgin principles and their function. The crucial feature of the virgin goddesses is their purity. Due to their purity, they fulfill the functions of being protective, elevating, and ordering. All these functions relate to unification or to avoiding multiplication so that the virgin goddesses appear to be quite male.

In the last section, I will discuss the problem of classifying the virgin goddesses as "male" or "female" in more detail. It will be argued that they reveal a complexity in Proclus' metaphysics that cannot be captured by a simple "male-female" scheme. However, the virgin goddesses' transgression of a simple "male-female" categorization is not connected to a revaluation of femaleness. Since the virgin goddesses will be shown to be removed from femaleness even more than from maleness, the positive connotations associated with virginity have no real consequences for the concept of femaleness.

Maleness and Femaleness in Proclus' Metaphysics

The difference between male and female entities is present throughout the metaphysical system that Proclus elaborates, beginning with the level of the Living Being Itself and illustrated most prominently in the paternal gods and maternal goddesses on the different levels of reality. In this section, first, I will show that the crucial difference between the male and female entities in the metaphysical realm is that the male entities are unifying powers while the female entities are multiplying ones.[4] Next, I will explain why—despite this determination—some male entities fulfill multiplying functions and some female entities unify certain beings. I will demonstrate subsequently that the determination of the male entities as unifying and the female entities as multiplying is hardly value-neutral. The unifying entities are closer to the One, and that is, to the Good.

The female deities are distinguished from the male deities by their multiplying and separating power as Proclus states in his *Commentary to Plato's Timaeus*:

> The division into male and female contains within itself the entire contents of the divine orders. For in the male is contained that which is the cause of the power of stability and sameness [τὸ μὲν γὰρ μονίμου δυνάμεως αἴτιον καὶ ταυτότητος] and that which furnishes being and attaches to all things the very first principle of their return, while the female embraces that which projects from itself all manner of processions and

> distinctions [τὸ δὲ προόδους παντοίας καὶ διακρίσεις], together with their measure of life and generative power.[5]

And according to the principle that every entity can provide the secondary entities only with characters it has itself (*El. Theol.* 18, 1–2), the female deities do not only multiply other beings but they are also themselves manifold in comparison to the male deities of the same level. The characterization of the male deities as unifying and the female deities as multiplying can be determined more precisely by considering the first manifestation of maleness and femaleness in Proclus' system.

> And the third [intelligible] god is father and mother. Since if the living being itself (τὸ αὐτοζῷον) is in this God, the cause of maleness and femaleness must exist primarily there, for they [maleness and femaleness] belong to the living beings.[6]

Thus, maleness and femaleness are not simply defined as unifying and multiplying powers but as unifying and multiplying powers established in living beings whereby living beings exist not only in the realm of nature but from the third triad of the intelligible realm on.

If male and female deities work together to procreate,[7] the male deity provides the offspring with unity and determination (*Theol. Plat.* III 32, 19–21), while the female deity provokes the unified and firmly established powers in the father to multiply and to proceed in lower levels of reality (*Theol. Plat.* V 36, 23–24): "For the intermediary deity [Rhea] multiplies [πολλαπλασιάζει] the uniform powers in Cronus [τὰς ἑνοειδεῖς τοῦ Κρόνου δυνάμεις]" and (*Theol. Plat.* 36, 14–15) "[Rhea] incites [προκαλουμένη] the remaining causes in him [τὰς ἐν ἐκείνῳ μενούσας αἰτίας]." In this procreative role, the female entities are also called "generative (γεννητικός)" (*Theol. Plat.* I 122, 5–10) and "fertile [γονίμος]" (*In R.* I 134, 12–17).[8]

The fundamental difference between being unifying and being multiplying is connected to further characterizations of the male and female deities that emphasize different aspects of this distinction.

As unifying causes the male deities are causes of sameness, and so therein the female deities—due to being multiplying—causes of otherness. This is shown in the *Theologica Platonica*, where Proclus explains the "female mode [θηλυπρεπῶς]" (IV 82, 4) as being "according to the power of otherness" (IV 82, 6–7).[9] Being multiplying is connected to otherness, since otherness arises if a unity is separated, and that is, multiplied.

> [The otherness] multiplies [πολλαπλασιάζει] the one that comes after this by proceeding generatively, and it incites [προκαλεῖται] being to the second and to the third procession by shattering [θρύπτουσα] being into many beings, and by cutting [κερματίζουσα] the one into particular unities.[10]

Similarly, being unifying is connected to sameness since entities are unified by being provided with identical characters.[11]

The difference between the male deities as unifying and female deities as multiplying causes is rooted in the first dyad, that is, in the first dichotomy between Limit itself and Unlimited itself.[12] This is where the primary difference between being unifying and being multiplying is established:

> For Limit is the cause of the stable, uniform and connecting deity [τῆς μονίμου καὶ ἑνοειδοῦς καὶ συνεκτικῆς θεότητος], but the Unlimited is the cause of the power which proceeds to all things and which multiplies [τῆς ἐπὶ πάντα προϊέναι καὶ πληθύεσθαι δυναμένης] and altogether it is the origin of the whole generative order [τῆς γεννητικῆς προκατάρχον ἁπάσης διακοσμήσεως].[13]

It is by participating in Limit that the unifying causes have their power. Similarly, all multiplying causes receive their power by participating in the Unlimited. That is to say, all male causes are manifestations of the first Limit and all female causes are manifestations of the first Unlimited (*In Ti.* I 130, 17–22).

As manifestations of Limit and the Unlimited the male and female entities are also associated with being monadic and being dyadic (*Theol. Plat.* I 122, 5–10).[14] It might appear paradoxical that the female is said to be analogous both to the whole dyad and to limitlessness that is a part of the whole. But it must be considered that the dyad can be examined in its relation to the One (or to the monad of the level in question) as well as in its inner structure. If it is observed in relation to the One, then the dyad is altogether the multiplying—and that is the female—principle since its duality is the principle of separation (*In R.* I 93, 4–8). But from the perspective of the inner structure of the dyad, limit appears as the unifying principle and the infinite power as the multiplying one.[15]

Furthermore, Proclus determines the difference between male and female deities with regard to the dynamic of remaining, procession, and reversion through which all causation within the metaphysical realm takes place. The male deities are characterized by remaining and the female deities by procession (*In Ti.* I 220, 4–10).[16] That is to say, the male deities remain and provide the power of remaining steady to the secondary beings, while the female deities proceed further and multiply what has been unified in the male entities, and they provide the power to proceed and to multiply to the secondary beings. Due to being associated strongly with procession, the female deities are also described as causes of life (*Theol. Plat.* IV 7, 5–13) and of movement (*In Crat.* 143, 11–15), while the male entities are characterized as causes of substance (*El. Theol.* 151, 3–4) and of repose (*In Ti.* II 92, 7–9).

To sum up, Proclus' metaphysics is based on a binary system of unifying limit and multiplying limitlessness. Proclus connects this basic distinction with gender. The stable, unifying causes that are established in living beings are determined as male and the multiplying ones as female.

But the determination of the male entities as unifying and of the female entities as multiplying cannot be understood in the way that the male entities have only the power to unify and that the female entities can only fulfill the function of multiplication. For if we look at Proclus' description of certain male and female deities more closely, we notice that unifying and multiplying powers are present in both of them in a mingled way. Cronos, for example, is the father of the intellective deities and unifies the whole realm. Nevertheless, he also seems to be responsible for certain kinds of separation and multiplication.

> It is likely that Cronus holds at his own level the highest causes of combinations and discriminations: for through the various sections of the heavens he leads forth into partition the wholeness of the intellect, becomes cause of generative processions and multiplications, and in general forms the dominant principle of the Titan generation, from which derives the division of real beings.[17]

And the multiplying and separating activities of the female deities are linked—especially on the higher levels of reality—with connective activities of several kinds. The female deities embrace the entities they multiply (*In R.* II 204, 29–205, 2), so that—despite being manifestations of limitlessness—they do not let the multiplication proceed ad infinitum. And since female deities are typically placed as intermediary terms of triads, they connect the extremes, as Rhea connects Cronos and Zeus by simultaneously inciting the procession of Zeus and enabling his reversion back to his father.[18] Additionally, female deities can even function as stable and monadic principles for the procession of certain entities, as, for instance, Rhea is described with regard to the female Titans.

> How could the number of the seven circles *not* be appropriate to the soul since it comes from the life-engendering goddess [Rhea]—who is herself a monad, dyad and number seven, encompassing (περιέχουσα) all the female Titans in herself?[19] (Baltzly's emphasis)

That is to say, even though Proclus determines the male principles as unifying and the female principles as multiplying there are male principles with multiplying functions as well as female principles with unifying functions.

The main reason[20] is that the difference between being unifying and being multiplying is primarily and purely established in the first dichotomy between Limit and Unlimited. All entities below these first principles are mixtures of limit and infinite power.

> For power is also before the male and the female and it is in both and with both (ἐν ἀμφοῖν καὶ μετ᾽ ἀμφότερα). Since power extends to all beings and all being participates in power, as the stranger from Elea says. For power is everywhere, but the female participates to a greater degree [μᾶλλον] in the peculiar nature of power and the male participates to a greater degree in the unity according to Limit.[21]

Thus, a male entity is not simply a unifying power and a female entity is not simply a multiplying power.[22] Instead, a male entity is a mixture that contains more unifying power because it participates more strongly in Limit, while a female entity is a mixture that has more multiplying power because it participates more strongly in the Unlimited (relative to the level of reality to which the mixtures in question belong).[23] Male principles are therefore best suited for a unifying function and female principles for a multiplying one, but due to the fact that they participate also—to a lesser degree than their male or female counterparts—on the other side of the first dichotomy, male entities can act as multiplying powers and female entities as unifying ones.

For the purpose of this paper it is most important that the multiplying role of certain male deities and the unifying role of certain female deities show that a real binary distinction exists only on the first level beneath the One, that is, in the dichotomy between Limit itself and Unlimited itself. The male deities as mixtures more characterized by limit and the female deities as mixtures more characterized by limitlessness are indeed diametrically opposed to one another. But they constitute two sides of a continuum rather than a strict binary distinction, and in the continuum there is also room for balanced mixtures. Thus, there are not only male and female deities but also androgynous ones (*In Ti.* I 46, 19–21).[24]

The determination of the male deities as unifying and the female deities as multiplying is hardly value-neutral but justifies the subordination of the female deities.[25] The inferiority of the female deities is shown by the fact that whenever male and female deities work together, the female deity operates in a secondary manner (*In Ti.* I 46, 21–25; Tarrant).

> Even where gender had been divided, male and female of the same rank have the same tasks, it is accomplished in an initial way [πρώτως] by the male, and in a subordinate way [ὑφειμένως] by the female. Hence in mortal creatures too nature has revealed the female to be weaker in all things than the male.[26]

Let's take a look at procreation within the metaphysical realm. When Proclus describes the conjunction of the encosmic Uranus and Gaia, he emphasizes that it is because of Gaia that the offspring are "rejoicing in their procession [προόδῳ χαίροντες]" (*In Ti.* III 185, 17; Tarrant) and "divorcing themselves from his [their father's] royal authority [διαιροῦντες ἑαυτοὺς ἀπὸ τῆς ἐκείνου βασιλείας]" (*In Ti.* III 185, 18–19; Tarrant).[27] The paternal influence, instead, seems to encourage the offspring to remain in the realm of the father (*In Ti.* III 185, 15–16).

Thus, even though both parents work together to procreate a secondary entity, the male cause is involved in the procession of the offspring only to a small degree. The father is the initial point of the procession of the offspring, but he mainly empowers the offspring to remain in the realm of the father and to receive unity and determination while the maternal cause incites the procession and the separation from the father and is thereby responsible for the loss of perfection which the offspring suffers because of its procession to a lower level of reality. The father fulfills the higher function of providing unity and stability while the mother fulfills the lower function of inciting the procession to a lower, and that is, to a worse state.[28]

The hierarchization of the male and female deities that is shown in the subordinate role of the female entities in joint activities is based on the general principle that what is more unified rules over what is more multiplied (*In Ti.* II 262, 18–21).[29] The superiority of what is unified compared to what is multiplied is based on the fact that the more unified an entity is, the more similar it is to the One, and that is, to the Good. This similarity is shown best in the paternal function of the male entities. The metaphysical fathers are described by Proclus as "manifesting the unified and boniform power of the One" (*El. Theol.* 151, 5–6; Dodds). They are not only similar to the One due to their unity but they fulfill also a function that is analogous to the function of the One by giving "existence [ὕπαρξις], power [δύναμις] and substance [οὐσία]" (*El. Theol.* 151, 3–4; Dodds) to all entities in their realm, as the One gives these things to the whole of reality (*El. Theol.* 151, 13–15).[30]

To sum up, the determination of the male deities as unifying and the female deities as multiplying is connected to a value judgment in favor of the male deities.[31] The female deities are characterized as inferior—that is, as more dissimilar to the One—and they have only a subordinate role when they work together with male deities. Especially interesting regarding the topic of this paper is that the degradation of the female deities is closely connected with their role in procreation. Female causes are inferior due to being manifold and multiplying, but it is exactly this characteristic that enables them to play a maternal role in the procreation of secondary beings.

Altogether, this section has shown that Proclus establishes his metaphysical system on the binary distinction of being unifying and being multiplying. This binary distinction exists purely only in the first dichotomy of Limit itself and the Unlimited itself. All entities below these first principles are mixtures of limit and limitlessness. The male entities are more characterized by limit and fulfill thereby (mostly) a unifying function, while the female entities are more characterized by limitlessness and operate (mostly) in a multiplying manner. This classification is not value-neutral. The male principles are superior to the female principles for they are more similar to the One, and that is, to the Good.

Proclus' Virgin Goddesses

The last section has shown that male and female deities are set apart from each other by the opposed features of being unifying and being multiplying. This section will explore what we can learn about the place of the virgin goddesses in this system from Proclus' own characterization of them. The relationship of the virgin goddesses to maleness and femaleness will be discussed in the last part of the chapter.

The distinctive feature of the virgin goddesses in Proclus' metaphysical system is their purity. In his *Commentary on Plato's Cratylus*, Proclus emphasizes that Artemis is a virgin due to her immaculateness.

> Plato presents here three properties of our lady Artemis: that of immaculateness (ἄχραντον), that of ordering and that of elevating. By virtue of the first the Goddess is said to desire virginity [παρθενίας ἐρᾶν].[32]

"And Athena is called "virgin" because she holds before her an immaculate and unmingled purity [ἄχραντον προβεβλημένη καὶ ἀμιγῆ καθαρότητα]" (*In Ti.* I 169, 5–6; Tarrant). Purity is spelled out in terms of being unmingled with lower entities: "For the divine purity isolates all the gods from inferior existences, and enables them to exercise providence toward secondary beings without contamination" (*El. Theol.* 156, 4–5; Dodds).[33]

Since being pure is the special feature of the virgin goddesses, they are part of Proclus' metaphysical system beginning from that level at which the perfection of the entities is diminished to such a degree that being unmingled with lower entities is no longer a matter of course for all entities. This is the case from the level of Rhea on—that is, from the intermediate position of the intellective triad on—since Cronos is the last entity in Proclus' system that is not in danger of getting mingled with secondary entities and that, therefore, doesn't need the protection of the Curetes (*In Crat.* 107, 34–38).[34] Thus, virgin goddesses exist starting from the intellective level and they can proceed from there as far as the level of the encosmic gods. Athena, for example, manifests herself on four different levels of reality.

> For just as in the case of the other gods, so there is a lot for Athena too as she proceeds from the intellective causes to the earthly region. Certainly she belongs in the first instance in the father [the Demiurge Zeus], at the second level she is among the hegemonic gods; thirdly she embarks on procession among the twelve rulers; and after this she reveals her independent authority in heaven.[35]

Their purity enables the virgin goddesses to fulfill three main functions, which are characterized as (1) protective, (2) elevating, and (3) ordering.

Virgin goddesses are not only pure, but they are also the cause of their own purity, which means that they are purifying. Being purifying is a particular form of being protective.

> Thus the protective is more universal than the purifactory: the distinctive office of protection, as such, is to keep each thing in the same station relatively to itself and its priors no less than to its consequents; that of purity, to liberate the higher from the lower.[36]

Accordingly, the virgin goddesses fulfill a particular protective function by saving themselves from contamination. Protecting oneself from getting intermingled with inferior beings relates to remaining so that the virgin goddesses are—in contrast to femaleness—not characterized by procession but by remaining. This is most clear in the case of Hestia who is described as the stable, remaining center of the earth while Demeter is the earth's fertile power (*In Ti.* III 137, 20–138, 3). And in accordance with the principle that every cause transfers its own characteristics to other entities (*El. Theol.* 18, 1–2) the virgin goddesses also protect other deities from contamination. Regarding this function, Athena is described as the leader of the Curetes and the guardian of the Demiurge (*In Crat.* 185, 19–23).

But virgin goddesses do not only protect themselves and other deities from getting contaminated by mingling with lower entities, they are also benevolent toward the lower entities since they elevate and order them (*In Crat.* 179, 1–4). Being elevating is a particular form of being conversive, that is, perfective.

> On the other hand it [the elevative cause] has a more specific rank than the conversive, since anything which reverts may revert either upon itself or upon the higher principle, whereas the function of the elevative cause, which draws the reverting existence upwards to what is more divine, is characterized only by the latter mode of reversion.[37]

Thus, on the one hand, the virgin goddesses guarantee the transcendence of the higher principles by protecting them from getting mingled with lower entities. But, on the other hand, they also enable the lower entities to participate and thereby create a link between lower and higher entities. While they are guardians for the higher causes, they are illuminators for the lower entities. Athena, for example, helps the encosmic gods to revert to the intellective realm (*In Prm.* 661, 8–15).[38]

Most interesting is that the elevating function of the virgin goddesses is described by Proclus as removing them from the "typical female activity" of multiplying. Regarding Artemis, he states that it is due to being elevating that "she is said to despise the procreative impulses [μισῆσαι λέγεται τὰς γενεσιουργοὺς ὁρμάς]" (*In Crat.* 179, 6–7; Duvick; for Artemis' contempt of procreation see also *In Crat.* 179, 32–36). This contrast between being procreative and being elevating might appear surprising since—as mentioned above—Rhea, a maternal goddess, is a cause of Zeus's reversion to his father and thereby fulfills a quite elevating function. But one must consider that Rhea belongs to a higher level of reality than the virgin goddesses in elevating functions. She seems to participate in Limit to such a high degree that she can connect her multiplying activity with causing reversion. However, on lower, less perfect levels of reality these activities fall apart. In the hypercosmic Core—an image of Rhea—the activities of causing generative multiplication and of causing reversion are split between the fertile Persephone and the virginal Athena (*In Crat.* 179, 22–25).

The virgin goddesses are also ordering deities. Their ordering function is not limited to preventing an intermingling of higher and lower entities—it is not identical with their purifying function—but it aims also directly at the lower entities. The virgin goddesses play an important role in making the cosmos a whole, as Proclus emphasizes with regard to Themis.

> Themis is appropriately included among the principles of the creation. It is she who is responsible for the demiurgic ordinances and thanks to her the order of the universe was indissolubly framed. For this reason she remains a virgin prior to the procession of the Demiurge.[39]

In the case of Athena, her ordering function is emblematized by her art of warfare.[40] Athena is characterized as war loving because of her providence for the contrarieties within the cosmos (*In Ti.* I 169, 6–8). It is thereby not her task to destroy one side of the contrarieties in favor of the other side. Instead, she unifies the manifold, conflicting powers in the cosmos while simultaneously preserving their difference.

> It is true that Ares too is fond of war and rivalry, but he is more closely related to separation and division, while Athena both conserves the rivalry [τὴν ἐναντίωσιν συνέχει] and lights the path to unity [τὴν ἕνωσιν ἐλλάμπει] for those she governs. Hence she has been said to be war-loving in respect of her unifying influence [καθ' ἕνωσιν], but in his case it is with regard to his dividing influence [κατὰ διαίρεσιν].[41]

Athena achieves unity among the conflicting powers in the cosmos by subduing them under the Demiurgic order (*In Prm.* 687, 16–18). That means that she allots each an appropriate place as, for example, she enforces that the better side of an opposition rules over the worse (*In Ti.* I 168, 6–8).[42]

All in all, the virgin goddesses in Proclus' metaphysics are determined by their purity, that is, by being unmingled with lower entities. Due to their purity they can fulfill a purifying role with regard to the entities of their own level and an elevating and an ordering function with regard to lower entities. It is striking that the virgin goddesses—although they are in some sense (at least by name) female goddesses—are not determined through the "typical female activity" of multiplying and even seem to be opposed to this activity. Since they are defined as pure, they seem to be dominated by remaining (as the male deities) and not by procession (as the female deities). Furthermore, as elevating causes, they provoke a movement that is opposed to the activity of multiplying. And as causes of order they are unifying. Athena's warfare does not lead to a multiplication of the cosmic forces but unites them.

Thus, we must consider whether the analysis of Proclus' characterization of the virgin goddesses' reveals them as virtual male deities who are female in name only. The difficulties of determining the place of the virgin goddesses regarding the polarity of maleness and femaleness will be discussed in the next section.

The Virgin Goddesses and the Binary

In the last section, we have seen that the virgin goddesses in Proclus' metaphysics are immaculate deities who are able—due to their purity—to fulfill protective (purifying), elevating, and ordering functions. It has been shown also that these functions seem to be closer to maleness than to femaleness because in ordering, elevating, and protecting, the virgin goddesses act as unifying causes or prevent multiplication. The difficulty of integrating the virgin goddesses into the classification of maleness and femaleness will now be discussed in more detail.

There are many aspects in Proclus' description of the virgin goddesses that give them quite a male appearance. Athena is explicitly described as "unfemale [ἀθήλυντον]" (*In R.* II 192, 18). Furthermore, she is disassociated from the female sphere due to being generated without a mother and due to being connected to the number "seven," which has male connotations because of its oddness.

> And the unfeminized character [ἀθήλυντον] of the heptad and its derivation from the monad alone [τὸ ἐκ μόνης εἶναι μονάδος] are celebrated, and it is above all the third monad and the heptad that constitute an image of Athena.[43]

Furthermore, the virgin goddesses are active in a way that is more similar to male than to female deities. Athena is described as a unifying cause, which is—like the male deities—characterized by remaining and which provides other entities with stability. This is a common feature of her purifying, her elevating and her ordering function.

> And if the universe is ever said to be "indissoluble" (*Tim.* 41a), she is bestower of its permanence [διαμονῆς]; and if it is said to dance for all time, she is leader of the chorus by a single reason-principle and a single order [καθ' ἕνα λόγον καὶ μίαν τάξιν]. She therefore watches over all the creation of her father, holds it together and turns it back to him and conquers all material indefiniteness.[44]

In a similar way, Hestia is clearly distinguished from the maternal goddesses Hera because she is characterized by remaining and unification.

> From herself Hestia provides unabating permanence [τὴν ἀκλινῆ διαμονὴν], the establishment [of beings] in themselves [ἕδραν ἐν ἑαυτοῖς] and indissoluble essence [τὴν οὐσίαν ἀδιάλυτον], while Hera provides procession and multiplication into lower levels of being and is the life-creating spring of the reason-principles and mother of the generative powers. This is why she is also said to cooperate with the demiurgic Zeus, since through their association she bears maternally what Zeus engenders paternally, but Hestia is said to remain in herself [μένειν ἐφ' ἑαυτῆς], since she keeps her virginity immaculate and is the cause of identity for all things.[45]

Thus, if we consider the tension of unifying and multiplying powers on which Proclus' metaphysical system is based,[46] the virgin goddesses belong to the unifying causes and side therefore with the male deities. On the lower levels of reality, at which point the perfection has already significantly decreased, they assist the male deities in their "struggle" with the multiplying powers. The unifying activities as well as the emphasis on the "unfemale" character of the virgin goddesses let them appear as de facto male entities given the definition of maleness as being a mixture in which the unifying element (limit) is especially strong.

But it would be hasty to determine the virgin goddesses as virtual male deities who are just given a female name. For as there are reasons to regard the virgin goddesses as male, there are also reasons to see them as female.

Athena and Artemis on the hypercosmic level[47] are part of the life-giving Core who is triadically structured as Artemis, Persephone, and Athena.[48] As a female, life-giving deity Core unites the maternal and the virginal.

> Whence Core too is said to remain a virgin [παρθένος λέγεται μένειν] by virtue of the Artemis and the Athena in herself, while by the fertile power [γόνιμον δύναμιν] of Persephone she is said to approach and to be attached to the third Demiurge [Hades] and, as Orpheus says, to bear [τίκτειν].[49]

Due to being part of Core, Artemis and Athena are also deeply connected with Rhea, since Core is described as proceeding directly from the life-giving monad.

> Just as the triad of the hegemonic demiurges comes to be out of the paternal monad, so also the life-giving order [Core] of the assimilatory gods proceeds out of the life-giving source [Rhea] which obtains among them [the intellective gods] the lot of the intermediary center, and, here again, a triad receives its existence from a single monad.[50]

Thus, although Athena is described as "motherless" and emerges in her first manifestation solely from the Demiurge, the hypercosmic Athena belongs also to the chain of the maternal goddess Rhea, due to being a part of Core.[51] And Artemis is also in her lower manifestation strongly associated with maternal goddesses. On the hypercosmic-encosmic level, she is part of the life-giving triad which is constituted by Demeter, Hera, and Artemis (*Theol. Plat.* VI 22, 3–11).[52]

Now if we take a closer look at the functions the virgin goddesses fulfill in these cases, we find again that they act in a way that lets them appear as strongly participating in Limit and therefore as quite male. In Core, the virgin goddesses are unifying powers. Core contains in herself—as all self-constituted principles (*El. Theol.* 42, 1–4)—the dynamic of remaining, procession, and reversion, whereby Persephone takes on the "female" part of procession, while Artemis and Athena are responsible for remaining and reversion.

> Whereas the Artemis and the Athena in her always preserve an unchanging virginity, for the former is characterized by her quality of stability [τὸ μόνιμον], the latter by that of reversion [τὸ ἐπιστρεπτικὸν], while the generative [γεννητικὸν] aspect is allotted in the middle order in her.[53]

And the hypercosmic-encosmic Artemis is the bottom of the life-giving triad and fulfills a perfective and guarding rather than a multiplying, generative function.

> But Artemis obtained the lot at the bottom, since she moves all the form-principles in nature to activity and the imperfection of matter to perfection. Therefore the theologians and Socrates in the *Theaetetus* call her "lochia" since she guards [ἔφορον] the physical procession and generation.[54]

Thus, the virgin goddesses are not totally disconnected from what is associated with femaleness. They are necessary constituents of altogether female triads on the lower levels of reality and thereby they are deeply connected with the female activity of causing procession and multiplication. But in the female triads, the virgin goddesses are not responsible for procession but either for remaining or for reversion.

Overall, it seems to be difficult to determine the virgin goddesses as simply "male" or "female." It might therefore appear likely that they are androgynous deities. As the male entities are characterized as mixtures that participate more in Limit and the female entities as mixtures that participate more in the Unlimited, the androgynous entities may be best characterized as balanced mixtures in which neither the unifying element nor the multiplying element is especially strong (relative to the level of reality in question).

But it is also problematic to determine the virgin goddesses as androgynous entities in this sense given that Proclus describes the virgin goddesses as strongly participating in Limit. As we have seen, the virgin goddesses "despise [μισῆσαι]" (*In Crat.* 179, 6) what is connected to limitlessness, namely, the multiplying activity that distinguishes femaleness. Moreover, if the virgin goddesses were androgynous in the sense of balanced mixtures, they would be more characterized by limit than the female deities but less than the male deities. But if we regard a male and a virginal deity of the same level—as Zeus and Athena on the intellective level—the virgin goddesses seems to be even more determined by limit than the male deity.

Zeus is—although he is a paternal, male deity—already strongly mixed with limitlessness. Proclus states that Zeus has generative powers (*In Crat.* 183, 30–31), that he is a cause of life (*In Crat.* 101, 21–28), and that he is not only monadic but also dyadic (*In Ti.* II 242, 2–4).[55] In contrast, the Athena on the intellective level appears to be totally disconnected from the generative activity. Furthermore, Zeus is perfect to such a low degree that he needs the protection of the Curetes to remain unmingled with lower entities (*In Crat.* 101, 34–38). Athena, as the leader of the Curetes, participates not only in Limit to such a high degree that she can preserve herself from contamination by lower entities, but she preserves also the Demiurge.

> And one of the principal intellective henads within him [within the Demiurge] is this immaculate and invincible divinity [ἄχραντος καὶ ἀδάμαστος θεότης], thanks to whom [καθ' ἣν] the Demiurge himself remains unswerving and unflinching [ἀκλινὴς μένει καὶ ἄτρεπτος], and all things that proceed from him participate in an unyielding power by which he thinks all things in transcendence, removed from all of reality. All the theologians call this divinity Athena.[56]

Thus, Athena does not appear as an androgynous deity in the sense of a balanced mixture when compared to Zeus. But she appears as quasi-male—or even *hyper*male—since she is more characterized by limit than even Zeus is, the father of the intellective gods (and of Athena herself). In a similar way, Themis—in her virginal manifestation—is described as a goddess who enables the Demiurge to take care of stability and permanence of the cosmos and who seems therefore more strongly associated with limit than he is (*In Ti.* I 396, 29–397, 3).

Thus, the virgin goddesses cannot be classified simply as male, as female, or as androgynous.[57] At first, the virgin goddesses appear to be male or quasi-male deities because they are unifying powers that strongly participate in Limit. Nevertheless, some virgin goddesses—as Artemis and Athena on the hypercosmic level—are parts of female triads. And furthermore, the classification of the virgin goddesses as male is difficult because the virgin goddesses are even more characterized by limit than the male deities of the same level, as, for example, the Curete Athena is more unifying than the Demiurge Zeus. Athena appears, on the one hand, as somewhat "*hyper*male" in relation to Zeus but, on the other hand, also as at least partly female if she is regarded as a part of Core.

A further difference from both the male and the female deities is that the virgin goddesses do not play a direct part in procreation. As mentioned above, the virgin goddesses have no part in the female contribution: they do not incite generative multiplication. But there is also no passage in which Proclus ascribes a paternal function to them. They do not sire together with a multiplying deity who incites them. Thus, the virgin goddesses seem to stand somewhat aside from the causal chains that enable procreation within the metaphysical realm. From there they assist the paternal and the maternal causes by their purifying, elevating, and ordering function without getting directly involved in their procreative activities.[58]

Overall, the virgin goddesses show that Proclus' metaphysical system contains a complexity that cannot be captured by a simple "male-female" scheme. On the first level beneath the One, we have a binary distinction of unifying limit and multiplying limitlessness, with all entities below this level being mixtures of both principles. Instead of a binary distinction, there is a continuum of mixtures. Male entities are more characterized by limit and female entities by limitlessness and in between there is room for balanced mixtures. But on the lower levels of Proclus' system, even this more complex picture is no longer capable of grasping the variety of entities. Starting with the intermediary level of the intellective gods, we have virgin goddesses who are strongly associated with limit but who cannot be characterized simply as male.

On the levels of reality which are (relatively) far removed from the One, the multiplying limitlessness gains power relative to the unifying limit, and the deities of these levels (even the male ones) have a stronger inclination toward procession and multiplication than the deities of higher levels. In this situation, they need the assistance of a new kind of deities, namely, of the virgin goddesses, who can dissociate themselves easier from the influence of limitlessness because they are not directly involved in procreation. The virgin goddesses can focus totally on remaining stable and pure while the paternal gods—despite their unifying function—must be open to the inciting activity of the maternal goddesses. Due to their purity, the virgin goddesses can then protect the other gods and goddesses from contamination and assist in the unification of the cosmos.

Conclusion

As our examination has shown, we must characterize the virgin goddesses in Proclus' metaphysics without classifying them as simply male or female. What can be said about these goddesses is that they are distinguished by their purity. Due to their purity, they can join male and female principles and protect them from getting mixed with secondary entities. The first Athena belongs indeed to a male deity (Zeus) and the second Athena to a female deity (Core), but despite this fact, Athena is established in both as a stabilizing element (*In Crat.* 185, 7–12). But virgin goddesses can exist also independently. In this case, they cause unity with regard to the cosmos and the lower beings in it (*In Crat.* 185, 7–12). Thus, due to their own crucial feature, that is, due to their purity, the virgin goddesses are deities who fulfill unifying functions by being protective, elevating, and ordering. Proclus uses certain elements from his "male-female" scheme to characterize the virgin goddesses, but they can be reduced neither to maleness nor to femaleness.

We have also seen that the female deities are characterized as inferior to the male deities. Due to their multiplying function they are dissimilar to the One (i.e., the Good). The virgin deities are not affected by this devaluation of the female deities because they are also unifying—even if not male—causes. But this does nothing to raise the value of femaleness, and there are two reasons for this.

First, the positive connotations connected with the virgin goddesses have no real consequences for the concept of femaleness since the virgin goddesses are set apart from femaleness due to the fact that femaleness is determined mainly through the multiplying activity in procreation from which the virgin goddesses are removed. In fact, although they are neither male nor female, they are closer to the male than to the female because they are stable, unifying causes.[59]

Second, Proclus does not state explicitly how similar the virgin goddesses are to the One in comparison to male and female deities of the same level. Certainly, their unifying function—in which they can even surpass the male deities—let them appear quite close to the One. But the One is also—in a hidden, unspeakable way—the cause of procreation, and to this extent, the male deities in paternal functions who are simultaneously unifying and causally involved in procreation seem to be more like the One than the virgin goddesses who stand beside the procreative chains.

To end this paper, I want to give a short upshot of this metaphysical system for women in the sensible world. The question is what significance Proclus' conception of the virgin goddesses has for women who—as Proclus recommends for all humans—gaze at the intelligible world and the deities there to gain a model for their own lives.

Surely, a deeper examination is necessary regarding the question of how far the distinction between male deities as unifying and female deities as multiplying carries on to men and women in the sensible world. To offer such an examination is beyond the scope of this paper. I can just hint briefly at three aspects in which Proclus might regard procreation in the sensible realm as closer connected with multiplication in the case of women than in the case of men, and due to which the idea of abstaining from getting entangled with multiplication by remaining virginal seems to carry on—at least partly—to women in the sensible world.

First, the male's contribution to procreation in Neoplatonic embryology is the potential, unified λόγοι in the semen, while the mother's contribution is the actualization and multiplication of these λόγοι.[60] Next, the mother's body is regarded as much more affected by procreation than the father's body in ancient medicine, and not just in the obvious sense that the mother's body carries the baby and gives birth to it, but the whole female body is conceptualized as somewhat "distorted" and "less unified" due to its procreative function and its requirements.[61] Finally, since—in Proclus' time—the care for the young child is regarded as part of the women's duty in the procreation and upbringing of children, becoming a mother is connected with a multiplicity of assignments, which binds the thoughts and activities of women to the sphere of the house, or more general, to the sensible realm and which get easily in conflict with the requirements needed to reach the highest unity of one's own life through a deep engagement in philosophy.[62]

If we keep this in mind while looking at the virgin goddesses in Proclus from the perspective of women in the sensible world, the virgin goddesses seem to present, on the one hand, a way of life that leaves behind what is regarded as bad about being a woman, namely, the entanglement with multiplication and procession, which in the sensible world amounts to the entanglement with nature, irrationality, the body, matter, or becoming in general. But this way of life demands transcending femaleness. It is therefore not a more emancipated way of being female, but a way of avoiding femaleness despite having a female body.

On the other hand, the virgin goddesses seem also to present a kind of dilemma. For whereas the male deities connect being unifying with being procreative, women seem to have to choose to either remain virginal and thereby to abstain from their procreative potential, or to procreate but thereby to get involved in multiplication, procession, or becoming. Both decisions seem to make them in some way dissimilar to the One and therefore inferior to the male, which can imitate the One most perfectly.[63]

Notes

1. I use the word *virgin* in this paper as a translation of the Greek *παρθένος*. But one should keep in mind that while *virgin* can refer to men as well as to women, *παρθένος* implies that the referent is a woman.

2. An exception seems to be Hestia who is associated with the "typical female" sphere of the private home and the hearth. However, as it is emphasized by Jean-Pierre Vernant, "Hestia-Hermès: Sur l'expression religieuse de l'espace et du movement chez les Grecs," *L'Homme* 3 (1963): 19, Hestia rejects at least one aspect of the "typical female" life due to her virginity, namely marriage, a social institution in which the woman was the "mobile element" since she moved from her parental home to the home of her husband's family, and which is therefore incompatible with Hestia's permanence and inalterability.

3. See, for example, Gillian Clark, *Women in Late Antiquity: Pagan and Christian Lifestyles* (Oxford, UK: Clarendon Press, 1993), 119; and Froma I. Zeitlin, *Playing the Other: Gender and Society in Classical Greek Literature* (Chicago: University of Chicago Press, 1996), 235.

4. I provide a more detail account on female (maternal) causes in Proclus in Jana Schultz, "Mütterliche Ursachen in Proklos' Metaphysik," *Philologus* 163.2 (2019).

5. *In Ti.* I 220, 4–10, Runia, Share. The determination of the female principles as multiplying is also discussed by Dirk Baltzly, "Proclus and Theodore of Asine on Female Philosopher-Rulers: Patriarchy, Metempsychosis, and Women in the Neoplatonic Commentary Tradition," *Ancient Philosophy* 33 (2013): 414.

6. *Theol. Plat.* IV 81, 20–23.

7. *Procreation* is used in this paper to signify a specific case of procession in the metaphysical realm, namely, a procession in which a male and a female deity work together to cause a secondary being that is not just a lower manifestation of themselves but another "kind" of deity, as, for example, Zeus is—although he has features from both parents—not just a lower Cronus or a lower Rhea. Instead he is characterized by the feature of being creative that belongs neither to his father nor to his mother (*In Crat.* 101, 21–27). The procession of Athena through the different levels of reality, on the contrary, is not a case of procreation in this sense, but of mere procession, since the results of this procession are just lower manifestations of Athena herself. As Danielle A. Layne, "Feminine Power in Proclus' Commentary on Plato's Timaeus," *Hypatia* 36, no. 1 (2021): 126 argues, the fact that entities are procreated that are not just lower manifestations of their father or mother is due to the activity of the mother, since the generative,

female power is associated with otherness in the sense that it enables the genesis of authentic others instead of mere images of the causes.

8. I offer a more detailed account of the collaboration of paternal and maternal causes in Proclus' metaphysics in Schultz, "Mütterliche Ursachen," 256–61.

9. For Proclus' determination of otherness as female, see also Werner Beierwaltes, "Andersheit. Grundriss einer neuplatonischen Begriffsgeschichte," *Archiv für Begriffsgeschichte* 16, no. 2 (1972), 181.

10. *Theol. Plat.* IV 80, 1–5.

11. *El. Theol.* 100, 4–6.

12. It is interesting that the opposition of Limit and Unlimited is one of the main structures of Proclus' metaphysical system, since this opposition is also one of the ten principles (ἀρχὰς δέκα) in the Pythagorean table of opposites. And here as well maleness relates to Limit and femaleness to the Unlimited (see Aristotle's report on the Pythagorean table of opposites in his *Metaphysics* (386a22–25)). For the Pythagorean influence on Proclus' conception of maleness and femaleness, see also Baltzly "Female Philosopher-Rulers," 414. However, the dyad of Limit and the Unlimited appears as a fundamental principle also in Plato's *Philebus* 23c9–10.

13. *Theol. Plat.* III 32, 13–19. For Limit as the cause of unity and Unlimited as the cause of plurality see also E. R. Dodds, *The Elements of Theology* (Oxford, UK: Clarendon, 1963), 247.

14. The determination of the dyad as a female principle is deeply rooted in the Platonic tradition. As John Dillon, "Female Principles in Platonism," *Itaca* 1 (1985): 113–15 points out the dyad is described as a female metaphysical principle already by Xenocrates (Frg. 133).

15. The analogy between the One and the Dyad, on the one hand, and Limit and Unlimited, on the other hand, is also emphasizes by Beierwaltes, "Andersheit," 179.

16. A connection between remaining and maleness and between procession and femaleness is also described by Radek Chlup, *Proclus: An Introduction* (Cambridge: Cambridge University Press, 2012), 124, but with regard to the paternal and generative function of these principles.

17. *In Crat.* 63, 16–20, Duvick.

18. The connecting activity of Rhea is most obvious in Proclus' *Commentary to Plato's Cratylus* where he states that everything which reverts to Cronus is connected with him through Rhea (143, 11–15).

19. *In Ti.* II 270, 9–13, Baltzly. These examples are surely not sufficient to expose the whole story of the connective activities of female deities in Proclus' metaphysics. But for the purpose of this examination it suffices to demonstrate that Proclus' characterization of the female deities as multiplying does not cover the whole range of their activities. For a detailed discussion of the binding powers of female deities see Layne, "Feminine Power," 128–29.

20. I provide a discussion of further reasons for male (paternal) causes sometimes acting multiplying and female (maternal) causes sometimes acting unifying in Schultz, 263–64.

21. *Theol. Plat.* IV 91, 21–26.

22. As Layne, 128 shows, the status of male and female entities as mixtures instead of pure manifestations of either Limit or the Unlimited can also been derived from the facts that all beings are images of Phanes, who is androgynous, since as the Living Being Itself he contains the male and the female.

23. One must keep in mind here that the higher levels of reality are more dominated by limit and the lower levels of reality are more dominated by limitlessness. Proclus states this in his *Commentary on Plato's Timaeus* with regard to the realm of soul and the realm of body: "For it is also true that what is definite [περατοειδὲς] here [on the bodily realm] is more undefined [μᾶλλον ἄπειρον] than what is indefinite [ἀπείρου] there [on the realm of soul], so that in every case the fall [of the soul] will be to something worse" (*In Ti.* III 283, 30–32). That means that, for example, the intellective gods are altogether more characterized by limit than the hypercosmic gods, but if we compare the intellective gods with each other, then the male intellective gods are especially determined by limit and the female intellective gods by limitlessness. In consequence, all female deities are indeed characterized by being multiplying and by being a manifestation of limitlessness relative to the other entities of their realm, but a female deity of a high realm (as the intelligible-intellective Adrasteia) might nevertheless participate more in Limit than a male deity of a low realm (as the encosmic Ares).

24. Baltzly, 414 argues that the existence of androgynous principles within the metaphysical realm shows that also the male and female principles are—despite their difference—strongly united on the higher levels of reality.

25. In this context it is interesting that the association of the female with otherness, differentiation, and multiplication in Hesiod's *Theogony* is already connected with the devaluation of women. Here, Pandora appears as the absolute (and negative) Other, since she is totally disconnected from the generative line that leads from the first gods to the mortal living beings (*Theogony*, 561–612; see also Zeitlin, "Playing the Other," 57). But limitlessness and otherness in Proclus' metaphysics are not an "absolute Other," since they are also caused by the One. Limitlessness and otherness are therefore not causes of evil (as Pandora) but rather necessary—even if inferior—parts of reality. See also Emilie Kutash, *The Ten Gifts of the Demiurge. Proclus' Commentary on Plato's Timaeus* (Bristol: Bristol Classical Press, 2011), 249. Regarding Hesiod's *Theogony*, one might wonder how Proclus regards Pandora in the context of the question of maleness and femaleness, especially because Athena and Pandora seem to be connected insofar as they are both "motherless daughters of Zeus" (see Nicole Loraux, *The Children of Athena: Athenian Ideas about Citizenship and the Division*

between the Sexes (Princeton: Princeton University Press, 1984), 79–80 and Zeitlin, 72–73). But since Athena—as we will see in the following sections—cannot really be regarded as female because of being a unifying deity, Pandora seems to represent in an extreme way what it is to be female for Proclus, that is, to multiply, for as the origin of all women she somewhat "multiplies the multipliers." (I owe thanks to Jessica Decker and Danielle Layne for this expression of Pandora's nature and, generally, for pointing me to the relationship of Athena and Pandora and its significance to the question of gender binarity in Proclus.) But, nevertheless, Pandora also cannot simply be determined as a woman, since she is rather a kind of android (see Elissa Marder, "Pandora's Fireworks; or, Questions Concerning Feminity, Technology, and the Limits of the Human," *Philosophy and Rhetoric* 47, no. 2 [2014], 387). Thus, it seems as if Athena and Pandora threaten to undermine Proclus' determination of femaleness as being multiplying and of maleness as being unifying from two sides. Unfortunately, however, in what we have left from Proclus' works, we do not find many passages in which he deals with Pandora. In his commentary on Hesiod's *Works and Days*, he equalizes Pandora with the nonrational soul (51, 3)—as Olympiodorus also argues in his *Commentary on Plato's Gorgias* (48.7, 1–18)—but he does not analyze, or even mention, the idea that Pandora is the origin of all women. Thus, we cannot know for sure how Proclus might have judged Pandora with regard to this aspect of Hesiod's myth.

26. For a detailed discussion of this passage see also Baltzly, 414–16.

27. For the maternal function of establishing the offspring as a separate entity see also James Wilberding, *Forms, Souls and Embryos: Neoplatonists on Human Reproduction* (New York: Routledge 2017), 44. I provide a more detailed analysis of the conjunction of Uranus and Gaia in Schultz, 267–68.

28. The connection of procession and the loss of perfection is described by S. E. Gersh, ΚΙΝΗΣΙΣ ΑΚΙΝΗΤΟΣ. A *Study of Spiritual Motion in the Philosophy of Proclus* (Leiden: Brill, 1973) 63. The superiority of the paternal role in procreation is connected to Jean Trouillard's observation ("La Μονή Selon Proclos," in *Le Neoplatonisme*, eds. P. M. Schuhl and P. Hadot [Paris: Centre National de la Recherche Scientifique, 1971], 230–31) that a cause is—in Proclus' system—the more powerful the less it acts. Beierwaltes, 187 describes a similarly justified value-judgment regarding sameness and otherness.

29. For a discussion of this principle see Kutash, *Ten Gifts*, 129.

30. The analogy between the One and the paternal causes is emphasized also by Ernst-Otto Onnasch and Ben Shomakers, *Proklos. Theologische Grundlegung* (Hamburg: Felix Meiner, 2015), 316.

31. There seems to be a tension between this general devaluation of femaleness in Proclus and the idea that the first gendered deity is the female Night. (For a detailed discussion of Night as the first gendered goddess, see Layne, 127.) For normally Proclus regards the properties that appear "earlier"

in his metaphysical system as higher than the properties that appear "later." A detailed discussion of this tension is beyond the scope of this paper. I can just offer two short remarks. First, it is striking that the female deities seem to undermine the principle that the "earlier" an entity appears in the metaphysical system, the higher its value, also on other occasions. For while the paternal gods are unambiguously superior to their offspring, Proclus marks the maternal goddesses as being superior as well as inferior to them (*Theol. Plat.* I 122, 13–20, see also Wilberding, *Forms, Souls and Embryos*, 43). Second, Phanes stands in a "male relationship" to Night—despite being androgynous—insofar as they work together as a paternal and a maternal cause (*In Ti.* I 450, 21–25). Thus, although Night is the first gendered goddess, the hierarchy between maleness and femaleness is somehow "saved" by the subordination of Night's maternal activity under Phanes' paternal activity.

32. *In Crat.* 179, 1–4; Duvick.

33. Proclus seems to refer to common notions of virginity in ancient Greek culture when he characterizes virgin goddesses as "uncontaminated" in the sense of being "untouched" by others. As Giulia Sissa argues in *Greek Virginity*, trans. Arthur Goldhammer (Cambridge: Harvard University Press, 1990), 5 and 159, female bodies were conceptualized within the semantic field of "open" and "closed," in consequence of which the virgin body was connected with closeness—that is, with being a self-contained whole—and the female body with openness. In a similar way, Zeitlin, 131, emphasizes that the virgin body was theorized as being a "whole unto itself, a sign of the self's integrity."

34. For an examination of the relationship of Cronus and the Curetes see also Luc Brisson, "La Place des Oracles Chaldaïques dans la Théologie Platonicienne," in *Proclus et la Théologie Platonicienne*, eds. A. Ph. Segonds and C. Steel (Leuven: Leuven University Press, 2000), 147 and "Kronos, Summit of the Intellective Hebdomad in Proclus' Interpretation of the Chaldaean Oracles," in *Platonic Ideas and Concept Formation in Ancient and Medieval Thought*, eds. Gerd Van Riel and Caroline Macé (Leuven: Leuven University Press, 2004), 194.

35. *In Ti.* I 140, 28–141, 3; Tarrant.

36. *El. Theol.* 156, 7–11; Dodds.

37. *El. Theol.* 158, 6–10; Dodds.

38. Robbert M. Van Den Berg, "Towards the Paternal Harbour. Proclean Theurgy and the Contemplation of the Forms," in: *Proclus et la Théologie Platonicienne*, eds. A. Ph. Segonds and C. Steel (Leuven: Leuven University Press, 2000), 432–33, and *Proclus' Hymns: Essay, Translations, Commentary* (Leiden: Brill, 2001), 289–90 emphasizes that this elevating activity gives Athena also a special function in theurgy. The human soul can revert to the Demiurge only by the assistance of Athena who connects the partial human intellect with the universal demiurgic intellect.

39. *In Ti.* I 396, 29–397, 3; Runia, Share.

40. Another emblem of Athena's ordering function is the art of weaving, which is on the intellective level a creative, intellectual activity (*In Ti.* I 135, 1–7). Through weaving Athena gains a model for ordering the contrary powers in the cosmos so that her arts of warfare and of weaving are deeply interconnected (*In Ti.* I 135, 12–15).

41. *In Ti.* I 167, 30–168, 2, Tarrant.

42. Regarding the relationship of virgin goddesses to maleness and femaleness, it is interesting that Athena's activity of gaining victory by allotting opposing powers to their appropriate place and by making them dependent on her father places her traditionally on the side of the male deities. In Aeschylus' *Eumenides*, in which male and female deities and humans struggle for dominance, Athena defeats the Erinyes by integrating them into the new—paternal—order (752–900; see also Zeitlin, 113).

43. *In Ti.* I 151, 14–15, Tarrant.

44. *In Crat.* 185, 33–38, Duvick.

45. *In Crat.* 139, 3–11, Duvick.

46. Kutash, 55 argues that in his interpretation of Plato's Atlantis myth in the first book of his *Commenary on Plato's Timaeus*, Proclus offers a notion of a rivalry which has its origin in the first Limit and the first Unlimited and which proceeds through all levels of reality.

47. Themis might appear to be even more characterized in a "female way" than Artemis and Athena, since she is called "mother" of the Fates when identified with Ananke (*In R.* II 208, 5). But Themis is described as a deity who manifests herself at one level as a virginal and at another level as a maternal goddess: "For this reason she [Themis] remains a virgin prior to the procession of the Demiurge, [. . .] but [then] she joints with Zeus in producing the triad of seasons" (*In Ti.* I 397, 2–5). And in this lower manifestation, Themis also engenders the Fates together with Zeus: "For the Demiurge too as Orpheus says, receives nourishment from Adrasteia, consorts with Necessity and generates Fate" (*In Ti.* III 274, 17–20). Thus, the "mother of the Fates" is not the same manifestation of Themis as the one who remains virginal.

48. The structure of the Coric triad is also described by Brisson, "La Place des Oracles Chaldaïques," 151 and by Chlup, *Proclus*, 126).

49. *In Crat.* 179, 17–20; Duvick, slightly changed.

50. *Theol. Plat.* VI 48, 14–19.

51. Spyridon Rangos, "Proclus and Artemis: On the Relevance of Neoplatonism to the Modern Study of Ancient Religion," *Kernos* 13 (2000), 57–58 refers also to Rhea as the origin of the hypercosmic Artemis when arguing that the virgin goddess Artemis is quite closely connected to the maternal goddesses in Proclus' metaphysical system.

52. For a detailed analysis of the hypercosmic-encosmic Artemis see Rangos, "Proclus and Artemis," 61–64.

53. *In Crat.* 179, 22–25; Duvick.

54. *Theol. Plat.* VI 98, 8–13.

55. Regarding the nature of Zeus, an interpretation along these lines is also offered by John Dillon, "The Role of the Demiurge in the *Platonic Theology*," in *Proclus et la Théologie Platonicienne*, eds. A. Ph. Segonds and C. Steel (Leuven: Leuven University Press, 2000), 346. He emphasizes that Zeus combines the powers associated with Limit and Unlimited to create the cosmos. Similarly, Jan Opsomer, "The Natural World," in *All From One: A Guide to Proclus*, eds. Pieter D'Hoine and Marije Martijn (Oxford: Oxford University Press, 2017, 150 describes the Demiurge as an entity in which the paternal and maternal series converge.

56. *In Ti.* I 166, 5–10; Tarrant.

57. We find in Proclus' characterization of the virgin goddesses something similar to what Loreaux, *The Children of Athena*, 64 states regarding the Athena in the myth of the autochthonous origin of the Athenian people, namely, that Athena as a virgin is a person who transcends all gender categories since she is both, masculine and feminine, and neither.

58. The topos of the virgin goddesses as assisting in procreation is also a common notion in Greek mythology. Artemis, for example, is a patroness of childbirth. See Rangos, 70–71. And Athena plays a crucial role in the procreation and upbringing of Erichthonius without actually giving birth to him. See Loreaux, 8.

59. This is quite a strange conclusion regarding the fact that the virginal deities are addressed as females, for example by being called "goddesses." But, on the other hand, the idea that a virgin is not (yet) a "real woman" or "really female" is not uncommon in ancient Greek culture and philosophical conceptualization. In *To Marcella*, for example, Porphyry prompts his wife to "flee from every effeminate element of the soul as if you are clothed in a male body" (296, 2–4; Wicker), while simultaneously praising the "virginal soul" (296, 4; Wicker), so that here also "virginal" seems to stand in contrast to femaleness rather than being a part of it. The conceptual separation of femaleness and virginity is based on a problematic reduction of femaleness to sexual activity and things associated with sexuality as, for example, the entanglement with irrationality and the realm of becoming. This connection is especially apparent in Philo of Alexandria's *De Cherubim* where being a woman and being a virgin are described as mutually exclusive, since womanhood is defined explicitly by menstruation, sexual activity, and pregnancy. See 50, 1–13, and also Dorothy Sly, *Philo's Perception of Women* (Atlanta: Scholars Press, 1990), 72–74.

60. For a detailed discussion of Proclus' description of the mother's contribution in embryology, see Wilberding, 36–37).

61. Zeitlin, 237 argues that the female body is conceptualized in ancient Greek culture as a "discordant harmony," as a "diversity in unity," and as much

less unified than the male body, since the female body is seen as subjected to "flux and change [which] put [the woman] at odds with herself." The idea of the female body as a diversity relates to its procreative function. In the *Hippocratic Corpus*, for instance, the female body and its diseases are considered as fundamentally different from the male body and the diseases of men, whereby especially the womb and menstruation are regarded as responsible for many kinds of distortion that are not all directly connected with procreation. See Helen King, *Hippocrates' Woman: Reading the Female Body in Ancient Greece* (London: Routledge, 1998), 69. For since the womb is considered as wandering, it is held responsible for diseases in all parts of the body (see *Nature of Women* 47, 1–49, 6). However, the ancient medicine schools differ regarding the question of whether remaining virginal helps to diminish the distortions of the female body or if virginity even advances them. In the *Hippocratic Corpus*, sexual intercourse and pregnancy are offered as a kind of therapy for distortions arising with menarche, including madness and striving for suicide (*Girls* 1, 51–55). Soranus of Ephesus, instead, claims that abstaining from sexual intercourse is healthy for women and for men (see *Maladies des Femmes* I 9, 79–81).

62. We find an example of such a conflict between the duties of a mother and the requirements of philosophy in Porphyry's *To Marcella*, where Porphyry emphasizes that Marcella cannot follow him on his travels to continue her philosophical education due to her responsibility for her daughters (275, 19–22). For himself, in contrast, Porphyry does not see a conflict between his role as a (step) father and his role as a philosopher. Plato indeed aims at disconnecting bearing a child and caring for it with his idea of upbringing and educating all children in common by the state (*R.* 460d2–7). But in the philosophical conceptions of most Neoplatonists, including Proclus, such an ambition of radically changing the social lives of men and women is not present.

63. I thank the DFG (German Research Foundation) for funding the research for this paper as part of the project *Die Frau und das Weibliche im Neuplatonismus* (GZ: WI 3873/4-1). I also owe thanks to Jessica Elbert Decker, Danielle Layne, Monica Vilhauer, and the participants of the online workshop connected to this volume for their remarks and comments on an earlier version, which were crucial in helping the paper take its current form.

Bibliography

Baltzly, Dirk, trans., *Proclus: Commentary on Plato's Timaeus. Vol. III, Book 3, Part 1: Proclus on the World's Body*. Cambridge, UK: Cambridge University Press, 2007.

———. trans. *Proclus: Commentary on Plato's Timaeus. Vol. IV, Book 3, Part II: Proclus on the World Soul*. Cambridge, UK: Cambridge University Press, 2009.

———. trans. *Proclus: Commentary on Plato's Timaeus. Vol. V, Book 4: Proclus on Time and the Stars*. Cambridge, UK: Cambridge University Press, 2013.

———. "Proclus and Theodore of Asine on Female Philosopher-Rulers: Patriarchy, Metempsychosis, and Women in the Neoplatonic Commentary Tradition." *Ancient Philosophy*, no. 33 (2013): 403–24.

Beierwaltes, Werner. "Andersheit. Grundriß einer neuplatonischen Begriffsgeschichte." *Archiv für Begriffsgeschichte* 16, no. 2 (1972): 166–97.

Brisson, Luc. "La Place des Oracles Chaldaïques dans la Théologie Platonicienne." In *Proclus et la Théologie Platonicienne*, edited by A. Ph. Segonds and C. Steel, 109–62. Leuven, Belgium: Leuven University Press, 2000.

———. "Kronos, Summit of the Intellective Hebdomad in Proclus' Interpretation of the Chaldaean Oracles. In *Platonic Ideas and Concept Formation in Ancient and Medieval Thought*, edited by Gerd Van Riel and Caronline Macé, 191–210. Leuven, Belgium: Leuven University Press, 2004.

Burgière, P., and D. Gourevitch, ed. and trans. *Soranos D' Éphèse, Maladies des Femmes. Livre I*. Paris: Les Belles Lettres, 1988.

Burnet, Iohannes, ed., *Platonis Opera Tomus II*. Oxford, UK: Clarendon, 1901.

Chlup, Radek. *Proclus: An Introduction*. Cambridge, UK: Cambridge University Press, 2012.

Clark, Gillian. *Women in Late Antiquity. Pagan and Christian Lifestyles*. Oxford, UK: Clarendon, 1993.

Colson, F. H., and G. H. Whitakter, ed. and trans. *Philo of Alexandria: De Cherubim*. In *Philo. Volume II*. Cambridge, MA: Harvard University Press, 1994.

Diehl, Ernestus, ed. *Proklos: In Platonis Timaeum Commentaria I–III*. Leipzig, Germany: Teubner, 1903.

Dillon, John. "Female Principles in Platonism." *Itaca* 1 (1985), 107–23.

———. "The Role of the Demiurge in the *Platonic Theology*." In *Proclus et la Théologie Platonicienne*, edited by A. Ph. Segdonds and C. Steel, 339–49. Leuven, Belgium: Leuven University Press, 2000.

Dodds, E. R., ed. and trans. *Proclus: The Elements of Theology*. Oxford, UK: Clarendon: 1963.

Duvick, Brian, trans. *Proclus: On Plato Cratylus*. London: Duckworth, 2007.

Festugière, A. J., trans. *Proclus: Commentaire sur la République, Livre I–III*. Paris: Les Belles Lettres, 1970.

Gersh, S. E. ΚΙΝΗΣΙΣ ΑΚΙΝΗΤΟΣ. *A Study of Spiritual Motion in the Philosophy of Proclus*. Leiden, the Netherlands: Brill 1973.

Jaeger, W., ed. *Aristoteles: Metaphysica*, Oxford, UK: University Press, 1963.

King, Helen. *Hippocrates' Woman. Reading the Female Body in Ancient Greece*. London: Routledge, 1998.

Kroll, G., ed. *Proklos: In Platonis Rem Publicam Commentarii I–II*. Leipzig, Germany: Teubner, 1899–1901.

Kutash, Emilie. *The Ten Gifts of the Demiurge: Proclus' Commentary on Plato's* Timaeus. Bristol, UK: Bristol Classical Press, 2011.

Layne, Danielle. "Feminine Power in Proclus' *Commentary on Plato's Timaeus*," *Hypatia* 36, no. 1 (2021): 120–44.

Lloyd-Jones, H., and Herbert Weir Smyth, ed. and trans. *Aeschylus II: Agamemnon, Libation-Bearers, Eumenides, Fragments*. Cambridge, MA: Harvard University Press, 1963.

Loreaux, Nicole. *The Children of Athena: Athenian Ideas about Citizenship and the Division between the Sexes*. Princeton, NJ: Princeton University Press, 1984.

Marder, Elissa. "Pandora's Fireworks; or, Questions Concerning Femininity, Technology, and the Limits of the Human." *Philosophy and Rhetoric* 47, no. 2 (2014): 386–99.

Marzillo, Patrizia, ed. and trans. *Der Kommentar des Proklos zu Hesiods "Werken und Tagen."* Tübingen, Germany: Narr Francke, 2010.

Morrow, G. R., and J. M. Dillon, trans. *Proclus: Commentary on Plato's Parmenides*. Princeton, NJ: Princeton University Press, 1987.

Nauck, A., ed. *Poryphyry. Pros Marcellan*, Leipzig, Germany: Teubner 1886.

O'Brien Wicker, Kathleen, trans. *Porphyry: To Marcella*. Atlanta, GA: Scholars Press, 1987.

Onnasch, E.-O., and B. Schomakers, ed. and trans. *Proklos: Theologische Grundlegung*, Hamburg, Germany: Felix Meiner, 2015.

Opsomer, Jan. "The Natural World." In *All from One: A Guide to Proclus*, edited by Pieter D'Hoine and Marije Martijn, 139–66. Oxford, UK: Oxford University Press, 2017.

Parente, M. I., ed. and trans. *Senocrate e Ermodoro. Testimonianze e frammenti*. Pisa, Italy: Edizione della Normale, 2012.

Pasquali, G., ed. *Proklos: In Platonis Cratylum Commentaria*. Leipzig. Germany: Teubner: 1908.

Potter, P., ed. and trans. *Hippocrates: Girls*. In *Hippocrates IX*. Cambridge, MA. Harvard University Press, 2010.

———. ed, and trans. *Hippocrates. Nature of Women*, in *Hippocrates X*. Cambridge, MA: Harvard University Press, 2012.

Rangos, Spyridon. "Proclus and Artemis: On the Relevance of Neoplatonism to the Modern Study of Ancient Religion," *Kernos* 13 (2000): 47–84.

Runia, David T., and Michael Share, trans. *Proclus: Commentary on Plato's Timaeus. Vol. II, Book 2: Proclus on the Causes of the Cosmos and Its Creation*. Cambridge, MA: Cambridge University Press, 2008.

Saffrey, H. D., and L. G. Westerink, eds. and trans. *Proclus: Théologie Platonicienne. Livre I–VI*. Paris: Les Belles Lettres, 1968–1997.

Schultz, Jana. "Mütterliche Ursachen in Proklos' Metaphysik." *Philologus* 163, no. 2 (2019): 250–73.

Sissa, Giulia. *Greek Virginity*. Translated by Arthur Goldhammer. Cambridge, MA: Harvard University Press, 1990.

Slings, R. S., ed. *Platonis Rempublicam*. Oxford, UK: Clarendon, 2003.

Sly, Dorothy. *Philo's Perception of Women*. Atlanta, GA: Scholars Press, 1990.

Steel, C., ed. *Proclus: In Platonis Parmenidem Commentaria. Tomus I–III*. Oxford, UK: Clarendon, 2012–2014.

Tarrant, Harold, trans. *Proclus: Commentary on Plato's Timaeus. Vol. I, Book 1: Proclus on the Socratic State and Atlantis*. Cambridge, UK: Cambridge University Press, 2006.

Tarrant, Harold, trans. *Proclus: Commentary on Plato's Republic. Vol. VI, Book 5: Proclus on the Gods of Generation and the Creation of Humans*. Cambridge, UK: Cambridge University Press, 2017.

Trouillard, Jean. "La Μονή Selon Proclos." In *Le Neoplatonisme*, edited by P. M. Schuhl and P. Hadot, 229–40. Paris: Centre National de la Recherche Scientifique, 1971.

Van den Berg, Robbert M. "Towards the Paternal Harbour: Proclean Theurgy and the Contemplation of the Forms." In *Proclus et la Théologie Platonicienne*, edited by A. Ph. Segonds and C. Steel, 425–38. Leuven, Belgium: Leuven University Press, 2000.

———. *Proclus' Hymns: Essay, Translations, Commentary*. Leiden, the Netherlands: Brill, 2001.

Vernant, Jean-Pierre. "Hestia-Hermès: Sur l'expression religieuse de l'espace et du movement chez les Grecs," *L'Homme* 3 (1963): 12–50.

West, M. L., trans. *Hesiod: Theogony and Works and Days*. Oxford, UK: Oxford University Press, 1966.

Westerink, G., ed. *Olympiodorus: In Platonis Gorgiam Commentaria*. Leipzig. Germany: Teubner, 1970.

Wilberding, James. *Forms, Souls and Embryos: Neoplatonists on Human Reproduction*. New York: Routledge, 2017.

Zeitlin, Froma I. *Playing the Other: Gender and Society in Classical Greek Literature*. Chicago, IL: University of Chicago Press, 1996.

Chapter Ten

Hekate and the Liminality of Souls

William Koch

> The son of Cronos did her [Hekate] no wrong nor took anything away of all that was her portion among the former Titan gods: but she holds, as the division was at the first from the beginning, privilege both in earth, and in heaven, and in sea.
>
> —Hesiod, *Theogony* 423–27[1]

> For all around the hollows of the cartilage of [Hekate's] right flank, / The abundant liquid of the Primal Soul gushes unceasingly, / Completely ensouling the light, the fire, the aether and the Cosmoi.
>
> —*Chaldean Oracles* F51[2]

Knotted Binaries and Beyond

It can be argued that Platonism, as found in both the dialogues of Plato and later articulations, such as the *Chaldean Oracles*, is based on binaries whose inconsistencies are knotted together by impossible but necessary liminal figures. The following will focus on the figures of soul and the goddess Hekate in the hopes of showing that far from simply pointing to the failures of Platonism when it comes to the problem of strict binary thinking, the identification of the soul with the goddess Hekate points to a solution. Specifically, this identification gestures to the possible rejection of Platonic binaries altogether via an implicit acceptance of Hekate's own Pre-Platonic form and its further survival in a cultural battle between later Platonic religious practices and beliefs based on the *Chaldean Oracles* and *The Greek Magical Papyri*. The heart of this solution is the subversion of binary thinking in favor of an earlier or Pre-Platonic view of reality free from the contradiction-haunted positing of transcendence.

The Problem of the Soul

Soul is the name of a problem in Plato, or at least in the later Middle and Neoplatonic attempts to develop a consistent metaphysics out of Plato's dialogues.[3] Soul is an entity that straddles the long list of constitutive binaries in Platonic philosophy—eternal and temporal, Being and Becoming, form and matter. Soul both binds these binaries together and passes between them. To offer a variation of Jacobi's famous observation concerning Kant, it can be claimed that one cannot enter Platonic philosophy without a concern for the soul, but one cannot remain within it and preserve the reality of the soul (due to the contradictions surrounding it).[4] However, if we surrender the soul we surrender the fundamental appeal of Platonism and, arguably, its coherence.

To expand briefly on these points, consider how the possession of soul undergirds our relationship to Forms, providing us with access to absolute knowledge, whether through recollection or intellection. We can know the Forms, or come to know them, only because we are not just passive material bodies but, rather, we are ultimately soul—an entity that resembles the eternal, perfect, invisible, intelligible, and unchanging more than it does the sensible.[5] The achievement that Socrates is meant to have accomplished, and that the students of Plato likewise attempted to repeat, is only possible because of the soul. However, there is arguably no place for the soul in what Platonic readers understood as Plato's "system." To explain, the soul is clearly not perfect and unchangeable insofar as its health or sickness or its harmony or disharmony are the baseline for Platonic ethics. Its ability to learn and to forget, as well as to recall, equally attests to its volatility. Despite this, the central importance of the soul's immortality and its ability to pass nearer and further from Forms, while remaining essentially the same in its transcendence of matter and return to the material, requires that the soul somehow also be unchanging.

This incoherence of the soul, despite its location at the very heart of the so-called Theory of the Forms, can be made very clear by asking a simple question: Is there a Form of the soul? The Forms are supposed to provide an origin for each thing's nature, they are what explain commonality amid things of the same type, and thus they provide for the essence of given entities. Since there are indeed many souls, and these souls share characteristics, it seems necessary that there be a Form that each resembles or partakes in. If this is the case, however, then the arguments for the personal immortality of the soul fail because the soul will have had an origin in the one eternal Form, Soul Itself. The goal of philosophy will not just be the purification of the soul, but rather its return to Soul Itself and thus its own loss of individuality. In other words, we run into "the problem of personality" here: the immortality desired is a personal one, but a return to the Soul Itself is a loss of all personality and, indeed, all particular and temporal characteristics. A thing may certainly have an essence, that is, a Form, and undergo change. But if the goal is to identify oneself with the unchanging and eternal essence, then the goal is also to do away with everything personal and particular about oneself. If, however, there is no Form of the Soul, as most of the arguments of the *Phaedo* indicate, due to the fact that such an absolute Soul would not provide the desired type of immortality, perhaps each soul itself is a Form (as Aristotle and some medieval Catholic philosophers argue). This would provide us with immortality, to be sure, as well as the connection to the eternal that the Theory of the Forms requires, but it would land us in a similar set of incoherencies. How can the soul undergo the changes that are so important for it if it is an unchanging Form? How can there be so many similar souls if each is a unique Form? What explains their similarities? It is worth remembering here that Forms seem necessarily to be unique if they are to avoid recourse to further Forms to explain similarity amid themselves. So, we cannot enter or understand the Platonic system without the soul, but we cannot maintain the soul within that system. The soul cannot be a Form, it cannot have a Form, and yet no class of things such as souls can exist without a Form and no connection to the Forms can be achieved by humanity without the soul.

Though these tensions show up throughout Plato's corpus, it is perhaps most clearly seen in the *Phaedo*. There it is repeatedly claimed that the soul is "akin" to the Forms or "resembles" them: "[T]he soul is most like the divine, deathless, intelligible, uniform, indissoluble, always the same as itself" (*Phd.*, 80b). Despite this, a direct identification of soul as Form, or the claim that there is a distinct Form of the soul, are not given. Instead we find arguments that make clear that if the soul is too much like the Forms, specifically if it were a harmony, then the differences between souls would be impossible.

> Can this be true about the soul, that one soul is more and more fully a soul than another, or is less and less fully a soul, even to the smallest extent . . . Then if a soul is neither more nor less a soul than another, it has been harmonized to the same extent . . . that being the case, could one soul have more wickedness or virtue than another, if wickedness is disharmony and virtue harmony? (*Phd.*, 93b, 93e)

Here we see that the very reasons a soul can't be a harmony are also reasons it can't be a Form. The concluding argument of the *Phaedo* suggests that Forms have something like privileged instantiations, non-Form entities that most perfectly and fully manifest the nature of the Form and so never partake of its opposite. The soul is, then, identified with the privileged instantiation of the Form of Life. But, as we have suggested, this is necessarily an inadequate source of human immortality since individual souls would have to come from the Form of Life and their ultimate goal would be to return to it, thus losing the very individual immortality Socrates is interested in proving. The soul both is and is not like a Form. It both has and cannot have an originating Form. For this reason, some have argued that the *Phaedo* is particularly plagued by fallacious reasoning, especially the final argument concerning the soul and the Form of Life.[6]

We can see the inconsistency in the nature of the soul very clearly if we look to its cosmological role in the *Timaeus*. In fact, nowhere do we see the liminal nature of the soul more clearly than here in what would become perhaps the most foundational dialogue for Platonism. Although important work has been done on the role of the material container or place called *chora* in the *Timaeus*—for example, in Luce Irigaray's *Speculum of the Other Woman*, John Sallis's *Chorology*, and Jacques Derrida's essay "*Khōra*"—the soul plays just as constitutive and question-worthy a role in the cosmology being constructed in the dialogue. Similarly, both cosmic soul and *chora* are identified as female in gender. Both mark a point of inconsistency, even impossibility, within the text.

When attempting to give an account of the cosmos, Timaeus suggests that the demiurgic creator would have chosen to make the cosmos as perfect as possible, and an intelligent thing is more perfect than an unintelligent one. The cosmos, then, can be conceived to be a body with a soul since "it is impossible for anything to come to possess intelligence apart from soul" (*Ti.*, 30b). The cosmos will be dualistic in regards to having a soul and body but also in terms of being created out of Being and Becoming or "*that which always is* and has no becoming, and *that which becomes* but never is" (*Ti.*, 27d–28a). These dualisms, however, are unstable ones with Being requiring a connection to Becoming in order to *inform* it. This connection is, of course, found in the demiurge but it is also found in the soul. The body of the cosmos, its material nature, is identified with a Becoming that never is. The plan and ultimate source of structure and essence is identified with Being and that which never changes. Between the two we find placed the soul.

> In between the *Being* that is indivisible and always changeless, and the one that is divisible and comes to be in the corporeal realm, he mixed a third, intermediate form of being, derived from the other two. Similarly, he made a mixture of the *Same*, and then one of the *Different*, in between their indivisible and their corporeal, divisible counterparts. (*Ti.*, 35a)

We see here clearly presented the inconsistency and liminal nature of the soul that holds just as much on the personal level as the cosmic. The soul is neither Being nor Becoming, neither material nor Form, it contains both sameness and difference. It is, in fact, an impossibly inconsistent entity despite the mathematical metaphors of ratio Timaeus attempts to use to construct coherence out of contradiction. The problem is that ratio, like harmony in the *Phaedo*, is constructed out of elements rather than having its own internal essence, such that the "unceasing, intelligent life for all time" (*Ti.*, 36e) which Timaeus wants for it is contrary to its composite and derivative nature. Ultimately the soul is described in several different and inconsistent ways throughout Plato's dialogue, depending on what work it is needed to do in a given argument. In *Phaedo* it is simple and noncomposite. In the *Republic* and *Phaedrus* it is made up of three parts. In *Timaeus* it is, at least at several key parts, derivative and again composite. These inconsistencies attest to the impossibility of the soul despite its importance for all the arguments in which it features. Giving the soul the slightest shake reveals it to be the piece that cannot fit within the master plan despite its necessity.[7]

It has been suggested, for example, by both Lacan and Derrida, that every system of meaning—including perhaps especially philosophical systems—has its apparent consistency guaranteed by a knot, a necessary symbol that unifies the whole while lacking any true support within it. This master signifier is both the necessary condition for the possibility and the impossibility of the system. The personal soul, I have attempted to demonstrate, plays this role within the standard understanding of Plato's system. On the cosmic level, the universal soul fills the role of master signifier.

Ultimately, Platonism will largely embrace not one but both of the impossible and inconsistent solutions to the problem of the soul. On the one hand, they will interpret Plato's divisions of the parts of the soul to mean that one part of the soul—the rational or intelligent part—is in fact unchanging and eternal in the same way as Form. The soul, in this sense, is very much like a Form, but only in one of its parts. This part, in turn, can undergo purification from its other parts, those more material in nature, and return to its origin in the Unchanging One. In other words, the soul is *in part* Form and seeks a return to the Form from which it derived or to which it has always been connected. Despite its focus on abstract entities, it proved necessary for Platonism—as Platonism made a play for a more central role in public intellectual and religious life—to personify the knot that covered over the system's inconsistency in the form of an already liminal and inconsistent goddess.

Hekate and the Cosmic Soul

The goddess Hekate occupies an inconsistent and liminal place in the pantheon of the Greeks in a manner not dissimilar to that of the soul in Plato's thought. To begin with, Hekate is overtly a liminal goddess. Sophocles refers to her with the title *Enodia*, or "of the road." Aeschylus describes her as standing before the doorways of every palace. And Aristophanes claims that a statue of Hekate stood before every door in Athens.[8] Later this will overtly become an identification of Hekate with crossroads, especially three-way crossroads, in Rome.

In the *Homeric Hymn to Demeter*, Hekate is present both as Persephone is taken to Hades and on her return, and it is stated that from that time "the lady Hecate was minister and companion to Persephone" (LCL 57, 321). The terms for minister, *propolos*, and companion, *horaon*, have a literal sense of going-before and following-after. Here there is both an overtly contradictory nature, Hekate goes both before and after, and a liminal nature, Hekate stands at the beginning and the end. The connection to Persephone, in turn, leads to an equation with both leaving life and returning to it, or the gateways of the underworld. The doorways of life—death and birth—are specially identified with Hekate as their guardian.[9]

Hekate's first appearance in literature, in Hesiod's *Theogony*, is marked by a similarly contradictory and liminal nature, though more subtly than in the *Homeric Hymn to Demeter*. In the passage from the *Theogony* that opens this chapter, Hesiod notes that when Zeus rose to rulership he did not take away any of Hekate's power or rights, despite her having derived those privileges from Cronos' earlier rule. Hekate maintains her privileges, the text notes, despite being an only child. The implication here is that she had no brothers to press her suit and threaten rebellion should she be overlooked or wronged. But, despite that, she was particularly honored by Zeus. This situation is odd, but it is all the odder because Hekate's privileges are not small. Rather, she is given a portion of each of the realms: the earth, sea, and sky. Indeed, in this regard, she has more wide-ranging power—if not greater power—than Zeus, Hades, and Poseidon each. This is a birth of the theme of Hekate being three-headed, with each head representing her power in one of the three realms, as well as her later identification with three-way crossroads. Hekate maintains this power in a manner that is, from Hesiod's view, clearly odd for a single woman without family support. Hekate' liminality, contradictory nature, and general strangeness even extend to transcending standard gender binaries in the same way she bridges the old gods and the new.

Hekate's role in the *Theogony* is strange enough that it has led to speculation that perhaps Hesiod himself had a unique relationship with Hekate, such that he purposefully overstated her power and position. In other words, his presentation of her does not reflect the common view in Greece. This consideration has been coupled with the claim that Hekate is not native to Greece but instead is of foreign, for example Anatolian, origin.[10] The ultimate truth of the claim that Hesiod's depiction of Hekate does not reflect Greek culture at the time or that Hekate is nonnative to Greece are not particularly important. What is important is the manner in which they underscore how odd her appearance is, both in Hesiod and outside of his work. She is strange enough that scholarship on her repeatedly expels her from the "official" or "real" Greek pantheon one way or another. In this she resembles Dionysus, a god who seemed to many (even to many Ancient Greeks) to be distinctly non-Greek and so was assumed to be a foreign import. Despite that, the worship of Dionysus can be confirmed in Greece since the Bronze Age. Hekate, like Dionysus, is both an outsider and an insider.

This liminal nature of the goddess Hekate, which both bridges and breaks binaries, was recognized by the Middle Platonic author of the *Chaldean Oracles*. More than this, her liminality's similarity to that of the soul was also recognized. The *Chaldean Oracles* directly equate Hekate with the cosmic soul found in the *Timeaus*. By the time of the heavily Platonic *Chaldean Oracles*, more than 900 years after the *Theogony*, the tensions between the appeal of Platonism and its actual implications had become very pronounced. Under Platonism the gods became increasingly abstract, distant, and transcendent, while middle figures multiplied in order to make up for the lack of immediate worldly gods. This is shown particularly in the increased role played by *daimons*, or intermediary part-divine entities that act as messengers and servants of the gods. The challenge that Platonism faced was being able to synthesize the metaphysics drawn from Plato's texts and Aristotelian elements with the religious sentiments of the populous. Platonic gods were ultimately insufficient for the task, and so semidivine *daimons*, with the personality so often lacking in abstract transcendent perfections and capable of direct interaction with humans, became central to Platonic religious and theurgical/magical practice.

Though it might sound strange to refer to Platonic religious practice, one of the main forces at work at the time of the composition of the *Chaldean Oracles* was an attempt on the part of Greek philosophy to respond to claims that Judaic thought was superior in its divine origin. The *Chaldean Oracles* represented, then, a grounding of Greek philosophy in divine revelation.[11] The *Oracles* present a Platonic cosmology, but one dictated by divine voices, the most prominent of which is the voice of Hekate, who dictates many of the oracles in her own voice. Beyond this, the Platonic intellectual and contemplative approach to the Unchanging was supplemented with both religious ritual and magical techniques, known as theurgy, which provided a ritual and material basis for the achievement of transcendence. Platonic theurgy also provided practical magical techniques for the solution of worldly problems, necessary elements in practical religion lost in the increasing abstraction of the gods to whom one was once able to make direct appeal for worldly assistance and support.[12]

Amid the intermediary principles in Middle Platonism, the most important is the cosmic soul, which connects the realm of intellection and sensibility and is identified with Hekate who is queen of the *daimons*. Hekate both connected the material cosmos with the originating unchanging perfections through which it was structured, as well as the souls of humanity with the transcendent perfections. In relation to the *daimons* and the individual souls of embodied entities, Hekate is identified with the moon, understood as the station through which souls pass in their journey either to or from the Intelligible. It is at the moon that the impure and changeable parts of the soul are divided from the perfect pure Form-like rational soul, or joined to it, depending on whether we are looking at the journey of death or birth. Hekate as goddess of the moon is, then, once more keeper of the doorway of death and birth.

In relation to cosmology, the cosmic soul is identified with the womb of Hekate, which receives the influence of the divine Father of the Intelligible realm and embodies and transmits this influence to the sensible realm.

> From him leap forth the implacable thunderbolts,
> And the lightning-receiving womb of the splendid light
> Of Father-born Hekate, and the girding fire,
> And the strong *pneuma* beyond the fiery poles. (*Chald.* Frag. 35)
> From here springs forth the genesis of varied matter;
> From here the sweeping lightning obscures its flower of fire
> As it leaps into the hollows of the Cosmoi; for from here all things
> Begin to stretch forth towards that palace beneath the wondrous rays.
> (*Chald.* Frag. 34)

The imagery of Hekate's womb stresses a creative mode for the intermediary cosmic soul.

> Into the Cosmic Soul were cast the eternal Ideas of the divine mind; the Cosmic Soul in turn cast images of these Ideas onto the shapeless Prime Matter, producing the Sensible World, which was ruled by Time. The intermediary function of the Soul thus took on a creative, transmissive aspect, reminiscent of the traditional feminine one of receiving fertilization and subsequently bearing life.[13]

This understanding of the soul as cosmic womb contains interesting echoes of the containing *chora* of the *Timeaus*, an enclosing nurturing space that grants body to the Intelligible in a manner that cannot be purely passive. This similarity also marks an extending of the role of *chora* in a more overtly female and active direction as it becomes the cosmic womb/soul. If, as Irigaray insists of the *chora*, "The figures of the nurse, the mother, the womb cannot be fully identified with the receptacle, for those are specular figures which displace the feminine at the moment they purport to represent the feminine,"[14] then the equation of Hekate with the cosmic soul and the cosmic womb locks down the meanings only suggested by the Platonic *chora* by joining it overtly with the cosmic soul and a female deity. Receptive but not passive, neither sensible nor intelligible, joining the eternal and temporal, and being the passage through which individual souls become depersonalized and more Form-like—Hekate plays the role of stitching together impossible contradictions. Hekate-as-soul marks the place of dualism's classic problems: How does the eternal and unchanging interact with the temporal, and how does the Intelligible and immaterial relate to the sensible and material? Far, however, from solving these problems she stands as the apotheosis of Platonism's failure. Like the soul, cosmic or personal, there can be no Chaldean system without Hekate, and yet she does not fit within it.

Hekate the Symptom and a Solution

In *The Feminine Symptom: Aleatory Matter in the Aristotelian Cosmos*, Emanuela Bianchi reads matter, in its active aleatory mode, as the symptom of the inconsistencies of Aristotelian thought on both sexual difference and the Form/Matter dualism. As symptom, it marks both disease and the point from which cure can come—the destabilizing space from which a new understanding of Aristotle and the thought that derived from him is possible. It was largely this book that inspired the reflections I am offering in this chapter. As mentioned, the *chora* has been read in a similarly symptomatic way for the Platonic corpus. My claim, however, is that more central and unavoidable than the *chora* as place of contradiction is the impossibility and necessity of soul in Platonic thought. This impossibility and necessity, overtly identified with a female goddess, echoes a similar impossible necessity in Bianchi's analysis of Aristotle. Specifically, in Aristotle's *Generation of Animals*, female animals are understood in this way. They are necessary for reproduction but also understood as a monstrous deviation from the natural priority of the male. The female, in this text, is always accidental while the male is essential—yet without the female no system is possible. The uniting of this impossible-necessity of the soul with the equally contradictory and liminal figure of Hekate points, not just to Platonism's inconsistency, but also to a counterposition that was very alive at the time of the dominance of the *Chaldean Oracles* and the transition from Middle Platonism to Neoplatonism. This counterposition arises in *The Greek Magical Papyri*.

The Greek Magical Papyri is a collection of papyri from Greco-Roman Egypt, which date from the second century BCE to the fifth century CE The collection is fascinating, not least of all because it presents a clear view of the wildly syncretic nature of much popular religion during the Hellenistic and Roman periods. The same prayer or spell might call on Egyptian, Greek, Persian, Judaic, Christian, and Babylonian divinities without any sense of inconsistency or conflict. There is, instead, a great unity to the seemingly disparate collection and to a large extent a clear worldview and metaphysics. As the editor of the papyri, Hans Betz, puts it, "We should make it clear, however, that this syncretism is more than a hodge-podge of heterogeneous items. In effect, it is a new religion all together, displaying unified religious attitudes and beliefs" (PGM xlvi). Key aspects of these unified religious attitudes and beliefs are: a focus on the practical nature of religion and magic—in other words, its ability to work change in the material world to the practitioner's benefit—and a focus on the supreme importance of the dead and underworld gods. Indeed, many gods that one would be surprised to find occupying an underworld role are overtly granted this position in the papyri, such as Isis, Aphrodite, Helios, and even the Jewish Iao. Some have argued, however, that far from representing new meanings granted to old and new gods, collections like *The Greek Magical Papyri* instead reveal the ancient and continued nature of a popular religion that had been concealed in more polished intellectual presentations of it even in the classical world. "[M]uch that we are accustomed to see classified as late 'syncretism' is rather the ancient and original, deep-seated popular religion, coming to the surface when the whitewash of 'classical' writers and artists began to peel off."[15] In contrast to both Betz and Barb, Eleni Pachoumi powerfully argues that the sense of unity present in the papyri attests to a deep Platonist influence on the popular religion.[16] What might at first appear as syncretism, Pachoumi argues, is motivated and guided by a Platonic concept of unity in abstract divine principles that drives unavoidably toward monotheism rather than the polytheism or henotheism of the ancient world.

Pachoumi's argument will be important for us, not in order to read *The Greek Magical Papyri* as Platonic texts, but, rather, in order to understand them as conversant with Platonic thought and largely constructed in the context of a conflict with Platonism. In other words, we can look to what elements of Platonism the papyri adopt and what elements they overtly reject, as well as what elements involve overlap, without necessary derivation from Platonism. Despite the papyri not being philosophical texts, we can nonetheless draw a counterposition to the dominant Platonism at the time from the implications of the papyri's worldview.

This ability to play *The Greek Magical Papyri* and the Platonism of the *Chaldean Oracles* against each other is strengthened by the fact that central to each text is the goddess Hekate. "The goddess Hekate, identical with Persephone, Selene, Artemis, and the old Babylonian goddess Ereschigal, is one of the deities most often invoked in the papyri" (PGM xlvi). As Hekate's identification with Selene should make clear, Hekate maintains her identification with the moon in both the papyri and the *Chaldean Oracles*. This identification of Hekate with the moon is unlikely to be from the *Chaldean Oracles*, since it was a very common theme before their composition, most particularly in Plutarch who overtly presents the idea that the moon is the liminal space through which ghosts and *daimons* pass with Hekate as its ruler, a position that both *The Greek Magical Papyri* and the *Chaldean Oracles* adopt.

> But there is a body with mixed characteristics that actually parallels the daemones—namely the Moon. And when men see that [the Moon], by being consistently in accord with those cycles through which the daemones pass, is subject to

apparent wanings and waxings and transformations, some call her an earth-like star, others a star-like Earth, and others still the lot of Hekate, who is both earthly and heavenly. Now if someone withdrew or removed the air that is between the Earth and the Moon, he would destroy the unity and communion of the Universe, for there could be an empty and unconnected space in the middle. In just the same way, those who refuse to leave us the race of daemones make the relations of the gods and men remote and alien.[17]

The unity of Hekate and the moon was clearly, already at the time of Plutarch, common place, as was the recognition that without the mixed (or we might say, inconsistent) liminality of the Moon, Hekate, and *daimons*, the entire cosmic system constructed under the influence of Platonism would collapse. In *The Greek Magical Papyri*, Hekate's relation to Persephone as well as both the *daimons* and the souls of the deceased is also strongly maintained, some of which harken back to her earliest identifications from Hesiod. The Hekate of the papyri, then, is very similar to the Hekate of the *Chaldean Oracles* in her connection to the moon and the souls of the dead, but this cannot be read as a Platonic Hekate. It would, perhaps, be better to claim that Hekate remains a non-Platonic element of the Chaldean system.

It seems reasonable to read the tendency of the papyri to equate disparate gods from different religions as an outcome of the Platonic idea of abstract principles, dare we say even Forms, unifying similar entities. Pachoumi does a great job of analyzing the unities amid different gods that do point toward a rather new idea of the gods. It takes a rather interesting theology to equate for example; Helios, Horus Harpocrates, "the Great Living God," God the Creator, Iao, Sabaoth, Adonai, and Mithras. There must be something of the great Platonic system able to unify all realities into a few simple principles at work here.

Despite that, however, it is hard to see much Platonism in the actual worldview presented in *The Greek Magical Papyri*. To begin with, the gods are depicted as present in the world in very personal, even terrifying, ways. In a papyri from the fourth century CE,[18] Hekate is described in the following way:

Dart-shooter, heav'nly one, goddess of harbors,
Who roam the mountains, goddess of crossroads,

O nether and nocturnal, and infernal,
Goddess of dark, quiet and frightful one,
O you who have your meal amid the graves . . .
O you with hair of serpents, serpent-girded, who drink
blood,
Who bring death and destruction, and who feast
On hearts, flesh eater, who devour those dead
Untimely, and you who make grief resound
And spread madness, come to my sacrifices . . . (PGM IV
2853–69)

It is hard to see an embodiment of some Platonic ideal in this eater of flesh and drinker of blood who haunts cemeteries and roams mountains. It is also worth noting that invocations within the papyri most often end with the deity being asked to come into the invoker's presence rather than seeking to raise the speaker to a higher plane of perfection. It is clear that the gods in most of the papyri are present in the world in idiosyncratic and personal, rather than abstract, ways. This is a world haunted by *daimons* and ghosts, but also by living deities who walk the same paths as humanity. The need for intermediaries here is very different than they are in Platonism. Far from a bridge to distant transcendental realms, the deities of the papyri serve as sources of authority over vagrant spiritual forces or protection against all too near divine threats. Consider, for example, the intimate relationship with the deity implied in this advice concerning what to expect following one of the papyri's rituals: "When you have said this and at the same time have opened your hands, the goddess will remove the [edge] of your hand from your breast. For you will see [a star being led] of necessity [to you], at which you are to look [intently], as it flashes [a picture] while rushing [toward you], so that you become stricken of God" (PGM LVII 22–26). The level of worldly contact here with the divine, occurring not in some transcendence but rather in the goddess taking you physically by the hand and drawing a star to you, is strikingly this-worldly focused.

As mentioned, the *Chaldean Oracles* hail from the second century CE. The elements of *The Greek Magical Papyri* that most extensively mention Hekate derive from the third and fourth centuries CE (most specifically Papyri IV from the fourth century, VII from the third, and LXX from the third or fourth). From the appearance of Hekate in Ancient Greece until her appearance in the *Chaldean Oracles*, a particularly interesting symbolic shift occurs. In Ancient Greece Hekate was commonly described or depicted as three-headed or triple-bodied. As mentioned, this led to her being associated with triple crossroads in Rome. This triple nature of Hekate reflects her identification in Hesiod as having power in sea, earth, and heaven—the three main domains of the Greek cosmos. Hekate in the *Chaldean Oracles*, and in Platonic contexts in general, is instead depicted as two-headed like the Roman god Janus. The two-headedness is common with deities of doorways, to be sure, but there is a deeper metaphysical and theological change that has occurred here. In general, the Ancient Greek cosmos is divided into threes, but there is a lesser division into two that is also present in it, specifically the divide between the world and underworld. The more ancient understanding of this binary is to equate power "within the earth" as power in the underworld as well as on the earth, with the sea and heavens making up the second and third terms. But an upper and under divide is certainly present despite this. In Platonism, however, the binary of higher and lower becomes the dominant one reflected in the intelligible and sensible, eternal and temporal, and Being and Becoming. Hekate's dual-headedness in the Chaldean system reflects her role as receiving and transmitting the fire from the Intelligible realm into the Sensible. It is the mark of her liminality and, though she is a third term uniting the other two, those two take priority. Though we have referred to her previously as having a liminal nature, there is a sense in which the triple nature of Hekate is more and other than liminal.

The suggestion that *The Greek Magical Papyri* offers an alternative to the Platonic view informed by more ancient worldviews, while it at the same time adopts aspects of Platonism in and through this conflict, is bolstered by the observation that Hekate is depicted as both dual and triple in the papyri.

> Triple-pointed, triple-faced, triple-necked,
> And goddess of the triple ways, who hold
> Untiring flaming fire in triple baskets,
> And you who oft frequent the triple way
> And rule the triple decades [. . .]. (PGM IV 2822–26)

> I call upon you who have all forms and many names, double-horned goddess, Mene, whose form no one knows except him who made the entire world, IAO, the one who shaped

> [you] into the twenty-eight shapes of the world so that you might complete every figure and distribute breath to every animal and plant, that it might flourish, you who wax from obscurity into light and wax from light into darkness [. . .]. (PGM VII 756–63)[19]

The presence of both the triple and dual nature of the goddess Hekate locates the papyri as an ancient survival engaged in a conflict with the transcendent theology of Platonic theurgy. The fact that the dominance of Hekate in the papyri postdates her centrality in the Chaldean system marks an ongoing battle and stubborn survival of Pre-Platonic world conceptions.

If, as I have argued, Hekate in the *Chaldean Oracles* in her dual nature represents the systematic impossible-necessity of the soul in the Platonic system, then Hekate in her triple form represents the counter-position inherent in *The Greek Magical Papyri*. There the soul is worldly, indeed the souls of the discontented dead represent serious dangers to the living as well as power for those who can control them through necromantic rites. The tripartite world of earth, sea, and heaven is one without transcendence, in which the underworld is a place in and on the earth, and the heavens rest on an earthly mountain. There is no problem of the eternal and temporal here, as gods might be undying but they are never truly eternal. There is no problem of the intelligible and sensible, as this dualism has no place in the indistinguishable unity of meaning and embodiment in the living cosmos free of hierarchical binaries.

Notes

1. Hesiod, *Theogony*, trans. Hugh Evelyn-White (New York: Macmillan, 2000), 423–27.

2. *Chaldean Oracles* Fragment 51 as quoted in Sarah Johnston, *Hekate Soteira: A Study of Hekate's Roles in the Chaldean Oracles and Related Literature* (Atlanta: Scholars Press, 1990), 62.

3. I do not take a stand in this chapter on Plato's ultimate position on the hypotheses and stories he has his characters present, but rather focus on the systems that Platonic thinkers who followed him attempted to create from his dialogues.

4. "[W]ithout the presupposition of the [thing in itself] I cannot enter the [critical] system, and with that presupposition I cannot remain in it." F. Jacobi, *The Main Philosophical Writings and the Novell Allwill*, translated and introduced by G. di Giovanni (Montreal: McGill University Press, 1994), 336.

5. The relationship between the soul and the Forms, as well as its resemblance to them, is the central structure of the *Phaedo*.

6. D. Keyt, "The Fallacies in *Phaedo* 102a–107b," *Phronesis* VIII (1963) 87.

7. For an extensive discussion of the ambiguous status of dualism in the *Phaedo* and *Timaeus* see Anne-Maria Schultz's and Hilary Yancey's "As Much Mixture as Will Suffice: Socrates' Embodied Intermediacy in Plato's *Phaedo* and *Symposium*," chapter 7 in this volume, and Monica Vilhauer's "Overturning Soul-Body Dualism in Plato's *Timaeus*," chapter 8 in this volume.

8. Johnston, *Hekate Soteira*, 23–24.

9. For a fascinating discussion of Hekate's liminality and how it fits into the Homeric and Presocratic context, see Jessica Elbert Decker's "The Roots of Life and Death in the Homeric Hymns and Presocratic Philosophy," chapter 4 in this volume.

10. For a discussion of this position, and an argument against it, see William Berg's "Hecate: Greek or Anatolian," *Numen* 21, no. 2.

11. Johnston, 72–73.

12. While it has often been argued that magic at the time of Middle Platonism and Neoplatonism can be divided between *goetia*, aimed primarily at lowly material worldly benefit, and *theurgy*, aimed at union with the divine or One through magical means, this distinction cannot be consistently maintained in the face of many worldly applications of theurgy on the part of Platonist writers.

13. Johnston, 17.

14. Luce Irigaray, Luce, *This Sex Which Is Not One*, trans. by Catherine Porter (Ithaca: Cornell University Press, 1985), 26.

15. A. A. Barb, "Three Elusive Amulets," *Journal of the Warburg and Courtauld Institutes* 27 (1964): 4.

16. Eleni Pachoumi, *The Magical Papyri: Diversity and Unity* (Newcastle: Newcastle University), 2007.

17. Plutarch, "On the Failure of the Oracles," 416 e–f, taken from Johnston, 32.

18. Ages for the various papyri are taken from William M. Brashear, *The Greek Magical Papyri: An Introduction and Survey; Annotated Bibliography (1928–1994)* (Berlin: De Gruyter), 1995.

19. Mene and Selene are syncretized in the papyri with Hekate in her role as goddess of the moon.

Bibliography

Barb, A. A. "Three Elusive Amulets." *Journal of the Warburg and Courtauld Institutes* 27 (1964).

Berg, William. "Hecate: Greek or Anatolian." *Numen* 21, no. 2 (1974).

Betz, Hans Dieter, ed. *The Greek Magical Papyri in Translation, Including the Demotic Spells*. Chicago, IL: Chicago University Press, 1996.

Bianchi, Emanuela. *The Feminine Symptom: Aleatory Matter in the Aristotelian Cosmos*. New York: Fordham University Press, 2014.

Brashear, William M. *The Greek Magical Papyri: An Introduction and Survey; Annotated Bibliography (1928–1994)*. Berlin, Germany: De Gruyter, 1995.

Derrida, Jacques. *On the Name*. Edited by Thomas Dutoit. Stanford, CA: Stanford University Press, 1995.

Evelyn-White, Hugh G. *Hesiod Homeric Hymns Epic Cycle Homerica*. New York: Macmillan, 2000.

Irigaray, Luce. *This Sex Which Is Not One*, translated by Catherine Porter. Ithaca, NY: Cornell University Press, 1985.

F. Jacobi. *The Main Philosophical Writings and the Novell Allwill*, translated and introduced by G. di Giovanni. Montreal, QC: McGill University Press, 1994.

Johnston, Sarah Iles. *Hekate Soteira: A Study of Hekate's Roles in the Chaldean Oracles and Related Literature*. Atlanta, GA: Scholars Press, 1990.

Keyt, D. "The Fallacies in *Phaedo* 102a–107b." *Phronesis* VIII (1963).

Lacan, Jacques. *Écrits: A Selection*, translated by Alan Sheridan. London: Tavistock Publications, 1977.

Lacan, Jacques. *The Seminar. Book III. The Psychoses, 1955–56*, translated by Russell Grigg. London: Routledge, 1993.

Pachoumi, Eleni. *The Magical Papyri: Diversity and Unity*. Newcastle, UK: Newcastle University, 2007.

Plato. *Complete Works*. Edited by John M. Cooper, and D. S. Hutchinson. Indianapolis, IN: Hackett, 1997.

Chapter Eleven

Christian Platonists in Support of Gender Equality

Bardaisan, Clement, Origen, Gregory of Nyssa, and Eriugena

Ilaria L. E. Ramelli

Introduction: Methodological Guidelines

This essay will endeavor to demonstrate how Christian Platonists (so-called Middle and Neoplatonists) used Platonic transcendence to enforce the relativity or illegitimacy of gender hierarchies in both theology and anthropology.[1] It will focus on Bardaisan, Clement, and Origen of Alexandria in the late-second to early-third centuries CE; Gregory of Nyssa in the late-fourth century CE; and Eriugena in the ninth. From the theological viewpoint, these Christian Platonists insisted on the genderless nature of the Divinity, which, in its transcendence (theorized within a solid Platonic framework), lies beyond any gender distinction. In this way, they removed the temptation to think about God as a male entity and model. Being Christian, they identified the divine Logos with Christ. But, notwithstanding the gender of the incarnate Christ (Jesus of Nazareth), as Platonists they emphasized the genderlessness of Christ-Logos-God, who can be metaphorically described in either female or male terms, as

Bardaisan, Clement, and Origen did. (Clement even depicted God the Father in female terms, as the Mother of Christ and of human beings, and Nyssen will call God "Mother" in more than one passage.)

Christ, in turn, is the paradigm of humanity, and if Christ is neither male nor female properly speaking (given that as God Christ transcends genders and as a human Christ has assumed all humanity and not only men), the grounds for an anthropological hierarchy that privileges men over women cannot subsist. These Christian Platonists' theological anthropology is modeled on Christ-Logos-Sophia and firmly grounded in their protological and eschatological view of the human being as primarily a rational creature (a *logikon*). In their view, gender differentiation arose only as a result of, or in prevision of, the fall, and will not endure in the end, just as it does not exist in Christ (Galatians 3:28: in Christ "there is neither male nor female"—within a sentence that reverses Aristotle's categories of discrimination).[2] Since Christ-Logos is the paradigm of humanity and the end (*telos*) is ethically normative, the consequences of these patristic thinkers' ideas about gender distinction are weighty.

Eriugena probably offers the strongest example of the merely provisional and secondary nature of gender differentiation, and this is perfectly consistent with his Neoplatonic system, structured on the three Neoplatonic movements: immanence, procession, and reversion (*monē*, *proodos*, and *epistrophē*). Gender hierarchies are meaningless, and indeed nonexistent both in the initial and in the final movement. Special attention will be therefore paid to Eriugena's theorization of the overcoming of all gender differences in the process of restoration-return. Now, since the *telos* is normative, Eriugena hammers home the principle—valid already during the historical time—that "the human being is superior to gender," that is to say, it transcends it (*homo melior est quam sexus*).

The Middle Platonists Bardaisan and Clement of Alexandria

Bardaisan of Edessa († 222 CE) is often represented as a Gnostic (Valentinian), but as I argued elsewhere, was in fact an anti-Gnostic and anti-Marcionite Christian Middle Platonist, who countered Valentinian determinism as Origen and Plotinus did.[3] Like Origen, he emphasized human free will against fatalistic determinism.[4] L. W. Barnard also thought that Bardaisan could not be a Valentinian: "There is nothing really to connect him with Valentinus."[5] In a fragment from his *De India* preserved by Porphyry in *De Styge*, regularly overlooked even in important studies,[6] Bardaisan describes a statue that represents Christ as cosmic Christ, in the shape of a cross, and as the sum of humanity, androgynous "in vertical": "The right part of its face is masculine, the left feminine. Likewise, the right arm, too, and the right foot, and the whole right side are masculine, whereas the left are feminine. Therefore, at this sight one was struck by this mixture, and wondered how it was possible to see such a difference of the two vertical halves in one and the same body in an indivisible way" (*Styg.* F 376 Smith). This statue has the whole cosmos carved on itself as noetic cosmos. All beings are represented on the cosmic statue: "On this statue the sun is carved on the right breast, all around, and the moon on the left one, and along the two arms . . . a great deal of angels are artistically carved and *all the beings that are found in the cosmos*, that is, the sky, the mountains, the sea, the rivers, the ocean, the plants, and in sum *all the beings that exist*." This statue therefore represents: (1) qua androgynous, the sum of the *microcosmos* (humanity); and (2) due to the representation of the cosmos on it, the whole of the *macrocosmos* (the universe). This because, for the Christian Bardaisan, it is Christ—Christ as all humanity and the cosmic Christ. In India both cosmological statues, with all creatures carved on them, and "vertically" androgynous ones have been found, but the cosmological are not androgynous, and the androgynous have no representation of the cosmos on them.[7] And none of the statues found represents a crucified person. Therefore, the synthesis of the cosmic and the androgynous statues in our Porphyrian fragment must be due to Bardaisan himself, who added, as a Christian, the element of the Cross. The statue of the cosmic Christ also represents all humanity, because Christ has assumed humanity as his body.

Thus, it represents the cosmos (having all beings carved on itself) and the human being (man and woman at the same time), as subsumed in Christ (as the shape of the cross indicates). In the fragment, the matter of the body of the cosmic Christ is unidentifiable; it is similar to imperishable/incorruptible wood, but it is not wood. Probably, the body of the statue represents the incorruptible human body as it was before the fall and will be again after the resurrection. This idea was developed by Origen and then Gregory Nyssen, and Bardaisan seems to share it.[8] Bardaisan posits a divine statue on top of the cosmic, androgynous

Christ-Logos, probably representing the Nous, divine and enthroned. Bardaisan's representation can be compared to that of the divine noetic human studied by Giulea.[9]

Bardaisan represents Christ as Logos-Wisdom/Sophia, male (Logos) and female (Sophia), just as Origen noted that Christ, being Wisdom, is female no less than male, and as God exceeds both genders.[10] The statue is the ideal paradigm (as κόσμος νοητός) used by Christ-Logos in the creation of the world, which was made "according to the Mystery of the Cross" (as attested by the so-called cosmological traditions reflecting Bardaisan's cosmogenesis). And this paradigm is Christ-Logos in that it is the cosmic Christ, since in "Middle Platonism" the Ideas are God's thoughts belonging to the divine Logos. Thus, Christ-Logos is both the creator of the cosmos and its ideal model. As a consequence, Christ-Logos incorporates both active principles that, according to Plato's *Timaeus*, intervened in the creation of the world: the *Demiurge*, the good God, and the ideal *paradigm* that the Demiurge followed in the creation. The passive principle is matter in Plato; in Bardaisan's cosmological traditions it is represented by the elements or "beings," which, however, are not uncreated as Plato's matter is, but are creatures of God. Here, again, we have a remarkable similarity with Origen, another Christian Platonist, who deemed matter a creature of God.[11]

An early-second-century homily, the *Second Letter of Clement to the Corinthians*, reports a logion of the Lord concerning the coming of the Kingdom. This happens "when the two will be one, the outside like the inside, and the male with the female neither male nor female" (12.2). This is also one of the Lord's logia in the Gospel of Thomas, which is now preserved in its entirety only in Coptic.[12] The Coptic has handed down 114 logia of Jesus. One of them is a dominical saying on the coming of the Kingdom that appears very similar to that of the *Second Letter of Clement to the Corinthians*: "when of the two you will make one, the inside like the outside and the outside like the inside, and the above like the below, and when you will make male and female one and the same being, so that the male is not male and the female not female" (22.3–5). This motif of making the two one surfaces repeatedly in Jesus's logia in the Gospel of Thomas: "Many who are first will become last. And they will become one and the same" (4); "When you were one, you became two" (11). And the terminology of the male-female binary that must be overcome in unity is the same as in Galatians 3:28, which in turn echoes Genesis 1:23. Likewise in Logion 106: "When you make one out of the two, you will become children of the human being," as Jesus is the Child of the Human Being, "and when you say, 'Mountain, move away,' it will move away," which in the canonical Gospels is related to perfect faith. The ideal is the prelapsarian human being, not yet divided into male and female by sin. The unity is to be recovered by the elect: "Blessed are the solitary and elect, for you will find the Kingdom. For you are from it, and to it you will return" (49); "Many are standing at the door, but it is the solitary who will access the bridal chamber" (75).[13] In both of the last two logia, *solitary* in Coptic is the transliteration of Greek *μοναχός*.[14] This is the person who has undone gender differences, as these did not subsist at the beginning and are undone "in Christ" (see the use of "in Christ" in Galatians 3:28). In Logion 77 Jesus explains: "I am the All" or "the Whole," which includes both the totality of the cosmos (as he says, he is in a piece of wood, a stone, and so forth: the creatures represented on Bardaisan's Christ statue) and the undivided totality of all humanity—exactly as in Bardaisan's fragment, quoted literally by Porphyry, about the cosmic Christ who contains the paradigms of all creatures and at the same time the totality of humanity, male and female, in a vertically androgynous form. It would be interesting to know whether the Gospel of Thomas was known to Bardaisan (or vice versa), or whether they have a common source. What is certain is that the Gospel of Thomas was known to Origen, who explicitly mentioned it in his first Homily on Luke.

Clement of Alexandria, a Christian Middle Platonist who also influenced Origen, displays a remarkable view of Christ as feminine as well as masculine, common to his semicontemporary Bardaisan. This concept will be taken over by Origen, who will also insist that Christ, being both Logos and Wisdom, is both male and female, or, better, transcends genders. Now, Christ represents a model for humans, and this model for Clement is not only masculine.[15] This is why Clement insists, following the Stoic Musonius, that virtue must be pursued by men and women alike, who must receive the same philosophical education.[16] For Clement, indeed, the true "Gnostic"—his ideal Christian sage—can well be a woman.[17]

Not accidentally, Clement quotes an Orphic fragment, later cited by the (turned Christian) Neoplatonic Synesius as well,[18] on God as "eternal, Father and Mother together," surrounded by angels, in *Strom.* 5.14.125.1. Clement supports this description as an expression of the generation from nothing in 126.2. Christ, the model for women and men, and God are often described by Clement in feminine terms. For example, Clement represented Christ's blood, shed for the salvation of humanity, as a mother's blood in childbirth,[19] or as a mother's blood transformed into milk for the nourishment of her infant.[20] The Logos is the breast of God the Father, providing God's children with milk: the food is the milk of the Father, from whom the babies suckle; they rush to the care-soothing breast of the Father, the Logos. He alone provides the infants with the milk of love, and only those who suckle this breast are really blessed.[21] Clement attaches again maternal breasts to the Father in *Paed.* I. 46.1, where he claims that the Father's nipples of love supply milk to babies who seek the Logos. As in Clement, in the Odes of Solomon 19, too, the Son is the cup, the Father is the one who is milked, and the Holy Spirit is "she, who milked him."[22]

Indeed, Clement overtly states that God is Mother as well as Father in *Div.* 37.2. As he explains, the ineffable part of God is Father, but the part that has sympathy toward creatures is Mother. By loving, the Father "became female" (ἐθηλύνθη), and the proof of this feminization of God is the child whom God brought forth. Clement probably had also in mind a Biblical (Septuagint) foundation for the maternal generation of the Son by God: "ἐκ γαστρὸς πρὸ ἑωσφόρου ἐγέννησά σε" ("From the womb, before Morning-star, I [God] brought you forth").[23] If God gave birth to the Son from the womb, God is obviously Mother, not just Father.

This point will be taken over in the fourth century by Macarius, *Apocriticus*, 3.23.8–9: Christ "gives birth" to the children of God "by some mystical principle" and "wraps them in ineffable swaddling clothes"; "She who gives birth to them is none other than the Wisdom of God . . . abundantly pouring out the two Testaments as if from two breasts." We shall encounter again Christ-Wisdom as feminine in Origen. Of course, angelomorphic Christology, too, well present in patristic theology, also contributed to a gender-neuter image of Christ.[24]

Like Clement, the *Acts of Thomas* also describe God, and specifically the Holy Spirit, in feminine terms, possibly because of the feminine gender of the Syriac name for "Spirit," *ruḥa*—thus, Syriac theology is rich in feminine descriptions of the Holy Spirit.[25] Most scholars think that the original redaction of these *Acts* was Syriac, although Lautaro Roig Lanzillotta (2015) deems them originally composed in Greek. In the Greek *Acts of Thomas*, 2.27, the Spirit is invoked as "compassionate Mother" and "Mother of the Seven Houses." And in 5.50 the Spirit is again invoked as "hidden Mother" and "Holy Dove, who bears the twin young." Exactly the same image of the Spirit as a Mother Dove who incubates two chicks appears in fragments of Bardaisan reported by Ephrem.[26]

In the time of Bardaisan and Clement, "Gnostics" also tended to represent God, including the "Father," as feminine,[27] and their views were well known to Bardaisan and Clement, as well as Origen. Interestingly, later on, the Christian Neoplatonist Synesius, a disciple of the philosopher and mathematician Hypatia,[28] put forward in Hymn 3[1] a Platonizing account of the Christian Trinity, in which the Son is the "hidden root" (Hymn 4[2].21) to whom the Holy Spirit, "mother, Sister and Daughter," gives birth (4[2].101–103). To emphasize the feminine nature of the Holy Spirit, Synesius calls it *pnoia* (grammatically feminine, just as *ruḥa* in Syriac), for example, in Hymn 4[2].98.

Even a contemporary of Clement such as Tertullian, who cannot certainly be considered a feminist by any standard, depicted the generation of the Son from the Father as a Mother's childbirth: the Father-Mother brought forth the Son "from the womb of his own heart" (*Adv.Prax.* 7.1). Tertullian, like Clement, was probably referring to Psalm 109.3 (LXX).

Origen of Alexandria: A Christian Platonist

Not only the anthropology of Clement, but also, and more clearly, those of Origen, Gregory Nyssen, the other Cappadocians, and Evagrius are modeled on Christ-Logos-Wisdom and based on their protological and eschatological view of the human being as rational creature (λογικόν). The rational nature is common to men and women alike. Within this framework, the differentiation of humans into male and female arose as a result of, or in prevision of, the fall, and will not endure in the ultimate end. This perspective is underpinned not only by Paul in Gal 3:28, but also by the saying of Jesus that in the resurrection humans will be like angels and will take neither wives nor husbands.[29]

Given that Christ is the model of humanity and the eschatological end is ethically normative, the consequences of these patristic thinkers' ideas about the adventitious and provisional nature of gender distinction are substantial, also with respect to the role of women as officeholders in the Church. Especially Origen, Nyssen, and Evagrius display a refined anthropology that entailed different kinds of bodies, pre- and postlapsarian (namely, before and after the Fall), and pre- and postresurrection;

only postlapsarian and preresurrection bodies are either male or female, while prelapsarian and postresurrection bodies are nongendered angelic bodies. Indeed, gender distinctions are absent from God and from the image of God.

Origen, the Christian Platonist, was a disciple of Ammonius Saccas, like Plotinus,[30] and may have been the same Origen, usually called "the Neoplatonist," of whom Porphyry, Hierocles, and Proclus speak.[31] Instead of metensomatosis (supported by "pagan" philosophers and possibly Philo, at least esoterically or heuristically, according to Sami Yli-Karjanmaa[32]), Origen proposed ἐνσωμάτωσις or "embodiment/incorporation."[33] In his perspective, souls do not enter a sequence of different bodies, as envisaged by the theory of metensomatosis, but rational creatures have only one body, which is transformed in accord with that creature's spiritual progress. Even the resurrected body will have different qualities from those of the mortal body, but it will be the same as the mortal body, not another.

Now, this body initially was nongendered, and will no longer be gendered in the end. Rational creatures were provided from the beginning with a body similar to the spiritual, nongendered, angelic body of the resurrection. After the fall, their fine, immortal body was changed into a perishable and gendered body, in the case of human beings; but these will eschatologically recover their immortal, angelic body.[34]

The "skin tunics" mentioned in Genesis 3:21 are not the body tout court, but gendered mortality, the result of sin.[35] For gendered bodies inevitably became necessary when death entered the world. Origen admits that the human being had a body before falling and receiving the skin tunics,[36] which represent, not the body in general, but specifically the heavy, gendered, and corruptible body given by God to humanity as a result of sin.

Procopius reports that, according to those who allegorized Scripture, the human being in paradise had a "fine" ("λεπτομερές") body, suitable for life in Paradise, called by some "luminous" ("αὐγοειδές") and immortal.[37] These allegorists, according to Procopius, said that initially the soul used the luminous body as a vehicle, and this body was later clothed in the skin tunics. On the basis of verbal correspondences, the ideas reported by Procopius probably go back to Origen. The Byzantine theologian Stephen Gobar, who knew Origen and the Origenian tradition well, also attests to Origen's identification of the skin tunics with mortality, heavy and gendered corporeality, and liability to passions, which came about after sin but will be shed at the resurrection.[38]

For Origen, the immutable, individual metaphysical form (εἶδος/*species*) of the body[39] guarantees that the risen body is the same as the present, mortal body as for individual identity, but it has better, more glorious qualities, which include genderlessness.[40] God initially created many intelligences, equipped with spiritual bodies (neither male nor female), since only the Trinity is entirely incorporeal. All intelligences were equal and enjoyed harmony and unity among themselves and with God.[41] But after sin, which came about as a result of a "cooling" ("ψύξις") of rational creatures' love for God, their wills became dispersed, and the spiritual bodies of some creatures (namely, humans) became heavy, mortal, and gendered bodies. But those (namely, angels) who did not turn away from God, or did so only minimally, maintained their spiritual, nongendered, and immortal bodies.[42]

Origen's anthropology, protology, and eschatology, as have been briefly outlined here, helped him attach relatively little importance to gender differences. Like other ancient philosophers such as Pythagoreans,[43] Stoics, Cynics, Epicureans, and Platonists, who also counted women as philosophers and head of schools (see below about Hypatia),[44] and Christian teachers, Origen also taught women at his school. According to Eusebius, this fact even induced him to his famous self-mutilation, aimed at preventing any possible gossip about relations with his female students (*HE* 6.8.1–3).

More importantly, with respect to the ordination of women, Origen claimed that Paul "teaches with apostolic authority that women too are constituted in the ecclesiastical ministry, and must be assumed into office."[45] Commenting on Romans 16:1, about Phoebe, an ecclesiastical deacon and president (προστάτις, the feminine of προστάτης, the title of Jesus himself), Origen remarks on her being constituted in the ecclesiastical ministry and stresses her *officium* and ecclesiastical *ministerium*, which he extends to other women too.[46] These "*ministrae in Ecclesia*" ("female ministers in the Church"), established on the basis of Paul's authority, hold an office that is not restricted to material cares, but, as Origen details, consists in spiritual ministry. Therefore, Origen claims that the women invested with this ministry deserve to be honored.

Also interestingly, Origen describes as ecclesiastical *ministeria* the episcopate, presbyterate, diaconate, and the orders of widows and virgins, without any distinctions in terminology or prescriptions between feminine and masculine orders.[47] Similarly, Origen lists the ecclesiastical orders without distinction between male and female ministries: "anyone who has married twice may not be a bishop, or a presbyter, or a deacon, or a widow."[48] This parallel between male and female ministries will occur again in seventh-century Modestus of Jerusalem: he describes Mary Magdalene as "the leader of the female disciples" ("ἀρχηγὸς τῶν μαθητριῶν") and attributes to her and all female disciples "the apostolic mission."[49] Modestus remarks that the Lord led male disciples and the Lady, his Mother, in a parallel way led female ones. Speaking of Deborah, the prophetess and judge of Israel, and the gift of prophecy bestowed on women, Origen overtly claimed that there is no gender diversity in matter of spiritual gifts: they come from "purity of mind, not gender diversity," *puritas mentis, non diversitas sexus*.[50]

Commenting on I Corinthians 14:34–35, Origen remarked that, as Paul attests, women can be prophets and teach other Christians very well, only not in assemblies of men.[51] Women can teach wonderful and holy things; only, they should not teach men, at least not at church. Soon afterward in the commentary, Origen read Titus 2:3–4, concerning "πρεσβύτιδες" ("female elders") who are "ἐν καταστήματι ἱεροπρεπεῖ" ("in a consecrated state"), as a clear reference to the ecclesiastical office of women presbyters qua proclaimers of God's Word. Origen indeed interpreted Titus 2:3–4 in reference to women presbyters' ministry and attached to them the specific office of teaching.[52] Origen similarly drew a parallel between the recommendations addressed to "πρεσβύτεροι" ("presbyters, elders") and those addressed to "πρεσβύτιδες" ("female presbyters, elders") in Titus 2:2–4: women presbyters are ordered by (Ps.) Paul to be also "teachers of good things, exactly in the same way as men presbyters are."[53] Origen draws a parallel that focuses on the task of teaching, common to men and women presbyters. Theodore of Mopsuestia may have referred precisely to Origen, whose ideas he knew well, when he observed that "some people" ("τινες") thought that Titus 2:3 testified to "the ordination of presbyters among women" ("χειροτονία ἐν γυναιξὶν πρεσβυτέρων").[54]

Also, Origen interpreted Philippians 4:3 in reference to women apostles. Talking about Persis, mentioned by Paul in Romans 16:12, whom Paul also calls "faithful/noble companion/colleague" ("σύζυγε"), Origen remarks that she has labored a great deal in the Lord in the apostolic mission.[55] For Origen there was no doubt that a woman, Persis, was a colleague of Paul in the apostolate, and was highly praised by Paul himself. Another woman apostle, whom Origen mentioned, was Junia, praised by Paul along with Andronicus as "ἐπίσημοι ἐν τοῖς ἀποστόλοις," "prominent/outstanding among the apostles."[56]

Origen's allegorical method ruled out a misogynist interpretation of passages that could be read as prohibitions against women's ecclesiastical leadership. For instance, Origen allegorized the first transgression of the woman mentioned in 1 Timothy 2:14 in reference to the bride of the Song of Songs, who in his exegesis symbolizes, not any woman, but each soul, of a man or a woman, when it sins, and the church gathered from among "pagans"—the real transgressors.[57] Likewise, following Philo (whose attitude toward women is ambivalent[58]), Origen allegorized the Genesis account about Adam and Eve by interpreting the man as rationality, intellect, and virtue, and the woman as flesh, bodily matter, vice, and pleasure.[59] Consequently, the Genesis fall story is not about differences between men and women, but about the effects of virtue and vice on every soul, irrespective of gender.

Also, 1 Timothy 2:15, stating that women will be saved through childbearing, was not taken by Origen as a reference to women, or a suggestion that childbearing, instead of ordained ministry or else, would be the task of women. Indeed, Origen entirely allegorized this statement, also because he, like Paul and many other early Christian thinkers, valued virginity as the highest way of life. Therefore, the literal sense of 1 Timothy 2:15 sounded absurd to him. He allegorized women as souls—of men or women alike—and childbearing as the birth of Christ and all virtues (which are Christ-Logos) in one's heart.[60] This idea will influence still Meister Eckhart.

In Origen's time, women presbyters taught, baptized, and offered the Eucharistic sacrifice within the "*ministerium leviticum*" ("priestly office"), as attested by Tertullian.[61] In the first half of the third century, Ammion, a female presbyter (πρεσβυτέρα), performed her ecclesiastical ministry in Phrygia. She was no wife of any presbyter, but a member of the clergy, since her epitaph was dedicated by her bishop. Likewise, between the second and third centuries in Egypt Artemidora *presbytera* was an ordained presbyter and not a presbyter's wife, since her inscription does not mention a husband priest, but only her parents. She probably was a consecrated virgin and presbyter, like Theosebia, to whom I shall return below. Similarly, Firmilian of Caesarea in a letter to Cyprian[62] attests that in Cappadocia a woman consecrated the Eucharist and baptized, performing the priestly office.

Early in the third century, the *Didascalia Apostolorum* listed virgins, widows, and πρεσβύτιδες or women presbyters as ecclesiastical orders, and regarded women deacons as an ecclesiastical order as well as male deacons. Women deacons are there said to be worthy of honor as the symbol of the Holy Spirit; their relation to their bishop is the same as that of Christ-God is to the Father. A Zayton relief represents a male bishop and a female bishop or leader of consecrated women as equal in rank and with identical characteristics, the same head covering, the same pectoral cross, and the same stole.[63] Many other examples of iconographic parallels between ordained men and ordained women in the ancient church have been pointed out.[64] Women too, like male deacons and presbyters, were ordained by bishops by *kheirotonia*, and belonged to the clergy. Some decades before Origen, Pliny the Younger and Apuleius[65] also attest to the presence of Christian female ministers. *Ministrae* in Pliny, early in the second century, refers to women deacons or presbyters. This also seems to be reflected in the *Acts of Thecla* and *Acts of Philip*.[66]

According to Origen, ordained ecclesiastical ministries, sacraments, and liturgy can be both physical/historical and spiritual/symbolical: the intellectual-spiritual aspect prevails over the liturgical-sacramental. In the spiritual Israel—the Church—the high priests are not the bishops or patriarchs or popes, but those who devote themselves to the study of Scripture.[67] Humans can be high priests according to the order of Aaron, but according to the order of Melchisedek only Christ is. All Christians share in the priestly office; a nonordained person—including women—can be worthier of ordination than one ordained. Only those who have an understanding of God are worthy of being called priests.[68] The true priest should be chosen on account of eminence in every virtue.[69] True teachers are not necessarily churchmen, and some ordained ministers are not teachers, because they do not possess God's Logos and Wisdom.[70] Only the sage is priest, because only the sage has the worship coming from the knowledge of God.[71] True Levites and priests are those who, independently of official ordination, devote themselves to the divine Word and truly exist for the service of God alone.[72] Some deacons, presbyters, and bishops in the earthly Church, who are unworthy, do not belong to the heavenly church; some who are not ordained in the former, but are worthy, are presbyters and bishops in the latter.[73] One should aspire to be called a presbyter/elder by virtue of the spiritual perfection of "the inner human being" (a Pauline and Philonic motif) rather than because of ordained office,[74] since perfection is not conferred on anyone by an ecclesiastical ministry.[75] Note that the "inner human" is neither male nor female.

Based on Galatians 3:28, Origen argues that the Church, as well as every soul, is beyond gender, just like Christ, who, being both Wisdom and Logos, can be called both Bride and Bridegroom.[76] We have seen that this characterization of Christ as male and female, or, better, beyond gender, was already present in Bardaisan. Christ is represented as a male (ἄρρεν) lamb, which the Hebrews used to sacrifice, not because Christ is male, but because he is, etymologically, courageous (ἀνδρεῖον, *Pascha* 22.6–7). Whenever the Savior sends someone for the salvation of humans, whether man or woman, this messenger is an apostle of Christ.[77] Origen considers the Samaritan woman and other women to be apostles.[78] According to Origen, the Church rests not only on Peter, but on a number of Peters/rocks, who can be women.[79] Therefore, Jesus gives the keys of the Kingdom and the faculty of binding and loosing not only to Peter, but also to these other Peters, men and women; conversely, an ordained bishop who judges unrighteously does not possess the power of the keys.[80]

In Origen's view, the eschatological end is normative because it coincides with God's eternal plan for humanity, and this contemplates no difference between man and woman, no discrimination, just as there is none "in Christ" (Galatians 3:28). Now, the Church must reflect Christ, since it is Christ's body. But Christ's body eschatologically extends to all humans or all rational creatures, and Christ's body does not include only men.

The Christian Neoplatonist Gregory of Nyssa, Follower of Origen

Like Origen, his admirer and follower Eusebius of Caesarea valued ascetics and intellectuals over bishops as "archons and hegemons" of the church, and monks as "the first rank" ("τάγμα") among those who have progressed in Christ.[81] Eusebius described female believers in Christ as "female priests of the Highest God" (*Theoph.* 5.14).

Methodius of Olympus, who was familiar with Origen and influenced in turn Gregory of Nyssa, offered a Christian remake of the *Symposium*, as Nyssen did of Plato's *Phaedo*. The speakers are all women and speak of divine love and virginity.[82] Theophila, the second speaker, also addresses issues of physical reproduction: Unlike ancient theories, such as the misogynist Aristotelian one, she posits that both parents, with their seeds, concur equally to the constitution of the newborn.

Origen's ecclesiology and anthropology, like all of his ideas, deeply influenced Gregory Nyssen too. Nyssen was probably Origen's most insightful admirer and follower. He avoided interpreting 1 Corinthians 14:34–35 or any other Biblical passage, as forbidding women to teach in churches. His minimalistic exegesis of that passage eliminates its potential ecclesiological implications against women, and altogether omits v. 34b, the most misogynist.[83] Gregory reads v. 35 as suggesting that, if some women want to learn anything they do not know, they should do so at home, not at church, where explanations would distract people. For Gregory, Paul's recommendation does not extend to all Christian women, nor does it establish norms against women's ecclesiastical teaching and preaching as presbyters. Gregory never refers to 1 Corinthians 14:34–35 anywhere else, nor does he ever cite 1 Timothy 2:11–15. Only once does he refer to v. 14,[84] not, however, to banish women from ordained ministries, but to claim that, since a woman was the first transgressor, a woman had to be the first witness and apostle of Christ's resurrection. Gregory recognized that women too—such as Mary Magdalene and Junia—were apostles.

Origen's ideas about material and spiritual ministries and sacraments and women's ecclesiastical offices were familiar to the Cappadocians. They read Origen in Greek, also in the light of their own, late-fourth-century ecclesiastical context, when ordained women are well documented.[85] In the second half of the fourth century, the Council of Laodicaea, Canon 11, testifies to the diffusion of "πρεσβύτιδες προκαθημέναι," "women presbyters who presided over churches." In the *Martyrdom of Matthew*, 28, a converted king is ordained πρεσβύτερος, his wife πρεσβύτις, his son διάκονος, and his son's wife διακόνισσα. The aforementioned *Acts of Philip*, in the late-fourth to early-fifth centuries, includes πρεσβύτιδες and πρεσβύτεροι, διακόνισσαι and διάκονοι, in the clergy, and depicts Mariamme, the apostle Philip's sister, as a better apostle than her brother.[86] The Synod of Nîmes (394), Canon 2, attests that women were enrolled in "*sacerdotale officium*" ("the priestly office"). Epigraphic confirmations include a *Laeta praesbytera*, who died at forty in the fourth/fifth century, and was not the wife of any presbyter, as her husband was no presbyter.[87] In the same period, near Poitiers in Gaul, a *Martia presbyteria* made or brought the oblations with Olybrius and Nepos "in the very same way" (*pariter*) as they did.[88] This indicates her presbyteral ministry and celebration of the Eucharist. Further iconographic and historical evidence of ordained women in the time of the Cappadocians and environs has been highlighted by recent studies.[89]

One remarkable case, which bears heavily on the Cappadocians' attitude toward female ordained ministry, is represented by Theosebia, a sister of Nyssen and Basil, extolled by Nazianzen in Letter 197 and Epigrams 161 and 164. She was probably a presbyter.[90] Nazianzen describes her, among other things, as "the truly sacred, truly colleague of a priest, endowed with a dignity equal to his, and worthy of the great Mysteries,"[91] namely, the Eucharistic consecration in the Mass. Theosebia's ministry entailed the celebration of the Mass, supporting pious women, including the "choir of virgins" she presided over at Nyssa, and leading the Divine Office.

Basil, Macrina and Gregory Nyssen's brother, and the friend of Nazianzen, often uses the adjective ὁμότιμος—the same used by Nazianzen for the equality of ecclesiastical dignity between Theosebia and Nyssen—to indicate the equality of dignity and honor between woman and man. Basil stresses the complete equality of both genders, deriving from the same human lump (φύραμα), with the same honor and dignity (ὁμοτίμως) and in perfect equality (ἐξ ἴσου).[92] Men, he warns, even risk being inferior in piety.[93] Basil insists that man and woman have one and the same virtue and one and the same nature, and that their creation was of equal honor and dignity (ὁμότιμος);[94] they have the same capacity and activity (ἐνέργεια), and will receive the same reward.[95]

Nyssen overtly calls God "Mother" in at least two significant passages of his last work. In *Homily* 7 *on the Song of Songs*, he declares that "God is neither male nor female: how could one think of anything of this kind concerning the divine nature, while not even for us humans this characteristic endures forever," but we shall transcend gender in the other world. Gregory continues: "If we call God 'Mother' or 'Love,' we shall not err: for God is Love, as John said."[96] And in *Homily* 6: human heart "will return to that condition [κατάστασις] in which it was from the beginning, when it was molded by Her who conceived it. For if one conceives the first Cause of our constitution as a Mother [μητέρα], one will not err."[97] Nyssen significantly dedicated these *Homilies on the Song of Songs* to Deaconess Olympias of Constantinople, who had been ordained by the predecessor of John Chrysostom and was a friend and affluent patron of John himself. In his preface, Gregory with deference and admiration calls Olympias "σεμνοπρεπεστάτη," "most dignified, most reverend." Σεμνοπρέπεια implies a respectful, ceremonial style of address, used for instance for a bishop by the same Nyssen[98] and by Nazianzen.[99] For Olympias, also an ordained ecclesiastical minister, Gregory even employs the superlative, showing further that for him gender is not a primary criterion with respect to ecclesiastical ministry—let alone to the dignity of a human being.

Nyssen also praised his older sister Macrina, a consecrated virgin and leader of a house-monastery, in *The Life of Macrina* and in the dialogue *On the Soul and the Resurrection*, where she is the main speaker, like Socrates in Plato's *Phaedo* and Diotima in the *Symposium*.[100] Macrina had been Gregory's revered teacher. Although she was not ordained, Nyssen represented her as a presbyter, invested with the offering of the Eucharistic sacrifice in her bio-hagiography,[101] and with the teaching of the Christian doctrine (in the form of Origen's doctrine) both in her biography and in *On the Soul and the Resurrection*. Gregory represents her life beyond gender as "performing Christology," as Amy Hughes has suggested.[102] For Gregory, just as for Origen, spiritual ministry was more important than officially ordained ministry. Thus, in Homily 3 *On the Lord's Prayer*, Gregory maintains that Christ allows every human to be a priest by virtue of the mystical sacrifice of her- or himself. Macrina and her fellow ascetics imitated the angelic life with their philosophical-ascetic life, thereby anticipating the life of the resurrection and restoration, when all men and women, through spiritual growth and purification, will return to the angelic life. Note that this life is ungendered.[103]

In the human being created in the image and likeness of God there was neither male nor female, as Gregory remarks; this division is a departure from the prototype—Christ—in whom there is neither male nor female.[104] What is in the image of God is the intellect, not the mortal body divided into genders, a division that is alien to God; it rather pertains to beasts. Humans after the fall assumed, instead of the angelic life, the irrational life of beasts.[105] The human being proper, that is, the intellect, is like the Creator; however, in the part that is divided into genders, that is, mortal corporeality, it is like animals. The priority belongs to the intellectual component (τὸ νοερόν), whereas the association with irrationality, and the division into male and female, came afterward. For Genesis first speaks of the creation in the image of God, and only later of "male and female," which does not apply to

God. Gregory observes that the intellect is present in all humans; gender difference was created afterward, as the last thing, added to the molded human, in view of the fall.[106]

Gregory cites Jesus's declaration that in the resurrection humans will be like angels and will not marry. Without the fall, humans would have multiplied like angels, and would have kept their original, angelic bodies. Now they multiply like animals, and this is why they need the male-female divide. But in the resurrection, they will recover their angelic, nongendered bodies. The risen body is the same as that of the first creation, a spiritual, angelic body, which due to the fall was transformed into mortal, gendered, and corruptible (*In Eccl.* 1). Especially in *On the Soul and the Resurrection*, Gregory affirms that the risen body is the same as the earthly body as for individual identity what Origen also claimed—but it is spiritual and immortal, with its qualities transformed.[107] The reproductive function, too, in the risen body will become the capacity for begetting virtue. The body will then be restored to its prelapsarian state of spiritual, genderless body, and the intellectual soul to its prelapsarian condition free from evil. This point will be developed by Evagrius.

Like Origen, Gregory identified the skin tunics of Genesis 3:21 not with the body tout court, but with the heavy, mortal, gendered body, and the passions connected to it, a fleshly mentality,[108] a dead and earthly kind of vision.[109] The "dead and repelling tunic" of "irrational skins" ("ἀλόγων δερμάτων") is "the form of the irrational nature in which we have been wrapped after we have become familiar with passion,"[110] and this irrational nature has also maleness and femaleness in common with animals. But at the resurrection, all the elements of the irrational, "animal" nature, which are accidental to human nature, will vanish. Bodily organs will lose the functions imposed on them by animal life, such as intercourse, conception, delivery, nutrition, and so forth; the risen will "move in the heavenly regions with incorporeal nature."[111]

Gregory, like Origen, relativized gender differences as a postlapsarian condition absent from God's initial plan, from Christ, and from the eschatological scenario. A consequence is their irrelevance to ecclesiastical ordination. Maximus the Confessor and Eriugena will also think along these lines (see below). Consistently, like Origen, for whom Christ is both male and female, Logos and Sophia, Gregory of Nyssa holds up Paul as a bride who imitated the Bridegroom by his/her virtues and is pregnant with the knowledge of the good—surely remembering Paul's claim that he has given birth, with labor's pains, as a mother, to those whom he has converted to Christ.[112]

Like Origen, each soul, of a man or a woman, can give birth to Christ, and this through virginity. What happened corporeally in the case of the immaculate Mary, when the fullness of the divinity shone forth in Christ through her virginity, happens also in every virginal soul who gives birth to Christ, although the Lord no longer effects a bodily presence.[113] That Mary's virginity connected her with the divine, as indicated by her special link with the Temple, was suggested already in the *Protevangelium of James*.[114]

Origen's and the Cappadocians' philosophical anthropology, grounded in the framework of Platonic transcendence, bears on their ideas, and practice, concerning women's leadership and ordination. They favored and—in the case of the Cappadocians—performed the ordination of women, as did their contemporary John Chrysostom, who respected and treasured the ordained deacon Olympia, who was also the revered dedicatee of Nyssen's *Homilies on the Song of Songs*, as mentioned above. Chrysostom also maintained the postlapsarian nature of gender differentiation.[115]

Eriugena: The Last Western Patristic Platonist and the Heritage of Origen, the Cappadocians, and Maximus

Maximus the Confessor, who exerted a major influence on Eriugena along with Christian Platonists such as Origen, Gregory of Nyssa, and Dionysius the Areopagite, taught that humanity unites within itself the opposite poles of the five divisions of beings: uncreated and created, intelligible and sense-perceptible, heavenly and earthly, paradisiacal and worldly, and male and female (*Ambigua* 41). This point will be developed by Eriugena at great length. The Logos, free from the curse that passes down through human generation,[116] by uniting humanity and divinity performed the unification of the above-mentioned five divisions, including that between male and female, since he lived sinlessly and without intercourse (*Amb.* 41).

John Scottus Eriugena (†877) is the last Patristic Platonist in the West and the most systematic Western Christian Neoplatonist before Meister Eckhart. In Book 5 of *Periphyseon*, he describes the return of every creature to God as universal restoration. This *reditus* to God is the reversal of the *exitus* from God in subsequent stages, according to a Neoplatonic scheme. The *reditus* passes through the human being, from whom the reunification of every creature to God will start. The recovery of unity will begin with the elimination of the distinction between man and woman, which was introduced because of sin, when, instead of an "angelic," "divine" form of multiplication, humanity was reduced to a "bestial" form of propagation (a concept found already in Nyssen). The gender division, which is ultimately a consequence of sin, is abolished in Christ (Eriugena also appeals to Gal. 3:28), and for all human creatures it will be eliminated when human nature will be restored to its original condition, which did not contemplate any gender dichotomy. The notion that human nature is one and originally undivided, and that the primary human being, in the image of God, is neither male nor female, is a tenet of Origen's and Nyssen's anthropology, taken up by Eriugena. Only the secondary, molded human was divided by God into genders, in view of its sin and the consequent necessity of reproduction due to mortality, but this secondary division will not endure in the end.

Christ unified man and woman with his resurrection, given that he rose, not as a man or a woman, but simply as a human being (*in homine tantum*).[117] Eriugena announces humanity's restoration to its original integrity,[118] as an overcoming of duality, first of all the gender duplicity. He describes the following stages of restoration, in a process of subsumption of inferior into superior that resembles that postulated by Evagrius: (1) the return of the earthly body to the four elements; (2) the resurrection of this same body; (3) its transformation into a spiritual, genderless body; (4) the return of the whole human nature to its primordial causes in God, that is, God's Ideas; (5) the return of the whole nature, together with its primordial causes (the Ideas), to God, so that God will be "all in all."[119] The difference between the two genders will be eliminated at the resurrection, and human nature will be restored to unity, to the blessed condition that would obtain if the human being had not sinned.[120] All inferior realities will be resolved into the respective superior ones: genders will be resolved into the human being because they are less important than the human being.[121] This is grounded in Christ's assumption of the whole of humanity, not only one gender: "If God's Logos took up humanity, it took up not a part of it—which would be nothing—but all of it, together."[122]

Concluding Remarks and Reflections

This kind of Platonist Christology enabled, at least theoretically, an anthropology that transcended gender differentiation and discrimination.

Eliminating sexual difference on the level of the divine may indeed have entailed for these Christian Platonists a disruption of the binary to some extent. This disruption works primarily at the level of the *model*, since God is the model for humans. If God, in whose image humans are made and in whose likeness they are called to become (in the Platonic and Christian ideal of "assimilation to God"), is above the gender binary (and can be called "Mother" as Nyssen repeatedly does), clearly this binary is not so important and does not belong to essential human nature. It is adventitious, like Plato's "barnacles and seaweeds"—taken over by Gregory for the lower functions of the soul. For Gregory of Nyssa, indeed, just as for Origen, the original human in God's image is the intellectual soul, while passions and sins are subsequent "accretions" to be shed;[123] *nous* after purification can recover the intelligence of the truth that is originally natural to it (*In Illud* 3). The inferior parts of the soul linked with the body and against nature are accretions—an image stemming from Plato *Rep.* 10.611D: "barnacles, seaweed, and stones," which encrust the soul in the Glaucus metaphor. These accretions are consequent on its association with the body, of which it will be divested when it leaves the body. These are Plotinus' "additions" (προσθῆκαι, *Enn.* 4.7.10; 5.5.2), not enriching but impoverishing the soul (*Enn.* 6.5.12), and earlier Numenius' "supplements," προσφυόμενα/προστιθέντα (F34 and 43 Des Places) and Basilides' "appendages" (προσαρτήματα, *ap.* Clement *Strom.* 2.20.113). Therefore, essential human nature is genderless *nous*; this is in the image of God, not gendered bodies, since God has no body.

Moreover, the gender binary is doomed to vanish eschatologically according to these thinkers. Now, if the eschatological *telos* is ethically normative (as it is at least for Origen, Gregory of Nyssa, and Evagrius), this means that from the ethical viewpoint, too, the binary is not so important. Indeed, Clement, Origen, Gregory, Evagrius, and Eriugena all maintained—with the Stoics and Plato—that virtues are the same for men and women alike.

To be sure, sometimes even these Christian Platonists fell into the traditional identification of females with the body and sensuality and males with the soul or *nous*: Origen does so in his allegoresis of Genesis, since he is following Philo. But their openness to women officeholders in the church was a proof that they took their God-above-gender as a model seriously, although they were immersed in a strongly gender-hierarchized society. They also had New Testament examples: Phoebe, Junia, Prisca, Aquila and so forth, as well as examples of women officeholders in the time of Origen and the Cappadocians, as seen, but also of Eriugena.[124] One more case in which they saw a convergence between Plato and Scripture: As Eriugena maintained, joining both traditions, *homo melior est quam sexus*, "the human being is superior to its gender" (*Periph.* 2.534a).

Notes

1. Although Plato was not immune to the misogyny of his time and thought that women had an imperfect logos, being dominated by the concupiscible part of the soul (*Tim.* 42C, 90E), he was not as misogynist as Aristotle (on whom see Ilaria L. E. Ramelli, *Social Justice and the Legitimacy of Slavery: The Role of Philosophical Asceticism from Ancient Judaism to Late Antiquity* [Oxford: Oxford University Press, 2016], ch. 1) and, as is emphasized by Apuleius, *De Platone* 1.4, Plato had both men and women as disciples, and many of them of both sexes flourished as philosophers. On the equality of women in the *Republic*, Elena Duvergès Blair's *Plato's Dialectic on Woman: Equal, therefore Inferior* (London and New York: Routledge, 2017) is critical, while Catherine Rowett's "Why the Philosopher-Kings Will Believe the Noble Lie" (*Oxford Studies in Ancient Philosophy* 50 [2016]: 67–100) is very positive. See, in the present book, Monica Vilhauer, "Overturning Soul-Body Dualism in Plato's *Timaeus*" (ch. 6).

2. As argued in Ramelli, "Constructions of Gender in Origen of Alexandria," invited lecture, Enoch Seminar, *Constructions of Gender in Late Antiquity*, Berlin-Potsdam, July 19–22, 2021, eds. Kathy Ehrensperger and Shayna Sheinfeld (forthcoming).

3. Full analysis appears in Ilaria L. E. Ramelli, *Bardaiṣan of Edessa: A Reassessment of the Evidence and a New Interpretation: Also in the Light of Origen and the Original Fragments from Porphyry* (Piscataway: Gorgias, 2009; electronic edition, Berlin: De Gruyter, 2019)—the argument in this book has been cited by Patricia Crone in "Daysanis," *Encyclopedia of Islam* (Leiden: Brill, 2012), 116–18; Heidi Marx-Wolf, "Bardesanes," in *The Encyclopedia of Ancient History* (Oxford: Wiley-Blackwell, 2013), DOI: 10.1002/9781444338386.wbeah05032; Ute Possekel, "Bardaisan and Origen on Fate and the Power of the Stars," *Journal of Early Christian Studies* 20, no. 4 (2012): 515–41: 522; Michael Speidel, "Making Use of History beyond the Euphrates," in Anette Merz and Teun Tieleman, eds., *Mara*

bar Serapion in Context (Leiden: Brill, 2012), 11–41; Han J. W. Drijvers, *Bardaisan of Edessa*, introduction by J. W. Drijvers (Piscataway: Gorgias, 2014), xv; Aaron Johnson, *Religion and Identity in Porphyry of Tyre: The Limits of Hellenism in Late Antiquity* (Cambridge: Cambridge University Press, 2013), 207, 209, 255, 284, 364; Dirk Bakker, *Bardaisan's Book of the Laws of the Countries: A Computer-Assisted Linguistic Analysis* (PhD diss., Leiden: University, 2011), 262; David Litwa, *Refutation of All Heresies* (Atlanta: SBL Press, 2016), 801; Clemens Scholten, "Der Abfassungszweckes sogenannten Haereticarum fabularum compendium des Theodore von Kyrrhos, 1," *Vigiliae Christianae* 70 (2016), 282–318, 283, 287; Patricia Crone, *The Qur'ānic Pagans and Related Matters*, vol. 1 (Leiden, the Netherlands: Brill: 2016), 316; Shaye J. D. Cohen, "Jewish Observance of the Sabbath in Bardaisan's Book of Laws of Countries," Harvard preprint: http://dash.harvard.edu/bitstream/handle/1/10861157/Cohen_JewishObservance.pdf?sequence=2, n1, 3, 12, 39. Further arguments on his philosophical setting in my "Bardaisan of Edessa, Origen, and Imperial Philosophy: A Middle Platonic Context?," *Aram* 30. no. 1–2 (2018): 337–53; on his relation to Gnosticism, my "Bardaisan: A Gnostic or a Polemicist against Gnostic Tenets?," *Aram* 33 (2020): 1–25.

4. Argument in my "Origen, Bardaisan, and the Origin of Universal Salvation," *Harvard Theological Review* 102 (2009): 135–68; "Bardaisan of Edessa on Freewill, Fate and Nature: Alexander of Aphrodisias, Origen, and Diodore of Tarsus," in *Women's Perspectives on Ancient and Medieval Philosophy*, ed. Isabelle Chouinard et al. (New York–Zürich: Springer Nature Switzerland, 2021), 169–76. On Origen: "The Legacy of Origen in Gregory of Nyssa's Theology of Freedom," *Modern Theology* (online 2022): 1–26: https://onlinelibrary.wiley.com/doi/full/10.1111/moth.12777

5. Leslie William Barnard, "The Origins and Emergence of the Church in Edessa during the First Two Centuries AD," *Vigiliae Christianae* 22 (1968): 161–75: 172.

6. Stob. *Anth.* [*Phys.*] 1.3.56; 1.66.24–70.13 Wachsmuth = Porph. fr. 376 Smith = 7 Castelletti. Porphyry was interested in caves such as that where the statue stood (see his *Cave of the Nymphs*) as well as in the interpretation of Plato's *Timaeus* in Bardaisan's description of the cosmic Christ as noetic cosmos and of the Father as showing the noetic cosmos to the Son for creation. Porphyry's passage is overlooked by most scholars, for example, in Wayne A. Meeks, "The Image of the Androgyne: Some Uses of a Symbol in Earliest Christianity," *History of Religions* 13, no. 2 (1974): 165–208; Charlotte Köckert, *Christliche Kosmologie und kaiserzeitliche Philosophie* (Tübingen: Mohr Siebeck 2009); see my review in *Augustinianum* 52 (2012): 550–52.

7. Cristiano Castelletti, *Porfirio, Sullo Stige* (Milan: Bompiani, 2006).

8. Ilaria L. E. Ramelli, "The Body of Christ as Imperishable Wood: Hippolytus and Bardaisan of Edessa's Complex Christology," in *Proceedings of the 12th Symposium Syriacum 2016*, ed. Emidio Vergani (Leuven: Orientalia Christiana Analecta, 2020), 1–33.

9. Dragos Giulea, *Pre-Nicene Christology in Paschal Context: The Case of the Divine Noetic Anthropos* (Leiden: Brill, 2014). On Nous in Origen and his followers: my "The Reception of Paul's Nous in the Christian Platonism of Origen and Evagrius," in *Der νοῦς bei Paulus im Horizont griechischer und hellenistisch-jüdischer Anthropologie*, eds. Jörg Frey and Manuel Nägele (WUNT 1.464; Tübingen: Mohr Siebeck, 2021), 279–316.

10. On Jesus as female Wisdom in early Christianity, see also Sally Douglas, *Early Church Understandings of Jesus as the Female Divine: The Scandal of the Scandal of Particularity* (London and New York: Bloomsbury, 2016), ch. 2, but she examines only OT, NT, and early texts until the second and very early third century, omitting many great Patristic Platonists (Origen is touched upon in ch. 4, Nyssen or Eriugena never), let alone Bardaisan himself. Christ's divinity is already proclaimed in the NT: Phil. 2:6–11, John 1:1–18, Col. 1:15–20, Eph. 5:14, 1 Tim. 3:16.

11. See Ilaria L. E. Ramelli "Origen, Greek Philosophy, and the Birth of the Trinitarian Meaning of *Hypostasis*," *HTR* 105 (2012), 302–50.

12. The title in the Coptic translation (NHC II) is: "These are the secret sayings that the living Jesus uttered and that Didymus Judas Thomas wrote down." The Greek fragment of the Prologue preserved in P.Oxy. 654.2–3 has only two names/appellatives, "Judas, who is also [called] Thomas." See Simon Gathercole, *The Gospel of Thomas: Introduction and Commentary* (Leiden: Brill, 2014).

13. This notion that the bridal chamber is reserved for those who renounce the exercise of sexuality on earth is developed in the *Acts of Thomas*, 1.12, a narrative usually labeled as "encratite."

14. See A. F. J. Klijn, "The 'Single One' in the Gospel of Thomas," *Journal of Biblical Literature* 81 (1962): 261–78.

15. Although "Christian leaders in Rome such as Clement and Justin virtually never mention their Christian women contemporaries" (Nicola Denzey Lewis, "Women as Independent Religious Specialists in Second-Century Rome," in Ulla Tervahauta et al., eds., *Women and Knowledge in Early Christianity* [Leiden: Brill, 2017], 21–38, 24). Only note that, while Justin was a Christian leader in Rome, Clement was in Alexandria for a long while before escaping persecution.

16. My "Transformations of the Household and Marriage Theory between Neo-Stoicism, Middle Platonism, and Early Christianity," *RFN* 100 (2008), 369–96; Alex Dressler, *Personification and the Feminine in Roman Philosophy* (Oxford and New York: Oxford University Press, 2016), mostly on Stoicism.

17. Clement, moreover, seems to build a kind of Stoic paradox: every noetic soul is priest. This includes souls of men and women alike, since noetic souls belong to both genders. He claims that the perfect Christian's "soul" has become "truly rational and high-priestly, because it is directly animated, so to say, by the Logos," who is Christ (*Exc. Theod.* 27).

18. *Hymn.* 5.63–64: "You Father, you Mother; you male, you female."

19. *Paed.* 1.42.2; 35.2–3.

20. *Paed.* 1.40.1.

21. *Paed.* 1.43.2–4. See also Verna Harrison, "The Care-Banishing Breast of the Father: Feminine Images of the Divine in Clement of Alexandria's *Paedagogus* I," *Studia Patristica* 31 (1997): 401–5.

22. See, for example, Judith Kovacs, "Becoming the Perfect Man: Clement on the Philosophical Life of Women," in S. Ahearne-Kroll, ed., *Women and Gender in Ancient Religions* (Tübingen: Mohr Siebeck, 2010), 289–413.

23. Psalm 109. 3 (LXX), NETS translation.

24. See Charles Gieschen, *Angelomorphic Christology: Antecedents and Early Evidence* (Leiden: Brill, 1998). On angelomorphic pneumatology-Christology, see Bogdan Bucur, "Revisiting Christian Oeyen," *Vigiliae Christianae* 61 (2007): 381–413: 391–92, and *Angelomorphic Pneumatology: Clement of Alexandria and Other Early Christian Witnesses* (Leiden: Brill, 2009), in which he studies angelic imagery applied to the Holy Spirit and shows that Clement maintained an angelomorphic pneumatology connected with spirit Christology, within a framework of "binitarianism" and the Jewish and Christian traditions on the seven *prōtoktistoi* angels. See also Justin J. Lee, "'Angelomorphic Pneumatology," *Vigiliae Christianae* 74, no. 4 (2020): 394–410, who finds some elements of angelomorphic pneumatology in Origen.

25. See Susan Harvey, "Feminine Imagery for the Divine," *St Vladimir Theological Quarterly* 37 (2004): 1–29. Sebastian Brock, "Come, Compassionate Mother, Come, Holy Spirit," *Aram* 3 (1991): 249–57, in idem, *Fire from Heaven: Studies in Syriac Theology and Liturgy* (Aldershot: Ashgate, 2006), 249–57; Susan Myers, "The Spirit as Mother in Early Syriac-Speaking Christianity," in S. P. Ahearne-Kroll, P. Holloway, and James Kellhoffer, eds., *Women and Gender in Ancient Religions: Interdisciplinary Approaches* (Tübingen: Mohr Siebeck, 2010), 427–62.

26. Full analysis of this fragment in Ramelli, *Bardaisan* 2009.

27. See, for example, the detailed analysis by Mariano Troiano, "Padre femenino: el Dios-Madre de los gnósticos," in Luciana Gabriela Soares Santoprete, eds., *Gnose et manichéïsme. Hommage à Jean-Daniel Dubois*, Turnhout: Brepols, 2016, 27–159; the late John Turner, "The Virgin That Became Male: Feminine Principles in Platonic and Gnostic Texts," in Ulla Tervahauta et al., eds., *Women and Knowledge in Early Christianity* (Leiden: Brill, 2017), 291–324, who finds that "those behind the first traces of the so-called Barbeloite speculation display the highest estimation of the feminine principle" (323).

28. On the figure of Hypatia, see now Edward Watts, *Hypatia: The Life and Legend of an Ancient Philosopher* (New York: Oxford University Press, 2017).

29. Matt. 22:30; Mark 12:25; my "Jesus of Nazareth," in *The Oxford Classical Dictionary* (Oxford: Oxford University Press, 2021).

30. On gender in Plotinus, see in this same book, Gary Gabor, "Plotinus on the Creation of Gender" (ch. 10).

31. Ilaria L. E. Ramelli, "Origen, Patristic Philosophy, and Christian Platonism: Re-Thinking the Christianization of Hellenism," *Vigiliae Christianae* 63 (2009): 217–63; "Origen and the Platonic Tradition," in *Plato and Christ: Platonism in Early Christian Theology*, special issue of *Religions*, ed. J. Warren Smith, 8(2), 21 (2017): 1–20: doi:10.3390/rel8020021; "The Construction of the Professional Identity of Origen of Alexandria and the Question of Which Origen," in *Problems in Ancient Biography: The Construction of Professional Identity in Late Antiquity*, eds. Elizabeth DePalma Digeser, Heidi Marx-Wolf, and Ilaria Ramelli (Cambridge: Cambridge University Press, forthcoming). A number of other scholars support the possible identity, among whom René Cadiou, *La jeunesse d'Origène: Histoire de l'école d'Alexandrie au début du III*[e] *siècle* (Paris: Beauchesne, 1935), 231–40; Richard P. C. Hanson, *Origen's Doctrine of Tradition* (London, 1954), 1–30; Henri Crouzel, "Origène et Plotin élèves d'Ammonios Saccas," *Bulletin de Littérature Ecclésiastique* 57 (1956): 193–214; Werner Jaeger, *Humanistische Reden und Vorträge*, 2nd ed. (Berlin: de Gruyter, 1960), 297–98: "The most important fact in the history of Christian doctrine was that the father of Christian theology, Origen, was a Platonic philosopher at the school of Alexandria"; Franz Kettler, "Origenes, Ammonios Sakkas und Porphyrius," in *Kerygma und Logos. FS Andresen* (Göttingen: V&R, 1979), 322–28; PierFranco Beatrice, "Porphyry's Judgment on Origen," in *Origeniana Quinta*, ed. Robert Daly (Leuven: Peeters, 1992), 351–67: 351; idem, "Origen in Nemesius' Treatise *On the Nature of Man*," in *Origeniana Nona* (Leuven: Peeters, 2009), 505–32: "Origen the Pagan, or the Neoplatonist, has never existed, and the Origen we meet three times in Nemesius' treatise is always the only Christian and Platonist Origen, known to Christian and pagan writers without any distinction" (531), and others; Thomas Böhm, "Origenes—Theologe und (Neu-)Platoniker?" *Adamantius* 8 (2002): 7–23 supports the identification, based on doctrinal identities; Daniel Boyarin, "By Way of Apology: Dawson, Edwards, Origen," *Studia Philonica Annual* 16 (2004), 188–217; Christoph Markschies, *Origenes und sein Erbe* (Berlin: De Gruyter, 2007), 3, deems the identification "not to be ruled out"; Ramelli ("Origen, Patristic Philosophy." "Origen the Christian Middle/Neoplatonist," *Journal of Early Christian History* 1 (2011), 98–130, and "Origen and the Platonic Tradition") offers arguments for a possible identification, also accepted by Johnson, *Religion and Identity*, 90, 153, passim; Michael Bland Simmons, *Universal Salvation in Late Antiquity: Porphyry of Tyre and the Pagan-Christian Debate* (Oxford: Oxford University Press, 2015); Heidi Marx-Wolf, *Spiritual Taxonomies and Ritual Authority: Platonists, Priests, and Gnostics in the Third Century* C.E. (Philadelphia: University of Pennsylvania Press, 2016), 43–44, and Elizabeth DePalma Digeser support the identity of the two Origens; Harold Tarrant, "Plotinus, Origenes and Ammonius on the King," in *Religio-Philosophical*

Discourses within the Greco-Roman, Jewish and Early Christian World, eds. Anders Klostergaard Petersen, George van Kooten (Leiden: Brill, 2017), 323–37: 324: "it is not sure that they are distinct"; PierFranco Beatrice, "Porphyry at Origen's School at Caesarea," in *Origeniana Duodecima. Origen's Legacy in the Holy Land*, ed. Lorenzo Perrone (BETL 302, Leuven: Peeters, 2019), 267–84 and "The Soul–Body Relation according to Nemesius of Emesa," in *Lovers of the Soul, Lovers of the Body*, eds. Svetla Slaveva Griffin and Ilaria L. E. Ramelli (Harvard University Press, 2021), 339–62; Claudio Calabrese, "La herencia clásica como instrumento para comprender a Dios. Clemente de Alejandría," *Theologica Xaveriana* 71 (2021): 1–26: 8; Stephen Clark, "Plotinus, Eriugena and the Uncreated Image," in *Eriugena's Christian Platonism and Its Sources*, ed. Ilaria L. E. Ramelli (Leuven: Peeters, 2021), 33–50, citation from 35: "The Christian theologian Origen may or may not be identical with Plotinus' friend and fellow-pupil, but both Origens (if they are distinct) were students of Ammonius Saccas."

32. Sami Yli-Karjanmaa, *Reincarnation in Philo of Alexandria* (Atlanta: SBL, 2015), esp. 216–48.

33. "Origen on the Unity of Soul and Body in the Earthly Life and Afterwards and His Impact on Gregory of Nyssa," in *The Unity of Soul and Body in Patristic and Byzantine Thought*, ed. Jörg Ulrich, Anna Usacheva, and Siam Bhayro (Leiden and Paderborn: Brill, 2021), 38–77.

34. Ramelli, "The ἀρχή and τέλος of Rational Creatures in Origen and Some Origenians," *Studia Patristica* 56 (2013), 167–226; "Origen," in Anna Marmodoro, ed., *A History of Mind and Body in Late Antiquity* (Cambridge: Cambridge University Press, 2018), 245–66; Griffin and Ramelli, *Lovers of the Soul*.

35. Homilies on Leviticus, 6.2.

36. Fragments on I Corinthians, 29.

37. Commentary on Genesis, 3. 21.

38. Ap. Photius *Bibl.* 232. 287b–91b, esp. 288a.

39. *Princ.* 2.10.2; Ramelli, "Matter in the Dialogue of Adamantius: Origen's Heritage and Hylomorphism," in *Late Antique Cosmologies*, eds. Johannes Zachhuber and Anna Schiavoni (Leiden: Brill, 2022).

40. *Comm. Ps.* 1, *ap.* Pamphilus, *Apol.* 141; Fr.140 on Luke 9:28; *Resurr.* 2 *ap.* Pamphilus, *Apol.* 132.

41. Ramelli, "Harmony."

42. Ramelli, "The ἀρχή and τέλος"; "Origen," in *A History*.

43. Sarah Pomeroy, *Pythagorean Women: Their History and Writings* (Baltimore: Johns Hopkins University, 2015).

44. Vicki Lynn Harper, "Women in Philosophy," in *Oxford Classical Dictionary*, online edition, (2016) DOI:10.1093/acrefore/9780193811 35.013.6894.

45. "*Apostolica auctoritate docet etiam foeminas in ministerio ecclesiae constitui . . . et tales constitui debere*," *Comm. Rom.* 10.17.

46. *Comm. Rom.* 10.17. See my "Diakonia in Origen: From Christ and the Angels to Men and Women," in *Deacons and Diakonia in Christianity from the Third to the Sixth Century*, ed. Bart Koet (Tübingen: Mohr Siebeck, 2022).

47. *Comm. Rom.* 8.9.

48. *Hom. Luc.* 17.

49. Τὸν δρόμον τὸν ἀποστολικόν, *ap.* Photius, *Bibl.* 275.

50. *Homilies on Judges*, 5.2.

51. Catena on I Corinthians A74.

52. Ramelli, "Colleagues of Apostles, Presbyters, and Bishops: Women *Syzygoi* in Ancient Christian Communities," in *Patterns of Women's Leadership within Ancient Christianity*, eds. Joan Taylor and Ilaria L. E. Ramelli (Oxford: Oxford University Press, 2021), 26–58.

53. Καλοδιδάσκαλοι ἀνάλογον τοῖς πρεσβυτέροις, *Comm. Io.* 31.12.132–33.

54. *Comm. Tit.* 2.3a.

55. *Comm. Rom.* 10.29. On Persis see David Eastman, "Epiphanius' and Patristic Debates on the Marital Status of Peter and Paul," *Vigiliae Christianae* 67 (2013): 499–516; Ramelli, "Colleagues."

56. *Comm. Rom.* 10.26; 39; see Eldon J. Epp, *Junia: The First Woman Apostle* (Minneapolis: Fortress, 2005); my review in *Rivista Biblica* 55 (2007): 245–49; Yii-Jan Lin, "Junia: An Apostle before Paul," *Journal of Biblical Literature* 139 (2020): 191–209.

57. *Comm. Cant.* 2.1. On Origen's exegesis of Scripture, see my "Origen's Philosophical Exegesis of the Bible against the Backdrop of Ancient Philosophy and Hellenistic and Rabbinic Judaism," main lecture, *The Bible: Its Translations and Interpretations in the Patristic Time*, KUL, October 16–17, 2019, *Studia Patristica* 103 (2021): 13–58.

58. He identified the female pole as passivity and sense-perception versus male activity and intellection, for example, in *Leg. All.* 2.23–24, *Opif.* 165, and *De Deo* or *De visione trium angelorum ad Abraham* 3, but he also portrays women, especially virgins, such as the Therapeutrides, very positively, capable of philosophy and the vision of God, in *De vita contemplativa*; QG 1.8, and *Cher.* 50. See Friederike Oertelt, "Gender, Religion und Politik bei Philon von Alexandria," in *Doing Gender, Doing Religion: Case Studies on Intersectionality in Early Judaism, Christianity and Islam*, eds. Ute Eisen and Angela Standhartinger (Tübingen: Mohr Siebeck, 2013), 227–50.

59. *Hom. Ex.* 2.2–3; cf. *Hom. Gen.* 4.4; 5.2. Philo also allegorized Adam as earth, though. See Sami Yli-Karjanmaa, "Call Him Earth: On Philo's Allegorisation of Adam in *Legum Allegoriae*," in *The Adam and Eve Story in the Hebrew Bible and in Ancient Jewish Writings*, eds. Antti Laato and Lotta Valve (Turku: SRHB, 2016), 253–93.

60. *Comm. Rom.* 4.6.160; *Hom. Jer.* 4.5; *Fr. Luc.* 32 Rauer. On virginity superior to marriage, as in Paul, in Origen's thought see, for example, *Comm. Matth.* 14.25.

61. *Virg. vel.* 9.1; *Praescr. haer.* 41.5; *Bapt.* 17.4; Ramelli, "Prophecy in Origen: Between Scripture and Philosophy," *Journal of Early Christian History* 7.2 (2017): 17–39.

62. Letter 75.

63. Pierre Perrier, *L'apôtre Thomas et le prince Ying* (Paris, 2012), 82.

64. For example, Mary Schäfer, *Women in Pastoral Office: The Story of Santa Prassede, Rome* (Oxford: Oxford University Press, 2013), with my review *Gnomon* 89.1 (2017): 42–46. A particularly clear example from Old St. Peter is on the cover of Taylor-Ramelli, *Patterns of Women's Leadership*, and in the analysis by Ally Kateusz and Luca Badini Confalonieri, "Women Church Leaders in and around Fifth-Century Rome," in *Patterns of Women's Leadership in Ancient Christianity*, ed. Joan E. Taylor and Ilaria L. E. Ramelli (Oxford: Oxford University Press, 2021), 228–60.

65. Pliny, Letter 10.96(97).7; Apuleius, *Met.* 9.14–15; see Ramelli, "Apuleius and Christianity," in *Echoes of Myth, Religion and Ritual in the Ancient Novel*, ed. Marília Futre Pinheiro, Anton Bierl, and Roger Beck (Berlin: De Gruyter, 2013), 145–73.

66. Ilaria L. E. Ramelli, "Mansuetudine, grazia e salvezza negli *Acta Philippi* (ed. Bovon)," *Invigilata Lucernis* 29 (2007): 215–28; "*Colleagues of Apostles*"; Rosie Ratcliffe, "The Acts of Paul and Thecla: Violating the Inviolate Body. Thecla Uncut," in *The Body in Biblical, Christian and Jewish Texts*, ed. Joan E. Taylor (London: Bloomsbury, 2014), 184–209; *Deacons and Diakonia in Early Christianity: The First Two Centuries*, eds. Bart J. Koet, Edwina Murphy, and Esko Ryökäs (Tübingen: Mohr Siebeck, 2018), and my review *Vigiliae Christianae* 75.3 (2021): 329–40.

67. *Comm. Jo.* I. 3.

68. *Hom. Lev.* 1.5.

69. Ibidem 2.1; 6.3.

70. *Hom. Luc.* 18.

71. *Comm. Jo.* 2.16.112–13.

72. *Comm. Jo.* 1.10–11.

73. *Comm. Matt.* 16.20–23; *Comm. Matt. Ser.* 12.

74. Homily 4 on Psalm 36, 3.

75. *Hom. Jer.* 11.3.

76. *Comm. Jo.* 1.6.14; *Hom. Gen.* 14.1. On the identification of Christ as female Wisdom in the first Christian centuries see also Douglas, *Scandal.*

77. *Comm. Jo.* 32.17.204.

78. *Comm. Jo.* 13.28.169.

79. *Comm. Matt.* 12.10–11; cf. *Comm. Matt. Ser.* 139.

80. *Comm. Matt.* 12.14.

81. *InPs.* 64.14, PG 23.644D, 689C.

82. See my "L'Inno a Cristo-Logos nel *Simposio* di Metodio di Olimpo: alle origini della poesia filosofica cristiana," in *Motivi e forme della poesia cristiana antica tra Scrittura e tradizione classica. Incontro di studiosi dell'Antichità cristiana, Roma, Augustinianum,* 3–5 Maggio 2007, ed. Vittorino Grossi (Rome: Augustinianum 2008), 257–80.

83. *In Eccl.* 7, GNO 5.409.15–21.

84. *C.Eun.* 3.10.16, GNO 2.295.9.

85. My "Theosebia: A Presbyter of the Catholic Church," *Journal for the Feminist Study of Religion* 26 (2010): 79–102.

86. Ramelli, "Mansuetudine."

87. CIL 10.8079.

88. CIL 13.1183; Kevin Madigan and Carolyn Osiek, *Ordained Women in the Early Church: A Documentary History* (Baltimore: Johns Hopkins University, 2005), 196.

89. Gary Macy, *The Hidden History of Women's Ordination: Female Clergy in the Medieval West* (Oxford: Oxford University Press, 2008); Schäfer, *Women.*

90. See Ramelli, "Theosebia," with full documentation; further arguments in "Colleagues" and "The Life of Macrina and the Life of Evagrius," in *Novel Saints*, ed. Koen de Temmerman (Turnhout: Brepols, forthcoming).

91. Τὴν ὄντως ἱεράν, ἱερέως σύζυγον καὶ ὁμότιμον, and τῶν μεγάλων μυστηρίων ἀξίαν, Letter 197.5–6.

92. *Hom. Julitt.* 241A.

93. *Hom. Julitt.* 241B.

94. *Hom. Ps.* 1 PG 39.216–17.

95. See also Verna Harrison, "Male and Female in Cappadocian Theology," *Journal of Theological Studies* 41 (1990), 441–71; Anna Silvas, "Basil of Caesarea and His View of Women in a Christian Anthropology," in *Men and Women in the Early Christian Centuries*, ed. Wendy Mayer (Strathfield: St Pauls, 2014), 149–59.

96. 1John 4:8.

97. *Hom. Cant.* 6 GNO 6.183.11–15.

98. Letter 21.

99. Letter 202. See my "Apokatastasis and Epektasis in *Hom. in Cant.*: The Relation between Two Core Doctrines in Gregory and Roots in Origen," in *Gregory of Nyssa: In Canticum Canticorum*, ed. Giulio Maspero, Miguel Brugarolas, and Ilaria Vigorelli (Leiden: Brill, 2018), 312–39.

100. "Gregory of Nyssa on the Soul (and the Restoration): From Plato to Origen," in *Gregory of Nyssa: Historical and Philosophical Perspectives*, ed.

Anna Marmodoro and Neil McLynn (Oxford: Oxford University Press, 2018), 11–141.

101. Derek Krueger, "Writing and the Liturgy of Memory in Gregory of Nyssa's Life of Macrina," *Journal of Early Christian Studies* 8 (2000): 483–510: 508–9.

102. Amy Hughes, "The Legacy of the Feminine in the Christology of Origen of Alexandria, Methodius of Olympus, and Gregory of Nyssa," *Vigiliae Christianae* 70 (2016): 51–76: 51 and passim.

103. On the contribution of asceticism to gender equality in late antiquity see Susanna Elm, *Virgins of God: The Making of Asceticism in Late Antiquity* (Oxford: Oxford University Press, 1994); Ramelli, *Social Justice*.

104. Galatians 3:28; *Hom. op.* 16.

105. *Hom. op.* 18.

106. *Hom. op.* 17.

107. See also *Mort.* GNO 9.62–63.

108. *Virg.* 12–13.

109. V. *Mos.* GNO 7.1.39–40.

110. Τὸ σχῆμα τῆς ἀλόγου φύσεως, ᾧ πρὸς τὸ πάθος οἰκειωθέντες περιεβλήθημεν, *An. et res.* 148.

111. *An. et res.*144B–48C.

112. *Hom. Cant.* 3.16, GNO 6.90–81. On Paul Reidar Aasgaard, "Paul as a Child: Children and Childhood in the Letters of the Apostle," *Journal of Biblical Literature* 126 (2007): 129–59, with bibliography. Grace Emmett, "The Apostle Paul's Maternal Masculinity," *Journal of Early Christian History* (2021): 1–23.

113. *Virg.* 2.24–28, GNO 8.1.254.

114. Megan Nutzman, "Mary in the Protevangelium of James: A Jewish Woman in the Temple," *Greek, Roman and Byzantine Studies* 53 (2013), 551–78 has shown that the depiction of Mary in the Temple in this second-century Christian text reflects historical data about the presence of Jewish women in the Temple and indicates familiarity with Jewish customs.

115. *Virg.* 15.2; *Hom. Gen.* 18.3–4.

116. *Amb.* 42; *Q.Thal.* 21.

117. *Periph.* 2.10.

118. *Ad pristinam integritatem restituatur* (*Periph.* 4.7).

119. I Corinthians 15:28, in *Periph.* 5.8.

120. *Sicut fieret si non peccaret*: *Periph.* 5.20.

121. *Inferior est sexus homine: Periph.* 5.893; *homo melior est quam sexus*: *Periph.* 2.534a.

122. *Si Dei Uerbum humanitatem accepit, non partem eius, quae nulla est, sed uniuersaliter totam accepit* (*Periph.* 5.27).

123. An. 52–56; 64 with the allegorical exegesis of the darnel parable.

124. Macy, *History*; Schäfer, *Women*; Taylor-Ramelli, *Patterns*.

Bibliography

Bakker, Dirk. *Bardaisan's Book of the Laws of the Countries: A Computer-Assisted Linguistic Analysis*. PhD Diss. Leiden, the Netherlands: University of Leiden, 2011.

Barnard, L. W. "The Origins and Emergence of the Church in Edessa during the First Two Centuries AD." *Vigiliae Christianae* 22 (1968): 161–75.

Beatrice, Pier Franco. "Porphyry's Judgment on Origen." In *Origeniana Quinta*, edited by Robert Daly, 351–67. Leuven, Belgium: Peeters, 1992.

———. "Origen in Nemesius' Treatise *On the Nature of Man*." In *Origeniana Nona*, edited by George Heidl and Robert Somos, 505–32. Leuven, Belgium: Peeters, 2009.

———. "Porphyry at Origen's School at Caesarea." In *Origeniana Duodecima. Origen's Legacy in the Holy Land*, edited by Lorenzo Perrone, Brouria B. Ashkelony, and Aryeh Kofski, 267–84. Leuven, Belgium: Peeters, 2019.

Berger, Teresa. "Women's Liturgical Practices and Leadership Roles in Early Christian Communities." In *Patterns of Women's Leadership in Ancient Christianity*, edited by Joan E. Taylor and Ilaria L. E. Ramelli, 180–94. Oxford, UK: Oxford University Press, 2021.

Blair, E. D. *Plato's Dialectic on Woman: Equal, therefore Inferior*. London and New York: Routledge, 2017.

Böhm, Thomas. "Origenes—Theologe und (Neu-)Platoniker?" *Adamantius* 8 (2002): 7–23.

Boyarin, Daniel. "By Way of Apology: Dawson, Edwards, Origen." *Studia Philonica Annual* 16 (2004): 188–217.

Brock, Sebastian. "Come, Compassionate Mother, Come, Holy Spirit." *Aram* 3 (1991): 249–57.

———. "The Holy Spirit as Feminine." In *After Eve: Women, Theology, and the Christian Tradition*, edited by Janet Soskice, 73–88. London, 1990.

Cadiou, René. *La jeunesse d'Origène: Histoire de l'école d'Alexandrie au début du IIIe siècle*. Paris: Beauchesne, 1935.

Castelletti, Cristiano. *Porfirio, Sullo Stige*. Milan, Italy: Bompiani, 2006.

Clark, Stephen. "Plotinus, Eriugena and the Uncreated Image." In *Eriugena's Christian Neoplatonism and Its Sources in Patristic Philosophy and Ancient Philosophy*, edited by Ilaria L. E. Ramelli. Leuven, Belgium: Peeters, 2021, 33–50.

Cohen, Shaul J. D. "Jewish Observance of the Sabbath in Bardaisan's Book of Laws of Countries." Harvard preprint http://dash.harvard.edu/bitstream/handle/1/10861157/Cohen_JewishObservance.pdf?sequence=2.

Cooper, A. "Nuptial Mystery or Sacrament of Sin? Maximus the Confessor on Marriage and Sexual Intimacy." In *Men and Women in the Early Christian Centuries*, edited by Wendy Mayer, 331–50. Strathfield, AU: St Pauls, 2014.

Costache, Doru. "Living above Gender: Insights from Maximus the Confessor." *Journal of Early Christian Studies* 21 (2013): 261–90.

———. "Gender, Marriage and Holiness in *Amb. Io.* 10 and 41." In *Men and Women in the Early Christian Centuries*, edited by Wendy Mayer, 351–71. Strathfield, AU: St Pauls, 2014.

Crone, Patricia. *The Qur'ānic Pagans and Related Matters*, vol. 1 (Leiden, the Netherlands: Brill: 2016).

Crouzel, Henri. "Origène et Plotin élèves d'Ammonios Saccas." *Bulletin de Littérature Ecclésiastique* 57 (1956): 193–214.

Douglas, Sally. *Early Church Understandings of Jesus as the Female Divine: The Scandal of the Scandal of Particularity*. London and New York: Bloomsbury, 2016.

Denzey Lewis, Nicola. "Women as Independent Religious Specialists in Second-Century Rome." In *Women and Knowledge in Early Christianity*, edited by Ulla Tervahauta, Ivan Miroshnikov, Outi Lehtipuu, and Ismo Dunderberg, 21–38. Leiden, the Netherlands: Brill, 2017.

———. "Women in Gnosticism." In *Patterns of Women's Leadership in Ancient Christianity*, edited by Joan E. Taylor and Ilaria L. E. Ramelli, 109–29. Oxford, UK: Oxford University Press, 2021.

Digeser, Elizabeth DePalma. "Origen on the Limes." In *The Rhetoric of Power in Late Antiquity*, edited by Elizabeth DePalma Digeser, Robert Frakes, and Justin Stephens, 197–218. London: Tauris, 2010.

———. *A Threat to Public Piety: Christians, Platonists, and the Great Persecution*. Ithaca, NY and London: Cornell University Press, 2012.

———. "The Usefulness of Borderland Concepts in Ancient History," in *Globalizing Borderland Studies in Europe and North America*, edited by Michael North and John Lee, 15–32. Lincoln: University of Nebraska, 2016.

Dressler, Alex. *Personification and the Feminine in Roman Philosophy*. Oxford, UK and New York: Oxford University Press, 2016.

Drijvers, Han J. W. *Bardaiṣan of Edessa*, introduction by Jan W. Drijvers. Piscataway, NJ: Gorgias Press, 2014.

Eastman, David. "Epiphanius and Patristic Debates on the Marital Status of Peter and Paul." *Vigiliae Christianae* 67 (2013): 499–516.

Elm, Susanna. *Virgins of God: The Making of Asceticism in Late Antiquity*. Oxford, UK: Oxford University Press, 1994.

Epp, Eldon J. *Junia: The First Woman Apostle*. Minneapolis, MN: Fortress, 2005.

Gathercole, Simon. *The Gospel of Thomas: Introduction and Commentary*. Leiden, the Netherlands: Brill, 2014.

Gieschen, Charles. *Angelomorphic Christology: Antecedents and Early Evidence*. Leiden, the Netherlands: Brill, 1988.

Griffin, Svetla Slaveva, and Ilaria L. E. Ramelli, eds. *Lovers of Souls and Lovers of Bodies: Philosophical and Religious Perspectives in Late Antiquity*. Cambridge, MA: Harvard University Press, forthcoming.

Hanson, Richard P. C. *Origen's Doctrine of Tradition*. 2nd ed. Cambridge, UK: Cambridge University Press, 2015.

Harper, Vicki Lynn. "Women in Philosophy." In *Oxford Classical Dictionary*, online edition, 2016. DOI:10.1093/acrefore/9780199381135.013.6894.

Harrison, Nonna Verna. "Male and Female in Cappadocian Theology," *Journal of Theological Studies* 41 (1990): 441–71.

———. "The Care-Banishing Breast of the Father: Feminine Images of the Divine in Clement of Alexandria's *Paedagogus* I." *Studia Patristica* 31 (1997): 401–5.

Harvey, Susan, "Feminine Imagery for the Divine." *St Vladimir Theological Quarterly* 37 (2004): 1–29.

Hughes, Amy. "The Legacy of the Feminine in the Christology of Origen of Alexandria, Methodius of Olympus, and Gregory of Nyssa." *Vigiliae Christianae* 70 (2016): 51–76.

Jaeger, Werner. *Humanistische Reden und Vorträge*, 2nd ed. Berlin, Germany: De Gruyter, 1960.

Johnson, Aaron. *Religion and Identity in Porphyry of Tyre: The Limits of Hellenism in Late Antiquity*. Cambridge, UK: Cambridge University Press, 2013.

Kateusz, Ally, and Luca Badini Confalonieri. "Women Church Leaders in and around Fifth-Century Rome." In *Patterns of Women's Leadership in Ancient Christianity*, edited by Joan E. Taylor and Ilaria L. E. Ramelli, 228–60. Oxford, UK: Oxford University Press, 2021.

Kettler, Franz. "Origenes, Ammonios Sakkas und Porphyrius." In *Kerygma und Logos. FS Andresen*, 322–28. Göttingen, Germany: V&R, 1979.

Klijn, A. F. J. "The 'Single One' in the Gospel of Thomas," *Journal of Biblical Literature* 81 (1962): 261–78.

Köckert, Charlotte. *Christliche Kosmologie und kaiserzeitliche Philosophie: Die Auslegung des Schöpfungsberichtes bei Origenes, Basilius und Gregor von Nyssa vor dem Hintergrund kaiserzeitlicher Timaeus-Interpretationen*. Tübingen, Germany: Mohr Siebeck, 2009.

Kovacs, Judith. "Becoming the Perfect Man: Clement on the Philosophical Life of Women." In *Women and Gender in Ancient Religions*, edited by S. Ahearne-Kroll, 289–413. Tübingen, Germany: Mohr Siebeck, 2010.

Krueger, Dereck. "Writing and the Liturgy of Memory in Gregory of Nyssa's Life of Macrina." *Journal of Early Christian Studies* 8 (2000): 483–510.

Lanzillotta, Lautaro Roig. "A Syriac Original for the Acts of Thomas?" In *Early Christian and Jewish Narrative: The Role of Religion in Shaping Narrative Forms*, edited by Ilaria L. E. Ramelli and Judith Perkins, 105–34. Wissenschaftliche Untersuchungen zum Neuen Testament 1.348; Tübingen, Germany: Mohr Siebeck, 2015.

Litwa, David. *Refutation of All Heresies*. Atlanta, Georgia: SBL Press, 2016.

Louth, Andrew. "The Ecclesiology of St Maximus the Confessor." *International Journal for the Study of the Christian Church* 4, no. 2 (2004): 109–20.

Macy, Gary. *The Hidden History of Women's Ordination*. Oxford, UK: Oxford University Press, 2008.

Madigan, Kevin, and Caroline Osiek. *Ordained Women in the Early Church: A Documentary History*. Baltimore, MD: Johns Hopkins University, 2005.

Markschies, Christoph. *Origenes und sein Erbe*. Berlin, Germany and New York: De Gruyter, 2007.

Marx-Wolf, Heidi. "Bardesanes." In *The Encyclopedia of Ancient History*. Oxford, UK: Wiley-Blackwell, 2013. DOI: 10.1002/9781444338386.wbeah05032.

———. *Spiritual Taxonomies and Ritual Authority: Platonists, Priests, and Gnostics in the Third Century* C.E. Philadelphia: University of Pennsylvania Press, 2016.

McVey, Kathleen. "Ephrem the Syrian's Use of Female Metaphors to Describe the Deity," *Zeitschrift für Antikes Christentum* 5 (2001): 261–88.

Meeks, Wayne A. "The Image of the Androgyne: Some Uses of a Symbol in Earliest Christianity." *History of Religions* 13, no. 2 (1974): 165–208.

Myers, Susan (2010). "The Spirit as Mother in Early Syriac-Speaking Christianity." In *Women and Gender in Ancient Religions: Interdisciplinary Approaches*, edited by James Kellhoffer. Tübingen, Germany: Mohr Siebeck, 427–62.

Nutzman, Megan. "Mary in the Protevangelium of James: A Jewish Woman in the Temple." *Greek, Roman and Byzantine Studies* 53 (2013): 551–78.

Oertelt, Friederike. "Gender, Religion und Politik bei Philon von Alexandria." In *Doing Gender, Doing Religion: Case Studies on Intersectionality in Early Judaism, Christianity and Islam*, edited by Ute Eisen and Angela Standhartinger, 227–50. Tübingen, Germany: Mohr Siebeck, 2013.

Perrier, Pierre. *L'apôtre Thomas et le prince Ying*. Paris, 2012.

Pomeroy, Sarah. *Pythagorean Women: Their History and Writings*. Baltimore, MD: Johns Hopkins University, 2015.

Possekel, Ute. "Bardaisan and Origen on Fate and the Power of the Stars." *Journal of Early Christian Studies* 20, no. 4 (2012): 515–41.

Ramelli, Ilaria L. E. "Mansuetudine, grazia e salvezza negli *Acta Philippi* (ed. Bovon)." *Invigilata Lucernis* 29 (2007): 215–28.

———. "Transformations of the Household and Marriage Theory Between Neo-Stoicism, Middle Platonism, and Early Christianity." *Rivista di Filosofia Neoscolastica* 100 (2008): 369–96.

———. "Philosophical Allegoresis of Scripture in Philo and Its Legacy," *Studia Philonica Annual* 20 (2008): 55–99.

———. "L'Inno a Cristo-Logos nel *Simposio* di Metodio di Olimpo: alle origini della poesia filosofica cristiana." In *Motivi e forme della poesia cristiana antica tra Scrittura e tradizione classica*, edited by Vittorino Grossi, 257–80. Rome: Augustinianum, 2008.

———. *Bardaiṣan of Edessa: A Reassessment of the Evidence and a New Interpretation: Also in the Light of Origen and the Original Fragments from Porphyry.*

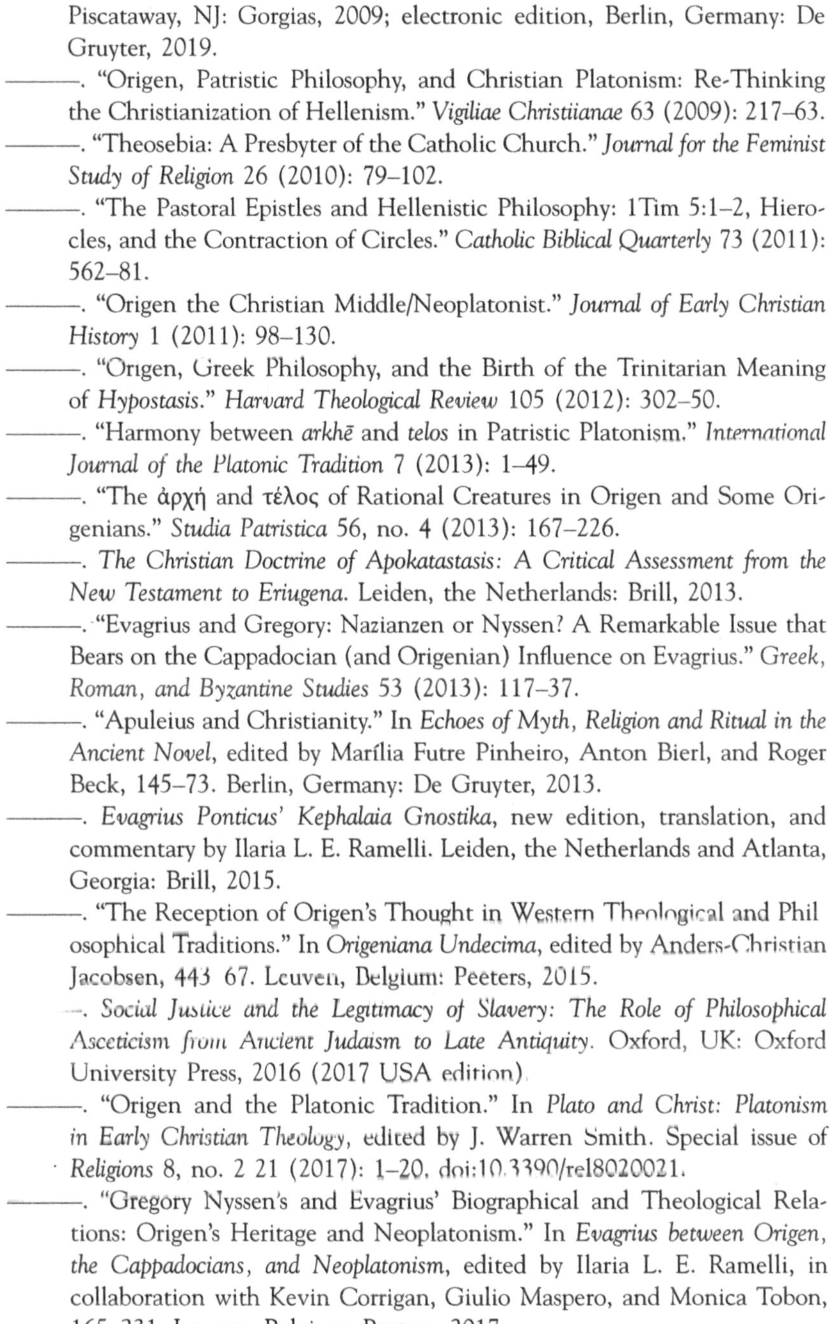

Piscataway, NJ: Gorgias, 2009; electronic edition, Berlin, Germany: De Gruyter, 2019.

———. "Origen, Patristic Philosophy, and Christian Platonism: Re-Thinking the Christianization of Hellenism." *Vigiliae Christiianae* 63 (2009): 217–63.

———. "Theosebia: A Presbyter of the Catholic Church." *Journal for the Feminist Study of Religion* 26 (2010): 79–102.

———. "The Pastoral Epistles and Hellenistic Philosophy: 1Tim 5:1–2, Hierocles, and the Contraction of Circles." *Catholic Biblical Quarterly* 73 (2011): 562–81.

———. "Origen the Christian Middle/Neoplatonist." *Journal of Early Christian History* 1 (2011): 98–130.

———. "Origen, Greek Philosophy, and the Birth of the Trinitarian Meaning of *Hypostasis*." *Harvard Theological Review* 105 (2012): 302–50.

———. "Harmony between *arkhē* and *telos* in Patristic Platonism." *International Journal of the Platonic Tradition* 7 (2013): 1–49.

———. "The ἀρχή and τέλος of Rational Creatures in Origen and Some Origenians." *Studia Patristica* 56, no. 4 (2013): 167–226.

———. *The Christian Doctrine of Apokatastasis: A Critical Assessment from the New Testament to Eriugena*. Leiden, the Netherlands: Brill, 2013.

———. "Evagrius and Gregory: Nazianzen or Nyssen? A Remarkable Issue that Bears on the Cappadocian (and Origenian) Influence on Evagrius." *Greek, Roman, and Byzantine Studies* 53 (2013): 117–37.

———. "Apuleius and Christianity." In *Echoes of Myth, Religion and Ritual in the Ancient Novel*, edited by Marília Futre Pinheiro, Anton Bierl, and Roger Beck, 145–73. Berlin, Germany: De Gruyter, 2013.

———. *Evagrius Ponticus' Kephalaia Gnostika*, new edition, translation, and commentary by Ilaria L. E. Ramelli. Leiden, the Netherlands and Atlanta, Georgia: Brill, 2015.

———. "The Reception of Origen's Thought in Western Theological and Philosophical Traditions." In *Origeniana Undecima*, edited by Anders-Christian Jacobsen, 443 67. Leuven, Belgium: Peeters, 2015.

—. *Social Justice and the Legitimacy of Slavery: The Role of Philosophical Asceticism from Ancient Judaism to Late Antiquity*. Oxford, UK: Oxford University Press, 2016 (2017 USA edition).

———. "Origen and the Platonic Tradition." In *Plato and Christ: Platonism in Early Christian Theology*, edited by J. Warren Smith. Special issue of *Religions* 8, no. 2 21 (2017): 1–20. doi:10.3390/rel8020021.

———. "Gregory Nyssen's and Evagrius' Biographical and Theological Relations: Origen's Heritage and Neoplatonism." In *Evagrius between Origen, the Cappadocians, and Neoplatonism*, edited by Ilaria L. E. Ramelli, in collaboration with Kevin Corrigan, Giulio Maspero, and Monica Tobon, 165–231. Leuven, Belgium: Peeters, 2017.

———. "Prophecy in Origen: Between Scripture and Philosophy," *Journal of Early Christian History* 7 (2017): 17–39.

———. "*Apokatastasis* and *Epektasis* in *Hom. in Cant.*: The Relation between Two Core Doctrines in Gregory and Roots in Origen." In *Gregory of Nyssa: In Canticum Canticorum. Proceedings of the 13th International Colloquium on Gregory of Nyssa (Rome, 17–20 September 2014)*, edited by Giulio Maspero, Miguel Brugarolas, and Ilaria Vigorelli, 312–39. Leiden, the Netherlands: Brill, 2018.

———. "Origen." In *A History of Mind and Body in Late Antiquity*, edited by Anna Marmodoro and Sophie Cartwright, 245–66. Cambridge, UK: Cambridge University Press, 2018.

———. "Gregory of Nyssa on the Soul (and the Restoration): From Plato to Origen." In *Gregory of Nyssa: Historical and Philosophical Perspectives*, edited by Anna Marmodoro and Neil McLynn, 110–41. Oxford, UK: Oxford University Press, 2018.

———. "Gal 3:28 and Aristotelian (and Jewish) Categories of Inferiority." *Eirene* 55 (2019): 275–310.

———. Review of Mark Edwards, *Aristotle and Early Christian Thought*. *Journal of Theological Studies* 71 (2020): 882–85.

———. "The Father in the Son, the Son in the Father in the Gospel of John: Sources and Reception of Dynamic Unity in Middle and Neoplatonism, "Pagan" and Christian." *Journal of the Bible and Its Reception* 7 (2020): 31–66.

———. "Bardaisan: A Gnostic or a Polemicist against Gnostic Tenets?" *Aram* 33 (2020): 1–25.

———. "Colleagues of Apostles, Presbyters, and Bishops: Women *Syzygoi* in Ancient Christian Communities." In *Patterns of Women's Leadership within Ancient Christianity*, edited by Joan E. Taylor and Ilaria L. E. Ramelli, 26–58. Oxford, UK: Oxford University Press, 2021.

———. "Clement and Metensomatosis: Comments on Sami Yli-Karjanmaa's Paper." *Studia Patristica* 110 (2021): 91–97.

———. "Diakonia in Origen: From Christ and the Angels to Men and Women." In *Deacons and Diakonia in Christianity from the Third to the Sixth Century*, edited by Bart Koet (Tübingen: Mohr Siebeck, 2022).

———. "The Reception of Paul in Origen: Allegoresis of Scripture, Apokatastasis, and Women's Ministry." In *The Pauline Mind*, edited by Stanley Porter and David Yoon, New York: Routledge, 2022.

———. "Constructions of Gender in Origen of Alexandria." *Constructions of Gender in Late Antiquity*, Berlin-Potsdam, July 19–22, 2021, edited by Kathy Ehrensperger and Shayna Sheinfield, forthcoming.

———. "Origen's and Gregory Nyssen's Critical Reception of Aristotle." In *Aristotle in Byzantium*, edited by Mikonja Knezevic, 43–86. Alhambra, CA: Sebastian Press, 2020.

———. "Soma (Σῶμα)." In *Reallexikon für Antike und Christentum*. Stuttgart, Germany: Hiersemann Verlag, 2021, 814–47.

———. "Matter in the Dialogue of Adamantius: Origen's Heritage and Hylomorphism." In *Late Antique Cosmologies*, edited by Johannes Zachhuber and Anna Schiavoni. Leiden, the Netherlands: Brill, forthcoming.

Ratcliffe, Rosie. "The Acts of Paul and Thecla: Violating the Inviolate Body. Thecla Uncut." In *The Body in Biblical, Christian and Jewish Texts*, edited by Joan E. Taylor, 184–209. London: Bloomsbury, 2014.

Rowett, Catherine. "Why the Philosopher-King Will Believe the Noble Lie." *Oxford Studies in Ancient Philosophy* 50 (2016): 67–100.

Schäfer, Mary. *Women in Pastoral Office: The Story of Santa Prassede, Rome*. Oxford, UK: Oxford University Press, 2013.

Scholten, Clemens. "Der Abfassungszweckes sogenannten Haereticarum fabularum compendium des Theodoret von Kyrrhos, 1." *Vigiliae Christianae* 70 (2016): 282–318.

Silvas, Anna. "Basil of Caesarea and His View of Women in a Christian Anthropology." In *Men and Women in the Early Christian Centuries*, edited by Wendy Mayer, 149–59. Strathfield, AU: St Pauls, 2014.

Simmons, Michael Bland. *Universal Salvation in Late Antiquity: Porphyry of Tyre and the Pagan-Christian Debate*. Oxford, UK: Oxford University Press, 2015.

Speidel, Michael. "Making Use of History beyond the Euphrates." In *Mara bar Serapion in Context*, edited by Anette Merz and Teun Tieleman, 11–41. Leiden, the Netherlands: Brill, 2012.

Tarrant, Harold. "Plotinus, Origenes and Ammonius on the King." In *Religio-Philosophical Discourses within the Greco-Roman, Jewish and Early Christian World*, edited by Anders Klostergaard Petersen and George van Kooten, 323–37. Leiden, the Netherlands: Brill, 2017.

Troiano, Mariano. "Padre femenino: el Dios-Madre de los gnósticos." In *Gnose et manichéisme. Hommage à Jean-Daniel Dubois*, edited by Anna van den Kerchove and Luciana Gabriela Soares Santoprete, 27–159. Turnhout, Belgium: Brepols, 2016.

Turner, John. "The Virgin That Became Male: Feminine Principles in Platonic and Gnostic Texts." In *Women and Knowledge in Early Christianity*, edited by Ulla Tervahauta, Ivan Miroshnikov, Outi Lehtipuu, and Ismo Dunderberg, 291–324. Leiden, the Netherlands: Brill, 2017.

Tzamalikos, Panayiotis. *Anaxagoras, Origen, and Neoplatonism: The Legacy of Anaxagoras to Classical and Late Antiquity*. Berlin, Germany: De Gruyter, 2016.

Watts, Edward. *Hypatia: The Life and Legend of an Ancient Philosopher*. Oxford, UK and New York: Oxford University Press, 2017.

Yli-Karjanmaa, Sami. *Reincarnation in Philo of Alexandria*. Atlanta, GA: SBL, 2015.

———. "Call Him Earth: On Philo's Allegorisation of Adam in Legum Allegoriae." In *The Adam and Eve Story in the Hebrew Bible and in Ancient Jewish Writings*, edited by Antti Laato and Lotta Valve, 253–93. Turku, Finland: SRHB, 2016.

Contributors

Sasha Biro is a teaching associate of philosophy at Marist College. Her research interests are embedded in the Continental tradition, focusing on practices of cultural and political narrative and the reception of antiquity in contemporary philosophical thought. She holds a PhD in philosophy from Binghamton University.

Jessica Elbert Decker is an associate professor of philosophy at California State University, San Marcos. Her research engages with Ancient Greek philosophy and mythology from a critical feminist perspective, and she is particularly interested in Ancient Greek poetic texts such as those of Presocratic thinkers, Sappho, Homer, and Hesiod. Her work has been published in numerous collected volumes and journals, including *Epoche: A Journal for the History of Philosophy*, *philoSOPHIA*, *Ancient Philosophy Today*, and *Women's Studies: An Interdisciplinary Journal*. She is the coeditor, with Dylan Winchock, of *Borderlands and Liminal Subjects: Transgressing the Limit in Philosophy and Literature* (2017), and her current project is a manuscript on the philosophy and method of Heraclitus.

Andrew Gregory is professor of history and philosophy of science in the Department of Science and Technology Studies at University College London. He has published extensively on ancient science and its relations to ancient philosophy, ancient religion, and ancient magic. His books include *Plato's Philosophy of Science*, *Ancient Greek Cosmogony*, *The Presocratics and the Supernatural*, *Anaximander: A Re-assessment*, and *Early Greek Philosophies of Nature*.

William Koch is an assistant professor at the Borough of Manhattan Community College in the CUNY university system. His recent publications include "Phenomenology and the Problem of Universals," in *Studia Phaenomenologica* and the coedited with José A. Haro volume, *The Films Lars von Trier and Philosophy*.

Danielle A. Layne is associate professor of philosophy at Gonzaga University. She has published widely on Plato and the Platonic tradition and is currently writing a monograph on the history and reception of philosophies of the erotic from antiquity to contemporary intersectional feminism.

Holly Moore is associate professor of philosophy at Luther College, where she teaches ancient philosophy, feminist theory, and critical theory. Her research focuses primarily on Plato's philosophical rhetoric and the way philosophical thought interacts with its expressive forms. She is currently working on a manuscript on Plato's rhetoric of slavery.

Ilaria L. E. Ramelli has been a professor of Roman history; senior visiting professor of Greek thought at Harvard and Boston Universities, of church history at Columbia, and of religion at Erfurt MWK; a full professor of theology and Endowed Chair at the Angelicum; and a senior fellow at Durham University (twice), at Princeton (2017–), at Sacred Heart University, and at both Corpus Christi and Christ Church in Oxford. She is also a senior member of the Centre for the Study of Platonism at Cambridge University, a Humboldt Forschungspreis fellow at Erfurt MWK, senior fellow at Bonn University (elect), professor of theology (Durham University, Hon.), and of patristics and Church history (KUL).

Anne-Marie Schultz is professor and Undergraduate Program director of Philosophy at Baylor University. She recently received the designation of Master Teacher. She is the author of *Plato's Socrates as Narrator* (Lexington, 2013) and *Plato's Socrates on Socrates* (Lexington, 2020).

Jana Schultz held a position as a postdoctoral researcher in the DFG project *Women and the Female in Neoplatonism* from October 2016 through July 2021. The project was placed first at the Ruhr-University in Bochum, and since 2018, at the Humboldt-University in Berlin. Jana Schultz's research focused on Plato and the Neoplatonic tradition, especially on Platonic and Neoplatonic metaphysics, psychology, ethics, and aesthetics. She is the author of *Formung und Umwendung der Seele:*

Eine Rechtfertigung ambivalenter Darstellungen in der Literatur im Rahmen von Platons Politeia (Lang, 2017) and coeditor with James Wilberding of *Plato's Non-Rational Soul (Logical Analysis and History of Philosophy 20)* (mentis, 2017).

Mary Townsend is an assistant professor of philosophy at St. John's University, Queens, NY. She works on issues of gender and politics in ancient and existential philosophy. She has also written on philosophy and culture for places such as *The Atlantic*, the *Hedgehog Review*, and *Plough Quarterly*.

Monica Vilhauer is the founder of Curious Soul Philosophy, which offers philosophy workshops and retreats for adults, as well as individual philosophical counseling on issues of meaning, purpose, ethics, values, identity, empowerment, and authenticity. She is a former associate professor of philosophy and author of *Gadamer's Ethics of Play: Hermeneutics and the Other* (Lexington Books, 2010). Her research areas are in ethics, existentialism, hermeneutics, philosophy of dialogue, and feminism.

Hilary Yancey graduated with her PhD in philosophy from Baylor University in 2020. She focuses her research in metaphysics, philosophy of biology and medical ethics, alongside ancient philosophy and philosophy of disability. She currently teaches in an adjunct capacity for Baylor University, as well as coordinating projects for the Honors College at Baylor.

Index

www.ingramcontent.com/pod-product-compliance
Lightning Source LLC
LaVergne TN
LVHW041110090826
844660LV00056B/103
* 9 7 8 1 4 3 8 4 8 8 7 9 0 *